D1175905

Apple of Gold

Apple of Gold

CONSTITUTIONALISM IN ISRAEL AND THE UNITED STATES

Gary Jeffrey Jacobsohn

PRINCETON UNIVERSITY PRESS

PRINCETON, NEW JERSEY

Library of Congress Cataloging-in-Publication Data

Jacobsohn, Gary J., 1946–
Apple of gold : constitutionalism in Israel and the United States
/ Gary Jeffrey Jacobsohn.
p.   cm.
Includes bibliographical references (p.   ) and index.
ISBN 0-691-08622-2
1. Israel—Constitutional law.   1. United States—Constitutional
law.   I. Title.
K3165.J33   1993
342.5694—dc20
[345.69402]   92-15743

This book has been composed in Linotron Caledonia

Printed in the United States of America

1   2   3   4   5   6   7   8   9   10

FOR JOSEPH AND MATTHEW

Contents

Acknowledgments

I HAVE BEEN FORTUNATE during the course of the preparation of this book to have had much good advice and encouragement. Of course it is not the fault of those who generously provided me with their suggestions that they were unable also to give me the wisdom to profit from them. I am, however, not totally lacking in good sense. Thus the book is much the better for my having pursued at least some of the recommendations of Pnina Lahav, George Gross, Sanford Levinson, Leslie Goldstein, Yochai Benkler, Walter Berns, and Moshe Landau. The latter, a former president of the Supreme Court of Israel, was particularly gracious in giving me the benefit of his vast experience and immense learning. Other justices, sitting and retired, who gave of their time were Aharon Barak, Menachem Elon, Gavriel Bach, Shimon Agranat, and Haim Cohn. I would also like to thank Helen Rivkin of the Israel Liaison Office of the American Professors for Peace in the Middle East for assisting me in arranging interviews in Israel. Finally, for their invaluable research assistance, I am indebted to two bright and energetic Williams College students, Michael Dawson and Adam Weiner.

My work has been facilitated by a fellowship from the National Endowment for the Humanities and by grants made available to me from divisional research funds at Williams College.

A revised version of some of the material in Chapter 5 has appeared in *Judicial Activism in Comparative Perspective* (New York: St. Martin's Press; London: Macmillan Publishing Co., 1991), edited by Kenneth M. Holland. Permission to incorporate this material is gratefully acknowledged.

Apple of Gold

Introduction

> The assertion of that *principle* at *that time*, was *the*
> word, *"fitly spoken"* which has proved an "apple of gold"
> to us. The *Union* and the *Constitution*, are the *picture*
> of *silver*, subsequently framed around it. The picture
> was made, not to *conceal*, or *destroy* the apple; but to
> *adorn*, and *preserve* it. The *picture* was made *for* the
> apple—*not* the apple for the picture.
> —*Abraham Lincoln*

TWO DECLARATIONS

On his trip from Illinois to Washington to assume the burdens of the
presidency, Abraham Lincoln stopped to deliver a brief address in Philadelphia's Independence Hall. In it he declared, "I have never had a feeling
politically that did not spring from the sentiments embodied in the Declaration of Independence."[1] Taken literally, this confession arouses, at the
least, mild skepticism, as Lincoln surely must have had many political
feelings that were in no discernible way spawned by the principles of the
Declaration. But considering the occasion and the location of the remarks,
and that Lincoln was obviously preoccupied by the nation's impending
crisis, to be critical of the speaker for having indulged himself in this small
way would be churlish and unseemly. Moreover, it is possible that Lincoln
was already anticipating the extraordinary sacrifices yet to be incurred, in
which case his noble sentiments may be seen as a manifestation of states-
manlike attributes that would one day be justly praised.

Skepticism in response to apparently inflated rhetoric is understandable, but it should not remain unquestioned. In speaking at the place
where both the Declaration and the Constitution had been composed,
Lincoln was giving voice to the most pervasive theme in all of his political
reflections, the inextricability of those two founding documents. Thus for

---

[1] Roy Basler, ed., *The Collected Works of Abraham Lincoln* (New Brunswick, N.J.:
Rutgers University Press, 1953), vol. 4, p. 240. It is recorded that this comment was greeted
with great cheering.

Lincoln constitutional meaning was scarcely imaginable without the Declaration as ultimate source of interpretive guidance. As he had demonstrated in his debates with Stephen Douglas and in many public statements, those of his political feelings that pertained to constitutional matters—in other words, high politics—were indeed traceable to the sentiments embodied in the Declaration. The "apple of gold" metaphor, appearing in a brief fragment that was never used in any of Lincoln's speeches, beautifully illuminates the constitutional role of these sentiments. "Liberty to all," he maintained, is the principle that the Constitution—the "picture of silver"—was specifically intended to preserve.[2] Without it Americans could have established their independence, "but *without* it, we could not . . . have secured our free government, and consequent prosperity."[3] Constitutionalism in the United States in essence becomes a matter of determining the meaning of the Declaration and clarifying its principle of liberty.

In that same speech in Philadelphia, Lincoln pointed out that the Declaration was not only a gift to the people of the United States, it also offered "hope to the world for all future time."[4] Its principles were worth defending precisely because they were of universal applicability; after all, the "Laws of Nature and of Nature's God" were not apportioned according to national boundaries. For this reason the document has served as a source of inspiration for peoples around the world. The U.S. Constitution, too, has been profoundly important in influencing the direction of constitutional evolution in many countries. Some of this, to be sure, is attributable to certain features—for example, federalism—that have a particular appeal in places where local circumstances recommend emulation of the American model. But to the extent that Lincoln was correct in viewing American constitutionalism as a protective enclosure for the principles of natural justice, it is clear that much of the broad appeal of the U.S. Constitution is related to its perceived value in securing the realization of those universal principles.[5]

In many polities, the core of American constitutionalism, its ethos of

---

[2] Ibid., p. 169. The fragment alludes to the biblical proverb that "A word fitly spoken is like apples of gold in pictures of silver" (Proverbs 25:11).

[3] Ibid.

[4] Ibid., p. 240.

[5] I should make clear here that neither Lincoln nor the Declaration stipulate that the American form of government is necessary to secure inalienable rights. Government must derive its powers from "the consent of the governed," but it may be organized in whatever way is "most likely to effect [the People's] Safety and Happiness." There may, in other words, be different "pictures of silver."

individualism, is embraced with much less enthusiasm. One such polity is Israel, whose 1948 Declaration of Independence inaugurated the third Jewish commonwealth, thus ending 1,878 years of Jewish statelessness. Although the early Israeli Supreme Court minimized the significance of the document—saying that "the only object of the Declaration was to affirm the fact of the foundation and establishment of the State for the purpose of its recognition by international law"[6]—later judicial decisions, along with many commentators, have argued for its central place in Israeli politics. Today there is widespread acceptance of the sentiment expressed in David Ben-Gurion's observation that "the legal and democratic system we wish to fortify is designed to give effect and permanence to [the Declaration]."[7] Echoes may be heard of what Lincoln had to say in reference to the American Declaration, that its principled assertions were of no practical use in effecting a separation from Great Britain and were included not for that but for future use.[8]

But what of this future use? An underlying concern of this study is to address this question by focusing on the contrasting Israeli and American experiences with the theory and practice of constitutionalism. The point of departure is the alternative constructions of national purpose and vision embodied in the documents that mark the official beginnings of the two countries. These founding papers establish new memberships in the community of nations, but they do more; they affix a particular political-moral character to their respective polities. As such, they introduce and outline the intellectual contours for constitutional discourse about how these societies arrange their fundamental rules and governing practices. All of which leads to the simple Tocquevillian insight that serves as the architectonic principle of this book: interpretations of diverse constitutional experience must be anchored in an appreciation of alternative conceptions of (in this case democratic) politics.

Constitutional experience is, for Tocqueville, mirrored in the "social condition" prevailing in a given society, a term intended to include the beliefs and ideas that help shape the political consciousness and identity of

---

[6] *Zeev v. Acting District Commissioner*, 72 (1) P.D. 85 (1948).

[7] David Ben-Gurion, *Rebirth and Destiny of Israel* (New York: Philosophical Library, 1954), p. 375. The point is made even more strongly by an Israeli legal scholar: "The Declaration of Independence is the formal source of legislative power in the State. This source, from which the entire system of government springs, is political and lies outside the Constitution." Eliahu Likhovski, "The Courts and the Legislative Supremacy of the Knesset," *Israel Law Review* 3 (1968): 346.

[8] Basler, *Collected Works*, vol. 2, p. 406.

a nation.[9] The revolutionary passages of Israel and the United States produced independence proclamations that reveal both the animating ideals of their respective regimes and the likely directions that their paths of constitutional development would take. Important differences are to be found here, but there is also considerable substantive overlap; the paths, in other words, are not destined to reach diametrically opposed constitutional destinations. Indeed, one of the reasons for choosing this particular comparison is that while the two polities present a sharp contrast in constitutionally relevant features of political culture, what they have in common not only makes a shared language of constitutional discourse possible, it offers the potential of using one approach to facilitate enhanced critical self-understanding within the other.

A preliminary analysis of the Declarations highlights the differences and similarities. In their opening lines the two documents establish contrasting emphases reflective of the thematic disparity underlying the revolutionary goals of their respective claims to independence. Unlike the American Declaration, which speaks in universalistic terms and in the abstract language of natural right, the Israeli counterpart commences with a simple affirmation of particularity: "The land of Israel was the birthplace of the Jewish people. Here their spiritual, religious and political identity was formed. Here they achieved independence and created a culture of national and universal significance." Not only are national values mentioned before universal ones (or at least values of universal significance), the latter are discussed in a national context, as creations of the Jewish people. The 1776 statement of course locates their source in the natural order of things, and in contrast to the Israeli version is essentially ahistorical. If the legitimacy of the Jewish state is ultimately rooted in the chronicle of a particular people, the claim of the American people to an independent state is based on principles that are notable for their timelessness.

It is not that history is absent from the American Declaration—the longest of its sections recounts in some detail the abuses perpetrated by the British king—but that it only illuminates the question of *why* the American people need to be independent, not *who* they are. Indeed, "American

---

[9] "Social condition is commonly the result of circumstances, sometimes of laws, oftener still of these two causes united; but when once established, it may justly be considered as itself the source of almost all the laws, the usages, and the ideas which regulate the conduct of nations: whatever it does not produce, it modifies. If we could become acquainted with the legislation and the manners of a nation, therefore, we must begin by the study of its social condition." Alexis de Tocqueville, *Democracy in America*, ed. Phillips Bradley (New York: Vintage, 1945), p. 48.

people" is not the term used; instead there are references to "one people" and to "the good people of these colonies," bloodless designations fully consonant with the abstract quality of the document's revolutionary appeal to principles of natural right. In contrast, the one mention of natural right in the Israeli Declaration is, from the perspective of Western political philosophy, a curious one, as it refers to "the natural and historic right of the Jewish people" to establish a state. Accustomed as we are to thinking of natural right in the idiom of Lockean individualism, its association here with a people is somewhat striking. Thus, whereas the American Declaration emphasizes self-evident truths bearing directly on the status of *individuals*, the Israeli document refers to "the self-evident right of the Jewish people to be a nation, like all other nations, in its own sovereign State."

While the first and longest part of the Israeli Declaration affirms the historic connection of the Jewish people to the land of Israel, the second section includes a paragraph commiting the new state to a set of principles very much in the spirit of the Western liberal democratic tradition. That paragraph reads:

> The State of Israel will be open to the immigration of Jews from all countries of their dispersion, will promote the development of the country for the benefit of all its inhabitants; will be based on the precepts of liberty, justice and peace taught by the Hebrew prophets; will uphold the full social and political equality of all its citizens, without distinction of race, creed or sex; will guarantee full freedom of conscience, worship, education and culture; will safeguard the sanctity and inviolability of the shrines and Holy Places of all religions; and will dedicate itself to the principles of the Charter of the United Nations.

For many Israelis, this is the core of the Declaration, its "apple of gold." It appears to embrace the Herzlian vision of a secular democratic state, thus representing the fulfillment of the Zionist dream. But the one lesson to be gleaned from any comprehensive history of the Jewish people is that there are several competing Zionist visions: *the* Zionist dream does not exist. What this means is that the significance attached to this paragraph will vary in accordance with the degree of compatibility between the liberal democratic vision and any given Zionist understanding. How one sees the Jewish state—as a place of refuge for persecuted Jews, as a homeland for the Jewish people to revive and develop a distinctively Jewish culture, as a holy land where God's chosen people can live their lives in accordance with divine law—will be decisive in determining the extent to which the passage's liberal sentiments assume interpretive prominence.

The absence in Israel of a formal written constitution, one that might function, in Lincoln's terms, as a "picture of silver" to the Declaration's "apple of gold," is in part attributable to the potential, if not necessary, irreconcilability of these various understandings. That the state should be a haven for the Jewish people might be construed as the Israeli "apple of gold," but beyond this basic core there has always been a significant division on the principles that should underlie the regime. Fortunately, we need not here resolve the question of Zionism's essence in order to appreciate the complex constitutional implications of the Israeli Declaration. It is clear in a way that simply does not pertain in the American case, that even in the version that most closely approximates the American emphasis on universal rights (where the above paragraph exerts a powerful claim on Israeli self-understanding), the rights of individuals are in important and perhaps contradictory ways bound up with the organic nature of the community and its constituent parts. While the promise of "full social and political equality" for all citizens represents a clear and substantial commitment to democratic values, the concurrent guarantee of "full freedom of . . . culture" also makes it very likely that the achievement of liberal goals pertaining to individual rights will have to accommodate communitarian goals with which they will often be in conflict. Upon first glance this may seem a small point, but within the broader context of the document as a whole, it suggests that at a minimum there will be a tension between the respective claims of group and individual. Such tensions exist in all societies—liberal ones included—but here, where the Declaration itself identifies the state with the destiny of a particular people, they possess, as we shall see, a special significance for the subject of constitutionalism.[10]

Perhaps most important, this identification means that the political prin-

---

[10] Not all Zionists who are liberal democrats will accept the necessity of tension here. Horace Kallen, for example, the American philosopher of secularist cultural pluralism, maintained in 1919 that "the whole of the Zionist ideology" could be summed up "in a slight modification of the Declaration of Independence: all nationalities are created equal and endowed with certain inalienable rights; among these rights are life, liberty, and the pursuit of happiness." Horace M. Kallen, "Zionism and Liberalism," in *The Zionist Idea: A Historical Analysis and Reader*, ed. Arthur Hertzberg (Garden City, N.Y.: Doubleday & Co., 1959), p. 529. This interpretation is indeed consistent with the guarantee of cultural equality in the Israeli Declaration; but even many liberals will concede that the officially declared Jewishness of the state ensures that in some sense (perhaps only minimally) one nationality is destined to be first among equals. For example, Amos Shapira, one of the authors of the much publicized and discussed draft constitution for Israel, said of his and his colleagues' efforts that they were "trying to raise in a dramatic gesture—by the adoption of a constitution—the traditional two flags of being a Jewish State and of being a Western-type liberal democracy, with all the

ciples that are also a part of the Declaration are of lesser consequence in providing substance to the identity of the nation than in the American case, where such principles are effectively the basis of nationhood. Samuel Huntington has argued, for example, that American national identity is understandable only in terms of the political principles of the Declaration, that Americans have nothing vital in common, no cementing unity, without the amalgam of goals and values that constitutes the American Creed. Thus he claims, "National identity and political principle [are] inseparable."[11] And we might add, they find their official expression in the Constitution, which in effect becomes, for Americans, the basis of community. For this reason it is nearly impossible to imagine the United States without a formal written constitution, and why, given the more organic, ascriptive quality of Israeli identity, it *is* possible to understand how Israel has developed without one.

TWO CONSTITUTIONS

It is a development, however, that has left many Israelis unhappy. Among them is the current president of the Supreme Court, who has expressed, both on and off of the Court, a strong preference for a formal written constitution.[12] Also unhappy is a highly respected former president,

---

inconsistencies of the two." *Jewish Week*, May 13, 1989. For the religious Zionist perspective on the tension, there is this comment of Zevulun Hammer, then minister for religious affairs, in which he addressed himself to what he characterized as the foremost challenge of a Jewish state: "At Mt. Sinai the Almighty spoke of the community. There is no Torah without a group. But he spoke in the singular: 'I am the Lord your God,' and, according to the midrash, was understood to have spoken to each individual. . . . In drafting the details of the law we will have to contend with the intellectual and moral challenge of being jointly faithful to the group and the individual. The importance of the individual cannot be an impediment to the formation of the Jewish—spiritual character of the community. Our intention is not that liberal vision of a mass of separate individuals. The life of the community must blend with the honor of the individual." *Yediot Aharanot*, November 24, 1989.

[11] Samuel P. Huntington, *American Politics: The Promise of Disharmony* (Cambridge: Harvard University Press, 1981), p. 24. For an insightful critique of Huntington's argument, see Rogers M. Smith, "The 'American Creed' and American Identity: The Limits of Liberal Citizenship in the United States," *Western Political Quarterly* 41 (1988): 225. Smith argues that ethnic and cultural factors have historically been important in understanding American national identity, and that Huntington exaggerates the significance of shared political ideas.

[12] *Jerusalem Post*, March 19, 1988. (International Weekly Edition.) In a 1984 Supreme Court opinion, Justice Shamgar previewed his preference when he reflected on "the importance and value of a written constitution, and [that] its absence in our system is con-

Shimon Agranat (born and educated in the United States), who told an interviewer, "The trouble is that we don't have a constitutional bill of rights, that we don't have a constitution. If we had, the law would be constantly tested against it and the basic civil liberties of the individual would be guaranteed."[13] Their frustration, and that of thousands of others who have recently joined in demonstrations demanding constitutional reform, is traceable to the Declaration of Independence, which explicitly refers to "a Constitution to be drawn up by the Constituent Assembly." This promise went unfulfilled, and while the Supreme Court has often functioned in a way that could lead one to forget that historical detail, advocates of a constitution that includes an entrenched bill of rights will ensure that, by keeping it high on the public agenda, it will not easily be forgotten.

One of the most ardent among this group is Shulamit Aloni, the leader of the Citizens Rights Movement, who argues that "no true democracy can exist where a constitution does not make explicit the fundamental human rights, rights that are inalienable."[14] Her professed goal is to fulfill the aspirations of the Declaration of Independence, not simply with respect to the specific pledge regarding adoption of a constitution, but more fundamentally in terms of what she sees as its commitment to liberal democracy. Others, of course, disagree; an indication of the range of constitutional opinion in Israel is revealed in the response of the leader of one of the religious parties to a query about a proposed bill of rights: "In my opinion, the current version of the human rights bill imitates the bill of rights of those civilized nations—that club to which we like to flatter ourselves as belonging. But it is no secret that we are different from other nations of the world; we have defined Israel as a Jewish state. . . . This is made quite explicit in no less than the country's Proclamation of Independence."[15] While these two comments come from individuals who represent opposite poles of Israeli opinion on constitutional and other issues, their remarks in this instance fall well within the range of mainstream opinion; moreover, many people adhere to both positions, which is to say, they embrace the

---

spicuous each time a constitutional issue arises in a legal proceeding." *Neiman and Avneri v. Chairman of the Central Elections Committee for the Eleventh Knesset*, 39 (2) P.D. 225, 237 (1984). Translation by Carmel Shalev. The case is included in an unpublished casebook, *Limits of Law*, edited by Aharon Barak, Joseph Goldstein, and Burke Marshall.

[13] *Jerusalem Post*, 6/6/87.

[14] *Jerusalem Post*, 10/13/84.

[15] From an interview with Avraham Ravitz, head of the Degel HaTorah party, in *Israeli Democracy*, Spring 1990, p. 23.

fundamental tension embedded within their founding document. Indeed, the dilemma over constitutional reform has been shaped by this tension.

Enter the U.S. Constitution. While the constitutional debate in Israel is not over the wisdom of embracing the American model, the latter's presence, particularly with respect to judicial review and the protection of individual rights, has been felt in important ways in the evolution of constitutional discourse in Israel. Unlike other examples of the influence of the U.S. Constitution abroad—most notably in the case of actual American interventions (e.g., the Philippines, Japan, West Germany)—the process in Israel has been fairly subtle, confined largely, although not exclusively, to the realms of adjudication and the legal academy. From these places American influence has radiated into the political arena; thus, for example, law professors, armed with American cases and jurisprudential theory, have played the catalytic role in mobilizing support for constitutional reform. Again, they have not been wedded to the American constitutional approach, but they have borrowed extensively from it (and to a lesser extent from other foreign systems).[16]

The process of constitutional transplantation is therefore a vital component of the constitutional reform debate and is similarly caught in the cross pressures of the Declaration's dual commitments. For my purposes, however, the subject of constitutional reform should be expanded beyond the various specific efforts that have been undertaken to codify a formal constitution, to include judicial decisions by the Israeli Supreme Court. This is because the Court has been a powerful actor in directing the course of constitutional development; its judgments are part of the constitutional fabric of the society. To take the principal example, in the absence of a formal bill of rights, the Supreme Court in Israel has created what commentators have characterized as a judicial bill of rights that in essence functions as part of the constitution of the state.[17] Primarily through cre-

---

[16] Borrowing legal concepts, ideas, and solutions from a foreign legal culture, what is sometimes referred to as legal transplantation, is not an area that has received a great deal of scholarly attention. One bibliographic study concludes, "What seems to be missing from legal literature, and is not common in historical, sociological, and anthropological literature, is a thorough study of legal ideas throughout their migration across political and cultural boundaries." Andrezej Rapaczynski, "Bibliographical Essay: Influence of the U.S. Constitution Abroad," in *Constitutionalism and Rights: The Influence of the United States Constitution Abroad*, ed. Louis Henkin and Albert Rosenthal (New York: Columbia University Press, 1990), p. 406.

[17] The actual source for the term is Justice Moshe Landau's opinion in *Vogel v. Broadcasting Authority*, 31 (3) P.D. 657, 664 (1976).

ative statutory interpretation, Israeli judges, consciously or unconsciously, are engaged in an ongoing process of constitutional reform. Their decisions regarding the applicability and appropriateness of foreign sources is the most important element in determining the scope of constitutional transplantation in Israel.

As the phenomenon of constitutional transplantation has mainly to do with the influence of one legal culture upon another, both its positive and negative dimensions need to be considered. Andrzej Rapaczynski writes in this context of "negative influence," referring to the process in which Country A's example is carefully considered and then rejected by Country B. As illustrations he cites the Indian decision not to include a due process clause in the Indian constitution, and the negative reaction of the French in the first half of this century to the American institution of judicial review.[18] In the Israeli-American context this phenomenon bears watching in light of the sociopolitical differences expressed in the Declarations of these two countries. How a particular constitutional solution will (or should) be received becomes a function of its compatibility with the abiding commitments of the regime. Thus the usefulness of American constitutional theory, practice, or precedent may be seen to vary with its potential fit within the political culture of the Israeli polity.

What I have sought to do in this book is contrast particular features of the constitutional cultures of Israel and the United States that are relevant to an assessment of constitutional transplantation. While these two polities constitute the specific focus of the analysis, my hope is to contribute more broadly to an improved understanding of the nature of constitutionalism. Too often comparative legal analysis of this subject proceeds in the absence of political understanding. Thus I begin in Chapter 2 by situating constitutionalism in the United States and Israel within the broader framework of their contrasting sociopolitical settings, each of which nourishes and sustains a constitutional government. The fact that these societies can reasonably be described as pluralistic only conceals the more significant fact that they represent different models of pluralism that may potentially affect the transferability of constitutional outcomes from one place to another. These two pluralisms are projections into the societal realm from the political ideas and aspirations of the two Declarations of Independence. Like these documents they have a good deal in common, but their differences speak directly to some basic assumptions of liberal constitutionalism.

First among them is the neutrality of public authority, with its policy of

---

[18] Rapaczynski, "Bibliographical Essay," p. 408.

official blindness to such ascriptive characteristics as race, religion, and ethnicity. Rights inhere in the individual; the collective rights of groups are acknowledged only in the sense of a freedom to advance corporate interests through appropriate political channels. This contrasts with a model in which communitarian pressures are sufficiently compelling that they recommend establishment of quasi-autonomous centers of rule-making authority that need not operate in accordance with the premises of the liberal state. But it is also an approach in which the state's own autonomy is compromised by its identification with a particular community. To be sure, in the case of Israel, the official autonomy of designated ethno/religious groups is limited, and the compromise of the state's neutrality is not extensive. Nevertheless, we are confronted with a set of political assumptions that are, for the most part, alien to the American experience. In constitutional terms, it thus forces us to consider how much of American constitutional law and theory depends on an adherence to the ideal of neutral principles in the conduct and administration of power in the public arena.

These contrasting pluralist models manifest themselves in the approaches taken by their respective societies in addressing the fundamental regime question: membership in the political community. This is the underlying assumption of Chapter 3, which is an inquiry into Israeli and American conceptions of political identity. If there is in Israel any constitutional development that may be said to flow directly from the Declaration of Independence, that qualifies as a "picture of silver," it surely is the Law of Return, which guarantees to any Jew who desires it automatic and immediate citizenship. Others may of course become citizens, but the raison d'etre of the state as a homeland for the Jewish people ensures that citizenship and nationality will possess distinctive meanings and legal significance. In the United States, citizenship and nationality are basically indistinguishable, even if historically immigration policies have often discriminated on the basis of place of origin. Thus acquisition of citizenship status is not a function of personal status; rather, it is one of volition, specifically the applicant's affirmation of the principles in the Constitution. This too reflects the theoretical emphasis in the country's Declaration of Independence, in this case on the social contract's premise of consent. And because membership in the political community *establishes* nationality (just as, in Lincoln's words, the Declaration established a "new nation"), this creedal assent symbolizes a fundamental teaching of the Declaration, which is that political principles are at the core of American national identity.

Chapter 3 also clarifies the significance of history. Invocation of the Law of Return requires a standard for determining who is Jewish. Policy makers

13

must choose from a range of possible tests for those seeking citizenship under the law, from a subjective declaration of Jewish affiliation to compliance with Orthodox religious law. Within world Jewry this has been a much-debated question, occasionally leading to nasty divisions between Israelis and diaspora Jews, especially Jews from the United States. The position embraced by most of the Americans generally reflects their political experience, which is to say they prefer a solution in which their Jewish identity, like their status as Americans, approximates a model of membership as a voluntary association. Many Israelis share this view, although even they have often failed to comprehend the strength of the American attachment to it, or the reasons—particularly those that may be inspired by a different secular experience—behind it. Israeli Jews, both the religiously observant and the majority who are not, are connected to their Jewishness in more primordial ways than are their American counterparts. As such they have much in common with their non-Jewish countrymen, whose identities have also been forged on the historically linked anvils of religion, land, and ethnicity. In part this accounts for their acceptance (or at least understanding) of a more objective membership test, one that subordinates present intention to past affiliation.

It also helps to distinguish the contrasting paths of Israeli and American constitutional development. The fact that Israelis did not comply with their Declaration's stipulation about adopting a constitution is understandable in light of the tensions embedded in that document. In Chapter 4 I argue that for the United States, a new nation seeking to establish a distinctive identity, the codification of a formal constitution was a necessary and urgent step in the achievement of this important goal. Moreover, to the extent that this identity was bound up in a coherent set of principles, it was important to constitutionalize the vision embodied therein, and thereby affirm the very foundations of American nationhood. On the other hand, while there were a number of good reasons for an early Israeli adoption of a constitutional document, in the end they only added up to a case for its desirability, not its necessity. And because national aspirations were rooted less in philosophy and more in history, namely the creation of a homeland for the Jewish people, the case for delay could be framed in aspirational terms: the wisdom of postponing the ultimate constitutional decision until many more members of the nation had joined the state.

This postponement has led some to claim that Israel is without a written constitution, a claim that turns out to be at best a half-truth. What the country lacks is a formal bill of rights and judicial review over legislation, two features that together are often considered the sine qua non of constitutional government. But here too things are more complicated than they may at first appear. There may be developing in Israel a kind of de facto judicial review, not entirely dissimilar to what emerged in the early days of the United States, where, as in Israel, no constitutional provision expressly authorized the practice. In fact what is emerging may turn out to be more consistent with the original spirit of *Marbury* v. *Madison* than the eventual path taken by the U.S. Supreme Court. In this regard, an analysis of the Israeli experience provides a splendid opportunity for a fresh examination of American arguments concerning judicial review that history has more or less left behind. So, for example, in Chapter 4 Hamilton's case against a bill of rights and Jefferson's defense of a departmental approach to constitutional interpretation are reconsidered as part of a broader inquiry into aspects of the contemporary debate over constitutional reform in Israel.

If there is one issue that dominates this debate it is the adequacy of current judicial safeguards of individual liberties. The recent history of the Israeli Supreme Court reveals an institution with a strong commitment to the pursuit of a rights-oriented constitutional agenda. The question is whether in the absence of a formal authority to enforce a list of constitutional rights against the actions of other governmental actors (particularly the legislature), a strong commitment is sufficient. Chapter 5 pursues this question by looking at the application of an American rights-based jurisprudential ethic to the Israeli constitutional environment. This application is evident in the increasing popularity of American constitutional theory and doctrine for those Israeli judges who explicitly view their role in terms of fulfilling the aspirations of the democratic component of the Declaration of Independence. They are aware of the potential conflict between this vision and the Declaration's other vision; however, their task, as they see it, is largely one of fulfilling the promise of the liberal part of the document, the part that enjoys considerably less priority elsewhere in the political system. What we will see is that, while there are very definite risks associated with an activist judiciary in Israel, such a role may actually possess greater structural justification in Israel than in the United States. In this institutional sense constitutional transplantation serves to enhance the appeal of the transplanted jurisprudence.

A critical dimension of this judicial role is its pedagogical mission. Judges committed to the democratic principles of the Declaration frankly acknowledge their obligation to articulate important political values as part of the process of educating their fellow citizens. In Chapter 6 I look closely at the area of constitutional concern (and hence political education) that has in Israel most heavily relied on American constitutional theory and doctrine—freedom of speech. It is an area that is particularly promising for any analysis of the intersection of constitutional doctrine and political culture; with respect to the larger comparative argument of the study, it directly addresses the conceptual differences between the respective pluralisms of Israel and the United States.

In this constitutional context, however, I should emphasize that in discussing prevailing doctrinal orthodoxy on freedom of speech, one needs to distinguish between the pluralism of the American founding period and the pluralism of the present. The radically individualist view that culminates in the advancement of personal autonomy as the constitutional value most jealously to be protected, represents a dramatic extension (verging on transvaluation) of the liberal premises of the American Declaration of Independence. The broad libertarian consensus that today mandates a First Amendment stance of content-neutrality is distinguishable from the natural rights philosophy underlying the Declaration. One critical point of distinction is that the older understanding had a place for civility, a virtue that has, for the most part, been sacrificed upon the altar of personal autonomy. Heterogeneity in a pluralist democracy requires extreme tolerance, which, according to the modern American view, must take precedence over whatever concerns we might have for the sensibilities of groups. On the other hand, an Israeli pluralism in which communal integrity is an essential defining attribute of the polity provides, in theory, for a more hospitable environment for nurturing a habit of civility. To the extent, then, that American free speech doctrine is held up as a model for Israeli emulation, the constitutional transplantation that follows may not produce a comfortable fit with the broader premises of the regime. However, as we shall see, these premises may point to constitutional outcomes that, for different reasons, comport with the free speech solution embedded in the older liberal vision of the Declaration of Independence.

At the end of this book I return to our point of departure, consideration of the two founding documents, the two Declarations of Independence. We will have taken the measure of the important differences in these documents, but as the issue of free speech suggests, noted too their converging implications. Perhaps then it will be clearer that the study of comparative constitutionalism has its greatest heuristic potential when it culminates in the symbiotic engagement of contrasting systems. By this I mean that the familiar manner in which a subject like legal transplantation is presented—what can or does one system appropriate from another?—is often too narrowly conceived to permit an appreciation of the fact that the lessons of comparative analysis proceed in two directions. My hope is that in the case of Israel and the United States, the juxtaposition of alternative pluralisms, the contrast of varying political sensibilities and commitments, will lead to a mutual enrichment of constitutional understanding.

Alternative Pluralisms

> Free institutions are next to impossible in a country
> made up of different nationalities.
> —*John Stuart Mill*

PLURALISM AND THE ANOMALY OF NATIVE AMERICANS

Among the many reasons that the decade of the sixties will long exert a hold over the American collective memory is its association with the expansion and legalization of rights. Amid the violence and turmoil of that time, courts and legislatures dramatically accelerated the process of extending constitutional rights to all Americans. For those who were the beneficiaries of this activity, the various efforts undertaken by public authorities to provide for a more just distribution of rights signaled the welcome prospect of their full inclusion in the system of pluralist democracy. To be sure, there were many shadings of opinion regarding the extent to which formal recognitions of rights would translate into meaningful inclusion, but few among the supporters of justice for minorities did not share in the celebration of such achievements as the Civil Rights Act of 1964.

The reason for the widespread sense of satisfaction is clear: however much work remained to be done, these victories represented progress toward fulfilling the societal goal of guaranteeing equal treatment to individuals. Thus, while particular enactments and judicial decisions were appropriately seen as advancing the interests of this or that group of people, the specific result celebrated was the delegitimation of group membership as a criterion in the making of public decisions about individuals. Indeed, the underlying aspiration of the traditional American constitutional approach to protecting the rights of minorities is the replacement of ascriptive recognition with a universal standard of transcendent equality. Entrance into the mainstream of American political, economic, and cultural life presumes a formal acknowledgment of the primacy of the individual to the group.

There is, however, one glaring exception—Native Americans. In 1968

Congress passed the Indian Civil Rights Act, which extended many of the guarantees of the Bill of Rights and the Fourteenth Amendment to Americans of Indian descent. It was the culmination of a lengthy legislative effort engineered by its principal sponsor, Senator Sam Ervin of North Carolina. But unlike the other civil rights enactments of that time, this one produced a decidedly mixed reception, with most of the criticism coming from those who were its intended beneficiaries.[1] This was perhaps not altogether surprising in light of the fact that much of the impetus for the legislation came from outside of the Native American community. Moreover, the legislative history indicates that Congress was itself sensitive to the fact that an extension of rights in this instance would be seen as a mixed blessing. Senator Ervin eventually accepted compromises that, in deference to communitarian sensibilities, modified his original commitment to full assimilation of Indian practices to the notions of individual rights prevailing in the larger society.[2]

Many of the critics readily conceded that altruistic motives lay behind the campaign for Indian rights, although some less charitable in their interpretation of events charged that the 1968 act represented just another chapter in the dismal history of "cultural assault" perpetrated by the dominant culture on Native Americans.[3] The common theme in the concerns expressed by the critics was that the Indian Civil Rights Act was grounded on premises that ignored the essential fact that Native Americans were a minority who did not fit the prevailing model of constitutional and political pluralism. "Individual rights so zealously and formally guarded by a system evolving in the English tradition . . . may not be transferable to a different environment. Only to the extent that the Indian system is based on similar

---

[1] There are a number of accounts of this legislation. See, in particular, Francis Paul Prucha, *The Great White Father: The United States Government and the American Indians*, vol. 2 (Lincoln: University of Nebraska Press, 1984); Donald L. Burnett, Jr., "An Historical Analysis of the 1968 'Indian Civil Rights' Act," *Harvard Journal on Legislation* 9 (1972); and Note, "The Indian Bill of Rights and the Constitutional Status of Tribal Governments," *Harvard Law Review* 82 (1969).

[2] According to Burnett's account, Senator Ervin's experience in North Carolina initially limited his perspective in confronting the problem of Indian rights on a national level. The Indians of his state were, unlike the situation generally, well integrated into the life of the broader community, a fact that influenced his determination to repeat the North Carolina experience on a national level. Burnett, "An Historical Analysis of the 1968 'Indian Civil' Rights' Act," p. 576.

[3] This characterization belongs to Wilcomb E. Washburn, *Red Man's Land/White Man's Law* (New York: Charles Scribner's Sons, 1971), p. 191.

values will the application of such constitutional guarantees be appropriate."[4] "The ideology of civil rights," it was argued, "was anathema to the majority of Indians."[5] Not surprisingly, activists in the civil rights movement were deeply perplexed by the reluctance of an oppressed people to join them in a united campaign to achieve the American dream. For example, Indian representation at the 1963 March on Washington was notably, and to blacks and liberals distressingly, small. "Many liberals saw only the struggle for individual rights, and refused to consider the equally important fact of community existence and the corresponding legal right of a community to exist for its own sake."[6] The Anglo-American concepts of personal freedom and individualism, and the constitutional commitments extending from them, were seen as posing a threat to those Indian traditions and practices that rested on communitarian assumptions fundamentally alien to the broader American experience.[7]

For example, would equal protection standards as applied to sexual discrimination invalidate tribal determinations of membership based on patrilineal criteria? Would such standards eliminate the differential treatment of Indians that had allowed tribes to receive important hunting and fishing privileges? Would the ethnic integrity of the tribe be undermined in the face of statutory prohibitions against racial discrimination that could be interpreted to forbid unequal treatment of cultural outsiders? Would the political speech of the outsider be upheld over the claim of tribal sovereignty? And would the religious authority of the tribe collapse under the weight of establishment clause constitutional tests? In regard to this last issue, Congress chose not to disturb the theocratic nature of much tribal authority by deleting guarantees against establishment of religion from the act's list of protected rights. There was, as the Supreme Court later pointed out, a deliberate congressional policy of selective incorporation "to fit the unique political, cultural, and economic needs of tribal governments."[8]

---

[4] Ibid., pp. 174–75.

[5] Vine Deloria, Jr., *Behind the Trail of Broken Treaties: An Indian Declaration of Independence* (Austin: University of Texas Press, 1985), p. 23.

[6] Ibid., p. 24.

[7] In general, see Vine Deloria, Jr., and Clifford M. Lytle, *American Indians, American Justice* (Austin: University of Texas Press, 1983). This has led one observer to argue, "As a matter of policy, Indians should be recognized as having a legitimate interest in maintaining traditional practices that conflict with constitutional concepts of personal freedom developed in a different social context." Mark S. Campisano, "The Indian Bill of Rights and the Constitutional Status of Tribal Governments," p. 1350.

[8] *Santa Clara Pueblo* v. *Martinez*, 436 U.S. 49, 62 (1978). For an excellent discussion of these unique needs, see Robert N. Clinton, "Isolated in Their Own Country: A Defense of

The fact that policy makers recognized the uniqueness of the Native American minority in formulating a civil rights policy is as interesting as the fact that many observers felt that the legislators had been insufficiently sensitive to all of the ramifications of this uniqueness. What is important is the anomalous status of Native Americans in American law and political theory, a status so exceptional as to emphasize the contrasting characteristics of the normal pluralist pattern of political relations in the United States.[9] The controversy over the Indian Civil Rights Act is not just another episode in the oft-observed tension in American life between the individual and the community; rather, it highlights the narrow parameters within which this struggle generally occurs, and suggests an alternative pluralism that is basically unfamiliar to the experiences and expectations of most Americans. Moreover, it challenges the way we are accustomed to think about constitutionalism.

It is widely understood that rights inhere in the individual, and that it is the purpose of constitutional government to respect and protect these rights. But the "quasi-sovereign" status of the Indian tribes casts a very different light on the question of rights and the concomitant role of government.[10] Native Americans are the only minority whose formal rule-making authority to regulate many of their own affairs is specifically recognized in law. As the Supreme Court has recently said, "Tribal courts have repeatedly been recognized as appropriate forums for the exclusive adjudication of disputes affecting important personal and property interests of both Indians and non-Indians."[11] This enables the tribe to defend its cultural autonomy in the face of widespread pressures to conform to societal norms and behavior. While the Indian Civil Rights Act clearly limits this auton-

---

Federal Protection of Indian Autonomy and Self-Government," *Stanford Law Review* 33 (1981). On the *Santa Clara* case, see John T. Hardin, "*Santa Clara Pueblo* v. *Martinez*: Tribal Sovereignty and the Indian Civil Rights Act of 1968," *Arizona Law Review* 33 (1979).

[9] This anomalous status in the law is reflected in the original Constitution. In Article I, section 8, Congress is given the power "to regulate Commerce with foreign Nations, and among the several States, and *with the Indian Tribes*" (emphasis added). Also, in Article I, section 2, the apportionment of representatives and direct taxes is based on a population that "exclud[es] Indians not taxed." Indians today do pay taxes, and they are counted in the census for purposes of determining representation in the House of Representatives. However, the diminished practical relevance of this constitutional reference should not obscure both its historical importance and its continuing theoretical significance in apprehending the unusual legal relationship between Native Americans and the polity as a whole.

[10] *Santa Clara Pueblo*, 436 U.S. at 71.

[11] Ibid., 65.

omy (Indians are, it should be noted, U.S. citizens), judicial interpretation of the law has been generally consistent with the apparent intent of the Congress not to interfere with the right of tribes to exercise sovereign-like authority in many important domains of social, economic, and political life.[12] Indeed, it is the rights of Indian tribes rather than individual Indians that have acquired formal legal protection in such important matters as marriage and divorce, hunting and fishing privileges, and education.[13]

Nowhere is this unique status better in evidence than in a recent policy initiative undertaken by the Bush administration, which in all other areas has been outspoken in opposing any notion of group rights. A three-year experimental self-government program under the aegis of the Interior Department enables certain tribes to relate to the United States as virtual sovereign nations (a status many tribes have long sought). They may establish their own budgets, conduct their own programs, and negotiate with the federal government for services. "With this experiment," according to the secretary of interior, "I forsee a day when we have true government-to-government relations."[14] In fact it is doubtful that this will occur, for it would mean, among other things, enforcing the terms of long-neglected treaties; but the policy clearly underscores the exceptional status of Native Americans in a liberal polity.

Arguments to resist assimilation into the cultural mainstream of American society have been made by a segment of all minorities in this country. They have been more or less successful depending on the objective circumstances of the group. But even where, as in the case of blacks, the minority has confronted great obstacles to its integration into the mainstream, the assimilationist argument has ultimately prevailed (with mixed practical success), and has been assisted, with notable exceptions, by public policies (including constitutional interpretation) that discourage separate development. Whether it is still true, as Gunnar Myrdal suggested decades ago,

[12] The courts have generally heeded the words of the U.S. Civil Rights Commission: "In enforcing the act, the courts will have the serious responsibility of drawing a balance between respect for individual rights and respect for Indian custom and tradition." Quoted in Burnett, "An Historical Analysis of the 1968 'Indian Civil Rights' Act," p. 555. Charles F. Wilkinson, a close observer of developments in Indian law, has written of the "anomaly of a federal civil rights act that provides only very limited remedies to enforce it." Charles F. Wilkinson, *American Indians, Time, and the Law: Native Societies in a Modern Constitutional Democracy* (New Haven: Yale University Press, 1987), p. 114.

[13] When several years ago the chairman of the Civil Rights Commission challenged the exercise of tribal authority in determining where the child of divorced parents should reside, it was he who ended up fighting for his job.

[14] *New York Times*, January 16, 1991.

that the American Creed is more meaningful to blacks than to whites (as a way of realizing unfulfilled aspirations) is perhaps debatable.[15] What is difficult to contest is that it has been the shared aspiration of minorities, and those who have sought to advance the interest of minorities, to destroy the barriers that prevent individual minority members from exercising a choice in regard to assimilation. With respect to Native Americans, however, resistance to assimilation has been so powerful as to reshape public policy into a pluralist mold that has as its goal the maintenance of the cultural integrity of the group. From time to time the federal government has developed programs seeking to integrate and atomize the Native American population by undermining tribal authority. But as the leading historian of governmental policy in this area has observed, "Attempts to divest Indians of their tribal relations and let them disappear as individual citizens into the body of the nation did not succeed."[16] The rhetoric of freedom, so often used to facilitate assimilation, has rung hollow in the face of the "primeval nationhood" that provides decisive definition to the Native American experience.[17]

This creates a constitutional anomaly. Officially sanctioned separate development is constitutionally tolerated only in the case of a minority whose claim to differential treatment as a group is directly related to its assertion of a separate national identity. The Supreme Court has acknowledged the historical basis of the claim. One of Chief Justice Taney's less notorious observations in the *Dred Scott* case was that Indians "were . . . a free and independent people, associated together in nations or tribes, and governed by their own laws." As such, "Indian political communities have always

---

[15] "The American Negroes know that they are a subordinated group experiencing, more than anyone else in the nation, the consequences of the fact that the Creed is not lived up to in America." Gunnar Myrdal, *An American Dilemma* (New York: Harper & Row, 1962). My guess is that the recent emergence of an Afrocentric orientation that calls into question the legitimacy of the American Creed has not penetrated very far into the black community.

[16] Prucha, *The Great White Father*, vol. 2, p. 1186.

[17] *Navajo Tribe* v. *Orlando Helicopter Airways*, 6 Am. Indian L. Newsletter 90, 92, quoted in Judy D. Lynch, "Indian Sovereignty and Judicial Interpretations of the Indian Civil Rights Act," *Washington University Law Quarterly* 1979 (1979): 899. According to Lynch, the phrase "refers to the tribes' original status as autonomous governmental bodies prior to the arrival of the white man on the American continent." It is the ultimate source of the sovereignty recognized by Chief Justice Marshall in the landmark case of *Worcester v. Georgia*, 31 U.S. (6 Pet.) 515 (1832). "Much of what is meant by 'sovereignty' is the power of the Indian polity to control its governmental affairs and employ that power to preserve or channel its 'cultural integrity.'" Monroe E. Price, *Law and the American Indian: Readings, Notes and Cases* (Indianapolis: Bobbs-Merrill Co., 1973).

been treated as foreigners not living under our Government."[18] More recently the Court has said, "As separate sovereigns pre-existing the Constitution, tribes have historically been regarded as unconstrained by those constitutional provisions framed specifically as limitations on federal or state authority."[19] In the case of other minorities, including those, like blacks, who were brutally victimized by the majority culture, the concept of a national identity has been meaningful principally in terms of the set of ideals that the pluralistic American polity has woven together to create unity out of diversity.[20] Native American separatism, dramatically symbolized by the reservation, and entailing unique, if limited, powers of self-governance, exists because the various Indian nations have, to a greater or lesser extent, retained their sense of independent nationhood and, with this, the capacity to embody the collective wills of their members. Public policies that would immediately arouse grave and widespread misgivings were they applied to any other ethnic or racial minority are tolerated in the case of Native Americans. This is the case both when they are singled out by the government for special treatment and when their tribes, in the exercise of quasi-sovereign authority, deny equal rights to nonmembers residing under their jurisdiction.[21] In part this reflects the support of most of these policies by the targeted group; in a broader sense, however, it reflects an awareness that the norms of a liberal pluralist society require modification

[18] *Dred Scott* v. *Sandford*, 60 U.S. (19 How.) 393, 403–4 (1857). Taney made the observation as a way of distinguishing Indians and blacks, toward the end of reinforcing his basic position regarding the latter group's inferior status under law.

[19] *Santa Clara Pueblo* v. *Martinez*, 436 U.S. at 56. The case involved the question of tribal membership, which the Court ruled was a fundamental right of an Indian tribe to determine. As we will see in the next chapter, this membership question has its analogue ("Who is a Jew?") in Israel. Wilkinson argues that our jurisprudence accepts this sovereignty because of its recognition that tribal authority is both "preconstitutional" and "extraconstitutional." *American Indians, Time, and the Law*, p. 112.

[20] A particularly good discussion of this phenomenon may be found in Kenneth L. Karst, "Paths to Belonging: The Constitution and Cultural Identity," *North Carolina Law Review* 64 (1986): 362. See also his broader study, *Belonging to America: Equal Citizenship and the Constitution* (New Haven: Yale University Press, 1989).

[21] The traditional test in this area requires that the Supreme Court exercise special scrutiny in examining laws affecting "discrete and insular minorities." Since Native Americans surely qualify for such status, it may be argued that tribal authority denying rights to non-Indians is itself a minority right requiring judicial protection. Or it might be said that since the status of tribes is in fact extraconstitutional, their exercise of discriminatory power falls beyond the reach of the usual tests. For a discussion of these arguments, see Wilkinson, *American Indians, Time, and the Law*, pp. 117–18.

when confronted by a nation coexisting with the larger nation within which it resides.

AUTONOMY

Justice Johnson's opinion in the famous case of *Cherokee Nation* v. *Georgia* presents this interesting parallel: "They [the Indians] are or may be deemed a state though not a sovereign state, at least while they occupy a country within our limits. Their condition is something like that of the Israelites, when inhabiting the deserts. Though without land that they can call theirs in the sense of property, their right for personal self-government has never been taken from them; and such a form of government may exist though the land occupied be in fact that of another."[22] Like the Indians, the right of the Israelites to self-rule inheres in their nationhood, a factor of sufficiently compelling quality that it legitimates a claim of governance even in the absence of territorial control. Thus the sentiment in the following formulation of a Cherokee Indian spokesman could just as easily have been made by a Jew about Israel: "In the language of my people there is a word for land: Eloheh. This same word also means history, culture, religion. We cannot separate our place on earth from our lives on the earth nor from our vision nor our meaning as a people."[23] Indeed, the example of Israel, its "relevance to the Indian status question," has not escaped the attention of advocates of Indian national rights. "Israel's achievement of independence, the international recognition of her sovereignty, and her membership in the United Nations are a dramatic vindication of the validity of traditional, historic claims to specific territory as the sovereign heritage of a particular people. Israel's victory is a great tribute to the strength of a culture and the tenacity of a people in pursuit of a homeland."[24]

Since 1948 self-rule and territorial control have coincided in spite of the reluctance of the surrounding states to accept Israel's status as a sovereign

---

[22] *Cherokee Nation v. Georgia*, 30 U.S. (5 Pet.) 1, 27 (1831). The predicament of Native Americans has also been compared to the contemporary plight of Palestinians in the Middle East. See Clinton, "Isolated in Their Own Country," p. 1019. Of course the political implications flowing from this comparison could assume several forms, ranging from autonomy within the state of Israel to the establishment of an independent Palestinian state.

[23] Quoted in Charles S. Liebman and Stephen M. Cohen, *Two Worlds of Judaism: The Israeli and American Experiences* (New Haven: Yale University Press, 1989), p. 68.

[24] Deloria, *Behind the Trail of Broken Treaties*, p. 183.

25

state. Also before that, during the period of the British mandate, the Jews exercised considerable autonomy in maintaining control over the internal affairs of their community.[25] Much as, in the words of the U.S. Supreme Court in 1896, "the powers of local self-government enjoyed by the Cherokee nation existed prior to the Constitution,"[26] for centuries under Ottoman rule the *millet* system operated, in accordance with which "those who did not belong to the dominant religion of Islam were allowed to administer their communal affairs under the authority of their ecclesiastical or religious heads."[27] This was a concession to the nonassimilative character of the area's heterogeneity, and in time became the expression of the nationalistic identity of religious minorities. Specifically as to the Jewish community, "[It] presented the least difficulty to the Ottomans in their reorganization of the non-Muslim religious groups because, among the Jews, ethnicity, religion, and community coincided. In fact, one may argue that the Jewish community was from the start close to the apparent Ottoman ideal of the synthesis of ethnicity, religion, and community that was to be the building material of its political edifice."[28] This experience was not discarded when Jews became a majority in a sovereign Israeli state.

While Zionism's intellectual and political roots were in Europe, its playing field was the Middle East.[29] No effort was made to uproot the historic

[25] On this point, see Joel S. Migdal, *Strong Societies and Weak States: State-Society Relations and State Capabilities in the Third World* (Princeton: Princeton University Press, 1988), pp. 142–76. See also Dan Horowitz, "Before the State: Communal Politics in Palestine Under the Mandate," in *The Israeli State and Society: Boundaries and Frontiers*, ed. Baruch Kimmerling (Albany: State University Press of New York, 1989). The considerable autonomy of the Jewish community should not conceal the fact, however, of deep divisions within that community—for example, old/new yishuv, sepharadim/ashkenazim, first/second aliya, left/right. For a thoughtful account of these divisions, see Dan Horowitz and Moshe Lissak, *Trouble in Utopia: The Overburdened Polity of Israel* (Albany: State University of New York Press, 1989), chaps. 2 and 3.

[26] *Talton v. Mayes*, 163 U.S. 376, 384 (1896).

[27] Elie Kedourie, "Ethnicity, Majority, and Minority in the Middle East," in *Ethnicity, Pluralism, and the State in the Middle East*, ed. Milton J. Esman and Itamar Rabinovich (Ithaca: Cornell University Press, 1988), p. 27. The many facets of the millet system are considered in Benjamin Braude and Bernard Lewis, eds., *Christians and Jews in the Ottoman Empire: The Functioning of a Plural Society*, 2 vols. (New York: Holmes & Meier, 1982).

[28] Kemal Karpat, "The Ottoman Ethnic and Confessional Legacy in the Middle East," in *Ethnicity, Pluralism, and the State in the Middle East*, ed. Esman and Rabinovich, p. 43.

[29] It is has been argued that there is an overlap between Zionism's roots in Europe and its eventual flowering in the group-oriented milieu of the Middle East. Shlomo Avineri, for example, has made the point that the links between religion and nationalism have their origin in the intersection of ethnicity and religion in Eastern Europe. For him Israei political culture

patterns of the area, in which a deference to the primordial attachments of religion and ethnicity was reflected in official support for sustaining and preserving the corporate identity of diverse groups in the polity. Of course there was more to the Israeli adoption of the essential features of the millet system than the desire for maintaining continuity with regional tradition. The establishment of a Jewish state implied both the acceptance, as a theoretical proposition, of some concept of group rights, as well as the nurturing, as a practical matter, of the cultural autonomy of the various population groupings who were non-Jewish.[30] The explicit recognition of the reality of difference is specifically institutionalized in the decision-making structure pertaining to questions of personal status. All the officially recognized religions maintain quasi-independent courts exercising jurisdiction over matters of marriage, divorce, adoption, inheritance, and charitable endowments. Through the Ministry of Religious Affairs funding is provided to these religions for the purpose of administering the facilities that perpetuate the separate existence of the particular communities. As a result, therefore, ethnoreligious groups compete with the state for the right to exercise coercive authority over individuals whom the group views as its members and whom the state recognizes as citizens of one polity. No such competition is permitted within the pluralistic configuration of the United States, where the ethnic or religious group is required to function in the much more limited fashion of the voluntary association.[31]

We arrive at much the same point if we note the problematic character, within the context of American pluralist assumptions, of the nexus between state and religion. For example, an American court recently declared, "The Establishment Clause . . . enshrines two central values: voluntarism and

---

is rooted in the traditions of Eastern European ethnonationalism rather than the secular individualism of Western Europe and the United States. See in this regard his portrait of Zionism in Shlomo Avineri, *The Making of Modern Zionism: The Intellectual Origins of the Jewish State* (New York: Basic Books, 1981), p. 12, where he makes the claim that the Jews of Eastern Europe followed the example of such national groups as the Poles and Lithuanians in forging their own modern national identity. Another useful account of the Eastern European roots of Zionism may be found in David Vital, *Zionism: The Crucial Phase* (Oxford: Oxford University Press, 1987).

[30] For an analysis that sees the public recognition of cultural autonomy as directly related to the "pluralistic-inequality structure of Israeli society," see Sammy Smooha, *Israel: Pluralism and Conflict* (Berkeley: University of California Press, 1978).

[31] See Michael Walzer's discussion in "Pluralism in Political Perspective," in *The Politics of Ethnicity*, ed. Michael Walzer, Edward T. Kantowicz, John Higham, and Mona Harrington (Cambridge: Harvard University Press, 1982), p. 16.

pluralism."[32] By this it meant, quoting Justice Black, that "a union of government and religion tends to destroy government and to degrade religion."[33] Understandably, then, the most notable difference between the enumeration of rights in the first ten amendments and the final list of rights included in the Indian Civil Rights Act of 1968 is the absence in the latter of an establishment clause; for as we have seen, it is the exceptional status of Native Americans that serves to delineate the contours of American pluralist practice. The constitutional barrier to religious establishment is intended to relegate the spiritual life to the realm of the private, which is consistent with a pluralist vision of carefully bounded public authority. It is a bar, as Michael Walzer has written, to "any attempt at communal provision in the sphere of grace."[34] This takes the place of an alternative set of boundary drawing. "A hard-edged, corporatist version of cultural pluralism, devolving important political functions to religious or ethnic groups, is beyond the range of the possible in the United States today. For ethnic corporatism to work, we should have to define the boundaries of each ethnic group, identifying its members and the characteristics that entitle them to membership."[35] American pluralism establishes a horizontal boundary between church and state in order to avoid enforcement of vertical boundaries between church and church that might compromise the principle of neutrality in affairs of the soul. "The Establishment Clause," according to Justice O'Connor, "prohibits government from making adherence to a religion relevant in any way to a person's standing in the political community."[36]

The familiar metaphor of a "wall of separation," for all of its shortcomings in representing the intentions of the framers, succeeds in conveying a cardinal principle of modern constitutionalist thought, namely that the state should not involve itself in matters that have been walled off for societal, which is to say private, attention.[37] For present purposes, it is a principle that incorporates more than the distinction between state and religion, for when one introduces considerations of race and ethnicity, it is

---

[32] *McLean v. Arkansas*, 529 F. Supp. 1255, 1258 (1982).

[33] Ibid., 1258.

[34] Michael Walzer, *Spheres of Justice* (New York: Basic Books, 1983), p. 245.

[35] Karst, "Paths to Belonging," p. 368.

[36] Quoted in Karst, *Belonging to America*, p. 101.

[37] For a thoughtful discussion of this principle, see Harvey C. Mansfield, Jr., "The Religious Issue and the Origins of Modern Constitutionalism," in *How Does the Constitution Protect Religious Freedom?*, ed. Robert A. Goldwin and Art Kaufman (Washington D.C.: American Enterprise Institute for Public Policy Research, 1987).

equally clear that they too, in accordance with the precepts of modern constitutionalism, are protected against much governmental intervention by a wall of separation.[38] One of the factors in the Middle East that explains the absence of a comparable wall is the difficulty in that setting of cleanly distinguishing between religion and nationality. Separating religion and state cannot therefore be accomplished without placing the cultural attributes of national identity outside the sphere of public authority, a placement that is, for most societies, scarcely imaginable. Where religion (as in the case of Native Americans) is so fundamentally entwined in conceptions of national identity, the insistence, for example, that there be no "governmental entanglement" in religion has an air of unreality about it.[39] This is often unappreciated by people whose experience offers a conception of citizenship and national identity that is fundamentally volitional in character, almost totally dependent on the affirmation of certain political ideas. For example, in a statement issued by organized American Jewry in 1964, the claim was made that "the overwhelming majority of Jews, whatever their religious commitment, support the basic Jewish position of separation of 'Church' and State, and of freedom of religious belief, practice and instruction for all."[40] This statement's accuracy (at least the first part) depends on the audience noting that a majority of Jews live in Western liberal democracies.

There should be no misunderstanding here. Israel, like most states in the area, is not a theocracy. It is a state, however, that takes official cognizance of religion and formulates public policy accordingly. Moreover,

---

[38] As Michael Walzer has observed, "Americans are communal in their private affairs, individualist in their politics. Society is a collection of groups; the state is an organization of individual citizens. And society and state, though they constantly interact, are formally distinct." Walzer, "Pluralism in Political Perspective," p. 17.

[39] At the Labor party convention held in November 1991, a resolution was passed that was described in the press as calling for the separation of state and religion. It was quickly denounced by party leaders who, in recognition of the political risks associated with such a pronouncement, vowed to have it overturned in the near future. One sentence in the resolution reads, "Religious pluralism and tolerance will be ensured by a constitution based on the principles of equality and freedom of choice, by keeping religion out of politics." *Jerusalem Post*, November 30, 1991. However, the author of the statement made clear that his language did not intend to remove marriage and divorce from under the authority of the religious courts. But as we shall see, the fact that these matters of personal status reside there is testimony to an inherent logic in the organization of the state that in the end provides a hollow ring to the call for separating religion from politics.

[40] Quoted in S. Zalmon Abramov, *Perpetual Dilemma: Jewish Religion in the Jewish State* (Rutherford, N.J.: Fairleigh Dickinson University Press, 1976), p. 375.

much of this policy embraces antiassimilationist assumptions antithetical to traditional American pluralism. One of the effects of the establishment clause is to facilitate, if not encourage, intermarriage, which is of course the most obvious measure of assimilation. By erecting a wall between state and religion it prevents the state from reinforcing other walls that religions themselves construct to exclude the outside world. In the case, for example, of an Israeli Jew who wishes to marry outside the faith but is unable to do so legally, that person's predicament results directly from the government's formal recognition and conferral of binding rule-making authority on the Orthodox rabbinate in affairs of personal status.[41] The American Jew in the same situation will very likely be discouraged by his or her rabbi from marrying, but any governmental action to support through law the religion's precepts on intermarriage would be seen as an unambiguous violation of the constitutional stricture against establishment. Thus the establishment clause supports the assimilative dynamic of the larger pluralism of which it is a part.

This difference in the two pluralist approaches also expresses itself in terms of how the polity deals with the question of exemptions from laws of general applicability. A 1962 Israeli statute, the Pig-Raising Prohibition Law, stipulated that "a person shall not raise, keep or slaughter pigs." The law applied to Jews and Moslems, but exempted Christian communities. The exemption was not an issue of religious freedom; Christians, after all, are not required to eat pork. Rather, it reflected the desire of the majority not to offend the sensibilities (and the pocketbooks) of an important religious and cultural minority. In the United States such a law would undoubtedly fail a constitutional test on establishment grounds. Indeed, even if eating pork *were* required of a particular religious denomination, the law might still be struck down in the clash between establishment and free exercise considerations. When Simcha Goldman, an Orthodox Jew and an ordained rabbi, claimed that an Air Force regulation preventing him from wearing his yarmulke (skullcap) indoors violated his free exercise rights, the U.S. Supreme Court held that "the First Amendment does not require the military to accommodate such practices in the face of its view that they

---

[41] Israel does not enforce the rabbinical views on intermarriage directly. It simply has no mechanism for civil marriage. A couple already married abroad will be recognized for all civil matters, and if their marriage requires dissolution, they will not be subject to the rabbinical courts, which would nullify the marriage, but rather to the civil courts, which would dissolve it. The power to decide jurisdictional questions in mixed-marriage dissolution is held by the president of the Supreme Court. The Dissolution of Marriage Act (Special Circumstances), 5729–1969, section 1(a).

would detract from the uniformity sought by the dress regulations."[42] Had an exemption been granted Goldman by the military, it is highly likely that it would have been struck down on establishment criteria. To be sure, religious exemptions have from time to time been upheld by the Supreme Court, but typically their validity hinges upon a secularization of the issue involved; thus it might apply to all those who can provide evidence that their consciences have been coerced by the state in violation of their sincerely held beliefs.[43] More fundamentally, in a pluralist society that remains publicly indifferent to one's group affiliation, exemptions from laws of general applicability are perhaps best viewed as an extension of grace to the individual; whereas in the polity that provides formal recognition to specified ascriptive groups, greater plausibility exists for asserting that exemptions are traceable to the collective rights of these groups.

An issue that highlights the contrasting nature of pluralist experience in the two countries is bigamy/polygamy. The Supreme Courts of Israel and the United States have addressed the question, and their respective treatments of the problem are revealing in theoretically interesting ways. The principal American case is *Reynolds* v. *United States*, in which the Court upheld a federal statute that made polygamy a crime. The plaintiff, a Mormon, had argued that the constitutional guaranty of religious freedom protected him against legislation limiting his liberty to have more than one wife. The Court's straightforward rejection of the claim focused on "whether those who make polygamy a part of their religion are excepted from the operation of the statute."[44] Its conclusion was that "it is within the

---

[42] *Goldman* v. *Weinberger*, 475 U.S. 503, 509–10 (1986). Congress eventually acted to permit members of the armed forces to wear religious apparel indoors if the item is neat and conservative. In the debate Congressman Stephen Solarz said, "I need not remind you that the most effective military force in the Middle East, the Israel Defense Forces, permits its members to wear yarmulkes. I do not think it has handicapped their ability to overcome their enemies in battle." Quoted in Louis Fisher, *American Constitutional Law* (New York: McGraw-Hill Publishing Co., 1990).

[43] See, in particular, the conscientious objector cases, especially *Welsh* v. *United States*, 398 U.S. 333 (1970), and *United States* v. *Seeger*, 380 U.S. 163 (1965). One way to avoid establishment problems is to define exemptions in terms of an expansive definition of religion that effectively dilutes it of religious content. Donald Kommers's observation is relevant here: "In dealing with minorities and various ethnic or religious groups . . . the [American] state is often obligated constitutionally to reject the model of cultural pluralism in favor of the assimilationist model . . . which 'detexturizes' our society and cuts us off from a rich heritage rooted in religion, ethnicity, language, and culture." Donald Kommers, "Liberty and Community in American Constitutional Law: Continuing Tensions" (Indiana University Bicentennial of the U.S. Constitution Lecture Series, 1986).

[44] *Reynolds* v. *United States*, 98 U.S. 146, 166 (1879).

legitimate scope of the power of every civil government to determine whether polygamy or monogamy shall be the law of social life under its dominion."[45]

Ten years later, in *Davis* v. *Beason*, the Court elaborated on its views. Justice Field argued that "to extend exemption from punishment for such crimes would shock the moral judgment of the community."[46] The community alluded to of course was coterminous with the nation, it being a virtual certainty that the local Mormon community would not have been shocked by an exemption from punishment for polygamy. "Probably never before in the history of this country has it been seriously contended that the whole punitive power of the government for acts, recognized by the general consent of the Christian world in modern times as proper matters for prohibitory legislation, must be suspended in order that the tenets of a religious sect encouraging crime be carried out without hindrance."[47] No doubt this observation gives expression to the widespread hostility directed toward the Mormons of this time. But it also manifests a philosophical opposition to the idea that the broader society owes consideration and deference to the fundamental beliefs of a religious community in matters touching on the public morality.

Of course no political system can commit itself categorically to incorporating into public policy all minority perspectives on public morality.[48] That would make civil society impossible. But once we discard the impossible extremes, there exists a spectrum of alternative approaches. In the Israeli case *Yosifof* v. *Attorney-General*, the issue of multiple marriages produced a revealingly "un-American" result. The case involved the terms of a statute passed under the mandate, a fact that might undermine its

---

[45] Ibid., 166.

[46] *Davis* v. *Beason*, 133 U.S. 333, 341 (1889).

[47] Ibid., 343.

[48] The limits of legal deference to cultural autonomy are vividly indicated in the Israeli case *Dalal Rassi* v. *Attorney-General* 7 P.D. 790 (1953). It may be found in E. David Goitein, ed., *Selected Judgments of the Supreme Court of Israel, vol. 1, 1948–1953* (Jerusalem: Ministry of Justice, 1962). The case involved a severe infliction of corporal punishment by a teacher in an Arab school. After stating that "the Court will always give full consideration to the effect of customs and traditions which have been accepted by the people as forming part of their way of life," the Court proceeded to apply a national standard in evaluating the punishment (p. 245). "The choosing of a punishment and the method of its infliction upon a wrongdoer are not matters affecting merely an individual or a number of individuals or a particular section of the community. They affect the State as a whole, the community as a whole" (p. 244). Finally: "It would indeed be a tragedy for the State and its inhabitants if acts of cruelty towards children or adults were to be permitted under the guise of religion or racial customs" (p. 245).

comparative value, except for the additional fact that it presents an underlying theory for the law of personal status that also applies to laws enacted since 1948.

Yosifof, an Israeli Jew, was convicted of the felony of bigamy. The core of his argument was that the section of the Criminal Code ordinance under which he was convicted discriminated improperly among the inhabitants of Palestine.[49] Because, in brief, it created an exception grounded in the law of personal status, it permitted a Moslem to have more than one wife but prevented him from acting in the same way. Marriage, he claimed, was an institution common to all communities, and the state (or mandatory power in this instance) could not legislate different principles for different communities. The Supreme Court accepted the antidiscrimination principle, but rejected Yosifof's claim.

In his opinion for the Court, Justice Landau placed the issue of discrimination within the context of "the social realities of the country."[50] He analogized the marriage law to the rule requiring that official court documents be issued in the language of the person to whom they are addressed. Such a rule, he maintained, distinguishes between classes of people by reason of language, but far from improperly discriminating, expresses "a desire to confer equal status upon all the official languages."[51] The critical word here is *status*, since in the case of marriage there is a much more obvious difference (than in the language example) in the treatment accorded individuals on the basis of their religious affiliation. But if the issue of equality is defined in terms of the status accorded to separate communities, then the fact that *individuals* experience a varied legal reality across communities does not substantiate a claim of improper discrimination.[52] Landau's argument assumes the following:

[49] He also claimed that the section exceeded the powers conferred on the legislature of the Mandate by the Palestine Order in Council, 1922. The Court acknowledged that if indeed there was such a conflict the section would be void *ab initio*, and it would also be invalid in the state of Israel (which otherwise recognized the validity of the Mandatory legislation).

[50] *Yosifof* v. *Attorney-General*, 5 P. D. 481 (1951), in Goitein, *Selected Judgments*, vol. 1, p. 185. Pnina Lahav has pointed out to me a dimension of the social reality not addressed in the Court's opinion. In the Sephardic world bigamy was acceptable. This community was literally ignored when this law was enforced after 1948, because for those responsible for law enforcement, there was one standard: Ashkenazi. The Sephardic way of life was considered primitive and unworthy.

[51] Ibid., p. 185.

[52] This is also put in the following way: "We must ask ourselves whether the men and women of the same community regarded as one unit are discriminated against. The answer to this question cannot be otherwise than in the negative." Ibid., p. 187.

A legislature does not operate in a vacuum, but is faced with an actually existing social state of affairs with its various manifestations, and must formulate legal forms to meet that situation, and also direct its development in the future. As far as the institution of marriage is concerned, the legislator found himself confronted, as raw material, with a reality consisting of varied outlooks which were fundamentally different. It found that the population of the country was not homogeneous, but that it consisted of different peoples and communities, each with its own laws and customs. Can we say that the Mandatory legislature committed a breach of the principle of nondiscrimination because it did not impose its will on the existing situation but to some extent yielded to reality?[53]

The population of the United States, too, is heterogeneous, but it is hard to imagine an American court upholding this sort of legislation. To support his argument in defense of the statute, the Israeli state attorney relied on judgments of the U.S. Supreme Court purporting to show that the equal protection clause of the Fourteenth Amendment does not prevent classification of different groups within the community. In accepting this line of argument, Justice Landau unfortunately did not cite specific cases, for while he surely would have had no difficulty sustaining the general point that not all governmental classifications are invalid, he would have had considerably more difficulty enumerating cases in which the Court has accepted racial, ethnic, or religious classifications as a legitimate basis for establishing a variable criminal code. Indeed, with the exception of law relating to Native Americans, the postslavery history of the United States does not reveal examples where legislatures have attempted to pass such laws. To be sure, the American federal system permits, in a way unavailable to the Israelis, the tailoring of laws to local communities; but here the relevant understanding of communities is geographic, not ascriptive.[54]

[53] Ibid., p. 185.

[54] Nathan Glazer has written that "the type of diversity that most concerned the framers of the Constitution was not that of race, religion, and ethnicity, but rather a diversity of political units." Nathan Glazer, "The Constitution and American Diversity," in *Forging Unity Out of Diversity: The Approaches of Eight Nations* ed. Robert A. Goldwin, Art Kaufman, and William A. Schambra (Washington, D.C.: American Enterprise Institute of Public Policy Research, 1989), pp. 60–61. Actually, it is difficult to separate the concerns of the framers as far as these two types of diversity are concerned; to a great extent, it was through a diversity of political units that they sought to minimize the potential dangers associated with the other kind of diversity. The American Supreme Court's decision in *Miller* v. *California*, in which the Court provided flexible standards for local regulation of pornography, may be viewed as a communitarian outcome. "It is neither realistic nor constitutionally sound to read the First

In his concurring opinion, Justice Silberg indicated that one of the appropriate functions of the state is "the maintenance and regulation of particular forms of living and cultural values in which that particular section of the community is interested, and which it holds dear."[55] This is not a function peculiar to the Israeli state. However, in contrast with the United States, two observations are worth making: first, that the American pursuit of cultural autonomy through public policy is a significantly less salient concern than in Israel; and second, that when it is of direct concern, the philosophical presuppositions of the system require that it be pursued in indirect ways with at best the oblique support of the law.

COMMUNITY

Whatever the degree of ethnoreligious autonomy (and legal equality) in Israel, it is not accompanied by real equality among officially recognized groups. Israel's Jewish community obviously enjoys a privileged status in a state whose raison d'etre is that it be the homeland for the Jewish people. Indeed, the laws of personal status, as well as their earlier incarnation in the millet system, can be understood as the logical extension of a system that in various ways commits itself to the special concerns of a dominant group. Communal autonomy thus supports political stability by providing non-dominant (and unassimilable) groups with mechanisms that enable them to minimize the effects of their inferior position in the larger society.[56] Or to

---

Amendment as requiring that the people of Maine or Mississippi accept public depiction of conduct found tolerable in Las Vegas or New York City. . . . People in different states vary in their tastes and attitudes, and this diversity is not to be strangled by the absolutism of imposed uniformity." *Miller*, 413 U.S. 15, 32–33 (1973). This respect for the diversity of political units is a very abstract form of communitarianism, which obviously misses a great deal in actual community sentiment. For example, the Orthodox Jewish community in New York would understandably bristle at the suggestion that its moral standards are to be reduced to the level thought by the Court to characterize New Yorkers generally.

[55] *Yosifof* v. *Attorney-General*, 5 P.D. 481, in Goitein, *Selected Judgments*, vol. 1, p. 195. It should be noted that the British Mandate Ordinance has been superseded, and that polygamy is now universally illegal. Penal Law, section 176. But in order not to encroach on Moslem law by giving a nonreligious meaning to the term *married* for purposes of bigamy, and yet not making bigamy a source of forced divorces in the Moslem community, the law makes it a felony for a man to divorce his wife without her consent and without a decision of the competent religious court.

[56] This factor has been cited as an explanation for the greater stability of Israel in comparison with Thailand, both of which have had to wrestle with the acute problems associated

put it another way, group autonomy may be valued more highly in a political context where a lack of autonomy characterizes the relationship between the state and one of its ethnoreligious communities.[57]

The autonomous, neutral state of liberal constitutional theory does not present an altogether appropriate model for the Israeli polity. Critics may question whether it is an appropriate model for any state (an issue that need not be confronted here); one can, however, compare polities in terms of the degree to which they identify with any particular population group residing within their jurisdiction. H.L.A. Hart, the legal philosopher who well represents an important version of the modern theory of liberal constitutionalism, was asked whether the national character of a country should be established by state law, and specifically whether Israel should be a de jure Jewish state. In his emphatic rejection of this idea, Hart argued that an Israeli state that was committed to Jewishness in the sense that it mandated compliance with various parts of the Jewish law would not be reconcilable with the principles on which the liberal state is based.[58] It was pointed out to Hart that "many people in Israel consider preserving the Shabbat, or even preserving Jewish marriage, as a cultural issue." His response: "Yes, but this is precisely where culture has no absolute priority. Where it impinges on moral judgment and denies desirable human liberties, I would subordinate the cultural aspects to the liberal principles, which are prima facie principles. Giving cultural consideration absolute priority would lead to a substantial retreat from the liberal conception of human rights and individual liberties."[59]

---

with the presence of an important ethnoreligious minority. See Erik Cohen, "Citizenship, Nationality, and Religion in Israel and Thailand," in Kimmerling, *The Israeli State and Society*, p. 84. For another interpretation of intercommunal stability in Israel, one that emphasizes segmentation, dependence, and co-optation as critical in maintaining control over the Arab minority, see Ian Lustick, *Arabs in the Jewish State: Israel's Control of a National Minority* (Austin: University of Texas Press, 1980).

[57] As scholars have noted, this political context prevails in the Middle East. For example: "In no polity in this region does the state enjoy sufficient autonomy from its ethnic communities that it can claim to be a neutral arbiter among them, building loyalty to political institutions that respect cultural pluralism while transcending particularistic solidarities. Ethnic solidarities are too prominent in the Middle East to permit this strategy of state-building." Milton J. Esman, "Ethnic Politics: How Unique Is the Middle East?" in Esman and Rabinovich, *Ethnicity, Pluralism, and the State in the Middle East*, p. 282. This should be contrasted with the more familiar pattern of Western democracies where, as Michael Walzer has pointed out in reference to the United States, "no single group can hope to capture the state and turn it into a nation-state." Walzer, "Pluralism in Political Perspective," p. 17.

[58] Interview with Herbert L. A. Hart, in *Israeli Democracy*, Winter 1987, p. 28.

[59] Ibid., p. 28.

No rights, of course, can be construed as absolutes (at best they can, in Ronald Dworkin's term, possess a trumping power); in Israel, however, it is far from clear that cultural (or national) claims are in fact *inferior* to, say, claims of conscience. Studies of Jewish public opinion in Israel reveal, for example, that shared ethnicity and a shared set of religious symbols are much more important than a shared set of values in providing unity for the Israeli society.[60] Thus, the subordination of "cultural aspects" to individual liberties on the basis of the assertion that the latter are "principles" has less justification in a polity where cultural imperatives may legitimately demand *principled* consideration.

From whence might such principles derive? Ultimately they are bound up in the historical experience of a given society, as the American—Israeli comparison suggests. Although the contrast is not perfect, it is helpful to view Israel as an example of a nation creating a state and the United States as a state creating a nation.[61] As Lincoln reminded us, that act of creation is a continuous one, its realization contingent on the fulfillment of certain foundational principles. On the other hand, "Israel is not a nation in the process of becoming. It is an instance of a not uncommon case: the political expression of a people already formed."[62] In the former case, the attributes of nationhood flow directly from the political conception of the state; to be an American is to embrace certain political principles. But the Israeli founding was different. "As a modern state, Israel was to be based on civil, legal-rational principles of legitimation; but these provided primarily the formal foundation of the state. Of greater salience for the founders and the Jewish population was the legitimation of the state in secularized traditional terms: the right of the Jewish people to national sovereignty in their own land."[63] This in itself does not establish the precise character of the regime, but it does ensure, unlike in the United States, official acknowledgment of both the particular as well as the universal; that is, it creates for the Jewish community a claim for principled consideration that must occasion-

[60] Liebman and Cohen, *Two Worlds of Judaism*, p. 122.

[61] Here I differ with Michael Walzer, who argues that with regard to the first immigrants, the Anglo-Americans, "politics still followed nationality." Walzer, "Pluralism in Political Perspective," p. 7. The state, to be sure, did not materialize out of nothing, but it does not follow that it was the nationality of the immigrants that led to the creation of this particular state. In this regard, the historian Louis L. Snyder has commented, "This was the first time in history that men had deliberately fashioned a nation; in the past, nations had simply grown as a product of history, religion, royal dynasties, or armies." Louis L. Snyder, *Varieties of Nationalism* (New York: Holt, Rinehart, & Winston, 1976), p. 207.

[62] Martin Peretz, "Comfort of Strangers," *New Republic*, June 24, 1991, p. 43.

[63] Cohen, "Citizenship, Nationality and Religion in Israel and Thailand," p. 69. This is to be contrasted with the United States, where, as Michael Novak has written, "ethnicity has not

ally compete with the principled claims of individual *citizens*, Jews and Arabs alike.[64] The argument among the Israeli majority is over which dimensions of Jewishness should receive public recognition, not whether such recognition is legitimate. In contrast, there is no serious debate within the Christian majority in the United States regarding the use of public authority for similar purposes; anyone suggesting that "we are a Christian nation" will most assuredly be dismissed as a crackpot.[65]

The seriousness of the assertion in Israel that "we are a Jewish nation" is reflected in an aspect of Israeli pluralism that has received considerable attention from Israeli scholars, namely the national goal of ethnic amalgamation. The Zionist ideology of the ingathering of the exiles has produced a melting pot ideal applicable to the Jewish population.[66] This assimilative aspiration has a reactive dimension to it as well: thus the reality of a nonassimilative group within the society accelerates the momentum for Jewish solidarity. "The marked rise in the Arab population demanded reemphasis of the collectivity's Jewish character, which constituted the common denominator between Ashkenazim and Orientals while excluding the Arabs . . . from the symbolic boundaries of the collectivity."[67] To be sure, this solidarity is severely tested by the significant level of socioeconomic stratification that remains within the Jewish community. Yet if there is an

---

been permitted to become an instrument of territorial sovereignty." Michael Novak, "Pluralism in Humanistic Perspective," in *Concepts of Ethnicity*, William Paterson, Michael Novak, and Philip Gleason (Cambridge: Harvard University Press, 1982), p. 39.

[64] On this subject, see Cohen, "Citizenship, Nationality and Religion in Israel and Thailand," p. 67.

[65] There is of course an ongoing debate over whether public authority can be employed to support religion. But even those who in fact believe that the United States is a Christian country rarely present an argument for government backing in these terms. In terms of political rhetoric it is simply a nonstarter.

[66] See, in particular, Hanna Herzog, "Political Ethnicity as a Socially Constructed Reality," in Esman and Rabinovich, *Ethnicity, Pluralism and the State in the Middle East*, p. 141. This melting pot should be contrasted with the much broader ideal prevalent in the United States. "The very essence of this American ethos [of a melting pot] contradicts the traditional Jewish emphasis on exclusivity and uniqueness." Amnon Rubinstein, *The Zionist Dream Revisited* (New York: Schocken Books, 1984), p. 171.

[67] Baruch Kimmerling, "Boundaries and Frontiers of the Israeli Control System: Analytical Conclusions," in Kimmerling, *The Israeli State and Society*, p. 273. Kemal Karpat argues that it is common in the Middle East generally for the sense of religious identity and communality to supersede feelings of ethnic and/or linguistic group solidarity. "The Ottoman Ethnic and Confessional Legacy in the Middle East," in Esman and Rabinovich, *Ethnicity, Pluralism and the State in the Middle East*, p. 37.

appropriate American analogy here, it is one offered by Alexis de Tocqueville. His depiction and analysis of equality of condition in the United States did not seek to deny the existence of objective inequalities; rather, his purpose was to focus on the subjective dimensions of equality, the egalitarian implications of a shared commitment to a common set of ideals. Similarly, the social and economic correlates of ethnicity in Israel are blurred (if not totally submerged) by a shared identification with an ancient religious and cultural tradition. It is the "common primordial sentiment" of Judaism (however defined) that is the driving impulse of Israeli politics.[68]

The Jewish communitarian tradition expresses itself in various ways. As Asher Arian has noted, the Yom Kippur service recites that "we have sinned" not that *I* have sinned, an illustration of religion as a community undertaking in which the identity of the individual is connected to membership in the group.[69] Charles S. Liebman cites a recent political example to illustrate the same phenomenon. In 1985 Israel exchanged 1,150 Arab prisoners who had been incarcerated for acts of terrorism for three soldiers captured during the 1982 war in Lebanon. The exchange has widely come to be seen as a big mistake. At the time, however, it received overwhelming public support, a reaction that Liebman found to be consistent with a dominant strand in the Israeli political culture. "Calculations of prestige, future cost, responsibility, were all secondary to the communal quasi-

---

[68] The phrase is borrowed from Arend Lijphart, *Democracy in Plural Societies: A Comparative Exploration* (New Haven: Yale University Press, 1977), p. 133. For an excellent discussion of primordialism in contemporary Israeli society, see Baruch Kimmerling, "Between the Primordial and the Civil Definitions of the Collective Identity: *Eretz Israel* or the State of Israel?" in *Comparative Social Dynamics*, Erik Cohen, Moshe Lissak, and Uri Almagor (Boulder, Colo.: Westview Press, 1985). Kimmerling correctly sees this primordialism in perpetual tension with Western notions of citizenship, but points out that since 1977 the former has been in the ascendance. See also Clifford Geertz, "The Integrative Revolution: Primordial Sentiments and Civil Politics in the New States," in *Old Societies and New States: The Quest for Modernity in Asia and Africa*, ed. Clifford Geertz (London: Free Press, 1963). Geertz suggests the ways in which primordial bonds come to supersede areas of difference. "[The] congruities of blood, speech, custom, and so on, are seen to have an ineffable, and at times overpowering, coerciveness in and of themselves" (p. 109).

[69] Asher Arian, *Politics in Israel: The Second Generation* (Chatham, N.J.: Chatham House Publishers, 1985), p. 218. Contrast this with Justice Douglas's statement in *Wisconsin* v. *Yoder*: "Religion is an individual experience." 406 U.S. 205, 243 (1971). Milton R. Konvitz points out that the most important prayers in the Jewish religion, whether recited privately or collectively, are plural in form and are offered in the name of the Jewish community rather than the individual. "[The Jew's] prayers are . . . communal and not private, integrative and not isolative, holistic and not separative." Milton R. Konvitz, *Judaism and the American Idea* (Ithaca: Cornell University Press, 1978), pp. 141–43.

familial sentiment that one does whatever possible for one's child without adding up costs. It was precisely what one expects of a family, not from a state."[70] From examples like this, Liebman contends that many, and possibly most, Israelis embrace a communal (based on kinship, loyalty, and status) as opposed to a Western (based on impersonal application of universal law) model of the state.[71]

Liebman's dichotomy is too sharply drawn and may obscure the fact that the Israeli polity represents a complex admixture of Western and Jewish elements. Yet it captures a fundamental reality of Israeli political culture, one that needs to be reckoned with in constitutional terms. One of the implications of that reality, as Liebman points out, is that "since membership in the community of Israelis is defined by Jewish identity, the non-Jewish minorities, almost by definition become second-class citizens."[72] Another scholar, Elie Kedourie, places this communitarian dynamic in the broader regional context of the Middle East: "The idea that a non-Muslim or a non-Sunni native of Turkey is a Turk in the same way as a Sunni Muslim is somewhat artificial. A 'Greek Turk,' an 'Armenian Turk,' and so on, may be legally intelligible concepts, but they are empty of political substance. Mutatis mutandis, the same is true for Iraq, Syria, or Israel."[73] The comparison is valid of course only in its isolation of a common exclusivist orientation associated with communitarian politics in the Middle East; it certainly could not be used to depict an equivalence in the policies of these regimes. Thus, Israel needs also to be distinguished from its neighbors in

[70] Charles S. Liebman, "Conceptions of 'State of Israel' in Israeli Society," *Jerusalem Quarterly* 47 (1988): 101. In their more recent work, Liebman and Cohen contrast this view of family with that of American Jews: "Unlike Israeli Jews, American Jews face pressures that militate against Jewish familistic feelings and behavior. American Jews need to square their Jewish familistic sentiments with American conceptions of equality and Western conceptions of liberalism and humanism. In these conceptions there is something archaic, unenlightened, and intolerant about asserting the primacy of one's kin or clan. In the liberal humanistic vision, the individual is the center of concern, not the family or the tribe or even the nation." Liebman and Cohen, *Two Worlds of Liberalism*, p. 26.

[71] Ibid., p. 102.

[72] Ibid. This is a point acknowledged by scholars of varying political persuasions. Horowitz and Lissak, who differ with Liebman in ideological perspective, point out that basic contradictions were always implicit in secular Zionist ideology, namely the commitment to a Jewish nation-state based on universal principles of justice. "This contradiction emerged with full force when it became apparent that the process of Zionist settlement would not be taking place in a 'land without a people,' . . . but in a country with an indigenous Arab population whose aspirations were incompatible with Zionist goals." Horowitz and Lissak, *Trouble in Utopia*, pp. 114–15.

[73] Kedourie, "Ethnicity, Majority, and Minority in the Middle East," p. 30.

terms of the degree to which it accepts the individualist norms associated with Western jurisprudence. If, as one political theorist has written, "strong community and liberal constitutionalism are fundamentally incompatible,"[74] then the critical constitutional question for Israel involves a determination of the strength of its communitarian commitment.

The considerations impinging on such a determination are highlighted in a 1978 Israeli Supreme Court case involving a dispute over the actions of a government corporation in restoring and developing the Jewish Quarter in the Old City of Jerusalem.[75] Jews had lived there for generations, but they were forced to leave by the Jordanians after the Arabs occupied the Old City in 1948. Arab residents in turn were required to leave after the 1967 Six-Day War, whereupon reconstruction of the area began. The criteria for purchasing an apartment in the newly renovated quarter clearly excluded Arabs, and so the petitioner, who was an Arab claiming to have previously occupied a residence there, maintained that his rights had been violated. The outcome of the case, in which the government's actions were upheld, may have been dictated more by the peculiar circumstances of the case (i.e., the questionable character of the petitioner) than by the requirements of Israeli law; the judicial opinions, however, reflect the dual commitments of the broader political culture.[76] Thus, Justice Bechor wrote in his opinion, "We have a distinguished rule that we should never give our assistance in any matter that amounts to discrimination between persons on grounds of their religion or nationality. But . . . we must not close our eyes to reality and to actual conditions."[77]

And what of these conditions and realities? Justice Shamgar pointed out

---

[74] H. N. Hirsch, "The Threnody of Liberalism: Constitutional Liberty and the Renewal of Community," *Political Theory* 14 (1986): 426. Hirsch argues that "the exclusion of nonmembers seems to be necessary for the maintenance of a viable political community" (p. 435). This issue is pursued in the next section.

[75] *Muhammad Sa'id Burkaan* v. *Minister of Finance*, 32 (2) P.D. 800 (1978).

[76] In interviews conducted with a number of Israelis connected to the legal profession, the author heard repeatedly that this decision by the Court was in fact anomalous. Thus cases dealing with the Old City should be construed very narrowly. Rather than viewing *Burkaan* as a fair housing case, it should, according to this understanding, be treated as a legitimacy test for the rebuilding of Jerusalem's Jewish Quarter, and Burkaan's claim should be seen as a challenge to the legitimacy of Zionism as a whole. David Kretzmer argues that while *Burkaan* "contains the seeds of an approach that could conceivably justify discrimination," it has not, with one possible exception, been followed in subsequent cases. David Kretzmer, *The Legal Status of the Arabs in Israel* (Boulder, Colo.: Westview Press, 1990), p. 81.

[77] *Muhammad Sa'id Burkaan*, 32 (2) P.D. at 805. Translation by Carmel Shalev, in Barak, Goldstein, and Marshall, *Limits of Law.*

in his opinion that the residential areas in the Old City had been divided
into quarters according to communities since the eleventh century. This
historical separation is one of the considerations that led him to this critical
contrast between Israel and the United States.

> Automatic transferral from place to place of all the varied forms and ways in
> which the rule of equality has been applied, without taking into account
> special conditions and circumstances, can be misleading to no small extent;
> for example compulsory integration of school children there, which forces
> the English language and Anglo-Saxon culture on each and every student
> and is regarded there as the height of equality, could be considered here to
> be compulsory assimilation if an Arab student were to be forced because of it
> to forego a separate school system in which studies are conducted in his own
> language and in accord with his own culture.[78]

While these sentiments might be construed in a contemporary American
context as a challenge to liberal democratic political beliefs, in Israel
Shamgar's observation is compatible with (if not required by) the communitarian assumptions that are significantly, if not exclusively, embodied
in that society's pluralist vision.

Those assumptions were in evidence in the more recent case involving
the Supreme Court's eviction of a group of Jewish settlers who had taken
over St. John's Hospice in the Christian Quarter of the Old City. Mayor
Kollek of Jerusalem justified the exclusion of Jews from the Christian Quarter by referring to the 1978 case and by appealing to the same principle of
separate development. This principle, he maintained (at least as applied to
the Old City), was "in keeping with both the wishes of the residents and
long-standing tradition." And in words that are relevant to the discussion of
free speech in Chapter 6, Mayor Kollek spoke of the need to ensure Jerusalem's "future as a city of religious tolerance and good neighborly relations."
He concluded, "Beyond the issue of law, there are the virtues of wisdom
and sensitivity."[79] Separate (but equal?) development may thus be consistent with principles of justice of a society in which distributive norms are
influenced by a logic of pluralism in which communal autonomy takes
precedence over assimilation.[80] Or as David K. Shipler suggested in his

---

[78] Ibid., at 808.

[79] All quotes are from Mayor Kollek's letter to the *New York Times* of May 1, 1990.

[80] Harold R. Isaacs has pointed out that such a logic of pluralism may becoming fashionable
in contemporary American intellectual circles. He argues that this "new pluralism" threatens
to "go back not only to 'separate but equal' but all the way to the Ottoman Empire, which left

study of Arab-Jewish relations in Israel, "The pluralistic, integrationist approach that has been the standard for American society has no relevance here."[81]

Separate educational facilities (which are not mandated by law but exist in accordance with the wishes of the overwhelming majority of both communities) are rooted in the prestate experience. Article 15 of the Mandate provided that "the right of each community to maintain its own schools for the education of its members in its own language, while conforming to such educational requirements of a general nature as the Administration may impose, shall not be denied nor impaired."[82] In the 1953 State Education Law, which applies to all schools, education is to be based, in large part, "on the values of Jewish culture . . . and loyalty to the state and the Jewish people." While "in non-Jewish educational institutions, the curriculum shall be adapted to the special conditions thereof," the coexistence of limited communal autonomy with the primacy of Jewish communal rule is reflected in this fundamental reality: that while biculturalism prevails in Arab schools, in the sense that students must learn Hebrew and Jewish subjects, no parallel requirement is prescribed for Jewish schoolchildren, whose exposure to Arab history and culture is extremely limited.[83] Dan Horowitz uses the term "dual authority politics" to describe the characteristic distribution of power in deeply divided bicommunal or multicommunal polities. By this he means that "political authority is divided between the sovereign political center, of the common polity on the one hand, and the institutionalized or semi-institutionalized political centers of the constitu-

---

all manners of civil status and communal justice to the separate communities while keeping all essential power in the hands of the regime." Harold R. Isaacs, "The New Pluralists," *Commentary*, March 1972, p. 78. While at the time this may have seemed an exaggerated fear, recent developments lead one to admire the prescience of Isaac's concerns.

[81] David K. Shipler, *Arab and Jew: Wounded Spirits in a Promised Land* (New York: Penguin Books, 1986), p. 273. Shipler elaborates: "Nationhood in the American concept may transcend race, creed, and ethnic origin, but in the Middle East the nation attempts to serve as an embodiment of those traits—not to promote harmony among diversity but to emphasize and express those differences" (p. 274).

[82] Quoted in Abramov, *Perpetual Dilemma*, p. 93. This prestate experience embodies an awareness of a point noted by Clifford Geertz, that "the school crisis is perhaps becoming the classical political—or parapolitical—expression of the clash of primordial loyalties." Geertz, "The Integrative Revolution," pp. 125–26.

[83] Indeed, the exposure of Arab children to Arab history and culture is also limited in the sense that very little attention is given in the curriculum to the phenomenon of Arab nationality. See in this regard Sami Khalid Mar'i, *Arab Education in Israel* (Syracuse: Syracuse University Press, 1978).

ent communities on the other hand."[84] His conceptualization, which emerges from the analysis of Palestine under the Mandate, illuminates such legislation as Article 15. Thus the "administration" that imposes general requirements is the "sovereign political center" that relates more or less equally to the various communal political centers. This has changed. Dual authority continues to exist in the Israeli polity, but the political (if not legal) reality of the sovereign center is that it overlaps with one of its communal subcenters. This inevitably confers on those in the other communities a status commensurate with the marginality of their symbolic recognition by the sovereign center—the status of an outsider.

REPUBLICANISM

Comparisons of Israeli and American models of pluralism are not simply academic exercises. This is particularly the case for American Jews, most of whom identify in one way or another with Israel and take a certain pride in the achievements of that country. As Americans, they quite naturally view political progress in Israel through the prism of their own democratic experience in the United States. In the words of a former head of the American Jewish Congress, "What we think is right and just in our own country must be right and just in Israel. What we find wanting in America—the imperfections of democracy that we recognize and seek to correct—must also be considered faulty and in need of correction in Israel."[85] Thus the more Israel resembles the United States in its politics, the more it becomes a source of pride and satisfaction for American Jews.

There is also another side to this relationship. Many American Jews who have visited Israel return to the United States deeply moved by what they have seen. Often what leaves the most lasting impression is the sense of community they have experienced, the perhaps unanticipated pleasure derived from exposure to a society whose members are linked in important ways by their Jewishness. Frequently these feelings are accompanied by criticism of an American society that seems to lack collective purpose. As Tocqueville expressed it, "Not only does democracy make every man forget his ancestors, but it hides his descendants and separates his contemporaries from him."[86] For some of these Jews the comparison leads them

[84] Dan Horowitz, "Dual Authority Politics," *Comparative Politics* 14 (1982): 329.

[85] Quoted in Abramov, *Perpetual Dilemma*, pp. 375–76.

[86] Alexis De Tocqueville, *Democracy in America*, vol. 1 (New York: Vintage Books, 1945), p. 106.

ultimately to "make aliyah" (emigrate to Israel), with its promise of an end to the emptiness of their atomistic lives. For others the Israeli alternative, while alluring, is not compelling enough to abandon the basic comforts and decencies of life in pluralistic America.[87]

The communitarian alternative has its attractions for others as well. In recent years some historians and constitutional theorists in the United States have attempted a "republican revival," seeking to dethrone the orthodox pluralistic vision of American history and constitutionalism. A dissatisfaction with the prevailing egoistic individualism of historical and constitutional interpretation has led them to resurrect (or, according to their critics, manufacture) the classical republican tradition of the founding period. Their challenge is an important one in contemporary constitutional scholarship; yet in the context of an American-Israeli comparison, it may appear as only a relatively mild disagreement within the family. Much as the application of an external perspective often makes political differences seem rather small in the United States, so too does such a perspective illuminate the comparison of alternative versions of the American constitutional experience.

The debate among constitutional theorists over the question of republicanism focuses on normative and historical issues, not over how best to describe the present constitutional reality. Thus, Frank Michelman, a leading republican theorist, assesses the prevailing state of affairs in terms with which most will agree. "Modern American political culture is militantly anti-organicist, committed to political democracy, hostile to social-role constraint, and broadly reconciled to deep and conflictual diversity of social experience and normative perspective. If any social condition defines modern American politics, plurality does."[88] Michelman and other contemporary republicans like to contrast this pluralist vision, with its emphasis on maximizing particular preferences at the expense of the common good, with an alternative vision that is much more community-oriented. It is a vision that, they argue, captures an important, if not necessarily dominant, strand in the political thought and commitments of the founding generation. As Cass Sunstein maintains, "Republican thought played a

---

[87] On this point see Kimmerling, "Between the Primordial and the Civil Definitions of the Collective Identity," p. 276. Kimmerling notes that for sectors of the world Jewish intelligentsia known for their universalism and humanism, the intensification of particularistic factors within Israel stands in the way of their immigrating to Israel. But it is these "family-like" aspects of the Jewish collectivity that continue to attract other sectors.

[88] Frank Michelman, "Law's Republic," *Yale Law Journal* 97 (1988): 1506. For some empirical evidence supportive of this characterization of American political culture, see Donald

central role in the framing period, and it offers a powerful conception of politics and of the functions of constitutionalism."[89]

Nothing less than a *powerful* conception would have even the remotest chance of destroying the assumptions commonly associated with constitutionalism (that is to be taken seriously). The literature of modern constitutionalism makes clear what these are: protection of individual rights against collective power, a framework of public authority that is to be officially neutral with respect to competing social goals, and a philosophical commitment or at least predisposition to serving the interests of the individual (or groups of individuals). Michael Sandel's description of a " 'procedural republic,' a public life animated by the rights-based liberal ethic," aptly captures the essence of this modern understanding.[90] Republicans, on the other hand, subscribe to a "concept of an autonomous public interest" independent of "the sum of private interests."[91] Their view of government is that it should be more than just an impartial arbiter of pluralist conflict; it should seek to articulate and defend the beliefs and aspirations of a community animated by an invigorated conception of democratic citizenship.

Critics of the republicans make at least two kinds of arguments. The first amounts to a charge of distorted history. The effort, for example, to portray the Anti-Federalists as a genuine republican alternative to Federalist interest liberalism is disputed. The attempt to "wring out of the Anti-Federalist writings an anti-liberal or anti-Lockian conception of republicanism" is one manifestation of the "contemporary infatuation with 'classical republicanism.' "[92] In fact, say the critics, the two contending political forces were united in their fundamental commitment to individual rights, differing only in the most effective political and constitutional strategy to achieve this end.[93] A second and related argument is that the tradition of classical

---

J. Devine, *The Political Culture of the United States: The Influence of Member Values on Regime Maintenance* (Boston: Little, Brown, 1972).

[89] Cass R. Sunstein, "Beyond the Republican Revival," *Yale Law Journal* 97 (1988): 1540.

[90] Michael Sandel, "The Political Theory of the Procedural Republic," in *Constitutionalism and Rights*, ed. Gary C. Bryner and Noel B. Reynolds (Provo, Utah: Brigham Young University Press, 1987), p. 141.

[91] Morton J. Horwitz, "Republicanism and Liberalism in American Constitutional Thought," *William and Mary Law Review* 29 (1987): 68.

[92] Thomas L. Pangle, *The Spirit of Modern Republicanism: The Moral Vision of the American Founders and the Philosophy of Locke* (Chicago: University of Chicago Press, 1988), pp. 33, 29.

[93] See, in particular, Herbert J. Storing, *What the Anti-Federalists Were For* (Chicago: University of Chicago Press, 1981). "Their disagreements were not based on different prem-

republicanism with which the founders were intimately acquainted was a fundamentally illiberal tradition that can serve as a model for contemporary republicans only if its problematic features are conveniently ignored. "The transformation of classical to modern republicanism . . . is not some refinement of classical doctrine. It is in large measure a new theory which borrows selectively, and seductively, from the past."[94] What these critics have in mind are the exclusivist, discriminatory tendencies of republican communalism, tendencies that liberal constitutional arrangements were largely designed to overcome. "America as we know it," says one skeptic of the republican enterprise, "began with the death of community."[95]

But the republican revival never threatens to disturb the fundamental assumptions of its adversaries. Sunstein, for example, speaks of a "liberal republicanism" and asserts that "republican beliefs in political equality and citizenship will generate strong antidiscrimination norms."[96] Here it would seem that the critics who discern a sort of transvaluation of classical republicanism are correct; otherwise it would not be so easy to ignore the current of intolerance that runs through classical republicanism as originally conceived. So dominant is the ethos of individualism in American political discourse that a critique which begins as a challenge to that ethos ends by largely accepting its major premises. In this respect the current debate parallels the earlier contest between Federalists and Anti-

---

ises about the nature of man or the ends of political life. They were not the deep cleavages of contending regimes. They were the much less sharp and clear-cut differences within the family, as it were, of men agreed that the purpose of government is the regulation and thereby the protection of individual rights and that the best instrument for this purpose is some form of limited, republican government" (p. 5).

[94] Richard A. Epstein, "Modern Republicanism—or the Flight from Substance," *Yale Law Journal* 97 (1988): 1636. See also H. Jefferson Powell, "Reviving Republicanism," *Yale Law Journal* 97 (1988).

[95] Hirsch, "The Threnody of Liberalism," p. 440. Even among Tocquevillian critics of American individualism, there is an awareness of the uglier possibilities associated with some forms of community. "We . . . face a profound impasse. Modern individualism seems to be producing a way of life that is neither individually nor socially viable, yet a return to traditional forms would be to return to intolerable discrimination and oppression." Robert N. Bellah, Richard Madsen, William M. Sullivan, Ann Swidler, and Steven M. Tipton, *Habits of the Heart: Individualism and Commitment in American Life* (New York: Harper & Row, 1985), p. 144.

[96] Sunstein, "Beyond the Republican Revival," p. 1571. H. Jefferson Powell says of Sunstein's effort, "Republicanism's common good is scarcely distinguishable from pluralism's aggregation and balancing of interests." Powell, "Reviving Republicanism," p. 1710.

Federalists, for while the latter attached greater emphasis to community, tradition, civic virtue, and moral education, both parties argued their differences within an essentially shared ideological context. As one empirical examination of American political culture concludes, "Stress in America has not been the result of conflict over the worth of the fundamental values but over their precise meaning and their relationship to each other."[97]

A comparative perspective is helpful. The Israelis who resist the communal model of the state, with its emphasis on primordial ties and ethnocentrism, are engaged in a much more serious dispute with their opponents than that which divided Americans in our early years or that today divides certain constitutional theorists. While liberal ideology has always existed in Israel, frequently serving (mainly through the courts) as an effective counterweight to more dominant collectivist trends, it does not provide, as it has in the United States, the intellectual context within which most, if not all, important political and constitutional debate occurs.[98] Jewish political culture can perhaps be described as republican,[99] but it is less the liberal republicanism of Madison, Hamilton, and Jefferson than it is the more communally oriented tradition of classical republicanism. As Daniel J. Elazar has shown, the backgrounds of the Israeli founders propelled them toward a more cooperative rather than individualistic sociopolitical model, and the strong collectivist thrust of this orientation was fundamentally consistent with the republican strain of Jewish political culture.[100] To be sure, the socialistic component of the early commitment has waned over time, but primordial bonds (expressed in both religious and secular nationalistic terms) have, if anything, been strengthened.

The normal in Israel is radical in the United States. American pluralism acknowledges groups as collections of individuals, not as units whose corporate identity carries with it any claim on the state for specific entitlement. While some today see this pluralism being overwhelmed by a rising tide of multicultural fervor, there is as yet little evidence that this is more than an ephemeral phenomenon, or that it is likely fundamentally to transform the widely shared values located at the core of the American political

---

[97] Devine, *The Political Culture of the United States*, p. 364.

[98] Baruch Kimmerling sees liberalism contending against three collectivist emphases—religion, socialism, and secular nationalism. "Balancing the Primordial and the Civil Definitions of the Collective Identity," p. 266.

[99] Daniel J. Elazar, *Israel: Building a New Society* (Bloomington: Indiana University Press, 1986), p. 160.

[100] Ibid., p. 3.

culture.[101] "Paradoxical as it may seem, the United States has a common culture that is multicultural."[102] Its diversity expresses itself in clamorous, angry, and frequently provocative ways; its commonality, while more muted, is firmly rooted in the soil of individualism. This of course is what makes an issue like affirmative action so controversial. Indeed, to the extent that programs designed to advance the interests of racial or ethnic groups are accepted as legitimate, they must be framed in the language of individual rights. Thus a recent defense of affirmative action by an eloquent spokesman for a more communally oriented American society stipulates that "affirmative action can be seen as a means to promote not separatism but integration—and, indeed, as an instrument in the long-term service of individualism."[103] The significance of the defense is best seen in the context of the distinction Milton M. Gordon makes between "liberal pluralism" and "corporate pluralism," the latter entailing a concept of group entitlement and the formal recognition of ethnic and racial characteristics by the state.[104] Gordon argues that "the logic of corporate pluralism is to

[101] The media of course has been quick to jump on the multicultural bandwagon. One example from *Time* illustrates very well the hyperbole that has been generated. "Gone . . . is the emphasis on the twin ideals that form the basis of the American experiment: that rights reside in the individual rather than with social or ethnic classes and that all who come to these shores can be assimilated by an open society that transforms disparate peoples into Americans." "Whose America?" *Time*, July 8, 1991, p. 13. No one can deny that ethnic groups (or at least their spokespersons) have become more assertive in expressing their separate identities, that, as Arthur Schlesinger, Jr., has observed, *unum* is being belittled while *pluribus* is glorified. While I think there is more to this than "a superficial enthusiasm stirred by romantic idealogues and unscrupulous hucksters," I tend to agree with him that "Americanization has not lost its charms," and that ethnic separatism has been more successful to this point at intimidation than conversion. Arthur M. Schlesinger, Jr., *The Disuniting of America: Reflections on a Multicultural Society* (Knoxville: Whittle Direct Books, 1991), pp. 78–79. For empirical support see Everett C. Ladd, "E Pluribus Unum Still: The Uniting of America," *The Public Perspective* 3 (1992).

[102] Diane Ravitch, as quoted in Schlesinger, *The Disuniting of America*, p. 81.

[103] Karst, "Paths to Belonging," p. 341. Consider also Michael Walzer's observation: "Selection by quota functions largely to provide a kind of escape from group life for people whose identity has become a trap. Its chief purpose is to give opportunities to individuals, not a voice to groups. It serves to enhance the wealth of individuals, not necessarily the resources of the ethnic community." Walzer, "Pluralism in Political Perspective," p. 22.

[104] Milton M. Gordon, "Models of Pluralism: The New American Dilemma," *Annals of the American Academy of Political and Social Sciences* 454 (1981): p. 185. The situation of Ashkenazi and Sephardi Jews in Israel is analogous to the prevailing pattern of liberal pluralism in the United States. Sammy Smooha's analysis of relations between these two populations provides an appropriate description of normal pluralistic competition in the United States. "The conflict is moderate, nonviolent, depoliticized [one might question this], and mostly

emphasize structural separation."[105] It is precisely because American constitutionalism (including its republican version) is so wedded to the model of liberal pluralism that affirmative action (again with the notable exception of Native Americans), which in some other setting might be unapologetically related to the enhancement of cultural autonomy, must be defended as a stepping stone to assimilation.

This is the case even where it would appear that corporate pluralism and structural separation are being upheld. Thus, the Supreme Court's decision in *Wisconsin* v. *Yoder* is commonly cited as an example of judicial deference to group autonomy, when in fact there is ample reason to believe that the outcome was a consequence of other considerations. The Court, to be sure, upheld the claim of the Amish for an exemption from Wisconsin's compulsory school-attendance law; but as commentators have noted, the Amish commanded the deference of the Court precisely because they exemplified those traits that define a good American.[106] They were granted their separateness out of an appreciation for the example they set for the society as a whole. They "reflect many of the virtues of Jefferson's ideal of the 'sturdy yeoman' who would form the basis of what he considered as the ideal of a democratic society."[107] What's more, they raise their children to be law-abiding, self-sufficient members of society. They are, despite their blatant rejection of mainstream American culture and society, splendid exemplars of the traditional American virtues of hard work, self-reliance, and deference to authority. The *Yoder* opinion, with its unabashed enthusiasm for good old-fashioned American values, is as much a vindication of authority as it is a victory for group rights. It is an assimilationist decision wrapped in the guise of cultural autonomy.

---

restricted to questions of resource competition—socioeconomic and power inequality. Integration is quite diverse and well balanced by extensive value consensus and crosscutting affiliations on the one hand, and elite co-optation, economic interdependence . . . on the other." Smooha, *Israel: Pluralism and Conflict*, p. 230.

[105] Ibid., p. 185. See also Robert N. Bellah, "Citizenship, Diversity, and the Search for the Common Good," in *"The Constitution of the People": Reflections on Citizens and Civil Society*, ed. Robert E. Calvert (Lawrence: University of Kansas Press, 1991). Bellah writes that "even the strongest communities seldom if ever meet the definition that is implied by the idea of communalist pluralism." As for the United States, "communalist pluralism is an inadequate expression of the reality of pluralism in America" (p. 50).

[106] See, e.g., Robert A. Burt, "The Constitution of the Family," *Supreme Court Review 1979* (Chicago: University of Chicago Press, 1980).

[107] *Wisconsin* v. *Yoder*, 406 U.S. 205, 226 (1972).

The absence of a constitutional grounding for group rights has not gone unnoticed.[108] The Constitution's silence in this matter is consistent with the basic commitment of modern constitutionalism to a "citizenship [that] transcends particularity and difference."[109] It is therefore natural that only a truly radical critique of liberal pluralism could establish the theoretical basis for the formal recognition of group claims on the state. In the work of Iris Marion Young, for example, we encounter such a critique, in which "differences are publicly recognized and acknowledged as irreducible."[110] Young stipulates that there are group-based perspectives and histories that can by their very nature never be completely understood by those whose identities are the product of a different group experience. The liberal policy of official blindness to race, gender, and cultural distinctions does violence, she maintains, to the various identities associated with such as-criptive designations. She proposes instead a concept of *"differential citizenship"* as the best way to secure justice in a heterogeneous society.[111] "To the degree that groups are culturally different . . . equal treatment in many issues of social policy is unjust because it denies these cultural differ-ences or makes them a liability."[112] The antidiscrimination principle of mainstream constitutional discourse and law needs to be replaced by a radical acceptance of social diversity.

Such radicalism, it is safe to say, is not going to be accepted by those who determine the shape and direction of American constitutional law, and this includes the republican critics, who believe in a universalist ideal accord-

---

[108] See, e.g., Owen M. Fiss, "Groups and the Equal Protection Clause," *Philosophy and Public Affairs* 5 (1975); Ronald Garret, "Communality and Existence: The Rights of Groups," *Southern California Law Review* 56 (1983); Hendrik Hartog, "The Constitution of Aspiration and 'The Rights That Belong to Us All,' "*Journal of American History* 74 (1987); and Nathan Glazar, "The Constitution and American Diversity," in Goldwin, Kaufman, and Schambra, *Forging Unity Out of Diversity.*

[109] Iris Marion Young, "Polity and Group Difference: A Critique of the Ideal of Universal Citizenship," *Ethics* 99 (1989): 250. Thomas L. Pangle makes clear, however, that the silence of the Constitution in no way reflects the amount of attention devoted to the subject by the framers. Indeed, it was their concerted effort to create a system that would secure a harmless diversity, thus avoiding the common affliction of previous popular governments. Shifting the focus from groups to individuals was a principal component of their long-term strategy. See Pangle, "Comment," in Goldwin, Kaufman, and Schambra, *Forging Unity Out of Diversity.*

[110] Young, "Polity and Group Difference," p. 258.

[111] Ibid., p. 251.

[112] Ibid., p. 271. For further discussion of these issues in a variety of policy contexts, see Martha Minow, *Making All the Difference: Inclusion, Exclusion, and American Law* (Ithaca: Cornell University Press, 1990).

ing to which different societal visions can be mediated through discussion and dialogue to arrive at the common good.[113] It is likely as well that the theory as presented would be rejected by most Israeli judges and intellectuals. But within the Israeli sociopolitical environment as a whole, the theory is not really radical at all; indeed, its translation from a normative to an empirical statement expresses well the reality of Israeli pluralism. Thus, for example, Israeli Jews are much less inclined to affirm the universalist sentiment included in the statement "As Jews we should be concerned about all people and not just Jews."[114] It is when one focuses on the underlying motivation behind the proposal for "differential citizenship" that the distinctions in the American and Israeli pluralist models are particularly apparent. Thus Young's critique of universal citizenship is the core of a strategy to improve the lot of oppressed groups in American society. Even if her social analysis was shown to be objectively valid, it is highly doubtful that most members of the groups she champions (e.g., women, blacks, Hispanics) would endorse such a departure from traditional American individualist aspirations. On the other hand, in Israel, where it is very easy to envision the argument for universal citizenship (i.e., no official recognition of groups) being used to advance the cause of social equality and justice for the downtrodden, a similar showing of validity would also have difficulty overcoming widespread and deeply rooted commitment to de jure communal organization.

CONCLUSION

Consider again the one great American counterexample, Native Americans. Differential citizenship is an acceptable solution in this case for the same reason that it is, to a greater or lesser degree, acceptable to most Israelis (Arabs and Jews), namely that individual identity is so intimately connected to group identity. At various times in our history public policy toward Native Americans was formulated without regard for this reality.[115] The failed allotment and termination policies, in their common assimilationist approach, assumed a model of social organization essentially consonant with the political culture of the broader society. The unfortunate

---

[113] See Sunstein, "Beyond the Republican Revival," pp. 1554–55.

[114] The survey result is reported in Liebman and Cohen, *Two Worlds of Judaism*, p. 138.

[115] For example, during the period of termination, this was official policy: "It is the policy of Congress, as rapidly as possible, to make the Indians within the territorial limits of the United States subject to the same laws and entitled to the same privileges and responsibilities as are

consequences of these efforts were attributable less to bad intentions than to good.

Comparative constitutional analysis would do well to bear this in mind. Changes in legal systems are often predominantly the result of borrowing from other systems.[116] To the extent that this is the case, constitutional actors must be aware of the relationship between law and political culture, and be sensitive to those aspects of political culture that can be influenced by the law and those that can be expected to be resistant to it. American constitutional theory and practice have long been a major source of inspiration for peoples around the world; when transplantations of institutions and approaches occur, it behooves those engaged in this process carefully to assess which elements of political culture are likely to matter most in determining a successful outcome.[117]

Israel is an especially fertile ground for this kind of analysis. "In the Law of the State of Israel the foreign elements predominate, and their foreign origin is obvious and unmistakable. This is the case to such an extent that in most spheres it is difficult to point to any significant contribution of our own."[118] This is changing. Thus the key provision of the Foundations of Law enactment of 1980 states, "Where the court, faced with a legal question requiring decision, finds no answer to it in statute law or case law or by analogy, it shall decide it in the light of the principles of freedom, justice, equity, and peace of Israel's heritage."[119] While this signals a renewed commitment to develop an indigenous Israeli legal tradition, one cannot help but observe that the principles referred to in the law will inevitably be contested, and that meanings will be assigned to them in the light of conceptions and experiences that extend beyond the borders of Israel. The vagueness of the reference to "Israel's heritage" was deliberate, with the result that different judges could interpret the Jewish tradition in different ways, religious and secular, liberal and communitarian. The provision demonstrates the dominance of Jewish culture in the Israeli polity, of the

---

applicable to other citizens of the United States, to end their status as wards of the United States and to grant them all of the rights and prerogatives pertaining to American citizenship." H.R. Con. Res. 108, 83rd Cong., 1st sess., 67 Stat. B132 (1953), as quoted in Wilkinson, *American Indians, Time, and the Law*, p. 188.

[116] See, on this subject, Alan Watson, *Legal Transplants* (Edinburgh: Scottish Academic Press, 1974), p. 22.

[117] On this point, see in particular Carl J. Friedrich, *The Impact of American Constitutionalism Abroad* (Boston: Boston University Press, 1967).

[118] Guido Tedeschi, as quoted in Watson, *Legal Transplants*, p. 95.

[119] Foundations of Law Act, 5740 (1980).

unity between the "political center" and one of the communities it incorporates; but its meaning is ultimately deferred for subsequent judicial interpretation.

The contrasts emphasized in this chapter are relevant to interpretive possibilities. Thus American approaches to constitutional questions should be viewed in the context of American "social condition," which, as we have seen in Tocqueville's account, includes critical beliefs and ideas. A conception such as equality may mean different things to different societies, but these differences do not negate the fact that there may also exist a core of transcendent meaning to the idea that can serve as a common denominator for those working within the legal process. This requires both a recognition of the alternative bases of the two pluralisms, as well as an appreciation for the transformative force of a powerful idea. How well this delicate balance is achieved will likely determine the success of constitutional transplantation.

The Who and the What of Civic Identity

> We Americans are the peculiar, chosen people—the
> Israel of our time; we bear the ark of liberties of the
> world.
> —*Herman Melville*

Two Elections

The New York–Jerusalem Shuttle

Nineteen Eighty-eight was not a good year for the Israeli tourist industry. One of the effects of the *intifada*, the Palestinian uprising in the West Bank and Gaza, was to convince many prospective visitors that there were probably better times to make a trip to Israel. However, following the Israeli election in November, there seemed to be a discernible, if short-lived, increase in the number of Jews visiting from around the world, especially the United States; indeed, their arrival by planeloads was scrupulously covered by the Israeli media. They had come because of the election results, results that did nothing to reduce anxieties about the *intifada*, but a great deal to heighten anxieties about the status of much of diaspora Jewry.

Unfortunately for the shopkeepers who catered to the normally substantial tourist trade, the visitors were focused exclusively on business. Their sole purpose was to kill the proposed amendment to the Law of Return that would, if adopted, accept as legitimate under the law only those conversions performed by an Orthodox rabbi.[1] This amendment had long been on the Orthodox agenda in Israel; the opportunity seriously to pursue it had been made possible by the inconclusiveness of the recent election. Thus, in the absence of an electoral majority, the small religious parties sought, as they had with mixed success in the past, to use their powerful negotiating

---

[1] The last revision of the Law of Return was in 1970, after the Supreme Court's controversial ruling in the *Shalit* case, which will be discussed later in this chapter. The Knesset accepted the halakic or Orthodox definition of a Jew (one whose mother was Jewish or converted to Judaism) without going along with the halakic definition of conversion. Among the arguments used to omit such a definition was the claim that including it would improperly intrude on the activities of diaspora Jewry.

position to extract a salient policy commitment from a willing coalition partner. And while Labor and Likud, the two major parties, were not in principle supporters of an amendment to the law, their leaders were hardly averse to gaining the decisive political advantage by promising to support the religiously inspired legal change. The less than edifying political spectacle that ensued culminated in the formation of another broad Likud-Labor coalition government, which had the effect of rendering moot the battle over the Law of Return. The amenders of the law would have to wait for another propitious political occasion to savor the fruits of victory.

What was not rendered moot, however, were the frayed relations that had developed between Jews in Israel and Jews in the diaspora. The fact that most Israelis joined American Jews in opposing any change in the law could not conceal the depth of the misunderstanding that the two constituencies manifested toward each other. Many Israelis found as incomprehensible the panic and outrage of American Jews, who in turn were disappointed by the lack of seriousness with which their Israeli counterparts viewed the issues involved.[2] From the time they disembarked from their planes, the Americans were struck by the Israeli failure to appreciate the symbolic significance of an official policy of nonrecognition of Reform and Conservative conversions. They were frustrated by the attempt on the part of many Israelis to minimize the effects of the proposed amendment. Thus, the fact that only a very small number of potential *olim* (emigrants to Israel under the Law of Return) would, as the Israelis were wont to point out, be affected by a change in the law, did not address the core issue, which was, as the Americans saw it, the delegitimation of much of world Jewry.

The dynamic of delegitimation contained both a religious and a political dimension. The visiting delegations were determined to elevate the sensitivities of Israelis in regard to the concerns the Americans had about policies that would effectively relegate their religious identities to second-class status. Less apparent to both sides, however, was the extent to which the controversy over religious identity overlapped with issues of political identity. American Jews and Israeli Jews have to varying degrees internalized the political values of their respective societies, so that their perspectives on a matter such as conversion are in part refracted through the prisms of their secular political experience. In the case of American Jews, for example, the proposed changes in the Law of Return directly chal-

---

[2] As one Israeli observer noted, "For most Israelis, the issue of 'Who is a Jew' seems about as interesting as the question 'Who is a Sagittarius?' " Yitzhak Sokoloff, "A Jewish Timebomb," *Jerusalem Post*, November 28, 1988.

lenged their identities as Jews; but on another less obvious level they also offended certain ideological attachments that were connected to their identities as Americans.[3] Not surprisingly, those Israelis who seemed most sympathetic to the American position on conversion were also those whose understanding of the fundamental principles of their polity most closely approximated the tenets of American democratic pluralism. Said one such person, "The Law of Return should not be changed, and the Rabbinical Courts legislation should not be passed, because it is in conflict with the basic Zionist agenda of a free, peace-seeking, pluralistic, democratic state, society, people." And specifically addressing the American audience: "We share an agenda. It includes values, and battles to implement them, that go far beyond the Law of Return."[4]

This convergence should not be mistaken for harmony. For some, particularly on the Israeli Left, the agreement on this question became the occasion to excoriate American Jews for their alleged shortcomings on other matters. Yossi Sarid, a Knesset member and leading figure in the Citizens Rights Movement, vented his anger by exclaiming, "People who for a generation or more took no interest in the question of *What* is a Jew— of what, if anything is special about being a Jew that differentiates us from everybody else—can't expect to generate interest in the question of *Who* is a Jew, because the two questions are inextricably linked: if it isn't clear *what* a Jew is—it makes no difference *who* he is."[5] Sarid, of course, also opposed the amendment, emphatically endorsing the position that anyone who is sincere in his self-identification as a Jew is entitled to that recognition. Whether intended or not, his criticism of American Jews possesses a distinctly American flavor, for in underlining the importance of substantive commitment—*what one chooses to be*—he appeals to a volitional element that can be found at the core of most theories of American exceptionalism.

A principal target of Sarid's wrath was Morris B. Abram, chairman of the Conference of Presidents of Major Jewish Organizations. Abrams's opposition to any change in the Law of Return expressed itself in the following way: "Israel has been adopted by Americans not only as the fulfillment of biblical prophecy and as the refuge for the victims of Hitler and other

[3] The studies conducted by Liebman and Cohen are illuminating in the context of this episode. They argue that "even among the more traditionally inclined Orthodox, the distinguishing characteristics of the religious life of American Jews can be conveniently summarized as personalism, voluntarism, moralism, and universalism." Liebman and Cohen, *Two Worlds of Judaism*, p. 158.

[4] Yael Dayan, "Agenda We Share with U.S. Jewry," *Jerusalem Post*, November 24, 1988.

[5] Yossi Sarid, "Only Yourselves to Blame," *Jerusalem Post*, December 1, 1988.

oppressors, but also as the new laboratory of prophetic idealism and liberal democracy—in short, as a replica of America in the Promised Land."[6] This interesting twist on the old Puritan depiction of America as the New Israel serves as the backdrop for the rejection of the proposed amendment because of its repudiation of the individualist ethos of progressive liberalism. That a law could mandate the method of conversion contradicted the American preference for freedom of choice and for consent as the critical legitimating principle of the regime. The statement recalls an earlier comment of an American Jewish leader, Rabbi Joachim Prinz, who in regard to another dispute involving Israel—diaspora relations—declared, "What we think is right and just in our own country must be right and just in Israel. What we find in America—the imperfections of democracy that we recognize and seek to correct—must also be considered faulty in Israel."[7]

The implicit assumption of these comments, that the Western liberal democratic tradition, best exemplified in the American experience, should be embraced with a similar passion in Israel, might be acceptable to Israelis who perceive the two countries as sharing an ideological agenda. Such individuals are likely to be somewhat more disposed to understanding American concerns over the Law of Return than their fellow Israelis; however, they are also likely to be more sensitive than American Jews to the case for amending the law (as well as irritated by the mildly arrogant tone of the two statements). Whatever their ideological orientation, they can be expected to be well versed in Israeli conceptions of national identity that in some important particulars are fundamentally at odds with American notions. These conceptions of identity extend from the alternative pluralist visions outlined in the previous chapter; thus, in contrast to an ideological conception of political identity that both exalts the deliberative capacity of the individual and separates it from its historical antecedents, the more anthropological Israeli conception rests in significant part on a shared historical experience that gives additional attention to fraternal and communal attachments at the expense of the subjective choices of individuals. It is the aim of this chapter to explore the implications of this difference.

Patriotism and Nationhood

If the Israeli election of 1988 focused considerable attention on an issue that served to raise important questions of national identity, so too did the

6 Morris B. Abram, "Why U.S. Jews Care about 'Who's a Jew,' " *Jerusalem Post*, December 2, 1988.

7 Quoted in Abramov, *Perpetual Dilemma*, p. 375.

American presidential election, which was held only one week after the balloting in Israel. The issue was patriotism, and it was skillfully (or if one prefers, cynically) exploited by the Republican party to the ultimate benefit of George Bush. It became a prominent part of a campaign that was widely perceived as having reached a new low in American electoral politics. It left one tempted to conclude that if indeed patriotism is the last refuge of a scoundrel, then it is the first recourse of a politician.

Yet if the politics was occasionally unseemly, it managed nevertheless to highlight the characteristically American absorption with patriotic symbol and ritual. Those who found themselves irritated with visits to flag factories and heated exchanges about the pledge of allegiance can surely identify with Alexis de Tocqueville, who, like many other foreign observers over the years, was struck by the frequent display of patriotic activity in the United States. "It is impossible to conceive a more troublesome or more garrulous patriotism; it wearies even those who are disposed to respect it."[8] As was learned in 1988, those who are not disposed to respect it, or at least take it seriously enough, are likely to pay a substantial political price. The force of this lesson was evident the following year when, after the Supreme Court's controversial decision invalidating Texas's flag desecration statute, Democrats rivaled Republicans in their haste to denounce the Court's work and to celebrate the stars and stripes. Nothing experienced by Tocqueville can compare with the effusion of patriotic rhetoric that for days filled the halls of Congress.

What accounts for this phenomenon? The answer, I would suggest, may be found in that very quality of patriotic display that produces much of the impatience and annoyance felt by its detractors. Thus some people are offended by what they perceive to be the artificial character of the rituals of patriotism, the transparently inauthentic expression that passes for love of country. The pledge of allegiance, for example, is uttered less out of conviction than out of compulsion (formal and informal); the worship of the flag coincides with its exploitation in the selling of everything from fried chicken to used cars. There is much sound and fury; what, however, does it signify?

Among other things, it signifies the very nature of American origins, origins that are themselves suffused with artificiality, which in this context does not connote a lack of genuineness so much as a founding in conven-

---

[8] Tocqueville, *Democracy in America*, vol. 2, p. 236. An interesting discussion of the symbols of American patriotism may be found in Wilbur Zelinsky, *Nation into State: The Shifting Symbolic Foundations of American Nationalism* (Chapel Hill: University of North Carolina Press, 1988).

tion. Lincoln said it best by noting that "our fathers brought forth on this continent, a new nation, conceived in Liberty, and dedicated to the proposition that all men are created equal." Its birth (and later, as portrayed in the Gettysburg Address, its "new birth") signaled a decisive break with the past; the womb from whence it came was essentially untested, thus ensuring that the durability of its issue would in time be seriously challenged. The theoretical foundation for this fresh experiment was the social contract, a contrivance of art, not nature. The Revolution, in short, was not a movement of national liberation; rather, it was a period of national construction whose building blocks were the products of human imagination. It was, as the historian Louis L. Snyder has pointed out, the first time in history in which people had deliberately crafted a nation.[9] Sustaining the conception of nationhood that resulted from this achievement, in which bonds of unity did not flow naturally from such primordial attachments as race, religion, or ethnicity, would lead, among other things, to an emphasis on patriotism, which may be construed here as a kind of artificial substitute for the natural ties of sentiment.

It is easy to sympathize with critics of patriotism who become distressed at the disjunction between form and substance, that is, the celebration of symbols as opposed to the ideas they are intended to represent. The flag, they often say, is less important than the ideas represented by the flag. While this makes an important point, it may inadvertently lead to a false dichotomy. Thus the rooting of our distinctive American peoplehood in ideas and principles is importantly connected to our heavy reliance on nationalistic symbol and ritual. No doubt for some the appeal of a noble idea is sufficiently powerful that it creates an identification with the nation requiring no mediating or intervening agent. For many, however, ideas are essentially words on a page, possibly respected when understood, but ultimately inadequate to the task of securing for the individual the sort of visceral connection to the national community that in most settings is achieved in other and more traditional ways. The principles of republican government will, as an abstract proposition, generate widespread support among the American people; to channel this support into a deeper emotional commitment leads, among other things, to the pledging of allegiance—first to the flag, and only then to the republic "for which it stands."[10]

[9] Snyder, *Varieties of Nationalism*, p. 207.

[10] Here I would disagree to some extent with John Schaar, who in his consideration of American loyalty contrasts two "opposing traditions," the first essentially rational and dedicated to certain philosophic principles, and the second the "idea of Americanism," which is

This connection between ideas and patriotic expression is also important in clarifying the concept of "Americanization," a term that, as Walter Berns has pointed out, "has no analogue elsewhere."[11] It is a term that has come to embody in the literature of American political culture the special character of American nationhood. "The United States defined itself as a nation by commitment to the principles of liberty, equality, and government on the basis of consent, and the nationality of its people derived from their identification with those principles."[12] The term connotes a *process* in which resources, public and private, are committed to the task of converting a country of immigrants into a national community. One is Americanized into a conception of nationhood whose existing members vary in their mastery of its essential attributes. In a sense, then, the nation is a work in progress, constantly perfecting itself, but never reaching complete fulfillment. Moreover, the specific function of Americanization in the immigration process is but one piece of a much larger effort in which the American people, in essence, move through various stages of nationhood, each stage reflecting the particular level that the society has reached in the realization of its nation-defining principles. It is again Lincoln who best captured the spirit of this understanding by interpreting the Declaration of Independence, the documentary source of American nationhood, as a statement of ideals "constantly looked to, constantly labored for, and even though never perfectly attained, constantly approximated."[13] Or as Perry Miller once observed, "Being an American is not something to be inherited so much as something to be achieved."[14]

Understandably, a great deal of the activity—some edifying, some not—

"irrational, nationalistic, and conformist." "The first views America as an uncompleted process; the latter views it as a finished and organic being." John H. Schaar, *Loyalty in America* (Berkeley: University of California Press, 1957), pp. 88–89. While there are certainly some obvious oppositional features in these two traditions, it is at least as important to appreciate their complementary aspects. In this sense they may both be understood within the context of an ongoing process, the goal of which is a fuller attainment of nationhood.

[11] Walter Berns, *Taking the Constitution Seriously* (New York: Simon & Schuster, 1987), p. 22.

[12] Philip Gleason, "American Identity and Americanization," in Paterson, Novak, and Gleason, *Concepts of Ethnicity*, p. 59.

[13] Basler, *Collected Works*, vol. 2, p. 406.

[14] Quoted in Werner Sollors, *Beyond Ethnicity: Consent and Descent in American Culture* (Oxford: Oxford University Press, 1986), p. 3. The philosopher George Santayana had the same thing in mind when he said that "to be an American is of itself almost a moral contradiction." Quoted in Arthur Mann, *The One and the Many: Reflections on the American Identity* (Chicago: University of Chicago Press, 1979), p. 69.

surrounding this goal-oriented conception of national identity involves the use and manipulation of patriotic exercises and symbols. When nationality coincides with ethnicity or religion, the need (in a constitutional regime) to encourage an active sense of belonging is mitigated by the innate ties that the individual brings to the community. The task of nation building, on the other hand, where the nation is younger than the state, and where a shared sense of common purpose must, for the most part, be assembled around a core of formal principles possessing a universal appeal, produces a more concerted effort to stimulate this sense of belonging through repeated affirmations of allegiance. In his study of polyethnic states, the Israeli political scientist Benjamin Akzin contrasts two patterns of development, "integration" and "unequal pluralism," and argues, "To the extent that the integrationist pattern prevails [as it does in the United States], it is the attachment to the State—*patriotism* . . . —that is pushed into the fore-ground, while the attachment to the dominant nationality—*nationalism*—though present, occupies a less conspicuous position in the background. Where the pattern of unequal pluralism shows up [as in Israel] it is the dominant nationality's nationalism that occupies the centre of the stage while the State is valued mainly because of its role as an instrument in the service of the nation."[15] Patriotism thus becomes a shorthand way of ex-pressing an American identity that rests on the neutralization of nation-alities in favor of a common allegiance to a political construct—the state—which embodies a concept of nationality fundamentally different from those that are in the process of being transcended.[16]

What remains to be considered is how these alternative conceptions of peoplehood influence the constitutional delineation of membership in the political community. In pursuit of this end the questions that one is accus-

[15] Benjamin Akzin, *State and Nation* (London: Hutchinson University Library, 1964), p. 44. Akzin points out, however, that while the United States began as a kind of repudiation of nationalism, it is now well on its way to becoming "nationalized" (p. 100). Relevant here is the distinction drawn by Louis L. Snyder between patriotism and nationalism. "Patriotism is concerned with the people's love for a *country*; nationalism refers to the historical sentiment of a *people*." Snyder, *Varieties of Nationalism*, p. 42.

[16] Meg Greenfield has eloquently captured the essence of this understanding of patriotism in America. She believes it a "stroke of genius" that we honor ancestors to whom "our only connection is spiritual and philosophical." Our patriotism is reflective of a "common acquired past and the common purpose that is meant to flow from it." This she sees threatened by the excessive separatism of the moment. "Even those among us who have had the worst of the American experience make a voluntary claim on these people [our adopted forbears], demand that the founders' posterity be held to the best of their ideals, never mind what has happened up till now." Meg Greenfield, "The Fellowship of Patriotism," *Newsweek*, July 8, 1991.

tomed to hearing are critical. Moreover, understanding the reasons for the questions is perhaps more important than eliciting answers to them. When we appreciate the bases for the queries "Who is a Jew?" and "What is American (or un-American) about _____?" we gain entry into the constitutional self-understandings of the Israeli and American polities.

"The Love of a Distant Brother": Membership and the Claim of History

Two of the most famous cases in Israeli judicial history center on the question of who is a Jew. The first, *Rufeisen* v. *Minister of Interior* (popularly known as the "Brother Daniel case"), considers whether a Polish Jew who has converted to Catholicism nevertheless qualifies for immediate Israeli citizenship under the terms of the Law of Return. The second, *Shalit* v. *Minister of Interior*, involves the question of the appropriate registration of two children who are the offspring of a Jewish father and a non-Jewish mother. The cases are notable both for the political controversy they generated and the insights they provide into the complex question of membership in the Israeli political community. Much can and has been said about them; the focus here will be on those elements directly bearing on the contrasting models of American and Israeli constitutionalism.

The Supreme Court ruled by a four-to-one majority against Oswald Rufeisen, but the justices were unanimous in their sympathy for the petitioner and in praise of his deeds. It is easy to understand why. Rufeisen was a heroic figure who, posing as a Silesian Christian, had courageously saved many Jewish lives during the time in which he served as an interpreter for the German police in Poland. This time was interrupted by imprisonment after an informant exposed him to the Nazis. He then escaped from prison and found refuge in a convent, where, in 1942, he converted to Christianity. After the war he joined the Carmelite order (becoming Brother Daniel), mainly because it had a chapter in Palestine, where he hoped eventually to serve. (Rufeisen, it should be noted, had been active as a youth in Poland in the Zionist movement and continued to assert his Zionist commitment after his conversion.) In 1958, following a number of unsuccessful attempts to emigrate, he was granted permission to pursue his dream in Israel. But his claim to automatic citizenship under the Law of Return and the Nationality Law was rejected by the minister of interior.

In his argument to the Court, Brother Daniel insisted that while his religion was Catholic, his one and only nationality was Jewish. "If I am not a

Jew what am I? I did not accept Christianity to leave my people. It added to my Judaism. I feel as a Jew."[17] The Court was clearly moved by the evidently sincere appeal of a genuinely good man. "Can [Brother Daniel] be denied the burning desire of his life to be completely identified with the people which he loves and to become a citizen of the land of his dreams, not as a stranger coming from without but as a Jew returning home?"[18] The answer, delivered decisively but with "great psychological difficulty," was yes.[19]

To arrive at this conclusion, the Court had to address one of the more interesting angles in the case, the convergence of Brother Daniel's claim with the Orthodox Jewish definition of a Jew. Brother Daniel was born of a Jewish mother and raised by his parents as a Jew; the fact of his later conversion to Catholicism could not, after all, negate these essential facts. While it is safe to say that Orthodox Jews did not rally behind Brother Daniel, their basic commitment to an Israel that was devoted to the enforcement of the halakic law meant that they could not without difficulty oppose his legal claim. Indeed, the Court's solution, which was to employ a wholly secular interpretation of the Law of Return, thus enabling it expressly to affirm the nontheocratic nature of the state, was perhaps a greater disappointment to the Orthodox than to Brother Daniel, who, it would seem, should have preferred a favorable decision firmly rooted in secular reasoning. The adoption of the religious interpretation of the law would have left him with a victory, but one tainted by its having come at the expense of an important principle.[20] For this reason, the dissenting judge, Justice Cohn, was in total agreement with the majority's position that religious law had no bearing on the outcome of the case.

But as to the appropriate secular interpretation, a significant gap separated the majority and minority opinions. Justice Cohn supported the claim of Brother Daniel by applying a "subjective test"—"that the right to return to Israel belongs to any person who declares that he is a Jew return-

[17] Quoted in Oscar Kraines, *The Impossible Dilemma: Who Is a Jew in the State of Israel?* (New York: Bloch Publishing Co., 1976), p. 24.

[18] *Rufeisen v. Minister of Interior*, 16 P.D. 2428, 2432 (1962). The fascinating story of Oswald Rufeisen's life is chronicled in Nechama Tec, *In the Lion's Den: The Life of Oswald Rufeisen* (New York: Oxford University Press, 1990).

[19] Ibid., 2432.

[20] Brother Daniel's first priority, however, was to win his case, and so he did resort to arguments based on religious law. This drew a rebuke from Justice Landau, who pointedly remarked, "As a person deeply conscious of his own self-respect, the petitioner should never have invoked the assistance of Jewish religious law." Ibid., 2444.

ing to his homeland and wishes to settle there."[21] His view is reminiscent in American constitutional law of the statutory interpretations of the Selective Service law during the war in Vietnam, in which conscientious objector status was found not to depend on any objective religious test.[22] For him the fate of Brother Daniel turned on the relative importance assigned to individual volition, and this in turn was a question properly resolved by interpreting the very establishment of the state of Israel as signifying a revolutionary break with the past, as "render[ing] imperative a revision of the values which we have imbibed in our long exile."[23] Therefore, whatever may have been the reasons for limiting subjective control over one's identity in the prestate period, these reasons need not decide such questions for a Jewish state that is in control of its destiny, that is in a position "to promote the fulfilment of its prophetic vision."[24]

As for the majority, the secular meaning of the term "Jew" in the Law of Return is to be derived from the common understanding of the "ordinary simple Jew."[25] The answer to the operative definitional question is not a matter for individual determination; rather, it is provided by the Jews

[21] Ibid., 2443. For Justice Cohn, this test also requires a demonstration of "good faith."

[22] For example, in *United States* v. *Seeger* the Supreme Court interpreted the statutory requirement of "belief in relation to a Supreme Being" to include any sincere belief occupying "a place in the life of its possessor parallel to that filled by the orthodox belief in God of one who clearly qualifies for the exemption." 380 U.S. 163, 166 (1965). See also *Welsh* v. *United States*, 398 U.S. 333 (1970).

[23] *Rufeisen*, 16 P.D. at 2441.

[24] Ibid., 2442.

[25] Ibid., 2437. This phrase is reminiscent of language used by the U.S. Supreme Court in a case that recalls a period in American history when racial qualifications were very much a part of the naturalization process. (Such qualifications were eliminated by the Immigration and Nationality Act of 1952.) The matter at issue concerned the qualifications of a Hindu, who, while technically a Caucasian, was not, according to Justice Sutherland, white in the "understanding of the common man." *United States* v. *Thind*, 261 U.S. 204, 209 (1923). "It may be true that the blond Scandinavian and the brown Hindu have a common ancestor in the dim reaches of antiquity, but the average man knows perfectly well that there are unmistakable differences between them today" (209). The analogue to the Israeli case's preference for common opinion over halakic law is Sutherland's rejection of science in favor of conventional understanding. This understanding is to be applied "whatever may be the speculations of the ethnologist" (215). The elimination of these race-based exclusions should be seen as propelled by those very principles to which naturalized citizens are sworn to allegiance. As Judith N. Shklar has has wisely noted, "No historically significant form of government or of citizenship is in principle incompatible with the exclusion of large groups of people, but natural-rights theory makes it very difficult to find good reasons for excluding anyone from full political membership in a modern republic." Judith N. Shklar, *American Citizenship: The Quest for Inclusion* (Cambridge: Harvard University Press, 1990), p. 37.

themselves, by the consensus of the group. Whatever the Court's own views of the matter might be, the only definition that counts is the one that expresses itself in "the common parlance" of the Jewish community. In the circumstances of this case, Justice Silberg, writing for the majority, concluded that the communal understanding of the term does not include a Jew who has become a Christian.

This of course in no way answers the question of who is a Jew under the Law of Return; it only asserts that an apostate such as Brother Daniel is *not* a Jew. The Court at one point acknowledged the deep divisions of opinion within the Jewish community with respect to a positive definition of Judaism, and it prudently abjured the temptation to choose among them (with the exception that in disagreeing with the minority opinion it implicitly rejected the volitional or subjective definition). In effect, then, the Court's resolution of the issues raised by Brother Daniel amounts to discerning the least common denominator among Israeli Jews; that is, finding what it is "that is shared by *all* Jews in Israel (save a mere handful)."[26] If the "one thing" that constitutes a common bond among Jews is antithetical to the membership claim of Brother Daniel, then his case collapses. Justice Silberg's understanding of this common bond is "that we do not cut ourselves off from our historic past nor deny our ancestral heritage. We continue to drink from the original fountains. The shape has changed, the channels have been altered, but we have not sealed the wells for without them we would be but 'as the poor that are cast out.' Only the simple believe or think that we are creating here a *new culture*; for this it is much too late. A people which is almost as old as the human race cannot start *ab ovo*, and our new culture in this land—at the highest—is merely a *new version* of the culture of the past."[27]

Brother Daniel cannot avail himself of the rights in the Law of Return because, as Justice Landau's concurrence explicitly stated, "He has denied his national past."[28] In this respect the Law of Return is very much an

---

[26] *Rufeisen*, 16 P.D. at 2438. One critic of the Court's decision has expressed concern over his approach, saying that "if taken seriously, [it] would involve a relinquishment of the judicial responsibility to clarify and enlighten current public sentiment rather than merely to reflect it." Marc Galanter, "A Dissent on Brother Daniel," *Commentary* 36 (July 1963): 12.

[27] *Rufeisen*, 16 P.D. at 2438.

[28] Ibid., 2447. A similar result may be observed in the 1989 "Jew for Jesus" case, *Beresford v. Ministry of Interior*, 23 (4) 793 (1989), where the Court ruled that Messianic Jews cannot claim automatic Israeli citizenship under the Law of Return. It held that belief in Jesus made one a member of another faith, despite the fact that the petitioners claimed to be Jewish and were, like Brother Daniel, born to Jewish parents. Again the Court seemed to defer to the

extension of the Declaration of Independence, which in its first half presents a history of the Jewish people. This history, according to Landau, reveals that for the Jewish people "nationalism and religion are inseparably interwoven."[29] As a result of his religious conversion to Catholicism, Oswald Rufeisen severed his ties to the Jewish people; when he became Brother Daniel he repudiated the history that gives definition and meaning to membership in the Jewish community. The fact that he may sincerely "feel as a Jew" cannot overcome the objective reality of his deed, which, intended or not, challenges the continuity of Jewish life. Or in the words of Justice Silberg, "Certainly Brother Daniel will love Israel. This he has proved beyond all doubt. But such love will be from without—the love of a distant brother. He will not be a true inherent part of the Jewish world."[30]

Thus, in spite of his uncontestedly sincere affirmations of affinity to the Jewish people (supported by many acts of great courage) and his evident devotion to Israel (he had attempted to emigrate in 1948 in order to participate in the War of Independence), Brother Daniel can only stand, in relation to the Jewish people, and hence to the Jewish state as well, as a distant brother.[31] To be sure, he can acquire Israeli citizenship through naturalization (and has done so), but his claim to full membership in a political community that entails more than formal citizenship rights is thwarted by a counterclaim, the claim of history. History, as employed by the Court, possesses a cold logic of exclusivity—you are either a part of it or you are not. It establishes the conditions and the criteria for fraternity; the universalism of the "brotherhood of man," so important to liberal thought, must

---

common understanding of who qualifies as a Jew. And a similar denial of a national past was ultimately decisive in the Court's outcome. As Justice Elon put it, "Messianic Jews attempt to reverse the wheels of history by 2000 years. . . . But the Jewish people has decided during the 2000 years of its history that [Messianic Jews] do not belong to the Jewish nation . . . and have no right to force themselves on it" (830).

[29] *Rufeisen*, 16 P.D. at 2447.

[30] Ibid., 2438.

[31] In his study of the idea of fraternity, Wilson Carey McWilliams makes an observation that bears on the story of Brother Daniel: "It is never easy to identify one's brothers, and for modern man the task may seem impossible, or not worth the cost. Brethren have always required 'proofs' of one another, and being put to the test is an essential element of growing into fraternity. The ultimate test, of course, was the willingness to sacrifice life." Wilson Carey McWilliams, *The Idea of Fraternity in America* (Berkeley: University of California Press, 1973), pp. 90–91. In the *Shalit* case, Justice Silberg in effect responds to this test of brotherhood as a way of establishing a person's Jewish identity. "'Jewishness' is not a prize awarded to people as an honorary degree for their virtues and their efforts on its behalf." *Shalit* v. *Minister of Interior*, 23 (2) P.D. 477, 502 (1970).

give way to a more circumscribed perspective, where fraternal ties ultimately depend on the manner in which people connect to a communal
past.[32] More, however, than fraternity is involved; the very survival of the
Jewish people is predicated on a history that has always served as a common
source of collective identity. Brother Daniel's "sincere affection" for the
Jewish community cannot take the place of an "absolute inner identification,"[33] which is absent in his case but present within even the most secular
Jew. "Whether he is religious, non-religious or anti-religious, the Jew
living in Israel is bound, willingly or unwillingly, by an umbilical cord to
historical Judaism from which he draws his language and its idiom, whose
festivals are his own to celebrate, and whose great thinkers and spiritual
heroes . . . nourish his national pride."[34]

The choice of metaphor is revealing, particularly in comparative terms.
If one reflects on Lincoln's juxtaposition of "a new nation" with a "birth of
freedom," one sees how sharply this contrasts with a "national pride" that
receives nourishment from "an umbilical cord" to a distant past. In the first
instance we are encouraged to think of a polity that, untethered from the
past, was positioned to build its own history; in the second we are to
imagine a polity that from the moment of its inception embodied a history
that was to be a powerful force in determining its future. Thus James
Madison could confidently reject the opinions of those who dismissed the
framers' "experiment . . . merely because it may comprise what is new."[35]
And Thomas Jefferson could voice the characteristically American sentiment, "I like dreams of the future better than the history of the past."[36] It is
slightly ironic that this oft-expressed American attitude, involving a hope-
ful breaking with the past, has frequently been analogized to ancient Israel.
"Having repudiated Europe and severed ties with the past, America was
able to float free in historical time and, like the Hebrews, to believe in an

---

[32] Or as Justice Silberg later indicated in *Shalit*, "The culture of the past is first and
foremost our definitive national identity laid down at least 2400 years ago." *Shalit*, 23 (2) P.D.
at 503. On liberalism and fraternity, see McWilliams, *The Idea of Fraternity*, p. 569.

[33] *Rufeisen*, 16 P.D. at 2438.

[34] Ibid. It is worth noting here that American holidays and festivals, in contrast with those
of Israel, are on the whole somewhat less involved with the commemoration of particular
historical events. Even the great exception, the Fourth of July, is celebrated as much for the
ideas associated with independence as for the actual break with England.

[35] Henry Cabot Lodge, ed., *The Federalist* (New York: Knickerbocker Press, 1888), no. 14,
p. 81.

[36] Quoted in McWilliams, *The Idea of Fraternity*, p. 171.

essentially ahistorical reality."[37] As a people, therefore, the American nation, like the ancient nation of the Jews, could do precisely what Justice Silberg denied is possible for the modern Jewish nation, "start *ab ovo*."

It is in this sense that Justice Cohn's dissent resonates more harmoniously within an American frame of reference. He did not repudiate history—he insisted that his position was consonant with the vision of the prophets of Israel—but he postulated an understanding of historical continuity that incorporates within it a favorable account of revolutionary change. In conjunction with this, he also embraced a stance toward history in which one looks back in order to discover the ideas or principles that should guide the present in establishing what ought to be.[38] *What* is Jewish is ultimately more important than *who* is a Jew. For Cohn, the establishment of the state does not create "merely a *new version* of the culture of the past"; the umbilical cord metaphor is an inadequate device to convey the possibilities confronting the new polity.[39] And among the possibilities is a conception of community that gives priority to the *will* of those wishing to be recognized as full members of the community. Brother Daniel's fate is consequently not bound unwillingly to historic Judaism, if that means that he is precluded from exercising his sovereign choice with respect to contemporary Judaism. His is not the "love of a distant brother"; the distant past does not automatically establish the boundaries of communal membership in the present.[40]

---

[37] Charles A. Miller, *The Supreme Court and the Uses of History* (New York: Simon & Schuster, 1969), p. 172. Miller also refers to the view of ancient Israel and the United States as two chosen peoples. Being "responsible to a divine destiny" they were both, according to this notion, "exempt from the ordinary course of history" (p. 172). Other scholars have also focused on the conscious distancing of the American founding from the past. For example, John Schaar writes, "America was founded on explicit repudiation of tradition, dogma, and reverence for ancient institutions." Schaar, *Loyalty in America*, p. 87.

[38] One student of the American political culture has written, "In equating America with an idea—more accurately, with a cluster of ideals—the Revolutionary generation insured that their posterity would be in search of themselves as they ought to be." Mann, *The One and the Many*, p. 69. It is an observation that Justice Cohn would have no difficulty applying to Israel.

[39] Support for Justice Cohn's position on the possibilities opened by the subjective view on Jewish identity may be found in Galanter, "A Dissent on Brother Daniel," p. 15.

[40] Not surprisingly, American courts have been required to consider the question of "Who is an Indian?" For example, Martha Minow has an interesting discussion of the Mashpee Indian land dispute, in which the 1790 Non-Intercourse Act was appealed to on the ground that it protected tribal groups from exploitation by white developers. The only question was

PLURALISM, PEOPLEHOOD, AND POSITIVISM

The story of Benjamin Shalit is mundane in comparison with that of Oswald Rufeisen, but whatever it may have lacked in personal drama was more than made up for in political excitement. It was the kind of excitement that courts, always vulnerable to political assault in a constitutional democracy, studiously seek to avoid. The Israeli Supreme Court was in this respect no exception, but in the end it had no choice but to take up an issue, the explosiveness of which it knew had the potential for precipitating a governmental crisis of the first magnitude.

The facts of the case can be simply stated. Benjamin Shalit, a native-born Israeli Jew married to a non-Jewish naturalized Israeli citizen, sought to have the couple's two children registered as Jews in the Population Register. More specifically, as nonbelievers, the Shalits wanted their son and daughter to be listed under the relevant law as "of Jewish nationality and without religion." This desire was frustrated by a clerk of the Ministry of Interior who, following directives of the ministry, refused to register them in this way. The reason for the refusal was that Mrs. Shalit was not Jewish. The appeal to the Court thus confronted the justices with the problem of whether the status of Jewishness could exist independently of any religious content. That they appreciated the significance of the issue is revealed in the fact that the president of the Court proceeded in an unprecedented way by convening nine of the ten justices then on the tribunal, all nine of whom eventually contributed opinions.[41]

The Court divided five to four in the petitioner's favor, but not in a way that produced a definitive judicial response to the "Who is a Jew?" controversy. Shalit was permitted to register his children in accordance with his wishes, but this specific outcome was based largely on technical grounds having to do with the legal authority of the registration clerk to reject a registrant's declaration. "It is in fact a mistake to think that the matter

---

whether the Mashpee Indians could be considered members of a tribe, inasmuch as their tribal status and identity had been made ambiguous by intermarriage with whites and blacks. Should ethnic self-identity or external community understandings prevail? A Massachusetts jury eventually ruled against the Mashpees, while agreeing with some of their historical interpretation. See Minow, *Making All the Difference*, pp. 351–56. The issue here, determining who belongs to a particular group, is of course one of the most contested questions in the contemporary debate over affirmative action.

[41] Most cases are decided by three- or five-judge panels, depending on the importance of the case.

under consideration requires us to determine who is a Jew."[42] This was not enough, however, to defuse the political crisis that predictably followed the announcement of the decision; under the threat by the Orthodox to bring down the government, the Knesset passed legislation directly addressing the Court's decision. It amended the Law of Return by defining as a Jew "a person who was born of a Jewish mother or has become converted to Judaism and who is not a member of another religion."[43] The Population Registry Law was also amended so as to preclude the registration as a Jew, both in terms of nationality and religion, of anyone failing to satisfy the test of the amended Law of Return. In effect, then, the secular position on the separability of religion and nationality was rejected.

"It is absurd," wrote a non-Orthodox rabbi in the *Jerusalem Post*, "that a parliamentary body in a pluralistic, democratic state should decide the identity of a section of the population."[44] This reaction to the legislation of 1970 reflected the view of many Israelis, particularly those of liberal persuasion. It also reflects, as we have seen in the previous chapter, an understanding of pluralist democracy that fits comfortably within the constitutional environment of American society. Any law in the United States that sought to provide ascriptive definition for the identity of a group of people would have to contend with the prevailing commitment of the polity to liberal, republican philosophical and constitutional principles. Moreover, the Law of Return is not just *any* law; it occupies a place in Israeli jurisprudence equivalent in some ways in status to the U.S. Constitution. While most Israelis probably did not support the 1970 amendments, some of the arguments advanced in support of the changes possess a certain logic that can readily be assimilated to the very raison d'etre of the regime. This is clear from the various opinions in the *Shalit* case. Coalition politics, in which the religious parties often successfully pursue policies opposed by

---

[42] *Shalit*, 23 (2) P.D. at 505.

[43] Law of Return (Amendment no. 2), section 4b, 1970. This amendment was in fact a compromise that, because it did not mandate conversions according to halakic law, did not entirely please the Orthodox community. It became the basis for the most recent "Who is a Jew?" struggle. In the interim there have been many attempts by the religious parties to amend the law to make it conform completely with halakic law. They have all failed, but their margin of defeat has narrowed. The Supreme Court has been busy as well. In 1987 it overturned the Interior Ministry's refusal to register an American-born Reform convert to Judaism as Jewish. And in 1989 it ordered the Interior Ministry to accept non-Orthodox converts to Judaism as citizens under the Law of Return.

[44] Quoted in Amnon Rubinstein, "Who's a Jew, and Other Woes," *Encounter*, March 1971, p. 91.

the majority, may account for the passage of the amendments; but the assumptions embodied in the amendments are in themselves consistent with, if not mandated by, fundamental tenets of the constitutional polity.

One of the more intriguing aspects of these opinions is the manner in which they endeavor to reconcile the outcome in the Brother Daniel case with the circumstances in *Shalit*. The Court, as the opinion of Justice Berinson points out, was "faced with the same question [as in the earlier case] but the other way around: a boy born in this country to a Jewish father and a non-Jewish mother, who according to Jewish law is not a Jew, neither from a religious nor from a national point of view."[45] In the first case the Court had opted for a secular interpretation of the law while also rejecting the subjective test for determining its applicability. This was made possible by the fact that the Court could appeal to a popular consensus in order to establish the appropriate *objective* criteria according to which an apostate's application under the Law of Return could be evaluated. A secular, objective test was relatively easy to derive in determining who is not a Jew in the case of someone who had converted to Christianity. But Shalit's case presented the Court with a much more difficult assignment. Here it was impossible to rely on the common understanding of the "ordinary simple Jew." The Israeli Jewish community was fundamentally divided on the question of whether the halakic test should be the basis for determining policy in the civil arena. As the president of the Court, Justice Agranat, wrote, it was a question that "lies entirely in the ideological sphere."[46]

For those, like Justice Cohn, who subscribed to a subjective test, the lack of consensus in Israeli society, when viewed in conjunction with the application of a secular legal interpretation in *Rufeisen*, clearly indicated only one logical outcome: the Shalits should be able to register their children in accordance with the sincere dictates of their conscience. Justice Sussman, for example, found that "the multiplicity of meanings of the word [*Jew*] makes it impossible for [the] question [Who is a Jew?] to be answered."[47] But unlike Justice Agranat, who emphasized that the Court in *Rufeisen* had opted for "an objective criterion firmly rooted among members of the Jewish people,"[48] Sussman (and even more explicitly, Justice Berinson)

---

[45] *Shalit*, 23 (2) P.D. at 605.

[46] Ibid., 574. This was also the view of Justice Landau who, in *Rufeisen*, had deferred to the popular consensus. "What can the court contribute to the solution of an ideological dispute such as this which divides the public? The answer is—nothing, and whoever expects judges to produce a magic formula is merely deluding himself in his naivete" (520).

[47] Ibid., 512.

[48] Ibid., 574.

underscored the secular orientation of the earlier Court. It is implicit in their opinions that the divisive nature of the issue raised by Shalit effectively removed the last barrier to the adoption of a secular and subjective interpretation. This naturally leads one to the opinion of Justice Silberg, whose ruling had been the principal basis for deciding Brother Daniel's case. How would he resolve the tension that had emerged from the twin pillars of his earlier judgment?

Silberg's opinion was a dissent, but it is critical to any comparative assessment of Israeli and American conceptions of civic identity. While it failed in this instance to carry the day (although the subsequent action of the Knesset might suggest otherwise), its argument illuminates some key political precepts underlying membership in the Jewish state. This is signaled at the very outset of the opinion: "The question which we have to consider here surpasses in import and significance anything this court has dealt with since it first became an Israeli court. . . . [O]ur examination [of] its ideological constituents calls for the most profound and penetrating self-scrutiny of our existence as a people, our essence as a nation and our Zionist-political task in the renaissance of this country."[49] Such an examination led Silberg to resolve the abovementioned tension by retaining both the objective test *and* the secular interpretation of the *Rufeisen* decision. Objective criteria in this case, unlike in *Rufeisen*, were based on the halakic test, which needed to be incorporated within a secular interpretation of the Population Registry Law, emphasizing its functional (as opposed to its religious) utility in rendering meaningful the concept of nationality.

The basic rationale of the Silberg opinion is that the Zionist enterprise, which is crucial to the existence of the Jewish people, requires a concept of national identity that has at its core a common strand uniting all members of a distinctive people. This common strand must be able to serve as an identifying mark for Jews around the world, most of whom do not live in Israel. "The nation whose characteristics we seek is not the small group, the Israel group, *which as a nation does not exist at all*, but the large Jewish nation of some 13 million, whose members are scattered all over the world, including the State of Israel."[50] Why then does the halakic test recommend itself for this purpose? Partly, to be sure, for ideological reasons: in connecting religion to nationality it affirms the Zionist claim to the land of Israel. But also because it "is a very simple one for determining the nationality of a Jew. It is clear-cut and readily applicable to every Jew, whether from north

[49] Ibid., 492.
[50] Ibid., 495.

Iceland or from south Yemen, whether he is one of the righteous of the world or a hardened sinner."[51] Its appeal, in other words, is not theological (as illustrated by its rejection in *Rufeisen*); on the contrary, its attraction lies in its instrumental value, in its capacity to serve the ends of the Jewish state.[52] It is an essentially positivist solution that disconnects inner identification from nationality (as also occurred in the case of Brother Daniel), affirming a purely external criterion that relegates the will and intent of the individual to a place of no practical legal consequence.[53]

The deeper philosophical and constitutional implications of this view may be found in the dissenting opinion of Justice Kister, who consciously engaged in a comparative analysis focusing on the distinction between nationality and citizenship. Once this distinction is made, it follows from his argument that the adoption of the subjective test advanced by the Shalits would introduce an alien, or at least an incongruous, element into the Israeli constitutional system. That test of course is premised on the commonly held view that the term *Jew* has a variety of meanings. Kister's rejection of the test is predicated on the parallel observation that the term *nationality* also possesses a variety of meanings, and that the selection of the appropriate one as applied to Israel will indicate the correct legal response to the question of who is a Jew.

Justice Kister pointed out that "in some countries the meaning of 'nationality' is equated with that of the 'State' and national affiliation with State citizenship. That is so *inter alia* in France, England and the United States. Although various ethnic groups and people of different races dwell in these countries, where a public certificate uses the term 'nation' the reference is

---

[51] Ibid., 501.

[52] The recent emigration to Israel of thousands of Soviet and Ethiopian Jews, in which the Jewishness of many of the arrivees was called into question, causes one to wonder how well the interests of the state are in fact being served.

[53] In his argument to the Court, Shalit maintained that his children had more of a right to be considered Jews than did an Al Fatah terrorist named Nimri, who had been recognized as a Jew because his mother was Jewish. Justice Silberg's response to this argument possesses a distinctly positivist flavor. "Can the son of a Jewish mother, who joins the El Fatah terrorists and strives with all his might and main to destroy Israel, be called a Jew by nationality, whereas a person, the child of a non-Jewish mother, who sheds his blood for this country and is prepared to sacrifice his life for it, is to be held a gentile, a non-Jew? Is this conceivable?" Answer: "The son of a Jewish mother, a member of El Fatah, is a despicable wicked Jew. . . . As against this, the petitioners' children are delightful though unfortunate non-Jewish children who, because of the stubborn opposition of their parents towards religion, are regretfully not entitled to admission to the Jewish fold." Ibid., 502.

to the State and 'nationality' refers to citizenship."[54] When one speaks of a French or American national, one is referring to citizens of those countries. In Israel, on the other hand, "nationality" is used to describe a people, or an ethnic group, and the term is not synonymous with citizenship. When the Israeli Arab author Anton Shammas says that Israel "is a country where nationality does not coincide with citizenship," his purpose, to convey a sense of the Arab in Israel as outsider, is different from Kister's, but his assessment of the constitutional implications of a Jewish state is essentially the same.[55] Shammas understands too, like Justice Silberg, that Israel "belongs to the Jewish people wherever they are";[56] hence the distinction between the two terms is directly related to the official policy involving the ingathering of the exiles.

Where nationality and citizenship convey identical meanings, the alteration of one's political identity (through acquisition of a new nationality or renunciation of an existing one) is a volitional act that, unencumbered by ascriptive constraints, is fundamentally a matter to be resolved through subjective means. "Declaration of a wish to join a particular nation is only of importance when 'nation' is used in the sense of 'State' and when national affiliation means citizenship."[57] Consider in this regard the nineteenth-century American case *Minor* v. *Happersett*, involving a woman's right to

[54] Ibid., 541. See also Salo W. Baron, "Who Is a Jew?: Some Historical Reflections," *Midstream* 6 (Spring 1960): 12.

[55] Anton Shammas, "A Stone's Throw," *New York Review of Books*, March 31, 1988, p. 9. In another important case, *Tamarin* v. *State of Israel*, 26 (1) P.D. 197 (1972), Justice Agranat provided additional insight into this issue. The case involved an individual who had petitioned the minister of interior to change his nationality registration from "Jewish" to "Israeli." The Court held that nationality was distinct from citizenship and coterminous with ethnicity. Agranat was concerned that a ruling in the petitioner's favor would divide the Jewish people into Israeli and Jewish nations, and that this would undercut the principles on which the state was created. "There is no Israeli nation separate from the Jewish people." "The Jewish people is composed not only of those residing in Israel but also of Diaspora Jewry." Quoted in Kraines, *The Impossible Dilemma*, p. 67.

[57] *Shalit*, 23 (2) P.D. at 574. Further parallels in the arguments of the Arab author and the Israeli justice—Shammas: "There are no Israelis in Israel, in the sense that there are Americans in the United States." Kister: "Clearly there is no single Israeli people in the sense that the Arabs, Jews, Druze, and Armenians constitute one nation divided into ethnic groups which are not to be regarded as nations." Ibid., 568. With respect to Arab nationality, Oscar Kraines has pointed out that the "Who is a Jew?" question does not have an Arab analogue. Thus members of the "Arab nation" may, for example, be Moslem or Christian. Under Israel's Population Registry Law, Israeli Arabs are recorded as Arab in nationality, but unlike Jews, they are registered in a variety of ways under religion. Kraines, *The Impossible Dilemma*, p.

vote, in which Chief Justice Waite articulated an understanding of national identity that supports the distinction made by Justice Kister: "There cannot be a nation without a people. The very idea of a political community, such as a nation is, implies an association of persons for the promotion of their general welfare. Each one of the persons associated becomes a member of the nation formed by the association. He owes it allegiance and is entitled to its protection. Allegiance and protection are, in this connection, reciprocal obligations. The one is a compensation for the other; allegiance for protection and protection for allegiance."[58] This is the conception of nationhood modeled along the lines of a voluntary association, in which membership is based on calculations of mutual advantage. It recalls Hume's observation that "a nation is nothing but a collection of individuals."[59] The nation here is an inclusive concept entailing, in theory, the acceptance of anyone who is prepared to accept the reciprocal obligations that are the only conditions for membership in the political community.[60] "The struggle for citizenship in America has . . . been overwhelmingly a demand for inclusion in the polity, an effort to break down barriers to recognition."[61]

Charles Liebman has observed that "[Americans] would consider [ethnic as opposed to religious] schools divisive because they do not consider nationality a legitimate basis for exclusiveness."[62] Ethnicity is of course an

---

92. Relevant here is David Kretzmer's observation: "Registration of 'nation' is irrelevant in determining the rights and obligations of citizens, but it strengthens the dichotomy between the state as the political framework of all its citizens, and the state as the particularistic nation-state of the Jewish people." Kretzmer, *The Legal Status of the Arabs in Israel*, p. 44.

[57] *Shalit*, 23 (2) P.D. at 542.

[58] *Minor* v. *Happersett*, 88 U.S. 162, 166–67 (1874). James Kettner's scholarship on early American conceptions of citizenship conveys a similar understanding of political obligation. He says of the colonists that "they ultimately concluded that all allegiance ought to be considered the result of a contract resulting on consent." James H. Kettner, *The Development of American Citizenship, 1608–1870* (Chapel Hill: University of North Carolina Press, 1978).

[59] David Hume, "Of National Characters," in *The Philosophical Works. Vol. 3*, ed. Thomas Hill Green and Thomas Hodge Grose (Darmstadt, Ger.: Scientia Verlag Aalen, 1964), p. 244.

[60] See on this point T. Alexander Aleinikoff, "Citizenship, Aliens, Membership and the Constitution," *Constitutional Commentary* 7(1990). Aleinikoff argues that constitutional norms governing federal immigration policy are shaped by a "membership model" of citizenship. "The Constitution is understood as recognizing or establishing a 'national community,' and one belongs to that community by being a citizen" (pp. 9–10). Aleinikoff is highly critical of the result of this way of thinking, which is that "the immigration power [is] largely immune to the constitutional norms applied to other congressional powers" (p. 10).

[61] Shklar, *American Citizenship*, p. 3.

[62] Charles S. Liebman, *The Ambivalent American Jew: Politics, Religion, and Family in American Jewish Life* (Philadelphia: Jewish Publication Society of America, 1973), p. 43.

important component of American political culture, but it has always coexisted, as current debate in the country surely indicates, in some tension with the universalist appeal of American citizenship. As Harold Isaacs has noted, "The uniqueness of the American experience had to do with the uniqueness of the American credo: it was the only society in the world that had taken as its explicit goal the building of an open society, the making of one 'nation' out of many."[63] Thus, we can restate Liebman's observation by noting that when nationality corresponds with citizenship, the existence of schools organized in accordance with the alternative conception of nationality rooted in ethnicity may be seen as a potential threat to a citizenship based on principles of inclusiveness.

The association model suggests an even more familiar metaphor in liberal political philosophy, the social contract. Not surprisingly, therefore, we find Justice Kister making the following reference to it:

> Certainly in those states where affiliation in its sense of citizenship prevails, the conceptual basis is always or generally the subjective approach which has its source in Rousseau's *Contrat Social*. According to this view, the State was set up as a result of the inhabitants' agreement, and its citizens may always dissolve the contractual bond that created it and combine to set up another State. . . . [C]itizenship, a person's belonging to a particular state, is explained as coming from choice; a person may choose to cut the link but so long as he is a citizen he must obey the law.[64]

Kister concluded his reflections on the social contract with the thought that "in our State . . . 'nationality' serves to describe belonging to an ethnic group and not to the State, and therefore we cannot utilize the theory of Rousseau and others."[65] This is debatable. While the American Declaration of Independence, unlike the Israeli Declaration, explicitly invokes the language of the social contract, the philosophy of Rousseau and others (most notably Locke) is surely present (even if not so prominent) in the promises of equal rights mentioned in the Israeli founding document. As Daniel J. Elazar has noted, "Israel was founded on the basis of a political compact that is [in part] a social contract through which its citizens have

---

[63] Harold R. Isaacs, *Idols of the Tribe: Group Identity and Political Change* (New York: Harper & Row, 1975), p. 193.

[64] *Shalit*, 23 (2) P.D. at 541–42.

[65] Ibid., 542. Sanford Levinson has noted, apropos this rejection of consent theory, that being a Jew is "essentially . . . an ontological status rather than the free choice of the individual in question." Sanford Levinson, *Constitutional Faith* (Princeton: Princeton University Press, 1988), pp. 90–91.

established the terms of civil peace upon which the state rests."[66] In developing an analytically useful distinction, Kister overstated his argument. But it is an argument that nevertheless deserves to be taken seriously, for it does capture an important difference in conceptual understanding of the terms of membership in the political community that are reflective of the alternative pluralisms described earlier.

Modern social contract theory is a product of the seventeenth century. "Probably in no century before or since was there so self-conscious a break with the past or so resolute an effort to win freedom from the dead hand of custom and tradition."[67] The spirit of the age was one that rejected "the blind acceptance of that which has no better credentials than its mere existence."[68] It is in this sense that Justice Kister was correct in drawing a connection between the subjective test of nationality and those societies, particularly the American, that so clearly embody the spirit of this Enlightenment age. In this regard, Justice Agranat's characterization of the "modern view" of the issues raised by Shalit is very much to the point: "The present generation has 'equal rights' with the generations of the past and therefore is not bound to perform the 'totality' of precepts laid down by the latter. The present has its own dynamic and our generation is free to act in accordance with its own outlook and by having regard to modern needs."[69] This freedom applies to membership in the Jewish community; thus, the Shalits, according to this presentist view, should not be constrained by definitions emerging from the "dead hand" of the distant past.

The support for their claim that can be adduced from social contract

---

[66] Daniel J. Elazar, *The Constitution of the State of Israel* (Jerusalem: Jerusalem Center for Public Affairs, 1986), p. 1. The basis of the Zionist claim for an independent state may be grounded in contract theory, but the specific claim to such a state in the land of Israel is more clearly identified with covenantal theory, in which the source of the claim is located in the covenant between God and the Jewish people. The former is a natural, secular theory, whereas the latter is theological. Of course, for the Jews, the theological has become entwined with the historical, leading to a situation in which Justice Kister and others perceive the nationality of the Jewish people as inescapably connected to a religious definition. On this question, see Sol Roth, *Halakhah and Politics: The Jewish Idea of the State* (New York: Yeshiva University Press, 1989).

[67] George H. Sabine, *A History of Political Theory*, 3rd ed. (New York: Holt, Rinehart & Winston, 1961), p. 431. In the late eighteenth century the principal rival to the natural rights theory was utilitarianism, which, however, like its rival, shared a universalist orientation that viewed social and cultural differences as normatively insignificant. See Christopher J. Berry, "Nations and Norms," *Review of Politics* 43 (1981): 76–77.

[68] Sabine, *A History of Political Theory*, p. 432.

[69] *Shalit*, 23 (2) P.D. at 595. T. Alexander Aleinikoff argues that the "citizen-as-membership" model is ultimately traceable to the political theory underlying liberal democracy:

theory may also be found in the contemporaneous seventeenth-century Protestant emphasis on the primacy of the individual conscience in matters of scriptural interpretation and church membership.[70] There is a correspondence, for example, in John Locke's reflections on government and his views on religion. "A church . . . is a society of members voluntarily uniting to this end."[71] "No man by nature is bound unto any particular church or sect, but everyone joins himself voluntarily to that society in which he believes he has found that profession and worship which is truly acceptable to God."[72] And perhaps of most relevance to the case at hand, "Nobody is born a member of any church."[73] Seymour Martin Lipset has written that "the United States became the first nation in which religious groups were viewed as purely voluntary associations."[74] From the beginning of the nation's history, religious and political ideas played off against one another, eventuating in a coherent philosophical synthesis that provided content to the emerging American national identity.

All of which might lead Justices Silberg and Kister to say, "Our national identity is also a reflection of the interplay of religious and political ideas. But unlike the American example, religion in Israel is more than an influence on national identity; it is a constituent part of that identity. Lockean voluntarism is fine in the case of a religion that stands independently of the fate of a particular people. But this position cannot be fully sustained in the Israeli context, where religious and national identities are so intimately entwined." Their answer, then, to the *Jerusalem Post* letter writer is that a

the notion of popular sovereignty. Aleinikoff "Citizens, Aliens, Membership, and the Constitution," p. 14. This is another way of formulating Justice Agranat's characterization.

[70] In his study of American Protestantism's attitudes toward Israel and the Jewish people, Hertzel Fishman discerned a strand of opinion that resented the ethnic and national aspects associated with the Jewish religion, that was uncomfortable with the phenomenon of Jews as a people. "Protestantism's liberal attitude toward Jews as individuals stands in sharp contrast to its persistently hostile attitude toward Jewish peoplehood." Hertzel Fishman, *American Protestantism and a Jewish State* (Detroit: Wayne State University Press, 1973), p. 35. A particularly revealing item appeared in the thirties in the *Christian Century*: "Can democracy suffer a hereditary minority to perpetuate itself as a permanent minority with its own distinctive culture, sanctioned by its own distinctive cult forms? . . . They have no right *in a democracy* to remove their faith from the normal influences of the democratic process by insulating it behind the walls of a racial and cultural solidarity" (p. 31).

[71] John Locke, *A Letter concerning Toleration*, ed. Mario Montouri (The Hague: Martinus Nijhoff, 1963), p. 23.

[72] Ibid.

[73] Ibid.

[74] Seymour Martin Lipset, *The First New Nation: The United States in Historical and Comparative Perspective* (New York: Basic Books, 1963), p. 160.

parliamentary body in a pluralistic, democratic state may legitimately decide to identify a section of its population when there is compelling reason to believe that public indifference to such questions of identity will pose a substantial threat to the very essence of the regime. They, however, must be mindful of the fact that commitment to this essence is not exhausted by satisfying its communitarian requirements, that secular, democratic aspirations are also a vital component of the political culture. The challenge of balancing these commitments in a manner that retains respect for the constitutional sanctity of both of them will doubtless ensure the continuing presence of this issue on Israel's political and legal agenda.

"Citizenship Means Something"

It is not only Israeli judges who seek to distance themselves from the social contract. In his last book, *The Morality of Consent*, Alexander Bickel delivered a scathing critique of what he called the contractarian model, a societal metaphor representing the relationship between individuals and government as one defined in all essential matters by law—law that originates in the imagined legal transaction of a contract. "The concept of citizenship is, therefore, central [to the model], defining the parties to the original contract and the membership of society."[75]

It is fortunate, Bickel went on to argue, that the centrality of the concept was not an accurate description of its place in the American constitutional order: "I find it gratifying . . . that we live under a Constitution to which the concept of citizenship matters very little, that prescribes decencies and wise modalities of government without regard to the concept of citizenship."[76] Bickel considered citizenship to be a legalism and a theoretical abstraction; thus it was a perfect target for his preferred Burkean alternative to contractarianism. Burke's "Whig model" possessed attractive virtues lacking in the rival approach, principal among them being a sensitivity to the complex nature of political consent. It led him to conclude that "citizenship is at best a simple idea for a simple government."[77]

The view that citizenship plays only a marginal role in American constitutionalism does not lack for textual support. Most significantly, constitu-

---

[75] Alexander M. Bickel, *The Morality of Consent* (New Haven: Yale University Press, 1975), p. 5.

[76] Ibid., pp. 53–54.

[77] Ibid., p. 54.

tionally protected rights, with rare exception, are bestowed on persons without regard for whether they enjoy the status of citizens. To be sure, the Fourteenth Amendment contains important language defining who citizens are; but this was done more to rectify a historic injustice than to establish new practical meaning to the privileges associated with citizenship. Indeed, the Supreme Court's steady incorporation of more and more Bill of Rights protections under the due process clause of the Fourteenth Amendment has proceeded largely without cognizance of the distinction between citizen and noncitizen. With the extension of equal protection to children of illegal aliens, it is certainly tempting to echo the sentiments of Bickel and others who question whether any significant meaning can be attached to the status of citizenship.[78]

It would not be irrelevant to point out, however, that the exercise of the franchise is predicated on the holding of citizenship. Yet the import of this entitlement (which, it bears reminding, required four additional amendments) is easily minimized, as Bickel does in his defense of civil disobedience, by portraying electoral majorities as fictions—contractarian legal fictions—whose real effects are not weighty enough to make citizens want to revel in the contemplation of their privileged status.[79] At least in the United States, where an embarrassingly small percentage of the citizenry actually exercise their right to vote, one would be hard put to sustain a case, in contractarian terms, for the centrality of citizenship on the basis of its connection to the franchise.

As tempting as it is to adopt Bickel's view, his account of citizenship may be challenged on the basis of his own set of assumptions. Thus, to confine a consideration of the significance of the concept of citizenship to the specific legal consequences that flow from it is to establish somewhat artificial (or at least incomplete) evaluative measures dictated by an essentially contractarian vocabulary. As Judith Shklar has reminded us, the struggles of groups to gain the franchise were not motivated solely, or perhaps even primarily, by the anticipation of instrumental benefits, but rather by the expressive potential of the franchise as a mark of social standing.[80] Bickel's assessment is also contestable—and has so been contested—on inter-

---

[78] See *Plyler* v. *Doe*, 457 U.S. 202 (1982), involving a suit brought on behalf of all school-age children of Mexican origin residing in Texas as illegal aliens. It should be pointed out, however, that the Court has itself not always been comfortable with its pronouncement in *Graham* v. *Richardson*, 403 U.S. 365 (1971), that aliens are a "discrete and insular minority" for whom a heightened judicial solicitude is appropriate.

[79] Bickel, *The Morality of Consent*, p. 100.

[80] See Shklar, *American Citizenship*, pp. 25–62.

pretive grounds, in which the constitutional references to citizenship are read more expansively than is the case in Bickel's narrow reading.[81] But the Israeli comparison suggests another way of addressing the important issue raised by Bickel, one that places the phenomenon of citizenship within the broader political context of national identity. It is in this context that one can better appreciate that, in the words of Justice Bradley's dissent in *The Slaughter-House Cases*, "citizenship means something."[82]

In Israel, citizenship entails similarly limited legal consequences. It is difficult to disagree with the Israeli constitutional scholar Amnon Rubinstein, who wrote in 1976 that "the importance of nationality [citizenship] as a criterion for determining the rights and obligations of persons who are in Israel is not great."[83] This is illustrated in the various drafts of a basic law on fundamental rights that have from time to time been debated in Israel. The most recent one, approved by the cabinet in 1989, contains an enumeration of some twenty rights, most of which guarantee protection for "persons" rather than "citizens." This includes, among others, such basic liberties as free exercise of religion, sexual equality, free expression, privacy, property, and bodily integrity. A distinction is made between citizens and non-citizens only in the case of freedom of movement, freedom of employment, freedom of assembly, and freedom of unionizing. The right to vote, of course, has already been restricted to citizens.

For the Jewish people, citizenship in the modern nation-state has been a much contested concept that continues to stimulate debates within and about Zionism. While some Jews celebrated the citizenship they acquired in the wake of the Enlightenment, others were upset that the individual freedoms associated with their newly won status came at the expense of their corporate Jewish identity, which underwent relentless assault, in formal and informal ways, from the nation-state. As Shlomo Avineri has

---

[81] See, for example, Karst, *Belonging to America*, and Note, "Membership Has Its Privileges and Immunities: Congressional Power to Define and Enforce the Rights of National Citizenship," *Harvard Law Review* 102 (1989).

[82] *The Slaughter-House Cases*, 83 U.S. (16 Wall) 36, 114 (1873).

[83] Amnon Rubinstein, "Israel Nationality," *Tel Aviv University Studies in Law* 2 (1976): 189. Consider in this regard the 1989 "Black Hebrews" case, involving the claim by that sect (of American blacks who see themselves as the true descendants of the original Hebrew inhabitants of Israel) that despite their unlawful residence in Israel, they were entitled to certain basic rights, including the right to work. Justice Bach's decision for the Court relied heavily on American precedents that had affirmed the rights of illegal aliens, including the right to an elementary education. But it concluded, again following American constitutional precedents, that this did not hold in the area of employment, where the rights of citizens would be directly affected. *Avshalom Ben Shlomo v. Minister of Interior*, 43 (3) P.D. 353 (1989).

observed, "The inclusivism of the universalistic principles of the French Revolution was tempered everywhere by the historicist exclusivism of much of modern nationalism."[84] Jews could lead comfortable lives if they conformed to the ways and expectations of the larger national culture, that is, if they abandoned whatever claims they had to their own nationhood. The French Revolutionary Assembly declared them to be a "nation within a nation." It was only in accordance with Count Clermont-Tonnerre's famous formulation that their existence was assured: "To the Jews as a nation—nothing; to them as individuals—everything."[85]

It is not surprising, then, that a certain ambivalence should have developed among many Jews about the concept of citizenship, or even that this ambivalence should have extended to the Jewish state itself. As we have seen, the laws of personal status evolved from the Ottoman millet system; but they also reflected a sensitivity to the historic Jewish predicament, from which the desire to preserve zones of communal autonomy was a perfectly natural extension. Recall once again the parallel example of Native Americans. By statute they were extended American citizenship in 1924. In the ensuing years attempts to reduce or eliminate tribal autonomy have relied heavily on an appeal to their citizenship, advocates of this course of action contending that the "quasi-sovereign" status of the tribes translated into second-class citizenship for the Indians. Many Indians see in these efforts malevolent motives clothed in the respectable and altruistic garb of citizenship. Their rejoinders resonate with Bickelian echoes; they view citizenship as a convenient abstraction behind which those seeking to destroy the only authentic indigenous American culture can achieve their objective.

Jews are Israel's native Israelis. Whatever the political and historical objections to this observation, it is a legal fact. This is suggested by what at first glance may appear to be a trivial comparison: that within their respective countries, Indians and Jews are the only groups, none of whose members has acquired citizenship through the process of naturalization. The underlying assumption of the Law of Return is that immigrating Jews are simply returning to their native soil; moreover, the law, in not differentiating between Jews born in Israel and those who have arrived from other lands, assumes that all Jews acquire their citizenship from the right of

---

[84] Avineri, *The Making of Modern Zionism*, p. 11.

[85] Quoted in Lucy Dawidowicz, *The Jewish Presence: Essays on Identity and History* (New York: Harcourt Brace Jovanovich, 1978), p. 10. Yet, as the Dreyfus affair illustrated, even the radically assimilated, totally emancipated Jew was not assured his security, a fact that made an indelible impression on Theodore Herzl among others.

return.[86] In both the United States and Israel, citizenship through naturalization represents only a very small percentage of the total citizen population. But in the United States this was not always the case, which is why, as James H. Kettner's work has shown, Americans, beginning in colonial times, employed the naturalization model as their starting point for evolving a new concept of consent-based citizenship.[87]

Thus, another way of recognizing the anomalous status of Native Americans is to appreciate the symbolic meaning of their noninvolvement with the process of naturalization. Similarly, the Jewish character of the state of Israel is represented by the fact that Jews are presumed citizens by virtue of who they are rather than what they profess and, to a lesser extent, what they do. For example, unlike those qualifying under the Law of Return, persons acquiring citizenship through naturalization are required to renounce their prior nationality.[88] They are also to be distinguished from other immigrants by the declaration of loyalty to the state of Israel that is required of them.[89] The practical significance of this, while very little, reveals something important about citizenship in the polity, namely that *its* significance does not extend beyond the specific legal entitlements attendant on it. The failure to exact even the most minimal demonstration of allegiance on the part of one immigrant population, while making such demonstration a requirement for the admission of all others to membership in the political community, means that citizenship cannot play the unifying role that is open to it in other contexts. The loyalty of those for whom Israel is not a homeland is not presumed; for them citizenship carries with it some entitlements, but it is not a source of bonding or identification with those for whom citizenship is the final stop in a long journey home.

In contrast, the law governing acquisition of membership in the American nation requires that an individual be "attached to the principles of the Constitution of the United States."[90] Over the years judicial interpretation has prevented this requirement from becoming a real obstacle to the attainment of citizenship through naturalization. Bickel was surely correct in observing about this interpretation that "qualifications that seek to pour

---

[86] Rubinstein, "Israel Nationality," p. 162.

[87] Kettner, *The Development of American Citizenship, 1608–1870*, p. 9.

[88] Nationality Law of 1952, sec. 5(a)(6). In contrast, the repudiation of prior political loyalties is required of all naturalized American citizens, that is, all immigrants who desire citizenship. This means that under the naturalization laws of the United States, one is precluded from possessing dual allegiances.

[89] Ibid., sec. 5(c).

[90] 8 U.S.C. 1427(a) (1983).

ideological and political meaning into the concept of citizenship meet with judicial resistance."[91] He was pleased with this development, and found in it additional support for his contention about the minimal content of the concept of citizenship. But he was too quick to draw the conclusion he did from it. He attached too much importance to the Court's statutory construction and not enough to its constitutional determination. Thus, while the Court has interpreted the naturalization law in a manner that would make it very difficult for someone to fail the "attachment test," it has never invalidated the test or the oath of allegiance that is based on it. Through its efforts it is possible for a William Schneiderman, someone, that is, with communist sympathies, to acquire citizenship; but for the vast majority of applicants, whose political beliefs can probably best be described as unformed, the oath of allegiance makes more sense as an introduction to a new national identity rather than as a hurdle to be overcome by supplying politically correct answers.

In his dissenting opinion in *Schneiderman v. United States*, Justice Stone asked, "What could be more important in the selection of citizens of the United States than that the prospective citizen be attached to the principles of the Constitution?"[92] The answer may not be the one intended by the rhetorical question: to wit, what is more important is that the *eventual* citizen be attached to the principles of the Constitution. Later in the dissent Stone observed that "the United States has the same interest as other nations in demanding of those who seek its citizenship some measure of attachment to its institutions."[93] To which it might be said that the United States conceivably has a greater interest than many other nations, for the reason that such institutional attachment is, in comparative terms, more vitally a part of the fabric of American nationhood. From this perspective, the oath of allegiance represents a commitment to embrace a set of principles that will become the basis for the shared sense of community that, in

[91] Bickel, *The Morality of Consent*, p. 50.

[92] *Schneiderman v. United States*, 320 U.S. 118, 176 (1943).

[93] Ibid., 172. The majority opinion by Justice Murphy did not dispute Justice Stone's observation in this regard. Among the pieces of evidence adduced by Justice Murphy to demonstrate that Schneiderman was so attached was the fact that Schneiderman "stated that he would bear arms against his native Russia if necessary" (128). This test, in which a person's willingness to make the ultimate sacrifice in defense of the nation testifies to his commitment to the defining principles of the nation, is consonant with the American practice of conceptualizing peoplehood in terms of ideas. It is a test that contrasts revealingly with the Israeli Supreme Court's treatment of Brother Daniel, as well as its consideration of the El Fatah terrorist born of a Jewish mother.

the American exceptionalist tradition, cannot and does not rely on history, religion, culture, or blood.[94] And perhaps equally important, it serves to remind those who are already a part of the political community that their national identity is manifest in a particular creedal affirmation, and that the arrival of new members will not, despite the diversity of backgrounds that will necessarily be incorporated into the polity, undermine the existing sense of what it means to be an American. As Michael Walzer has commented, "Admission and exclusion are at the core of communal independence. They suggest the deepest meaning of self-determination. Without them, there could not be *communities of character*, historically stable, ongoing associations of men and women with some special commitment to one another and some special sense of their common life."[95]

This oath is hardly unique; it closely resembles, for example, the oaths taken by *citizens* in assuming various public offices. Sanford Levinson has written at some length of the historical and philosophical importance of oath taking in the American polity. In particular, he associates this phenomenon with the liberal foundations of the regime, arguing that the oath supports the emphasis attached to consent as the basis of political obligation.[96] From the very beginning of the republic, American naturalization laws insisted on the individual's assent to the principles of republican government. "The Naturalization Act of 1802 was, in essence, a loyalty oath to the ideals of the Enlightenment, to which the American nationality had

[94] For some students of American citizenship, this situation requires addressing. T. Alexander Aleinikoff wishes to "end immigration exceptionalism by recognizing the weaknesses of earlier justifications and by resisting the siren song of membership theory." Aleinikoff, "Citizens, Aliens, Membership, and the Constitution," p. 34. His critique is mainly directed at the importance that both liberals and conservatives have invested in the concept of citizenship as a means for establishing a national identity. His description of the liberal interest in this project is particularly illuminating for the light it sheds on the Israeli-American comparison. Thus, for liberals, a "national community" that flows from citizenship is a liberating idea "because it overcomes the irrational, tyrannical, constricting aspects of 'tribal' loyalties" (p. 29). It emphasizes universalism and equality, while downplaying allegiances emerging from group affiliations. Aleinikoff does not worry that these ideals will suffer if we deemphasize the connection between citizenship and community; what is important, however, is that the connection exists and speaks to something essential in popular and jurisprudential understandings of American national identity. An eloquent articulation of the value of American citizenship as a basis for community may be found in Frederick Schauer, "Community, Citizenship, and the Search for National Identity," *Michigan Law Review* 84 (1986).

[95] Walzer, *Spheres of Justice*, p. 62.

[96] Levinson, *Constitutional Faith*, p. 113. Levinson also writes, "A willingness by immigrants to endorse the principles of Americanism became the benchmark of citizenship; residence requirements have always taken second place to affirmation of shared principle" (p. 97).

been linked since the War of Independence."⁹⁷ This association of law and political philosophy is worth juxtaposing with the comment of the eighteenth-century Jewish philosopher Moses Mendelssohn: "Judaism has no symbolic books, no articles of faith. No one has to swear to creedal symbols or subscribe, by solemn oath, to certain articles of faith. We do not require the affirmation of specific doctrines by oath. In fact, we consider the practice incompatible with the true spirit of Judaism."⁹⁸ While the "true spirit of Judaism" does not always prevail in modern Israel, it cannot be said to be offended by the oath required of naturalized citizens (who are in any case not Jews). That oath simply states, "I declare that I will be a loyal national of the State of Israel."⁹⁹ There are no creedal components to the oath, no articles of faith, no specific doctrines. The oath would seem, therefore, to have no other purpose than to legitimize a pledge of loyalty on the part of those whose devotion to the state of Israel is not simply implicit in the fact of who they are. Unlike the American oath, whose creedal dimension (vague though it may be) seems at once to reflect the contractarian origins of the state while pointing toward a future civic harmony, the Israeli declaration is consistent with a political understanding in which citizenship does not coincide with nationhood.

If in the American scheme of things the acquisition of citizenship is related to essential attributes of national identity, so too is its renunciation. What is taken for granted in much of the world today—the right of expatriation—was, at the time the United States first declared it to be "a natural and inherent right of all people, indispensable to the enjoyment of the rights of life, liberty, and the pursuit of happiness," commonly viewed as a sovereign prerogative.¹⁰⁰ Perpetual allegiance to the country of one's birth was the prevailing doctrine, which meant that expatriation could only be obtained with the express consent of the state. But when individual

---

⁹⁷ Mann, *The One and the Many*, p. 81. Mann points out that, with regard to the creedal requirement of the law of 1802, the United States was unique among countries of that time.

⁹⁸ Moses Mendelssohn, "Freedom of Religion—Absolute and Inalienable," in *Judaism and Human Rights*, ed. Milton Konvitz (New York: W. W. Norton & Co., 1972), p. 184.

⁹⁹ Nationality Law of 1952, sec. 5 (c). It is perhaps also worthy of note that this statute requires of all those acquiring citizenship by naturalization "some knowledge of Hebrew." Since Hebrew is the nation's main official language (although legally it does not have priority over Arabic), this requirement is not unreasonable. It is, however, not a citizenship requirement for Jews (for example, those who might have come from Brooklyn).

¹⁰⁰ The language is taken from the Expatriation Act of 1868. It supports the observation of Peter H. Schuck and Rogers M. Smith that "the Declaration of Independence was a Lockean justification of expatriation." Peter H. Schuck and Rogers M. Smith, *Citizenship without Consent: Illegal Aliens in the American Polity* (New Haven: Yale University Press, 1985), p. 49.

volition became the foundation for admission into the polity, it was only a question of time before its legitimacy was recognized when citizens sought to sever their relations with the polity. While there is validity in the claim that "immigration and emigration are morally asymmetrical,"[101] it is hard to see why in a liberal regime the principle of consent should not govern policies relating to both exit from and entry into the political community. This principle was officially acknowledged in the Expatriation Act of 1868, which for the first time codified "the idea that nationalities are changeable rather than irrevocable."[102]

Establishing the right of voluntary expatriation has proven easier than establishing the circumstances that justify the forced relinquishment of citizenship. The Supreme Court wrestled with the problem of determining whether certain acts, in the absence of a formal renunciation of citizenship, can be designated by the Congress for the purpose of triggering involuntary expatriation. In the end it overturned such efforts, the most important case involving a naturalized American citizen who had voted in an Israeli parliamentary election. According to Bickel's analysis of these cases, the Court in effect said "that Congress may not put that much content into the concept of citizenship. It seemed to reaffirm the traditional minimal content of the concept of citizenship, the minimal definition of allegiance."[103] However, Bickel also found the Court's rhetoric in conflict with its actions. Among the objectionable statements he cited was Justice Black's assertion, when speaking of the United States, that "its citizenry is the country and the country is its citizenry."[104]

But there is no contradiction. Bickel did not quote the preceding sentence, in which Justice Black commented, "Citizenship in this Nation is a part of a cooperative affair."[105] Citizenship, a legal status possessed by an individual, is considered here also in relational terms, and only then is it

---

[101] Walzer, *Spheres of Justice*, p. 40.

[102] Mann, *The One and the Many*, p. 178.

[103] Bickel, *The Morality of Consent*, p. 51.

[104] Ibid., p. 52, quoting from *Afroyim* v. *Rusk*, 387 U. S. 253, 268 (1967). Bickel drew an interesting and important parallel between the rhetoric of Justices Black and Warren and the language used by Chief Justice Taney in the *Dred Scott* decision. Taney had used "people of the United States" and "citizens" synonymously, which made it easier for him to deny any rights to blacks, except of course those specifically provided by whites. While it is true that he employed the concept of citizenship in an exclusionary way, the adoption of the Fourteenth Amendment has made the equation of peoplehood and citizenship a safer identification, and one that now contains *inclusionary* implications.

[105] *Afroyim*, 387 U.S. at 268.

equated with the country. Far from affirming the minimal content of citizenship, in denying congressional authority to divest a person of this possession, the Court was presuming a meaning that, in its fullness, entailed more than a list of specific entitlements. Divesting someone of his or her citizenship meant separating that person from a cooperative arrangement of people and ideas that was critical in the nurturing of an appreciation of who one is. "Because," as Kenneth Karst has written, "American identity *is* the civic culture, it enters into most Americans' lives as an important part of the sense of self."[106] The Court seemed to recognize that American citizenship is a source of identity as well as rights; hence its divestiture by the government placed a particularly onerous, and therefore unconstitutional, burden on the individual.

Or put another way, to be stripped of one's citizenship is to be deprived of one's sense of belonging to a people. In contrast, the survival of the Jewish people is often attributed to the capacity of the group to sustain a viable national identity in diaspora circumstances marked by an absence of legal support. In this particular sense, the stakes associated with citizenship are consequently not as high. "Judaism, like some nationalities, is a club which one can join but from which none can escape."[107] This does not mean that one cannot escape from the state of Israel. It, like other polities considered civilized, provides for the right of expatriation; although there are features that differ from the United States—for example, the fact that a resident national must present a "special reason" to justify the decision to renounce citizenship.[108] It is also possible under Israeli law to annul someone's citizenship if the person "has been abroad for seven consecutive years and has no effective connection with Israel, and has not proved that his effective connection with Israel was severed otherwise than by his own volition."[109] Thus in Israel it is marginally more difficult to give up one's citizenship and

[106] Karst, *Belonging to America*, p. 188.

[107] Rubinstein, "Who's a Jew, and Other Woes," p. 86.

[108] Nationality (Amendment) Law of 1958, sec. 10(b). For a citizen who is not an inhabitant of Israel no special reasons are required. As for the revocation of citizenship, until 1968 it could only be directed against naturalized citizens, but at present no such distinctions remain. One of the three grounds for involuntary loss of citizenship is that someone "has committed an act constituting a breach of allegiance to the State of Israel." This would appear to be related to Israel's security concerns rather than to any theoretically interesting assumptions about citizenship *per se*. In contrast see, in regard to the United States, *Trop v. Dulles*, 356 U.S. 86 (1958), where the Supreme Court held unconstitutional the involuntary expatriation of a wartime deserter.

[109] Nationality Law of 1952, sec. 11(2).

a little easier to have it taken away. Israeli law on expatriation may be said, then, to rely slightly less on the principle of consent than does American law.

But what of the situation of most citizens, those who are neither immigrants nor prospective candidates for voluntary or involuntary expatriation, where, in other words, the issue of consent is at best only indirectly involved? Are there any significant differences in the way the two countries employ the concept of birthright citizenship that might bear on the question of national self-understanding? The issue is one that has figured prominently in the debate over the illegal immigration problem in the United States, since the language of the Fourteenth Amendment is generally understood to confer citizenship on even those who are the offspring of parents whose presence in the country violates the law.[110] It is an issue of important theoretical interest, even though as a practical matter nation-states are obliged to recognize as citizens most of those who are born within their borders.

Students of American citizenship law have noted the somewhat anomalous character of birthright citizenship. Peter H. Schuck and Rogers M. Smith have argued that "despite the splendor of its constitutional pedigree . . . birthright citizenship is something of a bastard concept in American ideology."[111] They contend that the descent-based nature of such citizenship stands as an affront to the liberal, individualistic idea of consent; it is, in short, a peculiar, if understandable, method of allocating membership in the political community. They see in the ascriptive features of this allocation a violation of the political philosophy of John Locke, for whom "it was inconceivable . . . that the accident of birth in a land foreign to one's parents should create permanent obligations to that country."[112]

Of course nowhere in the world does consent take precedence over

---

[110] Two of the leading students of American citizenship law have written, "There is now no doubt that the constitutional rule of universal citizenship for all persons born in the United States is unaffected by the status of their parents. . . . Thus American citizenship is acquired by children born in the United States, even though their parents were always aliens, and even if the parents were themselves ineligible to become citizens of the United States." Charles Gordon and Ellen Gittel Gordon, *Immigration and Nationality Law* (New York: Matthew Bender, 1986), sec. 12, p. 6.

[111] Schuck and Smith, *Citizenship without Consent*, p. 2.

[112] Ibid., p. 25. A critical reviewer of Schuck and Smith's book has disputed their interpretation of Locke and birthright citizenship, arguing that the implications of birthright citizenship are indisputably liberal and hence quite Lockean. The argument involves seeing birthright as "a liberal property right against the government." David S. Schwartz, "The Amorality of Consent," *California Law Review* 74 (1986): 2150.

ascription in the distribution of citizenship to those born within a nation's borders. But ascription takes a variety of forms, and it is in this variety that interesting distinctions emerge. In particular, countries differ in the extent to which they rely on the principle of *jus soli* (citizenship dependent on geography) as opposed to the principle of *jus sanguinis* (citizenship dependent on inheritance or blood). The American priority is apparent from the Fourteenth Amendment, which provides: "All persons born or naturalized in the United States, and subject to the jurisdiction thereof, are citizens of the United States and of the State wherein they reside." Whatever qualifications may attach to the jurisdiction clause of that amendment, it is pretty clear that where one is born is more important than to whom one is born.[113] In Israel, on the other hand, the opposite applies. The offspring of an Israeli citizen is entitled to birthright citizenship, but not by virtue of being born in Israel. This may be made clear by pointing out a couple of salient features of Israeli law: first, the children of non-Jewish parents, who are noncitizens of Israel, do not acquire citizenship even if they are born in Israel; and second, a child of a Jewish woman (according to authoritative opinion) acquires citizenship even if the mother is only temporarily residing in Israel—for example as a tourist—and has no plans of settling in Israel.[114]

The difference is important. While both territoriality and inheritance are nonvolitional sources of political obligation, the first is more closely related to a conception of citizenship that has as one of its purposes the encouragement of a common national identity. Schuck and Smith observe that "attention to territoriality seems justified by the reality that persons within a given territory must inevitably and intensively interact with and affect one another, thereby creating a common life that ordinarily shapes their interests. Hence, defining political membership territorially expresses a recognition that all persons who share a specific locale over a period of time form an organic community, regardless of their inherited legal statuses."[115] The

---

[113] The key case is *United States v. Wong Kim Ark*, 169 U.S. 649 (1898).

[114] The opinion is that of the then attorney general and present Supreme Court president, Meir Shamgar. Rubinstein, "Israel Nationality," p. 162.

[115] Schuck and Smith, *Citizenship without Consent*, p. 39. This observation should be considered in the context of Chapter 2's references to the millet system. For example, one student of this system writes, "The newly born states [emerging from the Ottoman Empire] attached themselves to territorial bonds of secular citizenship and historical memories while their group identity internal cohesion and socio-political values as a nation were determined by their long experience in the *millet* system. Nationality, in the sense of ethnic-national identity, drew its essence from the religious-communal experience in the *millet*, while citizenship—a secular concept—was determined by territory." Kemal H. Karpat, "*Millets* and Nationality: The Roots of the Incongruity of Nation and State in the Post-Ottoman Era," in

observation has less application to deeply divided societies where a common life is not the inevitable consequence of people living within common territory. Indeed, it is unclear whether and to what extent territorial-based birthright citizenship is a cause or an effect of a life in common. What does seem clear is that establishing the principal claim to citizenship on the more or less neutral ground of geography manifests a presumption that all members of the political community can identify in a straightforward and uncomplicated way with the nation-defining principles of the regime. The reversal of *Dred Scott* meant that henceforward the ability of the native-born to share in the aspirational content of American national identity was to be formed only by one's relationship to the physical boundaries of the United States.

CONCLUSION

We might say that in American citizenship law territoriality is meant in a strictly geographical sense, whereas in Israeli law there is a dual territorial space, one extending over a geographical area, and the other extending over a cultural space defined along religious, lingual, and historical lines. Recall the comment of Justice Silberg, who declined to view the state of Israel in isolation from "the large Jewish nation . . . whose members are scattered all over the world." Many Israelis believe that this understanding actually legitimates their nation's interventions in other countries when the vital interests of Jewish populations are at stake. It is also an understanding that illuminates the relatively easy toleration of dual citizenship in Israeli law.[116] If the nation is commonly perceived in terms that transcend nation-state boundaries, then the presence of an additional citizenship does not pose the same kind of a challenge to the nation's integrity as it might if national identity descended from citizenship. When in 1985 the U.S. Department of State stripped Rabbi Meir Kahane of his U.S. citizenship because "his primary loyalty is to Israel," they may or may not have been

---

Braude and Lewis, *Christians and Jews in the Ottoman Empire*, vol. 1, p. 141. Karpat's assessment of these new states is also interesting: "Israel alone seems to have attempted to establish a certain harmony between the nation and the state, but her ability to maintain it indefinitely is doubtful" (p. 166).

[116] According to Amnon Rubinstein, the reason for this is the heavy Israeli reliance on the "law of blood," which, he contends, "particularly encourages the possibility of dual nationality." Rubinstein, "Israel Nationality," p. 177. In contrast, the United States permits dual citizenship only where the second nationality is acquired by an existing American citizen.

acting properly. But in so doing they were implicitly affirming that belonging to the American national community was not to be compromised by those dual citizenships that effectively mocked the ideational content of membership in the nation.[117]

In the United States there are also many people who believe that the internal affairs of other countries should be of concern to Americans. Indeed, the American relationship with Israel is largely predicated on the mutual perception that the two countries share a commitment to certain values. Thus, *what* a nation stands for is considered by the United States to be an important factor in formulating a foreign policy toward that nation. The willingness on occasion to defend particular principles abroad represents an affirmation by Americans of the worth of their own collective sense of self. It mirrors the emphasis in the Declaration of Independence on principles whose presumed universality means that they cannot be ignored even where circumstances of time and place do not allow for their immediate enforcement.

The "Who is a Jew?" controversy offered an insight into alternative conceptualizations of the meaning of citizenship. A recent survey of American Jews reached the following conclusion about the issue: "The theme running through these responses is one of fear of potential rejection by Israel. Respondents felt that, by passing the proposed legislation, Israel would be rejecting their brand of Judaism, their family members, their friends, and their claim to a special attachment to the Jewish state, which they regard as a center and refuge for all Jews, not just the Orthodox."[118] This is surely a reasonable conclusion, from which it is possible to develop a corollary conclusion that is also consistent with one's intuitive sense that the issue failed to evoke much empathetic understanding among the vast majority of Israelis. In this corollary account, American Jews feared another rejection, namely their commitment to liberal democratic principles. For most of them, their "special attachment to the Jewish state" had never been accompanied by any real reflection on the differences in the pluralist foundations

---

[117] For a stinging criticism of the Kahane decision, see T. Alexander Aleinikoff, "Theories of Loss of Citizenship," *Michigan Law Review* 84 (1986). Aleinikoff is certainly correct in finding that the State Department's denationalization ruling on the grounds of Kahane's membership in the Israeli Knesset was incoherent in light of its decision not to proceed in this manner against another Knesset member. But the real reason of course was that Kahane was *not* just another Knesset member; what he stood for rendered suspect his attachment to the principles of the Constitution.

[118] Steven M. Cohen, *Ties and Tensions: An Update—the 1989 Survey of American Jewish Attitudes toward Israel and Israelis* (New York: American Jewish Committee, 1989), p. 48.

of Israel and their own country. Their civic identity was happily unrelated to *who* they were. Their religious identity was closely connected to a state, which they viewed, particularly in contrast to its neighbors, as embodying the right sort of political ideas. If the very existence of a Jewish state in some ways contradicted one or two of these ideas, still its secular orientation was more than reassuring to American Jews, and to Americans in general. But the proposed legislation threatened all of this, especially the image of Israel as a "new laboratory of liberal democracy." By intervening in the intimate matter of *who* they were, the Israelis were in effect challenging *what* they believed in. Apart from everything else, what they believed in—the principle of free choice—was for *American* Jews a sufficient basis for their reciprocal intervention in Israeli political affairs. Their efforts bear some similarity to their government's in the conduct of its foreign policy: while vigorously pursuing their own interests, they drew on a liberal philosophic and moral tradition to establish that whatever intrusion into the affairs of another country resulted from such pursuit was ultimately in the best interests of both peoples.

Constituting the Polity

> Do we need a Constitution like the American? By all
> means let us profit from the experience of others and
> borrow laws and procedures from them, provided they
> match our needs.
> —*David Ben-Gurion*

A CONSTITUTION BY ANY OTHER NAME?

A young Israeli attorney general, Haim Cohn, once paid a visit to the U.S. Supreme Court. His purpose was to speak with the members of the Court about constitutional matters. More specifically, he had been sent by his prime minister, David Ben-Gurion, to pursue the question of a constitution for the state of Israel, a document promised in that country's Declaration of Independence, but as yet unrealized. The prime minister had always been an outspoken opponent of such a charter, and he was hoping that his attorney general's visit would produce a report confirming him in his strongly held belief. In carrying out his assignment, Cohn proceeded from justice to justice, inquiring of each his views on the appropriate course of action for Israel. From Justice Black he received a recommendation that was unlikely to appeal to Ben-Gurion: "Make a constitution immediately, and make it so stringent that no Supreme Court can evade it." As he made his rounds, sentiments of this sort were regularly voiced by other justices as well. Until, that is, he got to Justice Frankfurter, who said, "Never write a constitution. What you need are independent judges, not a written constitution." When the prime minister received his attorney general's report he expressed satisfaction that his stance on the undesirability of a written constitution for Israel had found such impressive support on the U.S. Supreme Court.[1]

---

[1] This story is based on an interview by the author with Haim Cohn. Mr. Cohn, known for his iconoclastic opinions, acerbic wit, and commitment to liberal ideals, eventually served with great distinction as a member of the Israeli Supreme Court. Justice Frankfurter's advice is consistent with a comment in an address he delivered in 1958: "As a matter of fact, they [the Israelis] haven't got a written constitution. And, incidentally, they can still survive, can't they, without a written constitution? Indeed, I am not sure that in their circumstances, with their

In this chapter I consider two related matters, the question of a formal written constitution and the practice of judicial review. The advice given to Cohn by Justices Black and Frankfurter will establish the parameters of the discussion. Justice Black was fond of quoting Thomas Jefferson; he especially liked the observation that "our peculiar security is in the possession of a written Constitution."[2] For Black, as his unheeded recommendation suggests, a codified charter not only protects our security from the excesses of legislative and executive governance, but also against invasion from the judiciary, that branch of government commonly viewed as solely responsible for imposing constitutional limits on the other branches. There is no evidence that Ben-Gurion, who strongly opposed judicial review ("The people as legislator must not be circumscribed"),[3] ever reflected on the possibility adverted to by Black, that a formal constitution may actually *support* the sovereign lawmaking authority of the people. As we shall see, judicial review has become an important factor in Israeli politics as a result of the efforts of "independent judges" of the kind envisioned by Justice Frankfurter. While much of the contemporary debate in Israel focuses on whether this review power provides adequate protection for individual rights, most of the debators would surely acknowledge that the power of the Israeli judiciary to determine quasi-legislatively (that is, mainly through statutory construction) what the law is far exceeds anything imagined by Ben-Gurion. Conceivably, then, Justice Black—who always maintained that his brother Frankfurter's constitutional philosophy led, despite his protestations to the contrary, to an expansion of judicial power at the expense of the legislative will—might say (were he around today) that Ben-Gurion's own goals, expressed in terms of popular sovereignty, would have been more fully realized had he followed his and Jefferson's advice.[4]

Jefferson's advice extended to the proposed Bill of Rights, which of course he championed with great eloquence and to great effect. To James Madison he wrote, "In the arguments in favor of a declaration of rights, you omit one which has great weight with me, the legal check which it puts into

---

problems, they are not wise in not having one as yet." Philip B. Kurland, ed., *Of Law and Life and Other Things That Matter: Papers and Addresses of Felix Frankfurter, 1956–1963* (New York: Atheneum, 1969), p. 119.

[2] Quoted in Hugo Black, "The Bill of Rights," *New York University Law Review* 35 (1960): 869–70.

[3] Ben-Gurion, *Rebirth and Destiny of Israel*, p. 371.

[4] For examples of Black's critique of Frankfurter's position, see *Adamson* v. *California*, 332 U.S. 46 (1947), and *Rochin* v. *California*, 342 U.S. 165 (1952).

the hands of the judiciary."[5] For Israelis, whose constitutional dispute is for all practical purposes a struggle over whether there should be a formal bill of rights, this observation speaks directly to the concern of Ben-Gurion and others that such an addition would effectively thwart the will of the majority. But in assessing the impact of such a document on popular governance, Jefferson's next sentence must also be considered: "This is a body, which if rendered independent, and kept strictly to their own department merits great confidence for their learning and integrity."[6] Jefferson's espousal of a departmental theory of judicial review, in which the reviewing authority of the Supreme Court is essentially confined to matters of a "judiciary nature," may today have greater relevance to constitutionalism in Israel than in the United States, where the doctrine of judicial supremacy (or at least finality in matters of constitutional interpretation) is pretty much taken for granted. Therefore, in considering the constitutional question in Israel in the light of American experience, we would be wise to remain open to options, or variants thereof, that in the United States may be thought after two hundred years to be of only antiquarian interest.

One of the options eliminated very early was a constitutional arrangement that omitted a specific enumeration of protected rights. Jefferson's archrival, Alexander Hamilton, had described the document emerging from the Constitutional Convention as "in every rational sense . . . a BILL OF RIGHTS"[7] but in the end Jefferson's view (which also became Madison's view) prevailed. But Hamilton's position is not irrelevant to the contemporary Israeli debate. For example, in 1974, Haim Cohn, now Justice Cohn, argued that all of the rights that would be explicitly guaranteed by a written bill of rights were in practice recognized, protected, and enforced in the absence of such enumeration. The "spirit of Israel law" (emanating in no small measure from the Declaration of Independence) has and will, he argued, guarantee the rights of Israeli citizens.[8] This opinion, much disputed in Israel, reminds one of Hamilton, who often invoked the "spirit" of the law. It also recalls Justice Cohn's earlier conversation with Justice Frankfurter, whose views on the written constitution (and whose opinions in due process cases) were very much in the Hamiltonian spirit. Both Cohn and Frankfurter could easily assent to Hamilton's assertion that "if the

[5] Jefferson to Madison, 15 March 1789, in Philip B. Kurland and Ralph Lerner, eds., *The Founders' Constitution* (Chicago: University of Chicago Press, 1987), vol. 1, p. 479.

[6] Ibid.

[7] Lodge, *The Federalist*, no. 84, p. 538.

[8] Haim H. Cohn, "The Spirit of Israel Law," *Israel Law Review* 9 (1974): 459.

constitution were even silent on particular points those who are intrusted with its power, would be bound in exercising their discretion to consult and pursue its spirit, and to conform to the dictates of reason and equity."[9] It was, in other words, unnecessary to specify rights that were already subsumed in the natural rights spirit of the Constitution. Moreover, the attempt to do so might actually produce unintended threats to individual liberties.[10]

Justice Black would, of course, have recoiled from such sentiments; why appeal to some vague spirit or natural law "excrescence" when specific language was available guaranteeing this or that right?[11] He might also have been particularly critical of the applicability of the Hamiltonian argument to the contemporary Israeli scene. "For why declare," Hamilton asked, "that things shall not be done which there is no power to do?"[12] The Federalists had pointed out that the notion of a bill of rights developed in England, where there was no written constitution. But precisely because Americans had constructed a constitution of limited, enumerated powers, they had no need, the Federalists argued, for a list of enumerated rights. This did not satisfy their opponents. As one said, "Any system therefore which appoints a legislature, without any reservation of the rights of individuals, surrenders all power in every branch of legislation to the govern-

---

[9] Harold C. Syrett, ed., *The Papers of Alexander Hamilton* (New York: Columbia University Press, 1961), vol. 3, p. 548.

[10] This is to be contrasted with Jefferson's opinion that "a bill of rights is what the people are entitled to against every government on earth, general or particular, and what no just government should refuse, or rest on inference." Jefferson to Madison, 20 December 1787, in Kurland and Lerner, *The Founders' Constitution*, vol. 1, p. 457. At a comparable period in Israeli constitutional development David Ben-Gurion criticized the proposed constitution with an argument similar to Hamilton's opposition to a bill of rights: "The liberty of the subject and the liberty of the people depend not on any pronouncements of freedom, nor on the finest of Constitutions but uniquely on the rule of law." Ben-Gurion, *Rebirth and Destiny of Israel*, p. 370. Ben-Gurion's point is actually closer to the British view as perhaps best expressed in Dicey's classic commentary: "The matter to be noted is, that when the right to individual freedom is a result deduced from the principles of the constitution, the idea readily occurs that the right is capable of being suspended or taken away. When, on the other hand, the right to individual freedom is part of the constitution because it is inherent in the ordinary law of the land, the right is one which can hardly be destroyed without a thorough revolution in the institutions and manners of the nation." A. V. Dicey, *Introduction to the Law of the Constitution* (London: St. Martin's Press, 1961), p. 201.

[11] *Adamson*, 332 U.S. at 75.

[12] Lodge, *The Federalist*, no. 84, p. 537.

ment."[13] Ultimately such arguments proved persuasive; should they not be even more persuasive in Israel, where there is no comprehensive written constitution, where the supremacy of the Knesset is a fact of political life?

The answer to this question is a complicated one, which this chapter will seek to illuminate. Its complexity is in part related to assumptions embedded in the question itself. For example, while it is fair to say that Israel lacks a comprehensive written constitution, it is highly misleading to portray this as an absence of written constitutional rules. Recently a visiting French jurist told his Israeli hosts, "Your problem is not that you are trying to adopt a constitution, but that you already have one and are trying to change it."[14] By this he meant that efforts to reform the Israeli system in the direction of a single, unified fundamental charter should be evaluated in terms of the actual constitutional changes that would result from such a development, rather than in the erroneously conceived context of a sudden departure from a constitutional tradition characterized by the absence of written limits on the exercise of power.[15] If the subject under consideration is the protection of individual rights, it surely matters if the status quo is described in a way that conveys the impression of a system of power unconstrained by constitutional checks.

But if parliamentary supremacy reigns, is there really any other way to convey a sense of the status quo? Yes would be the answer of many students of Great Britain; as Vernon Bogdanor observes, "The British Constitution is essentially a *political* constitution, one whose operation depends upon the

---

[13] Quoted in Gordon S. Wood, *The Creation of the American Republic, 1776–1787* (Chapel Hill: University of North Carolina Press, 1969), p. 538. Madison, whose role in regard to the Bill of Rights was critical to its adoption, said, "It may be less necessary in a republic, than a Monarchy, and in a federal Government than the former, but it is in some degree rational in every Government, since in every Government power may oppress, and declarations on paper tho' not an effectual restraint, are not without some influence." Madison to Richard Peters, 19 August 1789, in Kurland and Lerner, *The Founders' Constitution*, vol. 1, p. 491.

[14] Justice Robert Badinter, quoted in George Gross, "The Constitutional Question in Israel," in *Constitutionalism: The Israeli and American Experiences*, ed. Daniel J. Elazar (Lanham, Md.: University Press of America, 1990), p. 57.

[15] The 1787 Convention did not give Americans a Constitution; rather, it gave them a new Constitution, the acceptance of which was contingent on a successful demonstration of its superior qualities to the existing constitutional arrangements. Likewise, the significance of the current debate in Israel over this or that draft constitution lies not in the possibility of achieving governance under a constitution, but in the nature of the changes wrought by assembling all of the nation's fundamental rules in one document.

strength of political factors and whose interpretation depends upon the will of its political leaders."[16] It is frequently pointed out that a common historic political tradition of respect for law provides effective constitutional checks even in the face of a legislature that theoretically can do what it pleases. Is the same confidence justified, however, in the case of a society where tradition, demography, and culture do not follow the British example? Israel certainly differs significantly in these respects from Great Britain in spite of the enormous influence of the British legal tradition on Israeli institutions and practice. And yet, as we shall see, practices are being established in Israel that cast doubt on the omnipotence of the legislative branch. For example, it is still a debatable proposition whether the Israeli Supreme Court has the authority to nullify a legislative act of the Knesset on constitutional grounds.

But the specific questions relating to the prospects for and desirability of constitutional reform in Israel, while interesting in themselves, are not the real concern of this chapter. Rather, the main focus is a broader one—the subject of constitutionalism itself, or how the concerns of Black, Frankfurter, Jefferson, and Hamilton get addressed in two constitutional contexts that share a language of constitutional discourse while differing so profoundly in many politically relevant ways. American constitutional experience has been much commented on during the course of Israeli history, both in the context of discussions of constitutional reform and by Israeli judges seeking to define the limits of government in the absence of a charter of fundamental law possessing clear superiority to ordinary legislation. Israelis quite naturally have an interest in the lessens to be learned from the world's oldest written constitution; Americans *ought* to have an interest in the alternative experiences of others, if for no other reason than that it might provide a valuable opportunity for critical reflection on their own constitutional experience. I begin, then, with an analysis of the meaning of the constitution within the context of alternative pluralisms, followed by a comparative assessment of judicial authority.

Binding the Future

The story of Israel's failure to fulfill its Declaration of Independence's prescription for "a Constitution to be drawn up by the Constituent Assem-

---

[16] Vernon Bogdanor, "Britain: The Political Constitution," in *Constitutions in Democratic Politics*, ed. Vernon Bogdanor (Aldershot, Eng.: Gower Publishing Co., 1988), p. 71.

bly" is an oft-told tale.[17] Quite properly it is frequently cast as a political story, in which considerations of partisan advantage receive ample attention. For historians and legal scholars, even those inclined to resist cynicism, it is relatively easy to accept the allegations of Menachem Begin, then the leader of the minority Herut movement, that Ben-Gurion's opposition to a constitution was fundamentally attributable to his fear of losing all or some of his power. As Begin expressed it in debate in the First Knesset, "If the Constituent Assembly legislates a constitution, then the government will not be free to do as it likes."[18] The clear inference to be drawn from the tone and substance of the debates is that adherence to parliamentary supremacy is perfectly natural for the leader of the predominant political party, particularly a leader with no experience in the constitutional tradition of limited government.

Without losing sight of these obvious political calculations, we must still reflect on the arguments used by both sides to justify their respective positions. These justifications addressed genuine concerns, even if they also masked less principled considerations. One line of argument is particularly revealing in the insight it provides into alternative schemes of constitutional conceptualization. It was pursued in the debate in the First Israeli Knesset by a member of the governing Mapai party, who urged delay with respect to the constitutional question: "One does not create a constitution at the beginning of a revolution, but when it is completed. All constitutions are an attempt to 'freeze' certain principles, to preserve them, inasmuch as it is possible to preserve any particular thing in the life of a nation."[19] There were several additional reasons adduced for postpon-

[17] The usual point of departure is the United Nations' 1947 partition resolution, stipulating that the new Jewish and Arab states were to adopt democratic constitutions. Subsequent to the adoption of the U.N. resolution, the Jewish Agency for Palestine commenced the drafting of such a document, although preparation for this task had been initiated prior to the U.N. action. In addition, the Declaration of Independence contained language consistent with the partition resolution, including the provision for a Constituent Assembly whose sole function was to adopt the constitution. This assembly was elected in January 1949 (several months after the deadline set in the Declaration), and it immediately assumed a legislative function as well, an indication that the intent of the Declaration would not in the end be implemented. The Constituent Assembly enacted the Transition Law, providing broadly for the nation's governing institutions. The legislature was to be known as the Knesset, and the Constituent Assembly was officially designated the First Knesset. It never executed the specific task for which it was constituted.

[18] Itamar Rabinovich and Jehuda Reinharz, eds., *Israel in the Middle East: Documents and Readings on Society, Politics and Foreign Relations, 1948–Present* (New York: Oxford University Press, 1984), p. 45.

[19] Ibid., p. 42.

ing the adoption of a constitution; this one, which followed Ben-Gurion's argument that the drafting of a constitution should not precede the "In-gathering of the Exiles," was arguably of lesser importance than some others in influencing the subsequent course of events. Yet it speaks to some unique aspects of the Israeli constitutional experience.[20]

The proponents of a formal constitution had made several arguments in support of their position: that a constitution would protect individual rights by establishing written limits on the power of the majority; that it would stand as a symbol of Israeli independence and status within the international community; and that it would serve the pedagogical purpose of educating a diverse population in the political principles of their regime.[21] The opponents contended that the goals associated with the first two arguments did not require the "novelty" (Ben-Gurion's term) of a formal written constitution. These opponents, it is worth noting, represented an interesting alliance, consisting on the one hand of extreme secularists such as Ben-Gurion, and on the other of ultra-Orthodox Jews, who maintained that Israel had no need of *another* constitution, the Torah being a more than adequate fundamental law.[22] Indeed, it was the radically different understandings of the essence of the regime held by these alliance partners that explains why the third argument of the proponents was, from the opposition's perspective, flawed in its most basic assumptions.

Educating people in the principles of the regime assumes that such principles exist, or at least that they exist in a manner that can be inscribed coherently in constitutional form. But if the basic nature of the regime is in doubt (a Western state? a state of the Jewish people? a Jewish state? all of the above?), does it not make sense to postpone constitutionalizing, which is to say "freezing," a set of principles on which no consensus had yet

[20] As Ruth Gavison has observed, it is an "argument that would be inconceivable and clearly objectionable in almost any other country and it reveals one of the unique features of Israel." Ruth Gavison, "The Controversy Over Israel's Bill of Rights," *Israel Yearbook on Human Rights* 15 (1985): 135.

[21] Said a member of the left-wing Mapam party, "Our goal is to create one nation out of this mixed multitude. To achieve this goal, we must act on all possible fronts: the educational. . . ." Rabinovich and Reinharz, *Israel in the Middle East*, p. 45. For a more complete summary of the arguments for and against the constitution see, for example, Emanuel Rackman, *Israel's Emerging Constitution, 1948–1951* (New York: Columbia University Press, 1955). See also George Gross's fine essay, "The Constitutional Question in Israel," in Elazar, *Constitutionalism*.

[22] Said one member of the ultra-Orthodox Agudat Israel, "Any Constitution created by man can have no place in Israel." Quoted in Norman Zucker, *The Coming Crisis in Israel: Private Faith and Public Policy* (Cambridge: MIT Press, 1973), p. 67.

congealed? To the extent that a consensus existed, it was that the state of Israel was to be a homeland for the Jewish people; but if this was the case, why not postpone the constitutional decision until such time as a much larger percentage (i.e., much more than 7 percent) of the Jewish people resided within its borders? "The constitution is created for that population which was in existence within the borders of the state. . . . Our population is fluid. We are not at the end of a revolutionary process but at its beginning."[23]

During the debate, the American example was cited as one to be followed. After all, it took from 1776 to 1791 for the Americans to produce their constitution; why then, it was asked, expect Israelis to be more expeditious? A reasonable question, to be sure, but there are serious limitations to the appropriateness of the analogy. The U.S. Constitution was written in 1777, ratified in 1781, and then rewritten and reratified beginning in 1787. The Americans did what most successful revolutionaries have done subsequently, seize the opportunity provided by the occasion to codify the fruits of their victory. In their case they quickly became dissatisfied with their creation and went back to the drawing board. But their more successful venture in 1787 was not attributable to any massive infusion of new members into their ranks; rather, it resulted from specific lessons learned from actual experience under the earlier constitutional structure. In fact, the document was eventually sold as an improvement over its predecessor not because it had discovered the true meaning of the Revolution, but because it represented a better prospect for realizing its aspirations.

In this regard it is worth recalling Ben-Gurion's observation, cited in Chapter 3, in which he sought to distinguish between the revolutionary experiences of Israel and other countries, including the United States: "There the people rose against the government and a change in government signified attainment of the people's aim. But not we. We rose against a destiny of the years, against exile and dispersion, against deprivation of language and culture."[24] The observation is helpful in illuminating alternative understandings of nationhood, but in one respect, at least as applied to the United States, it is not quite accurate. While it is fair to say that the American Revolution was essentially political in nature, the claim that its success signified attainment of the people's aim is valid only if success is narrowly defined in terms of independence. But if the broader political goals of the Revolution, those announced to the world in the Declaration of

---

[23] Rabinovich and Reinharz, *Israel in the Middle East*, p. 42.
[24] Ben-Gurion, *Rebirth and Destiny of Israel*, p. 377.

Independence, are included among the aims of the people, then they were most assuredly not attained. One need look no further than to the existence of slavery to appreciate the magnitude of their unfulfilled aspirations.

Ben-Gurion might respond by saying that as far as the desirability of a constitution is concerned, this broader understanding alters nothing. He might say, for example, that the gap between reality and the principles that validated the Revolution required that a constitution be adopted in the United States as a means of closing the gap. In this he could appeal to Lincoln, who wrote of the signers of the Declaration of Independence: "They meant simply to declare the *right*, so that the *enforcement* of it might follow as fast as circumstances should permit. They meant to set up a standard maxim for free society, which should be familiar to all and revered by all; constantly looked to, constantly labored for, and even though never perfectly attained, constantly approximated, and thereby constantly spreading and deepening its influence, and augmenting the happiness and value of life to all people of all colors everywhere."[25] For Lincoln, this meant that those involved in the interpretation and enforcement of the Constitution were morally and legally obliged to pursue the aspirational content of the Declaration, and the legitimacy of their efforts in this regard hinged on their success.[26] Essentially, then, it was the purpose of the regime's founders to bind the future, to "freeze" a set of political principles that would serve as developmental guidelines for the nation. In the case of Israel, however, binding the future should, according to Ben-Gurion, await the now feasible goal of undoing the historic injustice of "exile and dispersion."

Proponents of an Israeli constitution might have a different take on all of this. They might start by pointing out that while the Declaration of Independence establishes an admirably high standard of political justice, the Constitution of 1787, with its recognition (if not endorsement) of slavery, manifests a clear set of moral compromises. It is thus obvious that the Americans adopted a constitution prior to their having resolved the greatest challenge to their professed principles, the presence on their soil of human bondage. The lesson to be learned, then, is that a consensus on critical questions of regime definition is not a prerequisite for constitution making. If, for example, the relationship between religion and the state is

[25] Basler, *Collected Works*, vol. 2, p. 406.

[26] I have explored Lincoln's position in much detail in my chapter, "Abraham Lincoln 'On This Question of Judicial Authority': The Theory of Constitutional Aspiration," in *The Supreme Court and the Decline of Constitutional Aspiration*, Gary J. Jacobsohn (Totowa, N.J.: Rowman & Littlefield, 1986), pp. 95–112.

an issue not amenable to satisfactory resolution in the forseeable future, then either remove it from the constitutional agenda or, as the American founders did with slavery, work to achieve a constitutional accommodation that ultimately, through subsequent amendment (e.g., something like the Civil War amendments), will work itself pure.

To this the following might be said. The American Declaration indicates clearly what direction constitutional evolution will have to take in order for the document to work itself pure. The constitutional compromises over slavery should, therefore, be seen as the pragmatic concession of principle to reality, namely that slavery was an existential fact that threatened to derail the entire experiment in popular government. As Herbert J. Storing explained, "Slavery was an evil to be tolerated, allowed to enter the Constitution only by the back door, grudgingly, unacknowledged, on the presumption that the house would be truly fit to live in only when it was gone, and that it would ultimately be gone."[27] Even the major concession of Article I, section 9, involving the migration and importation of slaves (euphemistically referred to as "such persons"), was, as Storing noted, "not a guarantee of a right but a postponement of a power to prohibit."[28] After 1808 Congress could regulate in a manner that would support what Lincoln later claimed was the true intent of the framers, to place slavery on the course of ultimate extinction. Or put another way, the compromise was accomplished in a constitutional form consistent with the goal of binding the future to the realization of universal principles of justice.

The Israeli Declaration, on the other hand, is, as we have seen, much more problematic as far as the consistency of its political vision is concerned. It is one thing to compromise principle in the face of political exigency; quite another to achieve a viable constitutional result in the face of competing, and potentially contradictory, visions. Moreover, where the definition of nationhood is straightforwardly understood in terms of a set of political ideals, binding the future through constitutional mandate becomes an intrinsic part of the self-understanding of the polity. Where, alternatively, the essence of the regime is so much bound up with the issue of *who* the majority of the citizens are, the adoption of a formal constitution may be seen as a less significant event in the inception of the postrevolutionary system. Indeed, the argument that the ingathering of the exiles,

---

[27] Herbert J. Storing, "Slavery and the Moral Foundations of the American Republic," in *The Moral Foundations of the American Republic*, ed. Robert H. Horwitz (Charlottesville: University Press of Virginia, 1977), p. 225.

[28] Ibid., p. 223. See also Walter Berns, "The Constitution and the Migration of Slaves," *Yale Law Journal* 78 (1968).

represented by the Law of Return, should precede the creation of a formal code of fundamental law is not without a certain compelling logic. It makes sense, that is, to want to leave the future relatively unfettered by principled constraints until more people can participate in defining the substance of the principles. Carried to the extreme this logic becomes a formula for indefinite postponement; and it may very well be that at a certain point (perhaps now) it is wise for the appropriate authority to make a more definitive constitutional declaration of its vision of the future. However, Ben-Gurion's contention, politically motivated though it may have been, was not an unreasonable claim at the time it was made.

The ultimate outcome of the First Knesset's deliberations over the constitutional question was the passage of a compromise proposal, known as the "Harari Resolution," that prescribes a process of incremental accumulation of individual chapters—or basic laws—that when terminated will together form the state constitution.[29] This vaguely worded and much criticized legislation left unclear the status of the basic laws, just as it was silent as to a timetable for completion of the constitution. It provided formal commitment (sincere or otherwise) to the principle of the written constitution, while maintaining maximum flexibility in the Knesset's capacity to determine its realization. It was essentially a formula to proceed with "all deliberate speed," although it lacked any mechanism to enforce compliance. It left the state with an evolving constitution that conceivably possesses superior status to ordinary law, but which, predictably, coexists uneasily with the tradition of parliamentary supremacy.

This piecemeal approach, in which every Knesset in effect serves concurrently as a constituent assembly with the power to enact basic laws, represents an appealing solution from the Ben-Gurion point of view. By functioning in the dual role as repository of both legislative and constitutional powers, the Knesset is unlikely to underestimate the value of consensus or fail to appreciate the significance of a changing body politic for constitutional development. And if, as one student of constitutionalism has suggested, a constitution is "a repository of society's hopes for its future,"[30] then it is prudent for a polity whose future cannot as yet be projected in the

[29] The Resolution reads: "The first Knesset charges the Constitutional Legislative and Judicial Committee with the duty to prepare a draft Constitution for the State. The Constitution shall be composed of individual chapters in such a manner that each of them shall constitute a basic law in itself. The chapters shall be brought before the Knesset to the extent which the Committee will terminate its work and all chapters together will form the State Constitution." 5 Knesset Protocols.

[30] Bogdanor, "Introduction," in his *Constitutions in Democratic Politics*, p. 10.

hopes of its highly conflicted people to retain flexibility in its constitution-making authority, which is to say, to ensure its capacity to revise its fundamental (or basic) law with relative ease. The Madisonian argument of *Federalist #49*, that "frequent appeals [to the people for constitutional change] would, in a great measure, deprive the government of that veneration which time bestows on every thing,"[31] did not apparently persuade Ben-Gurion. Indeed, he was a severe critic of the American amendment process, arguing that "only within the framework of laws that must be altered and improved from time to time as hurrying life demands . . ., only therein is civic freedom truly alive and are the rights of every man upheld."[32]

Of course the actual constitutive act of 1787 was about as bold an alteration (by nonviolent means) of constitutional practice as could possibly be imagined. Its boldness is mirrored in its patent illegality, as it amounted to a clear violation of the Articles of Confederation's provision for amendment. Compared to it, the failure of the Israeli Constituent Assembly to achieve the result specified in the Declaration represents at best a relatively minor act of noncompliance.[33] In other words, the cautious nature of Madisonian concerns about veneration and stability applies to the process of constitutional amendment, not to the act of constitutional creation; indeed it was Madison himself who took the lead in the Continental Congress in arguing for the radical departure undertaken by the recently concluded Constitutional Convention. While the putative purpose of the Revolution—restoration of traditional rights of Englishmen—was not *revolutionary*, the specific constitutional solution for achieving this objective was profoundly innovative. And as the inaugural *Federalist* essay indicates, the novelty of the solution is importantly connected to the character of its creation. "It has been frequently remarked that it seems to have been

[31] Lodge, *The Federalist*, no. 49, p. 315.

[32] Ben-Gurion, *Rebirth and Destiny of Israel*, p. 371. For an interesting perspective on the amending process that broadens the Madisonian understanding to include judicial interpretation of the Constitution, see Sanford Levinson, " 'Veneration' and Constitutional Change: James Madison Confronts the Possibility of Constitutional Amendment," *Texas Tech Law Review* 21 (1990). Ben-Gurion of course was speaking only of the specific procedures laid out in Article V of the Constitution.

[33] In fact it was claimed at the time by opponents of the constitution that the Declaration of Independence was not binding on the First Knesset, and consequently its members were under no obligation to adopt a written charter. Indirect support for this view may be found in the early Supreme Court's relegation of the Declaration to constitutional insignificance. On the subject of the tainted origins of the U.S. Constitution, see Richard S. Kay, "The Illegality of the American Constitution," *Constitutional Commentary* 4 (1987).

reserved to the people of this country, by their conduct and example, to decide the important question, whether societies of men are really capable or not of establishing good government from reflection and choice, or whether they are forever destined to depend for their political constitutions on accident and force."[34]

Reliance on reflection and choice, or what is the same, the imposition of a particular political vision on constitutional arrangements, is not incompatible with an account of the American founding that portrays the Constitution as the heir of a fully mature tradition. According to this interpretation, the achievements of the constitutional period are, as Donald S. Lutz has persuasively demonstrated, a kind of constitutional capstone representing the culmination of many years of colonial experience in government and law.[35] The Constitution was essentially an indigenous outgrowth that, while drawing on foreign sources, manifested a uniquely American mix of political principles and practices. Yet to understand the 1787 document as the inevitable stage of a historical progression is to ignore the deliberative options available to the framers, particularly with respect to the creation of a national government. Had the Constitution emerged more in line with Anti-Federalist thinking, it too would have been seen as falling within the constitutional tradition of the colonial period. But it would not have bequeathed to us a constitutional solution that, in its contribution to political science, was truly original in concept and scope.

Madison's conservatism regarding the amendment process is not unrelated to his boldness in constitution making. The latter activity did more than provide a set of rules for a new regime; it did, as Lincoln put it, culminate in the "picture of silver" that framed the "apple of gold." It constitutionalized the principles that gave to the people of the new regime the basis for a sense of nationhood. Not surprisingly, then, its leading advocate and intellectual benefactor would think it unwise to provide the people with unobstructed access to constitutional change. One is reminded of the advice not to mess with Mother Nature. In the case of the Constitution, the point would seem to be that when such a written document embodies principles that are the wellspring of the polity's national identity, it should not be altered for light and transient causes. Depriving "government of that veneration which time bestows on every thing" should therefore be especially avoided if the principles that animate and drive the government constitute the core of the society's collective sense of identity.

[34] Lodge, *The Federalist*, no. 1, p. 3.
[35] See Donald S. Lutz, *The Origins of American Constitutionalism* (Baton Rouge: Louisiana State University Press, 1988).

Or as Lincoln later put it, "As a general rule, I think, we would [do] much better [to] let it [the Constitution] alone. No slight occasion should tempt us to touch it. Better not take the first step, which may lead to a habit of altering it. Better, rather, habituate ourselves to think of it, as unalterable . . . The men who made it . . . have passed away. Who shall improve, on what *they* did?"[36]

In contrast, the Israeli experience displays greater conservatism in the initial phase of constitutional development, but less concern for the exalted place and survival of rooted constitutional norms. It is interesting, for example, that the Basic Law on the Judiciary specifically exempts the Supreme Court from any obligation to observe the principle of *stare decisis*.[37] And even if some basic laws have an entrenched character (itself a topic of considerable debate), in the sense that they take precedence over ordinary law, the process by which they may be altered or discarded is reflective of a much greater tolerance for constitutional innovation than is the case in the United States. To be sure, much of the early conservatism is attributable to a more complex legal environment confronting the founders of the new Israeli state in comparison with their American counterparts.[38] But perhaps more fundamental is the different roles that the constitution serves in their respective polities. For the American founders, a written constitution was the final legitimation of their Revolution, a revolution that gave birth to a new people. They needed it to affirm their existence as a nation. "In other countries, one can abrogate the constitution without abrogating the nation. The United States does not have that choice."[39] Or in John M. Murrin's artful formulation, Americans are notable in the "architecture of nationhood" for having "erected their constitutional roof before they put up the national walls."[40] The Israeli founders were architects confronting a different structural challenge. They were, as Daniel J. Elazar has aptly pointed out, in possession of an ancient traditional constitution rooted in history and religion,[41] within which was contained their "national

---

[36] Basler, *Collected Works*, vol. 1. p. 488.

[37] Paragraph 20 reads: (a) A rule laid down by a court shall guide any lower courts. (b) A rule laid down by the Supreme Court shall bind any court other than the Supreme Court.

[38] I have in mind here the multilayered system of British, Jewish, and Ottoman law, to say nothing of the specific realms of autonomous law relegated to religious communities.

[39] Huntington, *American Politics*, p. 30.

[40] John M. Murrin, "A Roof without Walls: The Dilemma of American National Identity," in *Beyond Confederation: Origins of the Constitution and American National Identity*, ed. Richard Beeman, Stephen Botein, and Edward C. Carter II (Chapel Hill: University of North Carolina Press, 1987), p. 347.

[41] Daniel J. Elazar, "Constitution-making: The Pre-eminently Political Act," in *Redesigning the State: The Politics of Constitutional Change*, ed. Keith G. Banting and Richard Simeon

walls." Their problem was to erect a constitutional roof over these walls while also integrating features of the modern liberal democratic style into their architectural planning. In order to complete the roof they would have to determine what was as yet unclear—how the merging of these two traditions would affect the configuration of the structure they were erecting.[42]

Looking Anew at Judicial Review

Conflict, Consensus, and the Role of the Court

In his most influential (and certainly most controversial) work, *The Liberal Tradition in America*, Louis Hartz introduced the concept of "Hebraism" in order to convey a sense of American exceptionalism, of Americans as a "chosen people." His characterization followed the Tocquevillian insight that Americans possessed the distinct advantage of having "arrived at a state of democracy without having to endure a democratic revolution." This fortunate circumstance of having been "born equal, instead of becoming so" meant that their social and political development could proceed largely in the absence of the bitterly divisive ideological battles that prevailed in most other places. It also meant, according to Hartz, that the crusading spirit of Americans would likely be tempered by an appreciation of the uniqueness of their own society. While the principles that formed the basis of American "moral unanimity" were thought to be universally valid, their universal application was quite another thing.[43] Thus Americans were a "chosen

---

(Toronto: University of Toronto Press, 1985), p. 233. Elazar's approach is to classify constitutions in accordance with the character and form of the polity the constitution is designed to serve. Among his five basic models are "the constitution as frame of government and protector of rights" and "the constitution as a modern adaptation of an ancient traditional constitution." The first fits the American example, the second the Israeli. I find his typology and its application to these two polities insightful, although I would be inclined to qualify it to the extent of highlighting the nation-defining aspects of the frame of government model. This might be done by elaborating on the rights that the government is obliged to protect.

[42] Ben-Gurion spoke of the written constitution as "a modern invention, not yet two centuries old, devised in the aftermath of certain political events." He then added, "We must consider very closely whether our State is in need of the novelty." Ben-Gurion, *Rebirth and Destiny of Israel*, p. 36. For him, in other words, the ancient traditional constitution, updated as circumstances required, was the proper Israeli approach to constitutionalism.

[43] Or as Hartz put it, the American sense of mission was not characterized by "Christian universalism," but by "a curiously Hebraic kind of separatism." Louis Hartz, *The Liberal Tradition in America* (New York: Harcourt, Brace & World, 1955), p. 37.

people" by virtue of having been blessed with ideal conditions for enjoying the blessings of liberty. Hartz quoted Gouveneur Morris as having given voice to this Hebraic sentiment when, as ambassador to France in 1789, he counseled the French against following the American example, declaiming in a snobbish sort of way, "They want an American constitution without realizing they have no Americans to uphold it."[44]

Hartz exaggerated the modesty of American missionary pretensions, and Morris's comment would require major qualification in order accurately to capture the spirit of American involvement in subsequent efforts in constitution making abroad. More fundamentally, Hartz's thesis has long been subjected (mainly in the context of the mounting of a "republican" challenge to the presumed hegemony of his liberal paradigm) to torrents of criticism, focusing on what is seen as the Hartzian failure to take sufficient note of conflict, and the corollary inflation of the importance of John Locke ("He is a massive national cliché")[45] to American political development. This is not the place to rehearse this familiar historiographical debate; suffice it to say that while a good bit of the criticism is on target, Hartz's argument is, as one of his more sympathetic critics has written, "animated by a basic instinct that is historically far sounder than that of most books written under the influence of more recent fashions."[46] Focusing on the centrality of the liberal theory of rights, even as one recognizes that it is at once more aspirational and more complex than Hartz might have had us believe, illuminates important aspects of constitutional development in the United States, including that "most puzzling of American cultural phenomena," judicial review.

As Hartz wisely pointed out, "Judicial review as it has worked in America

---

[44] Ibid., p. 38. The modern formulation of this sentiment has been best expressed by Daniel J. Boorstin in *The Genius of American Politics* (Chicago: University of Chicago Press, 1953). Indeed, "nothing could be more un-American than to urge other countries to imitate America" (p. 1).

[45] Ibid., p. 140.

[46] Pangle, *The Spirit of Modern Republicanism*, p. 27. I believe it is a fair criticism to make of Hartz that his emphasis on the presence of a broad Lockean consensus tends to minimize the significance of the debate that has prevailed in American history between proponents of alternative political visions. But as I suggested in Chapter 2, to the extent that competing principles have been engaged in a kind of historical dialectic, it has been a competition framed by a broader consensus committed to the fundamental tenets of liberal freedom. If Hartz exaggerated the differences between the United States and Europe, his work is a helpful reminder of the benefit to be derived in gaining perspective on our own divisions through a comparative understanding of regime differences. Here of course Hartz was wise to follow Tocqueville's lead.

would be inconceivable without the national acceptance of the Lockian creed, ultimately enshrined in the Constitution, since the removal of high policy to the realm of adjudication implies a prior recognition of the principles to be legally interpreted."[47] The exalted position of the Supreme Court is not simply attributable to the fact that it happens to be the nation's highest court; rather, it rests significantly on the acceptance of its unique role in enforcing, and hence validating, the nation-defining principles of the regime. The power to restrain the majority through the exercise of judicial review presupposes the existence of a moral consensus that is embodied in a constitution, and that may be safely entrusted to an institution possessing "neither Force nor Will." Or as Alexander Bickel, following Hartz, explained, "It is putting the cart before the horse to attribute the American sense of legitimacy to the institution of judicial review. The latter is more nearly the fruit of the former, although the 'moral unity' must be made manifest, it must be renewed and sharpened and brought to bear— and this is an office that judicial review can discharge."[48]

The argument that American experience with judicial review is in a profound way tied to the presence in the United States of a pervasive and dominant political creed (in Bickel's formulation, "enduring values") has obvious and important comparative implications. It has been suggested, for example, that "judicial review is America's most distinctive contribution to constitutionalism."[49] And if emulation may be taken as a sign of flattery, then it is perhaps the most admired feature of constitutionalism in the United States, for it has been imitated in countries around the world; indeed, even in the Soviet Union a constitutional provision allowed citizens to go to court to appeal official actions "in the manner prescribed by law."[50] But emulation is one thing, enjoying its fruits is another; thus the actual international experience with judicial review is as varied as the types of regimes in which it has been institutionalized. If Hartz and Bickel were correct, then a critical factor in any comparative assessment of the institution will be the extent to which a consensus may be said to exist with respect to a society's defining political principles.

[47] Ibid., p. 16.

[48] Alexander M. Bickel, *The Least Dangerous Branch: The Supreme Court at the Bar of Politics* (Indianapolis: Bobbs-Merrill Co., 1962), p. 30.

[49] Gerald Gunther, "Judicial Review," in *Encyclopedia of the American Constitution*, eds. Leonard W. Levy, Kenneth L. Karst, and Dennis J. Mahoney (New York: Macmillan, 1986), vol. 3, p. 1054.

[50] Louis Henkin, "Introduction," in *Constitutionalism and Rights: The Influence of the United States Constitution Abroad*, eds. Louis Henkin and Albert Rosenthal (New York: Columbia University Press, 1990), p. 15.

The contrast between the United States and Israel on this matter has been developed; it remains now to explore some of its ramifications for the question of judicial review. One way to do this is to examine an argument that builds on a different assumption than the one suggested here, namely that there is "a common historical basis for the development of judicial review" in the United States and Israel.[51] The argument is advanced in a provocative analysis by Robert A. Burt, who maintains that the emergence of judicial review in both countries is best understood as an institutional response to the presence of fundamental societal conflict. The "central truth" is that "deep-riven ideological disputes in a democratic society provide the impetus for the development of the institution of judicial review."[52] And so, according to Burt, the American and Israeli Supreme Courts have endeavored to transcend such divisions by invoking their nation's respective founding creeds in the context of bold and innovative assertions of judicial power.

Burt's case for parallel development draws on an interesting chronological correspondence in the Israeli and American experiences: the elapsed time from the founding document to the key judicial precedent is in both instances twenty-seven years (i.e., 1776 to 1803 and 1948 to 1975). While most commentators cite the case of *Bergman* v. *Minister of Finance* (frequently in conjunction with *"Kol Ha'am"* v. *Minister of Interior*), decided in 1969, as the critical legal event in the evolution of judicial review in Israel, Burt assigns greater significance to the landmark *Elon Moreh* case of 1979, in which the Supreme Court, following its initial steps of four years earlier, arguably embraced a role for itself as principal guardian of the constitutional system. It was a role thrust upon the Court by the 1967 Six-Day War, an event that had a transformative effect on Israeli society, including the impetus generated for the realization of an independent judiciary. "The political aftermath of the 1967 War raised profound and disquieting questions about the viability of democratic theory in Israeli society. The role that the Court has claimed for itself with progressively increasing clarity since 1979, as the independent embodiment of the rule of law, is in effect its answer to these questions."[53] Similarly, according to Burt, the partisan conflict that culminated in Jefferson's election in 1800 created the opportunity for John Marshall to establish and institutionalize the meliorative role of the judiciary. "The 1967 Six Day War and resulting military occupa-

---

[51] Robert A. Burt, "Inventing Judicial Review: Israel and America," *Cardozo Law Review* 10 (1989): 2015.

[52] Ibid., p. 2053.

[53] Ibid., p. 2028.

tion had the same underlying implication for Israeli society that the partisan struggle and resulting Republican electoral victory had in 1800 for American society: Both events raised serious doubts about whether the divisions were so sharp among a populace ostensibly subject to a common government that brute force was the only possible source of unified governmental authority."[54]

In the *Elon Moreh* decision, the Israeli Supreme Court did indeed venture into the thicket of intense ideological disputation. The case involved the seizure of Arab-owned land by the military commander of the occupied territories, followed shortly by civilian settlement by members of Gush Emunim, the religious nationalist group that views the West Bank (Judea and Samaria) as divinely promised land for the Jewish people. The seizure occurred under the justification of military necessity, but the Court, in its decision to order the eviction of the Jewish settlers, apprehended a political motive behind the initiative, one connected to a particular Zionist commitment to the settlement of Eretz-Israel in its entirety. Burt correctly highlights the boldness of a decision that directly challenged an important policy of a sitting government, although the extent of the challenge may be less than he suggests, and its comparability to two American cases—*Marbury* v. *Madison* and *Dred Scott* v. *Sandford*—may be questioned.

That the underlying issue in *Elon Moreh* bears directly on the democratic aspirations set out in the Declaration of Independence is indisputable. Thus a policy that implied eventual incorporation of a million or more Arabs into an enlarged Israeli state raises serious doubts about the long-term compatibility of the dual commitments of that country's founding document. What was always a tension would inevitably become an unbridgeable divide. To the extent, then, that the development of judicial review is seen as a response to this situation, a conflict-based theory of the origins of the practice appears eminently reasonable. Moreover, as a benchmark for comparative judgment, the very stark nature of the conflict involved in this political setting can serve to mitigate any tendency in other places to see political difference as evidence of deeply rooted conflict. Thomas Jefferson's famous pronouncement in his First Inaugural Address—"We are all Republicans, we are all Federalists"—is too easily dismissed as simply a rhetorical ploy to establish a foundation for governance in a bitterly divided young republic. On one level, certainly, this rings true; but it is a misleading truth if it obscures the reality existing at a

---

[54] Ibid., p. 2049.

deeper level, which is that the differences between Jeffersonians and Hamiltonians, Federalists and Anti-Federalists, are ultimately reconcilable within a broader consensus of agreement on political fundamentals. However, as one reflects on the Israeli scene, it is just this sort of agreement that is absent in the political context surrounding a case like *Elon Moreh*.

It is therefore not just the seemingly trivial facts of *Marbury* that contrast so sharply with the portentous matters involved in the Israeli case; it is also the contrasting nature of the respective underlying political struggles. The election of 1800 was one of only a few critical elections in American history, but like other political realignments (with the exception perhaps of Lincoln's election), it did not, in the end, represent a triumph of principle. It was, to be sure, an exceptionally nasty partisan affair that, as Burt suggests, may very well have caused some to wonder about the viability of the Union.[55] Jefferson's victory, however, did not signal the repudiation of, or ascendance of, any vital principle that was contestable at the time. Indeed, more revealing than the names each side called the other, was the fact that, as Richard Hofstadter noted, "each . . . saw the other as having a political aspiration or commitment that lay outside the republican covenant of the Constitution."[56] Each, in other words, sought to delegitimize the other by appealing to a common base of principle. Subsequent history is also revealing: if the Jeffersonian-Hamiltonian contest conjures up great conflict over principle (for example, regarding the federal government's role in the development of the country), it is worth remembering *whose* purchase Louisiana was.

[55] It is necessary to distinguish between the rhetoric of partisan politics and the reality of principled differences. The fact that one side is called "monarchist" by the other, and returns the favor by labeling the opposition "Jacobins," does not mean that there was any real basis for these charges.

[56] Richard Hofstadter, *The Idea of a Party System: The Rise of Legitimate Opposition in the United States, 1780–1840* (Berkeley: University of California Press, 1969), p. 90. More revealing, perhaps, than the parallel between *Marbury* and *Elon Moreh* is another one that might be made between the American case and an early Israeli case, *Jabotinsky* v. *Weizmann*, 5 P.D. 801 (1951), surely the most famous writ of mandamus case in Israeli constitutional history. Like *Marbury* it occurred in the setting of a political crisis, in this instance one engendered by the collapse of the first National Unity government. The justices rejected a petition that sought to have the Court order the president to extend an invitation to another member of the Knesset to form a government, after his first request of Ben-Gurion had failed to achieve that result. In both cases the Courts concluded that they lacked the authority to issue a writ of mandamus, and in both cases the decisions hinged on distinctions made between law and politics. But in Israel no ground was broken on the subject of judicial review. In my opinion, the politics of these cases presents more of a parallel than that which exists between *Marbury* and *Elon Moreh*.

As far as *Marbury* v. *Madison* is concerned, and in particular Marshall's skillful navigation of highly charged political waters, Louis Hartz's point is well taken: "We say of the Supreme Court that it is courageous when it challenges Jefferson, but since in a liberal society the individualism of Hamilton is also a secret part of the Jeffersonian psyche, we make too much of this. The real test of the Court is when it faces the excitement both of Jefferson and Hamilton, when the Talmudic text itself is at stake, when the general will on which it feeds rises to the surface in anger."[57] John Marshall did, as Burt emphasizes, use *Marbury* as an opportunity to affirm the primacy of the rule of law, but the immediate threat to that rule—the failure of a federal official to deliver some judicial commissions—was occasioned by partisan rather than principled considerations.[58] Very different from this was the threat to the rule of law presented in *Elon Moreh*, where individuals were deprived of their property rights on the basis of *who* they were rather than on the basis of *what* their partisan attachments were.

In this sense, then, a more fruitful comparison might be made between *Elon Moreh* and *Dred Scott*. In the latter decision it surely *is* the case that matters of high principle were at stake in a context where the denial of rights was directly related to circumstances of ascriptive status. It was also the first case since *Marbury* where the Court had exercised its power of judicial review to invalidate an act of Congress. And inasmuch as there is some evidence to suggest that the justices in the majority thought they were making a substantial contribution toward the resolution of the great conflict that was dividing the nation, support may be found for the Burt thesis about the origins and development of judicial review. All of this of

[57] Hartz, *The Liberal Tradition in America*, p. 12.

[58] An Israeli political scientist, Allen Shapiro, also finds the political upheaval surrounding *Marbury* to have been decisive in the development of judicial review. But interestingly, he sees the parallel to the Israeli situation differently; for him the Court did not assume a role of Olympian detachment, but rather it became a player in the partisan battles. Thus it "became a bastion of power of forces that had lost hold of the political centres and a spokesman for a vision of the new republic that had been defeated at the polls." "This," he goes on, "may be the true parallel to Israel's present stage of constitutional development." *Jerusalem Post*, December 2, 1988. In the United States, Leonard W. Levy has expressed the familiar view on this question: "The realities of political partisanship had as much to do with the growth of national judicial review as did abstract theories of constitutionalism." Leonard W. Levy, *Original Intent and the Framers' Constitution* (New York: Macmillan Publishing Co., 1988), p. 121. My argument is that Shapiro may be correct—that the Court is in the process of taking sides—but that its alignment should be viewed not so much as a partisan affair as a choice to emphasize one of the principled visions in the Declaration of Independence. This will be pursued further in Chapter 5.

course does not escape Burt's attention; in fact he refers to *Elon Moreh* as "Israel's *Dred Scott.*"[59] "The same considerations evident in the background of the Israeli Supreme Court's actions around 1967 dominated the deliberations of the United States Supreme Court in 1857 when it decided *Dred Scott.*"[60]

But there is also a great difference in these two cases, one that speaks directly to the contrasting constitutional environments within which judicial review must operate. It is inadvertently signaled by Burt, who says of *Dred Scott* that "the devisive underlying dispute in that case was between a conception of religiously based moral law that condemned slavery and the secular law of the Constitution that protected private property rights in slaves and thereby apparently ensured the continued political union of discordant peoples."[61] This suggests a parallel to *Elon Moreh*, where property rights of Arabs were in conflict with the biblical claims of Jewish settlers, and where, as in the American case, the Supreme Court intervened on the side of the secular law. The difficulty with this comparison, however, is that it was not *only* a religiously based moral law that condemned slavery, but also the secular law of the Constitution as interpreted in a particular way, namely as a document incorporating the natural rights commitments of the Declaration of Independence. To be sure, the radical abolitionists rejected the Constitution, a charter seen by them as a covenant with Hell, in favor of biblical scripture.[62] But Lincoln's consistent view, what we might call the abolitionist position with the best chance of success, was that the Constitution (the "picture of silver") was itself committed to the ultimate extinction of slavery.

It was for this reason that Lincoln opposed the *Dred Scott* ruling, arguing that the decision did not create any politically binding obligations for the coordinate branches of the federal government. His position was distorted at the time by his political enemies, notably Stephen Douglas, and it has

[59] Burt, "Inventing Judicial Review: Israel and America," p. 2067.

[60] Ibid., p. 2051. "The question of Jewish settlement in the occupied territories was . . . as central to the definition of Israel's national purpose as was, for America in the mid-nineteenth century, the status of slavery in its unsettled territories" (p. 2067).

[61] Ibid., p. 2074.

[62] Of course the defenders of slavery were not at a loss in justifying their peculiar institution as consistent with scripture. They claimed, in the words of one such defender, "that it was incorporated into the only National Constitution which ever emanated from God"; that "its legality was recognized, and its relative duties regulated, by Jesus Christ in his kingdom." Thornton Stringfellow, "A Scriptural View of Slavery," in *Slavery Defended: The Views of the Old South*, ed. Eric L. McKitrick (Englewood Cliffs, N.J.: Prentice-Hall, 1963), p. 86.

been much misunderstood in subsequent years; but in essence it amounts to this: that those sworn to uphold the Constitution have an obligation to advance the cause of constitutional principle, to the end of realizing the ideals of the Declaration of Independence. The Court's invalidation of the Missouri Compromise, accompanied by an opinion by Chief Justice Taney that Lincoln rightly saw as a repudiation of the substance of the Declaration, meant that a critical feature of the Constitution, its aspirational component, was being abandoned.[63] "[The signers of the Declaration] meant simply to declare the *right*, so that the *enforcement* of it might follow as fast as circumstances should permit."[64] Judicial review had to be consistent with the overriding obligation of all citizens—but especially governmental officials—to promote the progressive realization of those principles that gave definition to the nation.

Lincoln knew the Bible well, but his was a distinctly secular interpretation of the moral law incorporated into the Constitution. Taney had claimed that his opinion was in conformity with the Declaration, but in limiting its coverage only to white men, he effectively denuded it of its natural rights content. What so alarmed Lincoln in this was the real prospect that a general acceptance of the reasoning in Taney's opinion would re*constitute* the nation in accordance with an alternative, and much inferior, set of principles. If this prospect was obscured by Taney's deceptive legal claims, it was evident in the more straightforward repudiations of the Declaration found in the writings of other apologists for slavery. It is, for example, apparent in John C. Calhoun's *A Disquisition on Government*, where he speaks of the "dangerous error" of supposing "that all men are born free and equal," of which "nothing can be more unfounded and false."[65] The reason for this error, according to Calhoun, was the acceptance of "the assertion that all men are equal in the state of nature," a state that is totally "inconsistent with the preservation and perpetuation of the race."[66] For a polity

---

[63] For an elaboration, see Gary J. Jacobsohn, "Abraham Lincoln 'On This Question of Judicial Authority': The Theory of Constitutional Aspiration," *Western Political Quarterly* 36 (1983).

[64] Basler, *Collected Works*, vol. 2, p. 406.

[65] John C. Calhoun, *A Disquisition on Government* (Indianapolis: Bobbs-Merrill Co., 1953), p. 44.

[66] Ibid., pp. 44–45. Burt's understanding is different. For him the defenders of slavery simply interpreted the founding creed radically differently from their opponents. In regard to the Declaration of Independence, "The white South claimed political equality to protect the maintenance of slavery and ultimately to secede from the Union." Burt, "Inventing Judicial Review: Israel and America," p. 2095. This, however, minimizes the efforts of the South, as Hartz put it, to "break out of the grip of Locke." Hartz, *The Liberal Tradition in America*, p.

whose identity was bound up so closely in a particular set of ideas, Taney's opinion in *Dred Scott* was therefore a thoroughly subversive act, the toleration of which would further the preservation of the nation in name only.

Lincoln sought to counter this subversion by denying *Dred Scott* the finality that only a "fully settled" decision, that is, one consistent with constitutional aspiration, deserves. In so doing, he exemplified Bickel's understanding of the Court as the institutional voice of enduring values, but more important, he reminded us of the origins of judicial review in the United States, origins that played a part—albeit a symbolic one—in the birth of the nation. In his famous argument in the *Writs of Assistance Case*, James Otis exclaimed, "As to Acts of Parliament, an Act against the Constitution is void, an Act against natural Equity is void: and if an Act of Parliament should be made, in the very Words of this Petition, it would be void. The Executive Courts must pass such Acts into disuse."[67] John Adams, who had been in the audience, noted many years later, "Then and there the child Independence was born."[68] Or to put it differently: that an act of constitutional violation should be associated with the birth of a new nation (dedicated to a certain proposition) has both symbolic and real significance as far as the institution of judicial review is concerned, namely that its legitimacy, in the end, inheres in its furtherance of those ideas that nourish the American conception of nationhood. Thus it is clear from an important recent examination of the early American experience with judicial review that the pre-*Marbury* history is rich in establishing a vital connection between judicial review and the defense of first principles of natural justice.[69] To focus on *Marbury* v. *Madison* and the political conflict

---

177. Writing of the southern theorists of slavery, Hartz observed that they "dared to insist that life can be lived in an utterly different way from the way that Hamilton and Jefferson both agreed to live it" (p. 176). The point here is that the ultimate rejection of their theory was not the triumph of one interpretation over another, but rather the victory of one theory over a countertheory.

[67] Quoted in Thomas C. Grey, "Origins of the Unwritten Constitution: Fundamental Law in American Revolutionary Thought," *Stanford Law Review* 30 (1978): 869.

[68] Ibid., p. 869.

[69] Sylvia Snowiss, *Judicial Review and the Law of the Constitution* (New Haven: Yale University Press, 1990). Snowiss distinguishes three distinct periods in the early evolution of the American practice of judicial review. In the first period (from independence to the publication of *Federalist #78*), judicial review was still affected by the Blackstonian teaching on legislative omnipotence. Violation of the fundamental law had political significance, but the judiciary was not yet in a position to enforce pronouncements of voidness against legislative excess. "Unconstitutionality, at the end of period one and in the very act of writing the national Constitution, was thought not to be determined by judicial exposition of written supreme law

that brought it about is potentially to lose sight of the history that precedes it, a history in which judicial review emerges as an institutional expression of fundamental political agreement.[70]

Fundamental agreement rarely, if ever, connotes universal assent; thus a critic of Lincoln might very well make a case that Lincoln simply got it wrong, that the founding documents mean something very different from what he said about them. So someone might say that it is inconceivable on the basis of what we know of human nature that "all men are created equal" in the sense intended by Lincoln. Or someone else might say that on the basis of our history—most importantly the fact that slavery was legal at the time the Declaration and the Constitution were written—it could not have been their authors' understanding of the self-evident fact of human equality that it applied to members of the black race. Both of these arguments are serious ones, even if, as I think is the case, Lincoln convincingly disposed of them by revealing their ultimately subversive purpose. But what is noteworthy is that, with respect to the Declaration of Independence, these contrary understandings are not the result of an appeal to different sections of a document in tension with itself. And herein lies a critical, perhaps *the* critical, difference with the Israeli constitutional scene, in which the source of interpretive disagreement over first principles is itself foundational.

Let us, then, return to *Elon Moreh*, but before doing so directly, consider what the author of the Court's opinion, Justice Landau, has written elsewhere (and later) on the subject of judicial review: "I am worried about our adults, whether they know what the Declaration of Independence is about, both in embodying human rights and also in its opening passages; in affirming that the State of Israel is the state of the Jewish people, established by our founding fathers who were Zionists. How to bridge this tension between these two parts of the declaration is, of course, a question which has been with us for a long time and will continue to be with us for a long time to come, but this is a matter of living with the facts of life and is

---

but to consist of violation of long-standing and publicly acknowledged first principles of fundamental law, written or unwritten" (p. 43). See also Arkes, *Beyond the Constitution.*

[70] It is worth considering in this context the astute observation of John Agresto. Judicial review's "justification . . . must be in that original American desire to be bound by and to live according to certain ideas and principles of just social conduct embodied in the words of a constitutional text. The underlying promise of judicial review is that with it we may bring our philosophy, our principles, to bear on our actions, and thus work out our present and our future in terms of our inheritance from the past." John Agresto, *The Supreme Court and Constitutional Democracy* (Ithaca: Cornell University Press, 1984), p. 55.

inescapable."[71] As an outspoken proponent of judicial restraint, Landau's concern here is that the Supreme Court's considerable prestige will be jeopardized if the final settlement of political issues left unresolved by this tension becomes lodged in the Court. In *Shalit*, this concern prompted an important question: "What can the court contribute to the solution of an ideological dispute such as this which divides the public? The answer is— nothing, and whoever expects judges to produce a magic formula is merely deluding himself in his naivete."[72] But in an opinion by Justice Landau in *Elon Moreh*, the Court *did*, according to Burt, contribute to the solution of perhaps the most divisive ideological dispute in Israel; moreover, it did so in part on the strength "of the existence of a creedal basis for national unity formulated at a specific founding moment."[73]

What particularly impressed Burt was a passage in the Landau opinion in which the justice seemed to go out of his way to dispute the claims underlying the settlement policy implicated in the case at hand. He did so by appealing to "the authentic voice of Zionism which insists on the Jewish people's right of return to its land . . . but which has never sought to deprive the residents of the country, members of other peoples, of their civil rights."[74] This meant that Zionist principles were consistent with the international standards set out in the Hague Convention, standards that left the Court no choice (unlike the situation in *Shalit*) but to intervene on behalf of the rule of law. For Burt what is important is that this landmark case in the development of judicial review should be accompanied by a judicial pronouncement on Zionist principles, and that the Court should

---

[71] Moshe Landau, "The Limits of Constitutions and Judicial Review," in Elazar, *Constitutionalism*, p. 200.

[72] *Shalit*, 23 (2) P.D. at 520. On the question of judicial self-restraint, the justice acknowledges that he is often "out of step with the whole company of learned legal opinion here in the country." Landau, "The Limits of Constitutions and Judicial Review," p. 203. In this view he appeals to the oft-quoted sentiments of Judge Learned Hand: "This much I think I do know, that a society so riven that the spirit of moderation is gone, no constitution can save. That a society where that spirit flourishes, no constitution need save. That a society which evades its responsibility by thrusting upon the court the nurture of that spirit, in the end will perish." Quoted in ibid., p. 204. Of course in Israel a proponent of judicial activism might say that it is precisely *because* the conditions that nurture a spirit of moderation are so undeveloped that the Court must play a more prominent role. As we shall see in Chapter 5, something like this is present in the jurisprudential stance of Justice Aharon Barak. See also Shimon Shetreet, "Reflections on the Protection of the Rights of the Individual," *Israel Law Review* 12 (1977).

[73] Burt, "Inventing Judicial Review: Israel and America," p. 2095.

[74] *Dweikat v. Government of Israel*, 34 (1) P.D. 1, 12 (1979).

emerge as an agent of moral unity in the face of deep fissures in the body politic.

Landau was gently rebuked by one of his colleagues on the Court for unnecessarily entering into "political or ideological debate." But it is difficult to see how this entry—to the extent that it may be deemed political or ideological—rests on a creedal basis that can rightfully be construed as a source of fundamental political unity for the polity. The justice was doing what judges do best—asserting the primacy of the rule of law; it would be hard to imagine an Israeli judge *not* subscribing to a vision of Zionism that included protection for the civil rights of all people. But if, as Burt correctly asserts, the founding creed of the Israeli polity is that Israel is to be a "national home for the Jewish people" ("in America the creed was political equality"), then Landau could not have intended his observation to mean that "the creed had a single discernible meaning that could be definitively invoked to transcend political conflict."[75] That Justice Landau's intervention barely scratches the surface of fundamental political division becomes clear if one focuses on what is ultimately at the heart of the substantive issue in this case—Jewish ownership and control of land.

Indeed, it was toward the end of securing a "national home for the Jewish people" that the expropriation of Arab lands came to be associated with the Zionist movement. For example, in the 1950s and 1960s Arab land in the Galilee was expropriated by public authority in order to construct the development towns of Upper Nazareth and Carmiel.[76] One does not minimize the significance of the Court's ruling in *Elon Moreh* by suggesting that it does not really address the fundamental tension in the Declaration, the pursuit of equality for all people on the one hand, and as is manifest in this case, the development of the land of Israel for the Jewish people on the other. What distinguishes the taking of Arab land in the *Elon Moreh* case from other Jewish settlements (both in Israel proper and in the contested or occupied territories) was its blatant illegality, which the Court could not ignore (although it is possible that an earlier Court might have done so).[77]

---

[75] Burt, "Inventing Judicial Review: Israel and America," p. 2095.

[76] This process, as well as more recent developments, are described by David Kretzmer in *The Legal Status of the Arabs in Israel*, pp. 49–76.

[77] A 1955 case, *Committee for the Protection of the Expropriated Nazareth Lands* v. *Minister of Finance*, 9 P.D. 1261, is revealing in this regard. It involved the expropriation of Arab land by the Development Authority for the purpose of establishing a *kiryah*, that is, governmental offices and housing for public servants. The petitioners claimed that the transferral of lands from their Arab owners to Jewish settlers constituted discrimination against the

The 1967 war clearly exacerbated extremist tendencies in the Israeli polity, but it did not produce the deeply embedded societal divisions that generate them. These were always present and were implicit in the origins of the regime.

The war and its legacy may also have stimulated a number of justices to heighten the political profile of the Supreme Court by expanding the Court's powers of judicial review. In this sense, as Burt maintains, there may very well be a correlation between conflict and judicial review, or at least judicial activism. While in Israel the conflict may always have been present, at a certain point in its development its problematic character becomes so apparent and disturbing that many people—including judges—perceive the need to approach things differently. They may seek in fact to set into motion a process that holds out the hope of establishing a moral-political consensus that will eventually heal the increasingly dangerous rifts within the body politic. But my argument is that they will not be appealing to a foundational source of creedal unity; instead, whether acknowledged or not, they will be pursuing, as we will see more clearly in the next chapter, the constitutional implications that flow from one side of a divided political inheritance. In response to this initiative, more skeptical judges, such as Justice Landau, will come forth to remind their country-

---

Arabs in favor of the Jews. The Court, however, upheld the expropriation, arguing, among other things, that it was not its function to inquire into whether the purpose for which the land was acquired was a public purpose as required by the relevant ordinance. But it did proceed to consider whether the choice of the lands acquired was an arbitrary one. Interestingly, Justice Witkon's opinion relies in this regard on Justice Landau's discussion of discrimination in *Yosifof*, the bigamy decision discussed in Chapter 2. Landau, recall, placed the issue of discrimination within the context of "the social realities of the country." Witkon's opinion is less candid, for in borrowing the idea that not all differentiation between categories of people is "discrimination," he simply says, "In a sovereign state one does not recognize the autonomy of local residents, be they Jews or Arabs, to the extent that they are allowed to frustrate a plan that has been confirmed as a public purpose and decided upon for the benefit of the region and entire country. This concerns the priority of the central government over the will of the local people. No matter of discrimination is involved here." Ibid., V–24 (Barak et.al.) Translation by Carmel Shalev, in Barak, Goldstein, and Marshall, *Limits of Law*. While this may be technically correct, it neglects to mention that the benefits have mainly to do with the development of the nation as a homeland for the Jewish people. The case thus illustrates how a judicial decision that may very well be consistent with the rule of law may also be consistent with the special recognition given by the Declaration of Independence to the Jewish people. In the *Elon Moreh* decision, upholding the rule of law is consistent with the more egalitarian passages of the Declaration. In short, the principle of the rule of law does not, by itself, get at the underlying tensions in the Israeli constitutional system.

men and fellow jurists that there are definite limits to what the courts can do in the face of the tension embodied in the Declaration of Independence, and that the Court may be endangering what it *can* do by reaching too far.[78]

Bergman, Marbury, and Judicial Restraint

That such a message has come from Justice Landau is interesting, for in addition to his role in *Elon Moreh*, he is also the author of the Court's opinion in *Bergman* v. *Minister of Interior*, the Israeli decision most often compared to *Marbury* v. *Madison*. Decided in 1969, it has the potential for becoming what *Marbury has* become in American constitutional law, the leading precedent for a broadly based power of judicial review. Were that to occur within a time frame comparable to what has evolved in the United States, it would of course be many years before that potential (adjusting, as one would have to, for the absence of a formal written constitution) would be realized. And just as it is easy to imagine a surprised reaction from John Marshall in the face of how his opinion had been exaggerated with respect to the later claims made on its behalf, Moshe Landau could be expected to express a similar sense of wonderment at the inflated purposes to which his opinion had been put. Thus if Marshall had been around in 1958 to read the Court's opinion in *Cooper* v. *Aaron*, in which *Marbury* was taken to mean that "the federal judiciary is supreme in the exposition of the law of the Constitution,"[79] he might have seen fit to enter a vigorous disclaimer.

The Court in *Cooper* made its argument for judicial supremacy on the basis of Marshall's famous declaration that "it is emphatically the province and duty of the judicial department to say what the law is."[80] It is now largely taken for granted that the power of the Supreme Court to issue final and binding interpretations of the Constitution is a necessary corollary of judicial review. That Marshall's original formulation was written in the context of reviewing a section of a law that dealt specifically with the powers of the judiciary is long forgotten. And not only in the United States, as is

---

[78] In contrast, the U.S. Supreme Court, as its experience in *Dred Scott* reveals, threatens its legitimacy most when, in reaching too far, it fails to fulfill its role as institutional voice for those enduring values that constitute the American creed.

[79] *Cooper* v. *Aaron*, 358 U.S. 1, 18 (1958). His disclaimer might have been tempered somewhat by the particular circumstances of the case, in that the specific conflict involved a contest between federal and state authority. But was it necessary, he might have asked, to make such a bold claim on behalf of the Court in order to support the authority of the federal government?

[80] *Marbury* v. *Madison* 5 U.S. (1 Cranch) 137, 177 (1803).

illustrated in a recent Israeli case where the Marshall quote was used to make the point that "in a regime based on the separation of powers, the authority to interpret legislative acts—ranging from basic laws to regulations and administrative orders—is vested in the Court."[81] Furthermore, "Its interpretation is binding upon the parties, and . . . is binding upon the public in general."[82] The case involved a decision by the chairman of the Knesset to preclude a one-member (Meir Kahane) party faction from submitting a proposal of nonconfidence in the government. The intervention by the Court in what has at least the appearance of an internal legislative matter is reminiscent of the American case *Powell* v. *McCormack*, in which the Court said, again relying on *Marbury*, "It is the responsibility of this Court to act as the ultimate interpreter of the Constitution."[83]

This statement, too, was quoted in the Israeli opinion, accompanied by a reminder from its author, Justice Barak: "These words are not special to a legal system in which there is a formal constitution, and which recognizes judicial review of the lawfulness of legislation. These words are fundamental truths in every legal system in which there is an independent judicial branch."[84] Israel may not have a formal constitution, but it does have documents that have come to enjoy constitutional status, and that, when interpreted by the Court, have done much to establish the independence of the judiciary. The indirect use of the Declaration of independence in "*Kol Ha'am*" to invalidate an administrative action infringing on freedom of the press is perhaps the classic example. But despite its independence, the Court's authority to act as "ultimate interpreter" in constitutional matters involving the Knesset is far from being established, with the exception of legislation inconsistent with an entrenched clause of a basic law.[85] *Bergman*

---

[81] "*Kach Party Faction*" v. *Hillel*, 39 (3) P.D. 141, 152 (1985). Translation by Carmel Shalev, in Barak, Goldstein, and Marshall, *Limits of Law*.

[82] Ibid. Off the Court, too, in words that echo the reasoning in *Cooper*, Justice Barak has argued that "judicial law-making that comes from the interpretation of a constitution has the same normative standing of the constitution itself, and only a change in the constitution—or in the judicial rule itself—can change it." Aharon Barak, *Judicial Discretion* (New Haven: Yale University Press, 1989), p. 103.

[83] *Powell* v. *McCormack*, 395 U.S. 486, 549 (1969). This was the first case in which the Court asserted a claim of judicial supremacy in a dispute concerning its authority over the Congress. In *United States* v. *Nixon*, 418 U.S. 683 (1974), it reached the same conclusion with respect to the president, and in *INS* v. *Chadha*, 462 U.S. 919 (1983), the legislative veto case, it reaffirmed its superior role with respect to both coordinate institutions.

[84] "*Kach Party Faction*," 39 (3) P.D. at 153.

[85] On the current status of judicial review involving legislative matters, see David Kretzmer, "Judicial Review of Knesset Decisions," *Tel Aviv University Studies in Law* 8 (1988).

is the basis for this exception; however, a close reading of the case reveals how it could support a considerably broader claim. In this respect it may very well parallel the history of *Marbury*, another case whose relatively narrow holding includes language with an alluringly expansive potential.[86]

In the *Bergman* case the Court responded favorably to the petition of Aharon Bergman, who had sought to enjoin the minister of finance from acting under the provisions of the Financing Law of 1969. That law provided for governmental financing of political parties in election campaigns, but only for those parties represented in the outgoing Knesset. Bergman claimed that this unequal treatment violated the principle of electoral equality incorporated in section 4 of Basic Law: The Knesset, which reads as follows: "The Knesset shall be elected by general, country-wide, direct, equal, secret and proportional elections, in accordance with the Knesset Elections Law; this section shall not be varied save by a majority of the members of the Knesset." The last clause gives to the section its "entrenched" character, distinguishing it from ordinary legislation and providing the Court, according to Bergman, with the authority to overturn the Financing Law, which had not been passed by the required special majority. This the Court did, without addressing "some very difficult preliminary constitutional questions with regard to the status of the Basic Laws and the justiciability before this court of the question whether in practice the Knesset observes any self-imposed restriction by way of 'entrenching' a statutory provision such as section 4 of the Basic Law that is being dealt with by us."[87] The case was decided on the assumption that ordinary legislation of the Knesset can be struck down by the Court when it contravenes an entrenched provision of a basic law, but it is not, in itself, an authority for the correctness of that assumption.[88]

---

[86] Elsewhere, for example, Justice Barak has written, "Our *Marbury* v. *Madison* is about to be pronounced—or maybe it was several years ago. It will probably be decided before our constitution is written." Barak, "Freedom of Speech in Israel: The Impact of the American Constitution," *Tel Aviv University Studies in Law* 8 (1988). If the reference here is to *Bergman*, it might mean that, in Barak's view, the case could lead the Israeli Court where its American counterpart has led the American Court. This would certainly account for description of the Israeli Supreme Court as "ultimate interpreter." The current president of the Court, Justice Shamgar, has written, "*Bergman* did not pretend to be an Israeli *Marbury* v. *Madison* but after it, the idea of further development of judicial review of legislation could not be regarded as entirely unexpected." Meir Shamgar, "On the Written Constitution," *Israel Law Review* 9 (1974): 474.

[87] *Bergman* v. *Minister of Finance*, 23 (1) P.D. 693, 696 (1969).

[88] This decision by the Court not to address the question of the Court's authority to invalidate a law inconsistent with an entrenched provision of a Basic Law has come in for some

Opinions about what the Court actually did diverge markedly, ranging from the view that "*Bergman* is actually the least important basis for the Israeli Supreme Court's contemporary claims for increased judicial authority," to the view that it "revolutioniz[ed] the Israeli legal system by introducing *defacto* judicial supervision of the constitutionality of primary legislation."[89] It did seem to mean that the Knesset could bind itself, but beyond that, its implications for judicial review were uncertain.[90] As in *Marbury*, where a narrow interpretation of its meaning for judicial review would confine the holding to matters of direct concern to the judiciary, and a broad view would see it as a basis for judicial supremacy in all constitutional questions, Justice Landau's opinion possesses similar alternative possibilities. This may be seen in his treatment of the conflict between the two Knesset laws.

The attorney general had argued that no conflict existed, in that the principle of equality in the Basic Law was to be narrowly construed to mean only that each voter shall have one vote of equal weight (i.e., one person, one vote). But by an alternative reading of the statute accepted by the Court, section 4 should not be confined to technical provisions regarding the carrying out of elections, but should also cover the equal right to be elected, a right clearly denied by the Financing Law. Justice Landau acknowledged, however, that as an issue of statutory interpretation, this was a "borderline" call, an acknowledgment very different from Chief Justice

---

heavy criticism. For example: "Is . . . a Basic Law . . . 'superior' to an ordinary law? If so, then the court should have said so in clear terms and set the question at rest." Peter Elman, "Comment," *Israel Law Review* 4 (1969): 568. Justice Landau's avoidance of the justiciability issue was based on the fact that the attorney general had not contested this issue, and further, that the case was one of extreme urgency and therefore precluded the thorough examination that the question deserved. Nevertheless, his postponement of the question inevitably gave rise to a comparison with *Marbury*, in that both opinions challenged a powerful branch of government without providing that branch with a very good opportunity to respond effectively. See, for example, Burt, "Inventing Judicial Review: Israel and America," p. 2045.

[89] The first view is from Burt, "Inventing Judicial Review: Israel and America," p. 2043; the second from Amos Shapira, "Judicial Review without a Constitution: The Israeli Paradox," *Temple Law Quarterly* 56 (1983): 414.

[90] This is not to say that at the time of the decision the power of the Knesset to bind future Knessets was a settled question. Indeed, it was a much debated question in Israeli legal circles, but as Ruth Gavison has noted, "In fact, the debate about the Knesset's *power* [to enact an entrenched bill of rights] would seem to have been well-nigh decided by the political system. The Knesset has enacted entrenched provisions of basic laws, and the courts have opted for some version of recognition of the power of the Knesset to bind itself." Gavison, "The Controversy Over Israel's Bill of Rights," p. 115.

Marshall's decisive (although much more dubious) interpretation of section 13 of the Judiciary Act of 1789. But according to Landau, any doubt as to the meaning of the provision was to be resolved by applying the general principle of the equality of all before the law to the specific area of electoral laws. In this he rejected the claim by the attorney general that because the equality principle was not embodied in a written constitution or a basic law, it could not hinder the legislature from deviating from it.

Although it "is nowhere inscribed [it is a principle that] breathes the breath of life into our whole constitutional system. It is therefore right that just in the border-line case, when the provision of the enacted Law is open to two interpretations, we should prefer that which preserves the equality of all before the law and does not set it at naught."[91] That preference led the Court to invalidate the Financing Law, despite the fact that "the first inclination of the court must . . . be to uphold the law and not invalidate it, even when the contention against it is that it contradicts an 'entrenched' statutory provision."[92] This, then, raises an obvious question: if the unwritten constitutional principles referred to by Justice Landau are clear and powerful enough to overcome this "first inclination," then is it not proper to infer as a general jurisprudential proposition that when there is a statute of questionable consistency with an entrenched Basic Law, its validity may be established by application of the unwritten constitution? Or even more, if a law passed by the Knesset repudiates one of the life-breathing principles of the constitutional system, is it even necessary that there be an entrenched Basic Law for the Supreme Court to invalidate it? In this respect is not *Bergman* considerably more sweeping than *Marbury*? As one commentator has put it, "Where Chief Justice Marshall declared an Act of Congress void because it was in conflict with the Constitution, Mr. Justice Landau . . . declared an Act of the Knesset void despite the fact that Israel has not yet adopted a written constitution."[93]

---

[91] *Bergman*, 23 (1) P.D. at 698. See also Allan E. Shapiro, "Power to the Court Over the Knesset?" *Jerusalem Post*, February 22, 1992.

[92] Ibid., 699. This is perhaps what led one commentator to write: "Although the *Bergman* decision speaks the language of restraint, it actually engages in judicial activism *par excellence*." Shapira, "Judicial Review without a Constitution," p. 414.

[93] Melville B. Nimmer, "The Uses of Judicial Review in Israel's Quest for a Constitution," *Columbia Law Review* 70 (1970): 1218. The decision in *Bergman* might usefully be compared to an American decision, *American Party of Texas* v. *White*, 415 U.S. 767 (1974), in which the Court upheld a Texas statute that, among other things, denied ballot position to parties that failed to secure at least 2 percent of the vote in the previous election (although there were other routes for getting on the ballot). The decision may be seen as displaying more deference to the legislative branch than what occurred in the Israeli case, especially since the legislature was that of a state and not the Congress.

In fact there is nothing in Justice Landau's opinion to indicate that he had such expansive possibilities in mind, that he intended anything more than that where there are two possible statutory interpretations, the interpretation that conforms to the principle of equality is to be preferred. There is certainly no clear warrant for supposing that a Knesset law may be overturned on the strength, standing alone, of any unwritten constitutional principle. Landau himself argued in a subsequent case that "apart from the special problem of entrenched clauses, this Court does not assume for itself the jurisdiction to review the content of Knesset legislation."[94] But that is no guarantee that in the future the Court will not assume such a power, and that in doing so it will not appeal to the unwritten principles adverted to by the justice in *Bergman*. In Justice Menachem Elon's words, *"For the moment* this court exercises self-restraint and does not use the power of judicial review it has over legislative proceedings of the Knesset."[95] A Court, however, that is moving in the direction of "ultimate interpreter" could quite easily (although at present it might not be very likely) appropriate the language in *Bergman* to conclude that primary legislation offensive to the fundamental principles of the constitutional system cannot stand.[96]

---

[94] *Flatto-Sharon* v. *Knesset Speaker*, 35 (4) P.D. 118, 135–36 (1981). See also *Vogel* v.*Broadcasting Authority*, 31 (3) P.D. 657, 664 (1976), where Landau says, "Thus we have achieved a judicial quasi-bill of rights, similar to the written bill of rights of other countries. However, unlike some (though not all) of these documents, our bill of rights is subordinate to the sovereign will of the Knesset as the legislative branch."

[95] Dissenting opinion in *Miari* v. *Knesset Speaker*, 41 (4) P.D. 169, 264 (1985). It should be noted here that the Basic Law on the Judiciary contains language that could be interpreted to provide support for extensive judicial review over acts of the Knesset. Section 15(d)(2) reads: "The Supreme Court sitting as a High Court of Justice shall be competent to order state authorities and officials thereof *and other persons who carry out public duties under law* to do or refrain from doing any act in the lawful exercise of their duties, or if they were improperly elected or appointed to refrain from acting" (emphasis added). This section was used directly by Justice Barak to justify judicial review of the Knesset in his concurring opinion in *Miari* (265).

[96] After reviewing several cases in which the Court actively intervened in some important nonlegislative Knesset activities, David Kretzmer saw as possible, if not probable, that the Court would extend its power of judicial review to actual legislation. "One can easily conceive of the Court quoting from the judgment in *Marbury* v. *Madison* that '[i]t is emphatically the province and duty of the judicial department to say what the law is.' " Kretzmer, "Judicial Review of Knesset Decisions," p. 147. That this is not such a remote possibility may be seen in this excerpt from a 1987 opinion by the president of the Court, Justice Shamgar: "I do not find it necessary to consider here the broad constitutional question whether judicial review of this Court extends also to primary legislation of the Knesset, beyond review in connection with entrenched statutory provisions in a Basic Law." *Cohen* v. *Minister of Labor and Welfare*, 41 (2) P.D. 540, 543 (1987). While the Court has not gone on to consider the question, this statement suggests that, for some at least, it is still an *open* question. In January, 1992, Justice

As we have seen, Justice Landau's own reluctance to move in this direction is related to his concerns about the character of these fundamental principles. While the courts must enforce the principle of equality before the law in justiciable cases, there may be other principles (as well, perhaps, as this principle in certain situations) where enforcement by the Supreme Court would inappropriately enmesh the judiciary in controversies more amenable to political resolution. He has advocated a sort of bifurcated system for the exercise of judicial power, arguing that "the institutional part of the constitution should be entrenched and should be subject to judicial review," but that an entrenched bill of rights would lead to the unfortunate politicization of the Court.[97] In the context of *Bergman*, the Court's intervention might therefore be understood as a proper assertion of judicial power in defense of a vital institutional concern, namely the sanctity of the electoral process. But nothing in this intervention, Landau would no doubt claim, should be construed as necessarily legitimating interventions by the Court in other constitutional domains.

There is in this position an echo of the now arcane American doctrine of departmentalism, which denies that any one institution should possess final interpretive authority on all constitutional questions, and more particularly, that deference should be accorded each branch of government in matters concerning its own functions. Denying that the Supreme Court should be "ultimate arbiter of all constitutional questions," Thomas Jefferson maintained, "The constitution has erected no such single tribunal, knowing that to whatever hands confided, with the corruptions of time and party, its members would become despots. It has more wisely made all the departments co-equal and co-sovereign within themselves."[98] While this is a view most frequently associated with Jefferson, some constitutional scholars make the argument that it is an essential component of Marshall's opinion in *Marbury* v. *Madison*. Marshall "claimed no more than that each department shall have final authority to pass on constitutional questions affecting its own duties and responsibilities."[99] This is not the claim found in most contemporary *Marbury* justifications of particular exercises of judi-

---

Minister Dan Meridor submitted a proposed Basic Law: Legislation that would allow the Supreme Court, sitting as a constitutional court, to invalidate laws in violation of basic laws. Going beyond previous similar efforts, the constitutional court could also nullify Knesset laws that "contradict a principle of the fundamental principles of the state of Israel."

[97] Landau, "The Limits of Constitutions and Judicial Review," p. 204.

[98] Paul L. Ford, ed., *The Works of Thomas Jefferson* (New York: Putnam's, 1905), p. 12.

[99] Alfred H. Kelly, Winfred A. Harbison, and Herman Belz, *The American Constitution: Its Origins and Development* (New York: W. W. Norton & Co., 1983), p. 181. The most extended analysis of the departmental interpretation of *Marbury* is Robert Lowry Clinton,

cial review, but then, as has been said, "the mythic *Marbury* and the real *Marbury* inhabit different constitutional galaxies."[100] It is, for example, noteworthy that prior to the late nineteenth century Marshall's opinion was not cited as a precedent for judicial review; nor was it cited with any frequency in this regard until the 1950s.[101] Its absence in *Dred Scott* is especially significant, because that case was the first post-*Marbury* instance in which judicial review was used to overturn a congressional enactment, and also the first instance in the Court's history when it struck down a law that concerned matters falling outside the immediate purview of the judicial department.

As plausible as this understanding of *Marbury* is, the eventual demise of departmentalism (at least in its most fully developed Jeffersonian version) is not without a logic of its own. Marshall may very well have intended that the Court exercise judicial review only over acts of a "judiciary nature," but the practical as well as theoretical difficulties of determining jurisdictional boundaries in individual cases make it clear why such an intent would likely not in the end be faithfully observed. In addition, the historic connection between judicial review and natural rights jurisprudence suggests that confining the Court to narrowly prescribed substantive questions would be difficult to maintain.[102] Lincoln's opposition to *Dred Scott*—specifically his recommendation that the finality of the Court's judgment be withheld—did not flow from a sense that the Court had, in invalidating the Missouri Compromise, ventured inappropriately beyond the province of its own department. Rather, it reflected his deeply held belief that the Court's judgment was wrong; wrong, that is, in the most decisive way possible, because it repudiated the principles of the Declaration. For the same reason that he could not have endorsed judicial supremacy, he could not have endorsed the narrow view of *Marbury*; judicial finality is after all justified if it advances the aspirational goals of the Declaration and Constitution.

Justice Landau, on the other hand, *would* endorse what others might

---

Marbury v. Madison and Judicial Review (Lawrence: University of Kansas Press, 1989). See also William Wiecek, *Liberty Under Law: The Supreme Court in American Life* (Baltimore: Johns Hopkins University Press, 1988), pp. 38–40. For a different view of the case, see Edward S. Corwin, "*Marbury v. Madison* and the Doctrine of Judicial Review," *Michigan Law Review* 12 (1914). "Once we accept the doctrine of judicial review as part of the Constitution, the acquiescence of the political departments in the judicial review of the Constitution is required by the Constitution itself" (p. 551).

[100] Levy, *Original Intent and the Framers' Constitution*, p. 85.

[101] Clinton, *Marbury v. Madison and Judicial Review*, p. x.

[102] On this point, see generally Arkes, *Beyond the Constitution*.

characterize as a narrow construction of *Bergman* if for no other reason than that it could not then become a precedent for an expansion of judicial review into more controversial areas of nonentrenched basic law provisions, to say nothing of principles yet to be embodied in any Basic Law. One might say of his position, that like the advocates of a narrow reading of *Marbury*, he would prefer to confine the activity of the Court, as far as its review of legislation is concerned, to things of a "judiciary nature." His opposition to an entrenched bill of rights does not mean that the Court should stay out of rights enforcement (as is obvious from his own record on these questions), only that its institutional health depends on minimizing opportunities for direct confrontation with the legislature over such issues. In this it is worth recalling that Jefferson's advocacy of a declaration of rights emphasized "the legal check which it [would put] into the hands of the judiciary." In our own time this legal check has grown considerably, having become instrumental in putting into the hands of the judiciary many of the most divisive social and political issues confronting the American people. The judges have not, in other words, been "kept strictly to their own department," as Jefferson, perhaps unrealistically, thought they should.

That a similar evolution in Israel, where societal division cuts more deeply, might concern someone like Justice Landau, is understandable. One should of course question whether his own variant of a departmental solution, in which the judiciary is limited in its power by excluding for review legislative acts pertaining directly to individual rights, is any more realistic. Many would argue, for example, that Justice Landau has (to his considerable credit) done as much as anyone in Israel in creating a "judicial bill of rights," that, in other words, the Court has already become a principal player in the great issues that divide the body politic. While perhaps true, that may not be the best way to frame the issue. Developing a de facto bill of rights through statutory interpretation and administrative review does not entail the degree of certainty or finality that is involved in judicial review of primary legislation. Prudence thus dictates judicial restraint. Or to put it another way: judicial restraint in Israel means avoiding judgments of finality in the absence of a final settlement of regime principles.

CONCLUSION

Walter F. Murphy has argued that the question of *who* should be the authoritative source for constitutional interpretation is directly connected to the more basic question of *what* the constitution is.[103] For example, "Does a constitution point toward a vision or several visions of the good society?"[104] "Does it bind a people together into a nation?"[105] In this chapter I have proceeded in a similar fashion by considering the issue of judicial review in the context of the nature and role of the constitution in Israel and the United States. The fact that in the United States the Constitution assumes a more prominent role as a source for a shared political identity than it does in Israel has a bearing on how we should understand the act of constitutional interpretation. The *who* and the *what* of constitutional interpretation is in some manner related to the question of the *who* and the *what* of civic identity. If it is judicial review we are speaking about in this context, then the judges who perform this act, especially in the American system, are directly or indirectly engaged in a process of political legitimation.[106]

But this does not answer the question of ultimate interpretive responsibility. While Bickel and others are persuasive in showing why the Court is particularly well suited to articulate and defend "enduring values," it is Lincoln who demonstrated that the centrality of these principles precluded a judicial monopoly over constitutional interpretation.[107] His position did not deny judicial finality; it did, however, accept nonjudicial participation in the process by which it was ultimately achieved. To the extent that all branches (and, we might add, citizens) were involved in the common enterprise of attempting to realize constitutional ideals, they all had a responsibility to defend, in appropriate ways, their best understanding of these ideals. *Dred Scott* was of course Lincoln's great lesson in judicial fallibility, a specific version of a lesson detailed in the opening essay of *The Federalist*: "So numerous indeed and so powerful are the causes which serve to give a

[103] Walter F. Murphy, "Who Shall Interpret? The Quest for the Ultimate Constitutional Interpreter," *Review of Politics* 48 (1986).

[104] Ibid., p. 403.

[105] Ibid., p. 402.

[106] I mean this in a deeper sense than what is implied in Charles L. Black's understanding of the Supreme Court as a legitimating agent in American politics. "The Court, through its history, has acted as the legitimator of the government. In a very real sense, the Government of the United States is based on the opinions of the Supreme Court." Charles L. Black, Jr., *The People and the Court: Judicial Review in a Democracy* (Englewood Cliffs, N.J.: Prentice-Hall, 1960), p. 52. While not disagreeing with this, my point is that the Court is a legitimator of the principles by which Americans derive their collective sense of identity.

[107] Bickel, it should be noted, was very much influenced by Lincoln in these matters. Speaking of these great issues of principle, he observed that "the functions [of the branches of government] cannot and need not be rigidly compartmentalized." Bickel, *The Least Dangerous Branch*, p. 261.

false bias to the judgment, that we, upon many occasions, see wise and good men on the wrong as well as the right side of questions of the first magnitude to society. This circumstance, if duly attended to, would furnish a lesson in moderation to those who are ever so much persuaded of their being in the right, in any controversy."[108] Right and wrong were not terms that, when applied to founding principles, depended for their meaning on the particular judgments of individuals. Or as Justice Frankfurter said of the document incorporating these principles, "The ultimate touchstone of constitutionality is the Constitution itself and not what we have said about it."[109]

Thus it is that while the existence of a moral consensus embodied in a written constitution legitimates the exercise of judicial review by a counter-majoritarian institution, the possibility of error or willful distortion suggests the inappropriateness of an unqualified finality in constitutional interpretation. Regrettably, however, this is not a widely shared view, mainly because of a preference among many judges and scholars for constitutional theories that in one way or another embrace the teaching contained in the aphorism that the Constitution is what the judges say it is.[110] Americans are in need of a Court that is vitally engaged in the process of clarifying and elaborating those meanings that give definition to the nation as a whole; but for that reason they must also see to it that that engagement be part of a collaborative enterprise in which the finality of any constitutional judgment involving fundamental principle becomes more than a formalistic matter of determining who has the last word.[111]

The Israeli example can illuminate this problem. There the notion of a court as ultimate constitutional interpreter is particularly problematic in the light of that polity's historic difficulty in achieving a unified constitutional vision or consensus, to say nothing of its longstanding tradition of parliamentary supremacy. Right and wrong, when applied in Israel to founding principles, will largely depend on the perceived correctness of a choice between particularistic and universal filaments in the existent constitutional constellation. The position of judicial restraint reflects, among other things, an understandable desire to avoid making this choice. Indeed, such restraint is further justified if the alternative to it follows the

[108] Lodge, *The Federalist*, no. 1, p. 4.

[109] *Graves* v. *O'Keefe*, 306 U.S. 466, 491–92 (1938).

[110] I have reviewed these theories and their connection to the doctrine of judicial finality in *The Supreme Court and the Decline of Constitutional Aspiration*, pp. 114–29.

[111] For a thoughtful account of what such a collaborative enterprise might look like, see Agresto, *The Supreme Court and Constitutional Democracy*, pp. 125–38.

American pattern of a ratcheting up of the practice of judicial review into a defense of judicial supremacy. But this should not be seen as inevitable; judicial review, or more broadly, constitutional interpretation by the Court, has a much greater potential than in the United States for retaining a relatively modest role in the development of constitutional understanding. There is less reason for concern over an active judiciary if it is clearly understood that the specific results of its activity possess a politically tentative or intermediate status in the elaboration of regime principles. A Court pursuing the more libertarian aspirations of the nation's founding agenda can and ought to be checked by a Knesset that is more sensitive to the other parts of that agenda, as the latter in turn should be checked by the Court. If a genuine constitutional colloquy emerges from this process it may contain within it the possibility of achieving a greater unity of constitutional purpose. But it also contains within it a lesson for those polities that begin with this greater unity: they too can profit from a constitutional arrangement that allows them to achieve a higher level of clarity in the articulation, development, and application of constitutional principle.

Jurisprudence, Education, and the Constitution

> We are creating our own foundations. In a way, I, as a
> Supreme Court judge, have the sense that we are now
> the framers of our unwritten constitution.
> —*Justice Aharon Barak*

THE PROPERTY OF ENLIGHTENED NATIONS

The laws concerning national security censorship in Israel are suffused in
irony. They are rooted in Mandatory legislation that once was the special
target of outrage and contempt from those in Palestine who had been
engaged in the struggle to establish an independent Jewish state. That they
should now be the principal legal basis for censoring expression designated
a threat to the postindependence public order is a matter of great controversy and not a little soul searching.

But also opportunity. Precisely because the origins of these laws are so
tainted, their future may be determined without any sense of obligation to
the past. This was not always accepted by the Supreme Court; in the much
more restrained judicial environment of the early Court, Justice Smoira
wrote, "There is no room today for the submission that Emergency Regulations made in the time of the Mandate are no longer in force because they
were then used for anti-Jewish purposes."[1] Once employed to frustrate the
national aspirations of the Jewish people, they can become, in the re-
sourceful hands of today's judges, an important vehicle for elaborating the
principled commitments of the regime that triumphed in spite of them.
How better to establish a new constitutional mandate than by providing
fresh meaning to a discredited legacy. These laws, then, while technically
binding on Israeli judges, present rich interpretive possibilities for developing a distinctively Israeli constitutional jurisprudence.

[1] *Leon v. Gubernik*, 1 P.D. 58, 68 (1948). While today's Court would not dispute this, it
would, as we shall see, be more inclined to justify creative statutory interpretation on the basis
of this sordid history. As the president of the Court has argued, "It is within the power of the
Supreme Court to give a law a new direction when on principle and on reasoning it is right to
do so." Meir Shamgar, "The Supreme Court of Israel: Present Trends and Concepts," *Israel
Law Review* 20 (1985): 177.

Two inheritances from the British Mandate have been at the center of concern, the 1945 Defense Regulations and the 1933 Press Ordinance Law. Military censorship is traceable to the 1945 legislation, which includes a section that stipulates: "The censor may by order prohibit generally or specially the publishing of matters the publishing of which, in his opinion, would be, or be likely to be or become, prejudicial to the defense of Palestine or to the public safety or to public order."[2] Under the Mandate the censor was appointed by the high commissioner, but since independence the power to censor has been exercised under the authority of the minister of defense. Although the censoring power falls clearly within the jurisdiction of the military, the reference to public safety and public order in the authorizing language of the regulations suggests that the jurisdiction of the censor is not confined only to the publication of sensitive military secrets. Early concerns in Israel about the breadth of this power and its potential danger led to an effort to abandon the regulations in favor of a less sweeping censorship mandate that would be narrowly confined to security matters. This effort was dropped after the formalization of an Agreement between the Editors Committee (representing Israel Radio and the major Hebrew newspapers) and the minister of defense, in which the promise was made not to exercise the authority of the military censor against carriers of news who were members of the committee.[3] This meant that an expansive censorship regime could continue against the nonestablishment press, which in the present circumstances refers almost exclusively to the Arabic-language newspapers in East Jerusalem. Indeed, these papers are occasionally prevented from publishing material that has already found its way into the Hebrew press.

Under the Press Ordinance Law of 1933 censorship may assume a more drastic form, since the minister of interior (the high commissioner under the Mandate) is given the authority to revoke or refuse to grant a license to operate a newspaper. "If any matter appearing in a newspaper is, in the opinion of the [minister of interior], likely to endanger the public peace," he may "suspend the publication of the newspaper for such period as he may think fit."[4] While the *Kol Ha'am* decision did much to defang this law, the recent case of the Hebrew newspaper *Hadashot* graphically re-

[2] Defense Regulations, section 8, regulation 87(1).

[3] The Editors Committee has also supported voluntary censorship, a practice in which members (by unanimous consent only) agree not to publish information that government officials maintain would be damaging to the national interest. For this they gain access to information that the government withholds from the nonestablishment press.

[4] Press Ordinance, sect. 19(2)(a).

veals what may still happen in Israel to enterprising journalists. In 1984, when Palestinian hijackers of a bus filled with Israelis were killed by members of the Israeli security services, the initial report by the government that the killings had occurred in battle turned out to be a fabrication. A huge public scandal ensued after it was revealed that they had in fact been executed after their capture. For its role in reporting on this extremely embarrassing story (a breach of security according to the authorities), *Hadashot's* license to publish was suspended for four days, representing the first closing of a daily newspaper for censorship violations in thirty years. The suspension was upheld by the Supreme Court, which could very easily have employed respected precedent to rule otherwise.[5]

That they did not has much to do with the nature of Supreme Court decisionmaking, in that the Court's practice of not sitting *en banc* means that outcomes are heavily influenced by the particular judges (selected by the president of the Court) constituting the panel for decision in any given case.[6] But one cannot ignore the fact that this case was directly concerned with terrorism, an issue that more than any other underlines the omnipresent Israeli sensitivity about questions of security. As Judith Karp, Israel's deputy attorney general, points out, "[Israel's] entire democratic tradition has evolved alongside its security crisis."[7] She goes on: "The accumulation of years of security struggles leaves its psychological impact on the agencies of the state and the population, making it even harder to yield to abstract values."[8] Indeed, even where the Supreme Court has been eloquent in affirming the unique and intrinsic importance of these values, its acute awareness of the less abstract interest in the existence of the state and the continuity of the Jewish people has always been a prominent presence in its adjudicative calculations.

Thus in *"Kol Ha'am,"* for example, Justice Agranat borrowed freely from the rich free speech jurisprudential tradition of the United States, but when it came to formulating a specific doctrinal position for interpreting

---

[5] *Hadashot, Inc.* v. *Minister of Defense*, 38 (2) P.D. 477 (1984).

[6] The Court's traditional practice of sitting in panels of three justices for most of its cases has not escaped criticism. For example, Allan E. Shapiro has argued that as the Court's development as a constitutional court has moved to one of increasing significance, its opinions should be clearly identified in institutional rather than individual terms. In other words, its work arrangements should reflect its changing role. Allan E. Shapiro, "Changing Times and the High Court," *Jerusalem Post*, January 11, 1992.

[7] Judith Karp, "Finding an Equilibrium," *Israeli Democracy*, Fall 1990, p. 29.

[8] Ibid.

the Press Ordinance Law's language regarding publications "likely" to "[endanger] the public peace," he parted company with his ideological cousins from abroad, Holmes and Brandeis. Rather than insisting "that the danger to the public peace created in consequence of the publication is . . . proximate in time," he advanced the less "extreme" standard of "probability," which, though it represented a significant move away from the "bad tendency" test employed by the British during the Mandate, reveals a greater deference to security considerations than one is likely to find among liberal American judges. In the course of his opinion, Justice Agranat offered some unsolicited advice to the minister of interior, namely that he "pay attention" to the general principles espoused by Holmes and Brandeis; but in the end it was deemed unnecessary that the minister abide by the very demanding libertarian standard to which the principles had led these jurists. To be sure, the *Dennis* case, involving the application of the probable danger test by a deeply divided Supreme Court, had only recently been decided in the United States; but whereas "*Kol Ha'am*" has always been viewed as a progressive, visionary decision in Israel, *Dennis* was from the moment of its announcement roundly condemned in American legal circles as a retrograde capitulation to anticommunist hysteria.

The 1988 case of *Schnitzer* v. *Chief Military Censor* represents the most farreaching effort by the Court to limit the power to censor under the 1945 Defense Regulations. While it is too early to say how significant a precedent it is, it certainly bears scrutiny as demarcating the current outer limits of the free speech principle in the context of national security considerations. The case also vividly illustrates the interpretive process through which the Supreme Court has come to be regarded as the main bulwark of protection for individual rights in Israel.

A Tel Aviv newspaper that was not a member of the Editors Committee sought to publish an article critical of the head of the Mossad; but according to the military censor, it was an article prejudicial to the operational capability of the intelligence organization. Justice Barak's opinion for the Court is noteworthy for several things, not the least of which is its attempt to place the power to censor directly within a democratic political context. To accomplish this it was necessary to establish that the Defense Regulations emerged in a colonial setting antithetical to the animating principles of the subsequently independent polity: "The interpretation to be given to the Defense Regulations in the State of Israel is not identical to the interpretation which was appropriate in the period of the Mandate. The Defense Regulations today are among the laws of a democratic state. They need to be interpreted on the basis of the fundamental principles of Israeli law."[9] Since Article 11 of the Law and Administration Ordinance of 1948 establishes that the law existing in the country on the day of independence will remain in force "subject to the changes emanating from the establishment of the State and its rights,"[10] Barak could appeal to these "changes" as the basis for devising a more enlightened set of guidelines to govern the activities of the military censor.

To determine the fundamental values (in other words, what has changed) that will provide the context for balancing the interests in free expression and national security, the Supreme Court must have recourse to "basic principles of equality, freedom and justice, which are the property of all developed and enlightened nations."[11] This highlights the fact that for those judges, like Justice Barak, who wish to tighten restrictions against the use of the censorship power, a common strategy is to deemphasize the unique aspects of Israeli statehood in favor of those universal principles to which progressive liberal democratic states are or should be committed.[12] In applying this approach, the Court went on to declare "that a reasonable censor, acting in a democratic state, obliged to strike a balance between security and freedom of expression, would not have reached the conclusion reached by the respondent."[13] What might have been declared had the Court addressed itself to the actions of a reasonable censor acting in a "Jewish state surrounded by unremittingly hostile Arab neighbors" is of course highly speculative. For many, there is no conflict between the concepts of a democratic state and a Jewish state, and therefore a divergent result would and should not follow from the posing of an alternative conceptualization of the censorship question. After all, the particular security interests of Israel *were* here taken into account by the Court in its balancing exercise; hence there should be no grounds for anticipating an outcome other than what was achieved by emphasizing the democratic orientation of the polity.

[9] *Schnitzer* v. *Chief Military Censor*, 42 (4) P.D. 617, 628 (1989). The citations to this case are from a translation by Philip Simpson.

[10] Ibid., 625.

[11] Ibid., 627, citing Justice Haim Cohn's opinion in *Street* v. *Chief Rabbi of Israel*, 18 (1) P.D. 598, 612 (1963).

[12] In this regard it is perhaps worth noting how Justice Barak introduces his recent book: "This book is not about Israeli law. It is not about an Israeli judge. It is about the law and judging generally. The problems are universal." Barak, *Judicial Discretion*, p. xi. He goes on, however, to emphasize that for him the particular political culture in Israel must ultimately determine the use of judicial discretion in hard cases.

[13] *Schnitzer*, 42 (4) P.D. at 645.

This is all quite reasonable, except that it may obscure the fact that the manner in which competing interests are balanced is a function of the weight assigned to each interest, which in turn may be decisively affected by the initial formulation of the problem. Justice Barak drew inspiration from the democratic commitments of the Declaration, but it is easy to imagine a different panel of justices placing the censorship issue more centrally within the spirit of those passages in the document that emphasize the tragic history of the Jewish people and their consequent need to be secure in a state of their own.[14] In the *Schnitzer* case the Court's understanding of the problem led it to announce the following standard: "The question in each case is, whether a reasonable censor is entitled to reach the conclusion that, on the basis of assessment of the given facts, publication is likely to cause—i.e. there exists a near-certainty that publication will cause—severe or substantial damage to the security of the State."[15] This, as Barak points out, is a less severe standard than the American prior restraint rule (reflecting no doubt a more urgent sense of physical insecurity than exists in the United States); but in the end it must be seen as a potentially significant doctrinal support for the cause of press freedom.

This cause, however, cannot be served unless there is a sufficiently broad scope for judicial review to cover the authority of statutory agencies operating under the Defense Regulations. The limited nature of the Court's powers in this respect had been established at a very early date in the life of the state.[16] At least as important as its doctrinal contribution to prior restraint law was *Schnitzer*'s clear affirmation of a judicial role in reviewing administrative actions undertaken in a security context. "Security considerations enjoy no special status."[17] Following evolving standards of judicial

---

[14] There are other relevant passages. The Declaration establishes that Israel is to be the sovereign state of the Jewish people. That the founders of the state understood this affirmation of the raison d'etre of the state to entail very serious risks for the nation's future security is suggested by the document's "call upon the Arab inhabitants of the State of Israel to return to the ways of peace," and its "offer [of] peace and amity to all the neighboring States and their peoples." This is an invitation to harmonious relations that expresses more than an understandable yearning for a safe neighborhood; it is in addition a gentle reminder that the state was born into a hostile world of both internal and external threats to its very existence. A nation that is sensitive to its status as an unwanted presence in its part of the world is unlikely to surprise observers when it institutes a censorship regime that does not conform to all of the expectations associated with a democratic polity.

[15] *Schnitzer*, 42 (4) P.D. at 636.

[16] See on this point David Kretzmer, "Forty Years of Public Law," *Israel Law Review* 24 (1990).

[17] *Schnitzer*, 42 (4) P.D. at 639.

review in Great Britain, Justice Barak left no doubt that, as far as he was concerned, judicial deference in these matters was a thing of the past. "Regarding the scope of our intervention, there is one rule for all governmental authorities. They are all subject to the instructions of the law, and they are all subject to review by the court, according to the normal and accepted occasions of review which reflect the legal requirements of administrative jurisdiction."[18] Thus, while the Supreme Court has no real choice but to accept the validity of all of the statutory authorizations for censorship, it now has considerable leeway to affect, through interpretation, the actual course and extent of censorship in the sphere of national security. This has as yet not affected the exercise of censorship in the occupied territories, leading some to express legitimate concerns that attitudes about what is permissible outside the Green Line (Israel's pre-June 1967, borders as determined in the armistice agreements following the War of Independence) will corrupt mainstream Israeli thinking on the dangers of censorship; but there is no gainsaying the fact that a legal basis for heightened scrutiny has been clearly established.[19]

The evolution of Israeli jurisprudence since the establishment of the state in 1948 includes an expanding role for the courts in determining the shape and content of the law. In this chapter I discuss this phenomenon in relation to another frequently observed development—the growing use by Israeli judges of American legal precedents and scholarship. The Court in *Schnitzer* made very little explicit reference to American constitutional law and theory, but embedded in its argument and general approach are jurisprudential assumptions very much in the spirit of the liberal constitutionalism ascendant in the United States. As is evident from copious citation of American materials in earlier cases, by 1989 the Court had become well acquainted with the rights-oriented approach in the United States, so much so that it may now be considered unnecessary to rehearse in detail

---

[18] Ibid., 640.

[19] For an example of these concerns, see Pnina Lahav, "The Press and National Security," *Israeli Democracy*, Winter 1989. The potential for abuse in the domain of national security is very real. It can easily become an excuse for restricting embarrassing political revelations. In addition, as David Kretzmer has pointed out, the Israeli commitment to a Jewish state entails the use of a concept of security that encompasses broader considerations than direct threats to the physical security of the state. "Acts that strengthen the Jewish collective are perceived as acts that promote security. On the other hand, acts that tend to strengthen Arab nationalist aspirations among Israeli Arabs are regarded as threatening to the Jewish collective. They are seen as acts that ultimately affect the security of the state, even if they take the form of political expression." Kretzmer, *The Legal Status of the Arabs in Israel*, p. 136.

the foreign sources of interpretive assistance. My purpose is not to suggest anything as simplistic as that there is a causal relationship between American sources and Israeli outcomes; rather, it is to inquire into the value of constitutional theory to constitutional adjudication where the two have evolved in separate and different political contexts. Toward this end I look at three related dimensions of constitutional jurisprudence that have figured prominently in recent American constitutional theory and contemporary Israeli judicial practice: (1) the prescription for an aspirational judicial role in which the Supreme Court pursues just, coherent constitutional outcomes expressive of the best that is within a people as a community of principle; (2) the priority within the aspirational agenda of strengthening and expanding the constitutional protections surrounding individual rights; and (3) the adoption by the Supreme Court of a self-consciously pedagogic role as part of the advancement of a democratic political agenda. When examining them in the context of the two jurisprudentially salient features that distinguish the Israeli and American polities—the alternative pluralist political contexts in which constitutional adjudication is situated, and the absence in Israel of a comprehensive written constitution (and relatedly, the minimal formal authority possessed by the Supreme Court to exercise judicial review over legislation)—there emerges an intriguing development: while there is an awkward fit between American constitutional theory and Israeli constitutional reality, the former has a potentially useful role in the Court's participation as a partner in the making of a constitution.

THEORY AND PRACTICE

The role of the courts—particularly the Supreme Court—in American politics has been debated for as long as there have been courts in American politics. The institution of judicial review made this debate inevitable, for it meant that among the branches of the national government, one was destined to stand out as "deviant," at variance with the accountability principle of republican government, the regime's ultimate legitimating principle. Thus the Court's legitimacy required that its policy-making activity be circumscribed (while seen as an awkward, if necessary, consequence of judicial review) or, on the other hand, unapologetically defended as an essential countermajoritarian guarantor of individual liberties. The history of American constitutional jurisprudence consists in large measure of an ongoing intellectual struggle between these two contending positions.

In Israel, where, as we have seen, judicial review over legislation has not as yet been institutionalized, the controversy over the exercise of judicial power focuses less on the question of legitimacy, and much more on the issue of institutional equality, namely whether the Court should be granted the authority to exercise constitutional review over legislative enactments. Indeed, it is in part to avoid the divisiveness of a dispute over legitimacy that some who are opposed to the adoption of the American practice have developed their arguments. Nevertheless, in the absence of broad powers of judicial review the Israeli Supreme Court has embraced a role not altogether dissimilar to that of its American counterpart. It has often aggressively pursued a rights-oriented agenda that occasionally places it at odds with the Knesset. In fact, this role appears to be played with greater consistency than in the United States, where the activity of the Court is more subject to the vicissitudes of national politics.

This was not always the case; the early history of the Israeli Court reveals an institution much less venturesome in its pursuit of an independent role. The justices, for the most part, studiously sought to avoid controversy, a goal that could best be accomplished by pursuing the most formalistic jurisprudential path available to them. To some extent, as Pnina Lahav has argued, this conservative style resulted from the fact that the justices of the first Court were "members of the establishment" and therefore inclined toward judicial modesty.[20] But in large part it may be accounted for by the unique legal circumstances attendant the origins of the state, in which various layers of different law—Ottoman, Mandatory, British common law, and religious (Jewish, Muslim, and Christian)—continued, in varying degrees, to remain in force. The Law and Administration Ordinance of 1948 incorporated Palestinian law in effect on the date of independence. One of the main consequences of this was the heavy reliance by judges in the early years on English common law.[21] In time, however, the need to establish an indigenous Israeli law was increasingly felt, leading to a loosening of the binding nature of British precedents, a displacement of many prestate laws with new Knesset-passed legislation, and perhaps most important for the

[20] Pnina Lahav, "The Supreme Court of Israel: Formative Years, 1948–1955," *Studies in Zionism* 11 (1990): 53.

[21] Article 46 of the Palestine Order-in-Council of 1922 had assumed that local statute law was incomplete and thus in need of fortification from external law, namely English common law and equity. This provision was retained in the 1948 law. See in this regard G. Tedeschi and Y. S. Zemach, "Codification and Case Law in Israel," in *The Role of Judicial Decisions and Doctrine in Civil and Mixed Jurisdictions*, ed. Joseph Dainow (Baton Rouge: Louisiana State University Press, 1974).

long term, a gradual departure from the relatively passive judicial role characteristic of judges in the British common law tradition. In 1958, for example, Justice Agranat seemed to be encouraging a more aggressive judicial role by emphasizing language in the Law and Administration Ordinance that stipulated that prestate law would apply in the new regime "subject to such qualifications as local circumstances render necessary."[22] "The court must use the English law definition only to glean therefrom the underlying principle but, having done that it must apply the principle to the special conditions prevailing in Israel and in accordance with the concepts and views of Israeli society."[23]

In some areas of the law—particularly public law and administration—American legal precedents were held to be pertinent to the special conditions prevailing in Israel. An Israeli scholar noted in 1966 "the marked and growing predilection of our Supreme Court for the transatlantic version of the common law."[24] He demonstrated the increasing reliance of the Court on American authorities and the corollary decline in British influence. "Apart from the courts of the United States, the Israel Supreme Court possibly makes more frequent use of American jurisprudence than any other court in the common law world."[25] This trend has accelerated, in spite of the fact that Israel's "unwritten constitution" suggests a much greater similarity to the British system than to the American. The reason is simple: American law and jurisprudence provide a richer and more highly

---

[22] Jordan B. Cherrick, " 'Constitutional' Adjudication in Israel? The High Court Speaks Out for Prisoner' Rights," *International and Comparative Law Quarterly* 30 (1981): 839.

[23] *Stern* v. *Shamir*, 12 P.D. 421, 427 (1958), as quoted in Daniel Friedmann, "Independent Development of Israel Law," *Israel Law Review* 10 (1975): 519. It is worth noting that Israeli judges have been much more inclined than their English counterparts to resolve legal questions in accordance with principles of natural justice, although the term has evolved in a very strict sense, denoting, for the most part, the fair hearing and impartiality requirements in administrative proceedings and action.

[24] A. M. Apelbom, "Common Law à l'Americaine," *Israel Law Review* 1 (1966): 565. See also U. Yadin, "Judicial Lawmaking in Israel," in Dainow, *The Role of Judicial Decisions and Doctrine in Civil Law and in Mixed Jurisdictions*, p. 298. Yadin points out that the leading Israeli case in which judicial independence was proclaimed, *Cohavi* v. *Beker*, 11 P.D. 225 (1959), referred extensively to the corresponding development, in its time, in the United States.

[25] Apelbom, "Common Law à l'Americaine," p. 565. Apelbom was unable to find one instance where the Palestine Court, the Mandatory predecessor of the Supreme Court, had cited an American authority. In the first years of its existence the new Court cited American sources in approximately 2 percent of its cases, a figure that has steadily increased in subsequent years. Of course English case law, on the whole, is still cited more frequently than American case law.

developed model of a legal system committed to the enforcement of individual rights and a more fully articulated judicial philosophy devoted to the support of that commitment. As A. M. Apelbom has suggested, the very freedom to draw on American sources finds legitimation in a tradition whose commitment to binding precedent is, in contrast to other common law experience, more qualified.[26] American law provided attractive alternatives when the application of an English rule seemed undesirable, while also providing jurisprudential grounds for departing from the rule.

An additional attraction of the American system for Israeli judges is its hospitality to legal scholarship. Unlike judiciaries where the local legal culture does not encourage the use of academic writings in the adjudication of cases, judicial opinions in the United States and Israel are often liberally sprinkled with such references. Typical citations will involve analyses of technical legal questions, but frequently one encounters works of broader theoretical import. For example, the landmark 1953 Israeli civil liberties case *"Kol Ha'am" v. Minister of Interior* is well known for its extensive reliance on Zechariah Chafee's writings. Recent opinions make it clear that for at least some Israeli judges, especially those inclined toward broadening the boundaries of individual rights protection, the extensive American literature in constitutional theory is a subject of more than casual interest.

While it is risky to write in the singular about a complex subject such as American constitutional jurisprudence, I would argue that over the last twenty-five years or so a dominant school has existed in the United States, one advancing a model of the Supreme Court as a critical agent for principled social change of the sort that is measurable in terms of an expanding domain of individual rights. It is, for the most part, an activist Court that has been given theoretical justification. Although some within this school, most notably Ronald Dworkin, resist the activist label, objectively the judicial implications that flow from their analyses place them well within the activist side of the traditional activism/self-restraint dichotomy.[27]

There are very different kinds of activists; what serves as a common thread is an interpretive stance that views the Constitution as an instrument through which the courts have a responsibility to facilitate the realization of the nation's highest aspirations, aspirations that bear a striking

[26] Ibid., p. 576.

[27] See, for example, Bradley C. Canon, "A Framework for the Analysis of Judicial Activism," in *Supreme Court Activism and Restraint*, ed. Stephen C. Halpern and Charles M. Lamb (Lexington, Mass.: D.C. Heath & Co., 1982). Canon enumerates six dimensions for the assessment of judicial activism that, when applied to Dworkin's work, reveal an unmistakable pattern of judicial activism.

resemblance to the liberal, democratic prescriptions of contemporary moral philosophy. For Arthur S. Miller, a prolific and unabashed defender of the activist view, "The Constitution is always in a state of 'becoming,' always being brought up to date to meet the successive exigencies faced by the American people."[28] This notion, that the Constitution is a document to be shaped by judges in light of social needs, suggests a legislative and discretionary role distasteful to theorists such as Dworkin, whose denial of judicial discretion is predicated on the assumption that judicial statesmanship is a matter of discerning the contemporary implications of a principled and determinate Constitution. This leads Dworkin to view "activism [as] a virulent form of legal pragmatism."[29] Judges who practice it may rightly be seen as "impos[ing] on other branches of government [their] own view of what justice demands. Law as integrity [Dworkin's most recent formulation of his jurisprudential position] condemns activism."[30]

The emphatic rejection of judicial activism is more pronounced in Dworkin's recent writing than in his earlier work. Yet in matters of *stare decisis*, original intent, and deference to popularly created law, Dworkin fits, protestations to the contrary notwithstanding, unambiguously within the activist tradition. His recommended approach for judges is "constructive interpretation," which is the obligation "to make the object or practice being interpreted the best it can be."[31] The interpretive ideal of "integrity" requires that one locate some coherent set of principles about people's "rights and duties" for the purpose of providing the political community with its best possible constitutional outcome.[32] To be sure, these principles must have at least some "purchase in American history and culture;"[33] but this apparent constraint will not likely convince Dworkin's critics, even some of his more sympathetic ones, that he has, as he insists, avoided judicial discretion. For example, Justice Barak, whose jurisprudential orientation has many Dworkinian features, claims, in a recent book, to be unconvinced by Dworkin's assertions about discretion.[34]

[28] Arthur S. Miller, "In Defense of Judicial Activism," in Halpern and Lamb, *Supreme Court Activism and Restraint*, p. 169.

[29] Ronald Dworkin, *Law's Empire* (Cambridge: Harvard University Press, 1986), p. 378.

[30] Ibid.

[31] Ibid., p. 77.

[32] Ibid., p. 225.

[33] Ibid., p. 377.

[34] Barak, *Judicial Discretion*, p. 30. As a judge in a constitutional system framed by principles that are at least in tension with one another, Barak's critique of Dworkin, while meant to apply to all legal systems, is certainly understandable. "One often finds several conflicting principles that apply to a given problem. Principles tend to come in pairs of

The aspirational dimension is also present in the work of other contemporary constitutional theorists, for example, Michael Perry, Sotirios Barber, Sanford Levinson, and David Richards.[35] Perry's observation is illustrative: "What the constitutional text means to us . . . (in addition to the original meaning), are certain basic constitutive aspirations or principles or ideals of the American political community and tradition."[36] As the institution best situated and constituted to express these aspirations, the Supreme Court, in the view of these theorists, should assume a major part of the burden for advancing their achievement. To perform this task, however, presumes the existence of an "interpretive community." Again Perry: "In what sense and to what extent is American society a true political community, a 'judging community,' notwithstanding its morally pluralistic character? In the sense and to the extent the various moral communities that together constitute the pluralistic society share certain basic aspirations as to how the collective life, the life in common, should be lived. There *are* such shared aspirations: for example, the freedoms of speech, press, and religion, due process of law, and equal protection of the laws."[37]

The aspirations that are shared by members of this pluralistic community collectively constitute a rights-based jurisprudential ethic. It is the ethic extending from the moral supposition that all people are entitled to be treated with equal concern and respect, and is a hallmark of much contemporary constitutionalist understanding. While there is a substantive component that can be readily associated with these collective aspirations, in practice their fulfillment is found in a public authority that is to be officially neutral with respect to competing social visions and goals—that is, in the language of the First Amendment doctrine implicit within them, content-neutral.

The liberal, individualist premises that are at the core of this constitutional theory present a challenge to those operating within the political

---

opposites. How is the judge to decide among the opposing principles? Doesn't he have discretion in this situation?" (p. 32). As we shall see in the case of Justice Barak, when the conflicting principles are those emanating from the Declaration of Independence, he is inclined to exercise his discretion in favor of the democratic principle.

[35] Michael J. Perry, *Morality, Politics, and Law: A Bicentennial Essay* (Oxford: Oxford University Press, 1988); Sotirios A. Barber, *On What the Constitution Means* (Baltimore: Johns Hopkins University Press, 1984); Sanford Levinson, *Constitutional Faith* (Princeton: Princeton University Press, 1988); David A. J. Richards, *Toleration and the Constitution* (Oxford: Oxford University Press, 1986).

[36] Perry, *Morality, Politics, and Law*, p. 133.

[37] Ibid., p. 154.

framework of a pluralist universe that incorporates a vision of an extended community in which collective needs and visions often take precedence over individual ones. Political democracy in Israel depends, to be sure, on the guarantee of civil rights to all Israelis, but it also entails, among other things, the acceptance of the right of nonassimilating groups to their separate identities. The contrast with the United States is highlighted by Dworkin, who observes that "interpretive theories are by their nature addressed to a particular legal culture, generally the culture to which their authors belong."[38] It is altogether fitting, therefore, that when *he* addresses the issue of community and its relation to the problem of interpretation, he argues that "the idea of special communal responsibilities holding within a large, anonymous community smacks of nationalism, or even racism, both of which have been sources of very great suffering and injustice."[39] For Dworkin, such organic variables as religion, language, and ethnicity are peripheral factors that require vigilant attention by those who understand the latent potential for injustice within these necessarily exclusivist categories.

Constitutionalism in Israel must take these troublesome aspects of community more seriously. The United States was founded in order to pursue the liberal ideal of political freedom; on the other hand, the establishment of Israel, while also officially linked to this ideal, cannot be separated from the goal of fulfilling the national aspirations of the Jewish people. Constitutional law—indeed, law in general—must somehow reconcile liberal and communitarian precepts that are not nearly so accommodating to each other as they are in the United States. It is a matter of "internaliz[ing] concepts of individual rights in a society that placed priority on the collective."[40] What sets the context, then, for constitutional adjudication in Israel

---

[38] Dworkin, *Law's Empire*, p. 102. Of Dworkin's own theory it has been said that "it remains a theory that . . . fits only one particular society; it is not a theory that must necessarily be found in all legal systems." Philip Soper, "Dworkin's Domain," *Harvard Law Review* 100 (1987): 1182.

[39] Dworkin, *Law's Empire*, p. 196.

[40] Lahav, "The Supreme Court of Israel," p. 56. This refers, according to Lahav, to more than the need to pursue the political revival of the Jewish people. It also pertains to ideological issues involving the concept of the state, for, as she puts it, "The founders could not decide whether the collective existed for the individual or the individual was part of the collective, existing for its sake and deferring to its dictates" (p. 63). In a more recent article, Lahav discusses the jurisprudential tensions between "catastrophe" and "utopian" Zionism. The goal of the first is defense against the external threats to the Jewish people, a goal sharply contrasting with the messianic and liberal objectives of the second. However, at the time of the establishment of the state a strong collectivist theme united all Zionist ideologies. "The belief

are the dual, and occasionally conflicting, aspirations represented in its founding document. To see this more clearly I have chosen to focus on a specific case, not because it necessarily represents the prevailing thrust of Israeli public law, but because it reveals the attraction of American constitutional theory for Israeli constitutional practice, and because it illuminates both the benefits and pitfalls of relying on that theory.

The "Spacious View": Access to the Political Process

In 1984 the Israeli Supreme Court reversed two decisions of the Central Elections Committee for the Eleventh Knesset. It invalidated rulings by that body to exclude the right-wing "Kach" list (headed by the controversial Rabbi Kahane) and the left-wing "Progressive Peace" list from participation in the elections to the Knesset. The exclusions had been based on the following grounds: in the case of the Kach list, its racist and antidemocratic principles were seen as contravening the Declaration of Independence by denying the "basic foundations of the democratic regime in Israel"; and in the case of the Progressive Peace list, its principles (as propounded by some people who allegedly identified with enemies of the state) were also seen to conflict with the Declaration in that they threatened the existence of Israel as a Jewish state. The various opinions of the Court focused on two key issues, the authority of the committee to exclude lists under the Knesset Elections Law, and the import of a crucial precedent of the Court handed down twenty years earlier in a similar exclusion case, in this instance involving an illegal radical Arab list. The Court's treatment of the issues in *Neiman and Avneri v. Chairman of the Central Elections Committee for the Eleventh Knesset*[41] enables us to pursue an argument begun in the conclusion of the previous chapter: an activist judiciary functioning in a political context that is structurally and philosophically opposed to the doctrine of judicial finality is not as vulnerable to the sort of criticism that regularly surfaces in polities, such as the American, where the doctrine has been more readily assimilated into the nation's constitutional culture.

---

in the right of the Jewish people to political self-determination burned in the hearts of all Zionists. This set of beliefs operated as well against individualism and against the liberal conception of political and civil liberties. The community . . . stood above the individual." Pnina Lahav, "Foundations of Rights Jurisprudence in Israel: Chief Justice Agranat's Legacy," *Israel Law Review* 24 (1990): 221.

   [41] 39 (2) P.D. 225 (1984).

The Silence of the Legislature

If the power of judicial review were to disappear from the American political scene, it would not reduce the Supreme Court to impotence. The Court
would still retain the policy-making potential of statutory interpretation,
and the chances are that it would develop more imaginative ways to exploit
this power. This has certainly been the case in Israel, where the Court, as in
the United States, is widely recognized as an important player in domestic
politics.

In *Neiman*, the statute under which the Elections Committee (chaired
by a member of the Supreme Court) exercised its power to exclude the two
lists made no explicit provision for exclusion based on a list's platform or
objectives. This had been the main point of contention in the earlier case
(*Yardor v. Chairman of the Central Election Committee for the Sixth
Knesset*),[42] in which the majority (Justices Agranat and Sussman) found
nothing improper in the committee's reliance on an implicit statutory authorization, and the minority opinion of Justice Cohn insisted that in the
absence of any express language, the committee was limited in its confir-
mation power to reviewing only the formal qualifying conditions laid out in
the statute. Much of the focus in *Neiman* was on the outcome in the earlier
case.

The chairman of the Elections Committee in 1964 was Justice Landau,
who, as we have seen, has since become the most outspoken opponent of
adopting a bill of rights and extending the scope of judicial review. In his
ruling banning the Arab list, many of whose members belonged to an illegal
organization that denied the very existence of the state of Israel, he argued
that "we may read into the Elections Law an implied condition that an
illegal organization cannot be confirmed as a list."[43] Justice Cohn's dissent
in *Yardor* presented a positivistic defense of individual rights, an insistance
that the deprivation of a right could only result from specific legislation
passed by the legislature. The opinion recalls John Marshall's observation
that "when rights are infringed, when fundamental principles are over-
thrown, where the general system of the laws is departed from, the legislative intention must be expressed with irresistable clearness."[44] Justice
Cohn went on to repudiate any "natural law" approach that might be used

---

[42] 19 P.D. 365 (1965).

[43] Ibid., 373.

[44] *United States v. Fisher*, 6 U.S. (2 Cranch) 358, 390 (1805).

to fill the silence of the legislature, claiming that "those are not the ways of the State of Israel."[45]

Justice Sussman's view was different. He too posed the question of "whether the Committee may inquire into the qualification of the list according to an unwritten principle of law [the right of self-defense]."[46] His judgment that it did have this prerogative was emphasized in comparative terms: "If it is so in a country with a written constitution [the specific reference was to the Federal Republic of Germany], it is so, *a fortiori*, in a country which does not have a written constitution."[47] Why should this difference matter? Justice Sussman's opinion does not make this very clear, but elsewhere he provides an answer: "[The] superiority of the Israeli legislature, which is not constrained by a formal written constitution, justifies, in my view, this conclusion regarding the work of the courts: the judicial restraint in favor of which Justices of the United States Supreme Court preached, lest the national patterns be determined by people whom the public did not choose, and the Congress be powerless, this restraint is unnecessary in Israel, whose legislature is all-powerful."[48] The implication is that a judicial appeal to "supraconstitutional rules" has greater justification in a legal system where the final judgment as to the operative constitutional rules resides in the legislature than in a system where, practically speaking, the decisions of the Supreme Court in constitutional matters possess the attribute of finality. There is, then, a paradox: the constraints imposed on the courts by the constitutional principle of parliamentary supremacy legitimates a more active role for the courts in construing the law. Thus, even in regard to a principle of natural law, the Knesset can eliminate unwritten law as a source for judicial decisions by the simple act of legislation, in the case at hand, by expressly delineating the jurisdiction of the Elections Committee. In the United States, where the First or Fourteenth Amendments would control the question of electoral access to the political system, the Supreme Court, so the argument might go, would (or should) have less freedom to maneuver within the interstices or silences of the (written constitutional) law.

In the two decades between *Yardor* and *Neiman* the Knesset did nothing in legislative response to the 1964 decision to uphold the Elections Committee. A unanimous Court invalidated the committee's 1984 rulings, with

---

[45] *Yardor*, 19 P.D. at 382. Cohn, it is worth noting, did not always proceed down the positivist path.

[46] Ibid., 389.

[47] Ibid., 390.

[48] Quoted in Barak, *Judicial Discretion*, p. 194.

a majority of the five justices who participated deciding that, absent any specific legislative authorization, the only permissible substantive ground for disqualifying a list by the committee was if, as in *Yardor*, the list advocated the cessation of the existence of the state. As the president of the Court, Justice Shamgar, wrote, "Only an extreme situation permits judicial quasi-legislation beyond the written text."[49] As reprehensible as the platforms of the two lists in question were, they did not go this far, and so they could not be prevented from participating in the election. The precedent, in other words, was to be limited to the specific set of extreme circumstances confronted by the earlier Court.

However, the specific character of those extreme circumstances are subject to differing interpretations. For example, one can read Justice Agranat's opinion in *Yardor* as having given somewhat broader authority to the committee than the Court suggested it did in *Neiman*. Agranat had argued that the case was controlled by a specific "constitutional postulate," which, while involving the principle of self-defense, appeared to extend the principle beyond the fact of bare physical preservation.

> There can be no doubt—and this is clearly learnt from the statements made in the Declaration of the Establishment of the State—that Israel is not only a sovereign, independent and peace-loving state characterized by a regime of the people's government, but was also established as "a Jewish State in Eretz-Israel," for the act of its establishment was effected first and foremost by virtue of "the natural and historic right of the Jewish people to live as any independent nation in its own sovereign state, and that act was a realization of the aspirations of generations to the redemption of Israel."[50]

It is routine for the Court, particularly in recent years, to appeal to the Declaration of Independence as an aid in statutory construction; generally, however, its appeal is to the paragraph referring to individual rights. Here Agranat invokes an alternative section of the Declaration, one that, as we have seen, exists in some tension with the more frequently adverted to paragraph. Why, then, did the *Neiman* Court gloss over the issue of the Jewishness of the state and focus instead on the question of its existence? Was it simply that the existence of the state naturally presupposed its Jewish character?

The answer is perhaps contained in the opinion of Justice Barak, who is commonly viewed as the most activist Israeli Supreme Court justice. Barak

[49] *Neiman and Avneri*, 39 (2) P.D. at 243.
[50] *Yardor*, 19 P.D. at 385.

proposed a much more expansive interpretation of the committee's discretionary authority than anyone else. Accordingly, not only does the committee have the right to refuse to confirm a list because its platform denies the existence of the state, but it may also disqualify a list that denies the democratic character of the state—as long as there is a "reasonable possibility" that its ideas will be realized.[51] Thus, the Court may either narrow or broaden the statutory language, its choice in this regard being dictated by its assessment of what is required in the individual case to "realize the principles of our legal system."[52]

Justice Barak arrived at this determination with the assistance of the U.S. Constitution, which, he pointed out, has been held by a line of judges from Marshall to Holmes to Frankfurter to demand a "spacious view."[53] The laws regulating Knesset elections in Israel should be viewed as fundamental constitutional provisions subject to similar interpretive rules. Statutory silence is no bar to the Court's construing the law "in light of the Declaration of Independence, which expresses 'the vision and creed of the people.' "[54] Moreover, Barak's discussion makes it clear that this interpretive source is available to the Court both in the instance where the statutory language is ambiguous and inconclusive, as well as in the situation at hand, where the silence of the statute is clear in its meaning.

In making sense of all of this, the first thing to note is that, whatever disagreements they might have had, all the justices decided in the end to uphold the right of the lists to participate in the electoral process. In this case, both narrow and broad statutory construction led to a rights-oriented result, although a different judge applying Justice Barak's approach could easily have withheld the right to electoral participation. (Indeed, Justice Beisky indicated that the correct application of his colleague's interpretive stance should result in the exclusion of the Kach list.) This is not likely to happen, however, because in most cases the effect of a "spacious interpretation" that opens up the "democratic" paragraph of the Declaration as a source for judicial application is to expand the protections for individual rights. On the other hand, opening up those parts that affirm the Jewishness of the state are not so easily limited to protecting individual rights. This recalls the selective interpretation of the Declaration evident in Justice Barak's *Schnitzer* opinion. It is therefore not surprising that a majority in *Neiman*, abjuring in this instance the temptation to engage in an expan-

[51] *Neiman and Avneri*, 39 (2) P.D. at 315.

[52] Ibid., 306.

[53] Ibid.

[54] Ibid., 307.

sive statutory interpretation, would avoid characterization of the state's existence in terms that are potentially in tension with what many consider to be the primary role of the contemporary Israeli Court—to serve as guardian of the democratic component of Israeli democracy. Judicial activism in Israel, in short, means pursuing the rights-oriented implications of the Declaration of Independence; as a result, American constitutional theory has a very seductive appeal.

The Derivation of Constitutional Principles

"A statutory provision or judicial rule that limits a right is not interpreted broadly but rather, to the contrary, their proper interpretation is restrictive and pedantic."[55] Such is the interpretive orthodoxy expressed in *Neiman* by Justice Shamgar. On the other hand, the derivation of fundamental rights, such as the right to take part in elections, demands broad interpretive power: "Our conception of the law in effect in Israel is that it encompasses fundamental rules as regards the existence and protection of personal liberties, even if the bill of Basic Law: Civil and Personal Rights has not yet been enacted."[56] Thus, the silence of the legislator may not lead to the curtailment of rights; a similar silence need not prevent the judicial assertion and enforcement of rights.

Israeli judges tend to take rights seriously. Indeed, it is fitting that Justice Shamgar began his inquiry into the question of whether the committee may impose additional restrictions on the right to participate in Knesset elections by appealing to constitutional principles, specifically by quoting Ronald Dworkin: "Judicial decisions, even in hard cases, should be generated by principles not policy."[57] This is a distinction that lies at the core of Dworkin's prescriptions for an active judiciary. Policies establish goals to be reached by the community; they tend to follow from utilitarian calculations of aggregate good. Principles are different in that their validation depends not on popular approval but on their consistency with a coherent theory of political justice; as such they tend to be protective of the rights of the minority. Shamgar wisely does not commit himself to a blanket endorsement of the Dworkin approach, perhaps recognizing that such an embrace will at some point have to confront the tradition of parliamentary superiority. But his approach, at least in this case, is consistent in all important respects with Dworkin's.

[55] Ibid., 245.
[56] Ibid., 261.
[57] Ibid., 259.

Justice Shamgar has been an outspoken advocate for a written constitution, whose "absence in our system is conspicuous each time a constitutional issue arises in a legal proceeding."[58] Thus, it would be preferable if "the *constitutional* principles defining . . . fundamental rights be given explicit expression."[59] Yet in the absence of such express provision a judge must still, as Chief Justice Warren used to say, do the right thing. Here that involves establishing the right to participate in elections as a *fundamental* political right expressing the idea of equality, the essence of a democratic society. As a fundamental right, it possesses "superior legal status," which is why in the Israeli system any restriction of the right is contingent on explicit statutory language. In the American system such statutory language would (except in extreme circumstances) be trumped when confronted with a right of this elevated standing.[60] Therefore, to a much greater extent than in the United States, judicial activism in defense of the superior legal status of particular rights is a matter of creative statutory interpretation.

One can well imagine that this state of affairs would lead Israeli judges to look with envy on their American counterparts. "Everyone agrees," Justice Barak has said, "that in a constitutional government that recognizes judicial review of the constitutionality of a statute, the final decision about the fundamental values is in the hands of the court."[61] But the American judge, especially one following Dworkin's principled approach, might respond: "My job is both easier and more difficult than yours. We agree in the supremacy of constitutional principles—in their critical importance for resolving hard cases in the law. We also agree that equal concern and respect is the background assumption of the political system and therefore the principal source for deriving the content of our constitutional principles. Unfortunately for me, a Herculean effort is often necessary to demonstrate that these principles are actually in the Constitution. The text of the document is rarely conclusive, and I can always count on someone to provide evidence revealing a contrary intent behind the language. I can

---

[58] Ibid., 261.

[59] Ibid.

[60] President Shamgar does use language that could be interpreted to carry an implicit threat of judicial review. "It is clear that this Court will not intrude into the area of the legislature, but it is proper to stress again the caution that is required in this matter, lest any potential legislation makes a change in directions in a manner that we do not intend." Ibid., 278.

[61] Barak, *Judicial Discretion*, p. 199.

usually come up with strong counterarguments, but believe me, it's a struggle. How nice it would be if I could invent the Constitution as I went along, appealing to those moral and political principles that best comport with our contemporary sensibilities about democracy."

The Israeli judge would no doubt resist the notion that he or she was free to invent the Constitution; but there is a sense in which the idea is hardly preposterous. For example, Israelis frequently allude to a "judicial bill of rights," referring by that term to those liberties enjoying legal status by virtue of their recognition in judicial interpretation. A more general way of putting this is that in important ways Supreme Court justices in Israel are the coauthors of the text that they are interpreting. An American judge can go through all sorts of elaborate jurisprudential contortions to discover a right to privacy in a Constitution that makes no explicit provision for it. Critics will then have a field day condemning the judge for an improper act of judicial legislation, for in effect rewriting the Constitution. It will also be noted that this action is rendered even more problematic by the fact that the Court is presumed (rightly or wrongly) to speak with finality in constitutional matters. In the face of a similar act of judicial legislation in Israel, the critic's task will be more complicated. The judge there cannot be accused of rewriting a text (in the case of rights) that does not exist. And to the inevitable charge that the Court in creating such a right is usurping the authority of the Knesset, it can simply be pointed out that it is a strange, or at any rate benign, usurpation that can last only as long as the victimized body accepts through its own inaction the act perpetrated against it.

From this one could infer that while there may be very good reasons for legislative passage of a bill of rights, it is by no means clear that enhancing the authority of the Court is one of them. Certainly in the case of a right that is explicitly grounded in the text of a written constitution, the ability of a court to cite specific language from the fundamental law no doubt enhances the legitimacy of any action based on it. In this sense it *is* preferable, as Justice Shamgar averred, that explicit provision be given constitutional principles defining fundamental rights. But the experience of the United States is instructive, in that most of the controversy concerning the Court's role in American politics centers on the judicial derivation and enforcement of rights that are nowhere enumerated in the Constitution. The literature in contemporary constitutional theory—much of it outlining one or another aspirational interpretive approach—is as extensive as it is for a good reason, the need to defend activity that for many is so deeply troubling. Thus the observation (which amounts really to a complaint) of someone like Justice John Marshall Harlan requires an answer: "[I] know of nothing which entitles this Court to pick out particular human activities, characterize them as 'fundamental,' and give them added protection."[62]

Of course, as those familiar with Justice Harlan's significant contributions to substantive due process analysis well know, the justice was himself not reluctant to provide constitutional protection for unenumerated fundamental rights. He was also emphatically of the mind, despite section five of the Fourteenth Amendment, that the Court's power to define the substantive scope of due process and equal protection was final.[63] It was a conjunction of positions that stimulated Sanford Levinson aptly to consider Harlan the quintessential "Catholic" judge.[64] While he was also an eloquent exponent of judicial self-restraint, Harlan's "Catholic" understanding of a supreme judiciary possessed of the authority to define fundamental rights that are not textually explicit highlights the dilemma of constitutional interpretation in democratic regimes, a dilemma that fundamental rights theorists—especially in these relativistic times—have been notably unsuccessful in resolving.[65] There is no reason to think that Israeli practitioners

---

[62] *Shapiro* v. *Thompson*, 394 U.S. 618, 662 (1969) (dissenting opinion). Or as Justice Powell wrote for the Court in one of its most important equal protection cases, "It is not the province of this Court to create substantive constitutional rights in the name of guaranteeing equal protection of the laws. Thus, the key to discovering whether education is 'fundamental' . . . lies in assessing whether there is a right to education explicitly or implicitly guaranteed by the Constitution." *San Antonio Independent School District* v. *Rodriguez*, 411 U.S. 1, 33–34 (1973). Justice Harlan's criticism of the fundamental rights approach can be turned against him in assessing his concurring opnion in one of the cases cited by Justice Shamgar in *Neiman*, *Williams* v. *Rhodes*, 393 U.S. 23 (1968). The Supreme Court ruled unconstitutional an Ohio election law that made it exceedingly difficult for minority parties to satisfy ballot access requirements. In his dissent, Justice Stewart disputed Harlan's claim about the right of political association.

[63] *Katzenbach* v. *Morgan*, 384 U.S. 641 (1966) (dissenting opinion).

[64] Levinson, *Constitutional Faith*, p. 34.

[65] On this point see Paul Brest, "The Fundamental Rights Controversy: The Essential Contradictions of Normative Constitutional Scholarship," *Yale Law Journal* 90 (1981). In Israel it is not only the secular democrat on the Court who is inclined to follow a fundamental rights approach. The Jewish law tradition also encourages a noninterpretive approach. As Menachem Elon, Jewish law scholar and Israeli Supreme Court justice, points out, interpretation in Jewish law is called *Midrash*, "a word deriving from the verb *darosh*, meaning study and investigation of the inner and logical meaning of a particular text as opposed to its plain and literal reading." Menachem Elon, "Interpretation," in *The Principles of Jewish Law*, ed., Menachem Elon (Jerusalem: Keter Publishing House, 1974), p. 58. Thus while the sources for determining fundamental rights may differ (as well as overlap on occasion) among secular and nonsecular judges, the propensity for abandoning a narrow textual approach is common to both.

of constitutional law will be any more successful than their American counterparts. But in the absence of any major changes in the constitutional
system, the judges in Israel may not be pressed as hard to do so. It is, after
all, hard to be a Catholic judge in the Jewish state.

Balancing

"Would the State of Israel without the Declaration of Independence be the
same State of Israel?"[66] Justice Barak raised this question at the outset of his
effort to demonstrate why the committee should have the authority to
disqualify a list that threatens the democratic character of the state. It is
the sort of question that political philosophers have raised since at least as
far back as Aristotle. In the judicial context it inevitably leads to a heightened political profile for the judge who is willing to pursue all of its implications.

One can readily understand the Court majority's reluctance to confront a
question—the character of Israeli democracy—that is potentially so politically devisive. Confining the inquiry to the existence of the state is clearly a
safer strategy as far as the institutional prestige of the Court is concerned.
This is not to say that such a confinement is a guarantee against controversy;
the Court must still evaluate the Committee's ruling against its own assessment of the actual threat to the state's existence posed by the participation
of a particular list, and of course many people will very likely differ with its
assessment. Moreover, they may differ with the standard that the Court
applies to its judgment of the facts. Justice Shamgar, for example, adopted
the standard of *proximate certainty* (following an opinion of Justice Barak in
an earlier case) to evaluate the situation in *Neiman*. In his own evaluation,
Barak adopted instead the less strict test of *reasonable probability*, arguing
that his colleague's choice is more appropriate in the context of a specific
event rather than in the context of a comprehensive social system.

The process involved here, of balancing a variety of rights and interests,
is one that has come to be identified in Israel with Justice Barak, who, in a
series of opinions, has elaborated at length on the judicial considerations
involved in this approach.[67] Actually for Barak it is probably more accurate
to view balancing less as an approach (implying choice) than as an unavoid-

[66] *Neiman and Avneri*, 39 (2) P.D. at 314.

[67] See, for example, his opinions in these cases: *Kahane v. Broadcasting Authority*, 41 (3)
P.D. 255 (1986); *Laor v. Film and Play Supervisory Board*, 41(1) P.D. 421 (1986); *Sa'ar v.
Minister of Interior*, 34 (2) P.D. 169 (1979); and *Barzilai v. Government of Israel*, 40 (3) P.D.
505 (1986). And of course balancing was also a prominent part of the discussion in *Schnitzer*.

able adjudicatory task.[68] It is a task, however, from which he has shown little evidence of shying away. "When the judge encounters contradictory fundamental principles of his system—e.g., the existence of the State and the freedom of expression and vote—he must take them all into account. The judge must pose the principles together and give each its proper weight, and having done so he must balance the various principles."[69]

While the act of balancing may be viewed as a natural extension of the judicial function, it has understandably raised concerns about the subjective factor in judicial decision making. "Balancing has its dangers. It requires judges to find, define, articulate, and justify the weights given to interests and values out of very few straws. Balancing expands judicial discretion, frees it substantially from the need to justify and persuade."[70] Another familiar criticism is that "it appears to transfer to the judicial branch a method of decision making more properly reserved for the legislative branch."[71] Interestingly, the earliest critiques of balancing had judicial self-restraint as their target, often singling out Justice Frankfurter for his practice of deferring to the balancing done by the legislature.[72] They also found the balancing test weighted against individual rights; constitutional protections were diminished as a result of the tendentious way in which competing interests were often defined. In time, however, the criticisms changed direction; the balancing that was at the heart of the Warren Court's equal protection approach, in which the Court identified certain fundamental interests and measured them against competing state interests, became the focus of those who were alarmed at the accretion of power to the Court in recent decades.

The fact that balancing is typically presented in the language of moderation and reasonableness cannot belie that fact that it has become one of the

[68] *Neiman and Avneri*, 39 (2) P.D. at 309.

[69] Ibid., 308–9.

[70] Louis Henkin, "Infallibility Under Law: Constitutional Balancing," *Columbia Law Review* 78 (1978): 1047–48.

[71] Patrick M. McFadden, "The Balancing Test," *Boston College Law Review* 29 (1988): 641.

[72] "Ad hoc balancing gained its dismal first amendment reputation in large part because its chief proponent, Justice Frankfurter, held as well a theory of great deference to legislative determination. The two need not necessarily be conjoined." Frederick Schauer, "Categories and the First Amendment: A Play in Three Acts," *Vanderbilt Law Review* 34 (1981): 303. See also Laurent B. Frantz, "The First Amendment in the Balance," *Yale Law Journal* 71 (1962). In Israel, of course, deference is mandated by the absence of a formal written constitution; but judges still retain considerable power through their statutory interpretation. Apropos Justice Frankfurter, in *Neiman* Justice Barak quotes from one of the justice's most frequently criticized balancing efforts—*Dennis v. United States*. *Neiman and Avneri*, 39 (2) P.D. at 310.

160

principal instruments of judicial power. The more occasions a judge finds to choose, weight, and balance interests, the more significant he or she becomes in the policy-making process of a given society. But the nature of the society—especially the form of its constitution—is highly relevant to an evaluation of that policy making. "In all its forms [balancing] is essentially unrelated to text; in the case of the first amendment it runs into language that has to be accommodated. As substantive doctrine it further attenuates the links between judicial review and the text of the Constitution and erodes the assumption that the Court, if not tied by, at least works with and within the sacred text, on which its legitimacy and its acceptability still largely rest."[73] Justice Barak might take comfort in these words. While the legitimacy of his position as a Supreme Court justice is unquestionably related to his projection of an image of objectivity, its connection to the language of a particular text is less clear than in the American case. The principles he has chosen to balance derive from the Declaration of Independence, a document that enjoys a kind of quasi-constitutional status, analogous in some ways to the American Preamble. In insisting that "every law must be interpreted in light of the Declaration of Independence,"[74] Barak creates the best possible environment for judicial balancing. The Declaration is a charter that lists some general principles to which the regime is committed, which is different from a document such as the U.S. Constitution, of which it can with greater accuracy be said that its language is itself in part the product of a balancing process undertaken by its framers.[75] And inasmuch as there exists at its core a critical unresolved tension, the judicial act of balancing is inevitably connected to a determina-

[73] Henkin, "Infallibility Under Law," p. 1048.

[74] *Neiman and Avneri*, 39 (2) P.D. at 307.

[75] In his concurring opinion in *Williams* v. *Rhodes*, Justice Douglas wrote, apropos this observation, "It is unnecessary to decide whether Ohio has an interest, 'compelling' or not, in abridging those rights [to appear on the ballot], because 'the men who drafted our Bill of Rights did all the 'balancing' that was to be done in this field.' " 393 U.S. 23, at 39. Following the decision in *Neiman* the Knesset acted to amend the Basic Law: The Knesset. It now provides: "A candidates list shall not participate in elections to the Knesset if its objectives or actions entail, explicitly or implicitly, one of the following: (1) a denial of the existence of the State of Israel as the state of the Jewish nation; (2) a denial of the democratic character of the state; (3) incitement to racism." There is no language in the amendment that addresses the question of standards, for example, "reasonable probability" or "proximate certainty"; in effect, the Knesset has itself undertaken to balance the various contending interests. The new constitutional provision does not eliminate all possibilities for judicial discretion, but through its preemption of one of the critical balancing judgments, it clearly reduces considerably the scope of possibilities. And again it suggests that a move to a comprehensive written constitution would not necessarily enhance the power of the judiciary.

tion that will incrementally advance a particular understanding of the nature of the regime. When Barak claims that as a judge he is one of the framers of the constitution, he is not indulging in hyperbole.

THE "REPUBLICAN SCHOOLMASTER" REVISITED AND TRANSPOSED

Justice Barak's opinion was sharply criticized by Justice Beisky, who argued that the matter before the Court was "an essentially political subject that lies primarily in the field of the legislature."[76] By this he meant that it was a subject involving partisan considerations that should be resolved elsewhere. Had there been a rejoinder to this criticism it might very well have taken this form: while there is no denying that this (Barak's) interpretation will have implications of some importance to the current political scene (surely the majority view will also), the justification for this expansive exercise of judicial discretion is that it directly addresses the broader "political subject"—the nature of the regime. Behind this rationale lies a further assumption: the Court does not function only to resolve particular legal disputes, but also plays a critical role in political education.

The pedagogical mission of the Supreme Court is a familiar theme in American constitutional scholarship. The Court has been observed conducting "a vital national seminar,"[77] and its earliest justices have been described as "republican schoolmasters."[78] Ralph Lerner demonstrated that these judges made a self-conscious effort to provide Americans with a political education: "The national judiciary from the very beginning acted as 'teachers to the citizenry.' "[79] They did this by expounding (often through their charges to grand juries) on the principles underlying the Constitution. It is not a coincidence that this early period was also the time when many of the justices made frequent references in their judicial opinions to the principles of natural law that they felt illuminated the specific language of the constitutional text.[80] These references became increasingly rare after roughly the first three decades of constitutional adjudication, a

[76] *Neiman and Avneri*, 39 (2) P.D. at 329.

[77] Eugene Rostow, *The Sovereign Prerogative: The Supreme Court and the Quest for Law* (New Haven: Yale University Press, 1962), pp. 167–68; and Richard Funston, *A Vital National Seminar: The Supreme Court in American Political Life* (Palo Alto: Mayfield Publishing Co., 1978).

[78] Ralph Lerner, "The Supreme Court as Republican Schoolmaster," in *Supreme Court Review 1967* (Chicago: University of Chicago Press, 1967).

[79] Ibid., p. 129.

[80] See, for example, Suzanna Sherry, "The Founders' 'Unwritten Constitution,' " *University of Chicago Law Review* 54 (1987).

development that in part, may be understood as resulting from the judicial perception that the vital connections between the written and unwritten law had been made and widely incorporated into the political culture. Henceforth the Court could dispense with philosophical reflection, confining itself to interpretation of the written Constitution.

This pattern contrasts interestingly with the Israeli situation. There the adoption of a constitution was postponed to a date uncertain, and as it became increasingly apparent that this event would at best occur in the distant future, the Court has displayed an increasing proclivity for more expansive interpretive judgments based on general principles of democracy. For example, the first Court held that the Declaration of Independence "contains no element of constitutional law which determines the validity of various ordinances and laws, or their repeal."[81] In another case the Court said, in response to the suggestion that "we must interpret the expression 'justice' by reference to philosophical, religious and moral sources," that "we are not prepared to adopt this system of interpretation which is completely unlimited in scope and obscures the limits of judicial power."[82] While it is still technically the case that the Declaration cannot be employed to invalidate a law, it (and the philosophical network of ideas it embodies) has, as we have seen, become a major source for judicial policy making and judicial instruction in the principles of the polity.

In short, the "republican schoolmaster" role is relevant to the present constitutional situation in Israel. It might be argued that the Court has a special obligation to articulate and explain political principles that in the United States enjoy a kind of privileged status by virtue of their having been constitutionalized in a single, comprehensive document that is the object of worship and study. But there is more. Israel does not have a strong democratic tradition. Most of its people come from societies with little or no experience in the ways of constitutional government. "Democracy is not in our blood."[83] As a result, justices must consider with the utmost seriousness the connections between judging and teaching.

Teaching Democracy from the Bench

"The judge does not merely adjudicate. He also has an educational role."[84] Justice Barak, a former law professor and attorney general, has been the most important Israeli proponent of a judicial role that to some extent

[81] *Zeev v. Gubernik*, 1 P.D. 85, 89 (1948).

[82] *Jabotinsky v. Weizman*, 5 P.D. 801 (1951), in Goitein, *Selected Judgments*, vol. 1, p. 86.

[83] Interview of Justice Barak with the author, Jerusalem, December 4, 1988.

[84] Barak, *Judicial Discretion*, p. 221.

parallels the figure of the spiritual leader in rabbinic tradition. In his under-standing of the judicial task, the pedagogical dimension is self-consciously integrated into his writings, both on and off the Court. This involves the activities of teaching *and* learning. For example, in response to a query about why he frequently cites American cases and scholarship in his judicial opinions, he responded by explaining that democratic evolution in Israel should be informed by examples of what works in other nations possessing similar political values.[85] Lessons learned are the basis of lessons to be taught. Of course it is necessary, he added, to adapt those solutions to the Israeli context; the important thing is to discover the legitimate range of possibilities reflected in the constitutional environments of comparable polities. In considering the educative function of the Court, Barak main-tains that it is necessary to advance the legitimacy of fundamental princi-ples that enjoy at best a tenuous hold on popular belief. "It is important to establish the principles, and then if necessary to retreat from them."[86] By this he means that a bold assertion of principle is justifiable in pedagogical terms (i.e., providing general and understandable guidelines) even if pru-dence recommends its subsequent modification.

For example, in another case involving Rabbi Kahane, Justice Barak wrote, "The question before us is not one of tactics, but rather of principle. We are not concerned with theory of probability but with political theory. Judicial decisionmaking in constitutional matters cannot be confined to the narrow parameters of the concrete instance, but must consider the whole picture and the entire range of possibilities."[87] The case was the acutely sensitive one, cited in the previous chapter, concerning an internal Knesset ruling by the Speaker denying a one-member party faction the right to submit a proposal of nonconfidence in the government. The politi-cal theory at issue here related to "the essential values of our constitutional regime,"[88] which needed to be given extended affirmation even though this challenged the prerogative of the Knesset. It also entailed going be-

[85] Interview with the author, Jerusalem, December 4, 1988.

[86] Ibid. In this context consider this observation. "In the United States the history of political theory since the founding of the Republic has resided in the Supreme Court." Theodore J. Lowi, *The End of Liberalism: Ideology, Policy, and the Crisis of Public Authority* (New York: W. W. Norton & Co., 1969), p. 314. One measure of judicial activism is the extent to which the political theory reflected in the Court's decisions at any give time goes beyond simply expressing the prevailing political wisdom of the day. To what extent, in other words, does the Court (or individual justices) play a creative role in the evolution of its society's political theory? In the case of Justice Barak, to a very considerable extent.

[87] *"Kach Party Faction" v. Hillel*, 39 (3) P.D. 141, 165 (1985).

[88] Ibid., 164.

yond "the narrow parameters of the concrete instance" to deliver extended commentaries on theoretical issues raised in cases coming before the Court. In yet another Kahane case, this time involving the Broadcasting Authority's decision to exclude the controversial rabbi from the airwaves, Barak again assumed a characteristic didactic stance by providing a lengthy lesson in free speech theory. At the core of this extended analysis was the insight that "freedom of speech should be founded on a 'broad ideological basis.' "[89] Following in the tradition of Justice Agranat's "*Kol Ha'am*" opinion,[90] he drew extensively on American ideological sources. In so doing he perhaps also revealed why one should proceed cautiously in educating Israelis with lessons derived from the American experience.

A critical statement in the opinion has a familiar ring to it, especially to American ears. "Those who won our independence believed that the final end of the state was to make men free to develop their faculties, and that in its government the deliberative forces should prevail over the arbitrary. They valued liberty both as an end and as a means."[91] Many in Israel would doubtless question this assertion, believing that the final end of the state was the creation of a Jewish homeland (which might or might not value liberty as both means and end).[92] The statement, however, is part of a lengthier passage quoted by Justice Barak from Justice Brandeis's famous opinion in *Whitney* v. *California*.[93] It is an eloquent articulation of the individualist aspirations of the American Declaration of Independence.

[89] *Kahane* v. *Broadcasting Authority*, 41 (3) P.D. 255, at 271.

[90] "*Kol Ha'am*" Co. Ltd. v. *Minister of Interior*, 7 P.D. 871 (1953). For an interesting discussion of this case, see Pnina Lahav, "American Influence on Israel's Jurisprudence of Free Speech," *Hastings Constitutional Law Quarterly* 9 (1981). Lahav argues that "*Kol Ha'am*" was decided on a jurisprudential foundation creatively transplanted to the Israeli constitutional scene by the American-born and educated Justice Agranat. She finds that his opinion exemplifies the "Grand Style" in interpretation, one, that is, "which allows for policy oriented, sometimes radical, results, while retaining conservative judicial tactics" (p. 34). I will discuss this case in detail in Chapter 6.

[91] *Kahane*, 41 (3) P.D. at 271.

[92] For example, in response to Justice Barak's *Schnitzer* opinion, one commentator wrote, "The end [for Barak] is not a Jewish State, it is a democratic regime. It is mindboggling that after 2,000 years of being led like lambs to the slaughter, culminating less than 50 short years ago in the Hitlerian obscenity, a justice of the Supreme Court of Israel can so flippantly dismiss security. But even more astounding, this brilliant Jewish jurist sees a democratic form of government as being more important than a Jewish State." David Heimowitz, "Can Israel Be a Real Democracy?" *Jerusalem Post*, March 16, 1991. The author, an immigrant from the United States, was obviously not reluctant to criticize in this way a justice who, as a child, had made a dramatic escape from the Nazis.

[93] 274 U.S. 357, 375 (1927).

That the Israeli Declaration is a more complex document announcing both communal and individualist aspirations is well understood by Justice Barak. In emphasizing the liberal democratic strain in the Israeli Declaration, Barak is not seeking to distort the document, but he is, as he readily acknowledges, making selective use of it.[94] It is for this reason that he attempts to find independent grounds to support the democratic argument, because the presence of the Declaration's other sections tends to weaken an argument that is exclusively tied to the Western-oriented paragraph.[95]

While this selective use of the Declaration, coupled with an appeal to the principles and practices that define the essence of liberal constitutional democracy, may be taken as the outline for a judicial course on democracy, the scope of the course is not fully within the control of its teachers. Thus, the legislature's amendment to the Basic Law: The Knesset, specifically its exclusion from the electoral process of parties that deny the "existence of the State of Israel as the state of the Jewish people," represents an alternative lesson on the subject of the "final end of the state." It is a lesson that the Court must now incorporate into its own syllabus, as is evident in another recent elections case involving the decision of the Central Elections Committee to exclude the PLP (Progressive List for Peace) from the ballot in 1988 on the ground that it violated section 7A(1) of the amended Basic Law.

The Court decided three to two to upset the committee's ruling, but it did so only on the basis of the majority's conclusion that convincing evidence for the disqualification of a list was missing. On the larger issue of principle, there was fundamental agreement that a list may be disqualified if, as one commentator noted, it "rejects the ideological underpinnings of Israel as the state of the Jewish people, even if there is no subversive element involved, and no perceivable [or conceivable?] danger to state security."[96] Four of the justices indicated that a list could be disqualified even if the only thing that it did was advocate the repeal of the Law of

94 Interview with the author, Jerusalem, December 4, 1988.

95 For example, in a recent case, Justice Barak, after citing the Declaration of Independence as an expression of the nation's fundamental values, says, "The fundamental values have an existence that is external to this or that statute or document. . . . They stem from the very essence of the democratic regime, and from the very essence of the individual as a free person." *Poraz v. Mayor of Tel Aviv—Yafo,* 42 (2) P.D. 309, 330 (1988).

96 Kretzmer, *The Legal Status of the Arabs in Israel,* p. 30. The decision is *Ben Shalom v. Central Committee for the Elections of the Twelfth Knesset,* 43 (4) P.D. 221 (1988). The dissenters suggested that the advocacy of total equality between Arabs and Jews was tantamount to a denial of the state as a state of the Jewish people.

Return. As a result, then, of the Court's efforts in *Neiman*, the contours of constitutional interpretation have been changed (or at least clarified) by the Knesset, so that the more particularistic aspects of Israeli political identity could not easily evade the attention of the Court. As part of his or her educational mission, the activist judge is still free to emphasize the universalistic aspirations of Israeli constitutionalism, but henceforth these aspirations would in some manner have to be reconciled with other aspirations in which they stood in tension. To ignore them would be to provoke further legislative reaction, which is to say that in order to maximize their potential influence as educators, judges would have to strike a balance by respecting the ascriptive dimension of Israeli civic identity.

So it is that in regard to divisive social issues pertaining to the Jewishness of the state, Justice Barak emphatically advocates judicial *restraint*: "The judge must aspire to a solution that is compatible with the societal agreement or that at least does not contradict it. I think it is advisable to avoid choosing an option that sharply contradicts the public's fundamental conception. Thus, for example, judicial restraint is justified in Israel in the entire area of 'civil marriage,' for this matter is the subject of bitter public controversy."[97] This, however, is only part of the story, for on many issues of individual rights in Israel a societal consensus is also clearly lacking.[98] In these matters, according to Barak, the judge, the teacher to the citizenry, must engage in "instructional activity."[99] He must "raise the level of the society in which he lives."[100] The consensus that needs support and elaboration by the Court is one "that reflects the basic principles and the articles of faith of the enlightened public of the society in which [the judge] lives."[101] For the judicial activist, then, a more complete story is one in which enlightened judges (as in children of the Enlightenment) seek *to create* a broad societal consensus by educating the public in the ways of democracy.

There are of course different ways to instruct. Often a teacher provides lessons through example. A judge wishing to emphasize the importance of individual restraint in a democratic society might convey this mes-

[97] Barak, *Judicial Discretion*, pp. 213–14.

[98] On this point, see Michal Shamir and John L. Sullivan, "The Political Context of Tolerance: The United States and Israel," American Political Science Review 77 (1983).

[99] Barak, *Judicial Discretion*, p. 130. In these reflections on the connection between judging and societal mores, Barak's views are very reminiscent of the ideas of Benjamin Cardozo, particularly as the latter expressed them in his *Nature of the Judicial Process*.

[100] Ibid.

[101] Ibid., p. 215.

sage through the example of his or her own judicial restraint. What are commonly viewed as "technicalities"—limitations such as standing and justiciability—have a pedagogic potential that, under the right set of circumstances, may be exploited to good effect by the judge who takes seriously the role of educator.

But this orientation is perhaps too indirect in the framework of polities where a consensus on the value of individual rights is lacking. Here the judge might prefer a more direct approach, in which case procedural rules governing the consideration of substantive constitutional claims will be less strictly observed. And where, in addition, the judicial role in the creation of constitutional rights is seen as both necessary and proper, there is even less incentive to observe the proprieties of self-restraint. As Justice Barak has noted, "There is a difference between a judge whose judicial philosophy is based solely on the conception that the judge's function is to resolve disputes between holders of existing rights, and a judge whose judicial philosophy is rooted in the consciousness that the judge's function is to create rights and maintain the rule of law."[102] This argues for extreme judicial latitude in applying the rule of standing. Judges according to this view must not have their responsibility to enact and establish rights that reflect their understanding of the fundamental values of the regime undermined by adherance to procedural formulations more appropriate to a system in which such rights are firmly entrenched.[103]

The basic thought here is that "adjudication is not only declarative but also constitutive."[104] This constitutive act also serves the pedagogical purposes of the Court; that is, adjudication is not only declarative but also educative. Every occurrence of judicial creativity must be accompanied by an explanation that situates the newly established right within an evolving framework of fundamental values. What this entails can be grasped by imagining the U.S. Supreme Court in an interpretive context that did not include the Bill of Rights or the Fourteenth Amendment but did include (in a way that currently does not exist) the Preamble to the Constitution. In effect one would be imagining a situation not unlike what was originally

[102] *Ressler* v. *Minister of Defense*, 42 (2) P.D. 441, 458 (1988).

[103] An even greater latitude is called for with respect to the question of institutional nonjusticiability, where, according to Justice Barak, "There is nothing in the principles of democracy to justify institutional non-justiciability." Ibid., 493.

[104] Ibid., 464. Consider, too, this statement by Justice Shamgar: "Proper protection of the status of a given liberty is not achieved through mere declaration of its existence, although one should not fail to appreciate the didactic value of a declarative determination." *Mitrani* v. *Minister of Transportation*, 37 P.D. (3) 337, 355 (1983).

developed by the framers. As guardians of the Constitution, the justices would know that their task was an important one that had much to do with establishing justice and securing the blessings of liberty. They would also know that their constituency, the American people, would possess only the vaguest idea of the specifics of these aspirations. As a result, their gradual enunciation of the rights and responsibilities associated with the concepts of justice and liberty would have to *demonstrate* these connections in such a way that citizens could see how their enjoyment of these guarantees fulfilled the promise of the Constitution.

What, then, is the best way to ensure that adjudication is not only declarative but also educative? In the United States it was a widely shared belief on the part of the opponents of ratification, that the omission of a bill of rights represented a lost opportunity for civic education. It was thought that a specific enumeration of rights would facilitate the task of popular education in a new republic. "We do not by declarations change the nature of things, or create new truths, but we give existence, or at least establish in the minds of the people truths and principles which they might never otherwise have thought of, or soon forgot."[105] In Israel today the most frequently heard argument for adopting a bill of rights is essentially the same; it emphasizes the salutory effects of including such a charter among the documents from which the people, especially the young, might be instructed in the principles of democratic rule. There is considerable force in such an argument, and the educational potential of a bill of rights as a text that would be read and discussed in the schools (at least in the public schools) should not be minimized. Apart from its impact upon the legal system, this consideration itself might recommend passage of a bill of rights.[106] But what would its effect be on the teachers who wear judicial robes?

Many of the opponents of a bill of rights in the United States believed that it would become, as Hadley Arkes has pointed out, "a grand device of civic education that would misinstruct the American people about the

[105] Federal Farmer, no. 16, 20 Jan. 1788, in Kurland and Lerner, *The Founders Constitution*, vol. 1, p. 458.

[106] For proponents of a bill of rights, the educational benefits that could be anticipated as a result of such a development would replace the deficiencies of relying solely on the Declaration of Independence. "Regrettably, it cannot be said that the Declaration of Independence has served as an educational tool or as a source of guidance in the political, social and day-to-day life in Israel. Politicians and statesmen have not succeeded in elevating it to the status afforded it by judges." Shimon Shetreet, "Developments in Constitutional Law: Selected Topics," *Israel Law Review* 24 (1990): 413.

ground of their rights, and therefore about the ends or purposes of the government under the Constitution."[107] The Federalists "were dubious about the kind of legal sensibility that would be shaped by a Constitution that marked off rights in this way."[108] For them, the actual mention of a right in the Constitution is ultimately not what is important; the appropriate tests for determining the existence and extent of any freedom under the Constitution reside in canons of moral reasoning that take precedence over the fact of a right's specific enumeration. Arkes claims that their concerns have been vindicated, as can be seen, he suggests, in the sad spectacle of "lawyers and judges who no longer kn[ow] how to deliberate about questions of justice."[109] The effect of reducing rights to a compressed inventory is that it constricts our understanding of rights and encourages a shallow jurisprudence and, as a result, an essentially unenlightened teaching.

One can disagree with Arkes's assessment of contemporary American constitutional jurisprudence and still appreciate how the concerns he raises are worth pondering in Israel. When the adjudicative responsibility is understood to contain an educative dimension, one could well imagine a judge finding the absence of a specific enumeration of rights to be at once

---

[107] Arkes, *Beyond the Constitution*, p. 56. A comprehensive account of this question must take into consideration the recent work of Akhil Reed Amar, who has revealed the structural continuities between the Bill of Rights and and the original Constitution by highlighting the majoritarian essence of the former, including its concern for an educated citizenry. This education, according to Amar, is provided for less in the guarantee of individual rights than in the safeguarding of intermediate associations—church, militia, and jury—where citizens would be instructed in their rights and duties in active rather than passive ways. Akhil Reed Amar, "The Bill of Rights as a Constitution," *Yale Law Journal* 100 (1991): 1206–10. This interpretation is in at least one respect compatible with Arkes's views, in that it sees the Bill of Rights as a document that is more than a little suspicious of judges, whose interpretation of enumerated rights is certainly not the intended vehicle for public education. As to the relevance of Amar's account for Israel, and in particular its implications for civic education, the dependence on federalism for the efficacy of the solutions embedded in the Bill of Rights requires that one proceed with extra caution in deducing exportable lessons from that document.

[108] Arkes, *Beyond the Constitution*, p. 56.

[109] Ibid., p. 79. "The most damning thing that might be said . . . about the Bill of Rights is that it has been part of a curriculum of civic education in this country that has made it far less likely that we will bring to positions of authority people with the same furnishings of mind— with the same capacity to trace their judgments back to first principles—as the men who founded this republic" (p. 80). As a contrast to these views, consider the understanding propounded by Eugene V. Rostow: "Each Justice of the Court meets his highest challenge in seeking to interpret these words [of the Bill of Rights] in ways which contribute to the advancement of the rule of law, and to the advancement of the law itself. Thus can the Court help in the education of opinion and play its part in the colloquium through which the ideas of the community about law and justice are formed." Rostow, *The Sovereign Prerogative*, p. 142.

liberating and challenging. He or she would be required to elaborate on the rationale for any given assertion of right; the mere recitation of specific language, accompanied by an effort to establish its meaning through analysis of legislative intent, would be insufficient. As one reads Justice Barak's opinions, for example, one cannot help but wonder whether their quality as vehicles for democratic instruction would be diminished if he were constrained by the more taxing obligations of textual fidelity in constitutional interpretation. He, perhaps, would feel less constrained in exercising the power of judicial review, but this only raises a further question of whether the conjunction of heightened institutional power with constricted interpretive freedom is ultimately a good thing. Indeed, the willingness to indulge Barak's expansive (and typically illuminating) lessons in democratic understanding is no doubt affected by the awareness of its incomplete or provisionally binding nature. Viewed solely along the dimension of pedagogic value, the Federalist perspective is surely entitled to a respectful hearing in Israeli constitutional circles.

It is not surprising that John Marshall's oft-quoted observation that "it is emphatically the province and duty of the judicial department to say what the law is" should recommend itself to Justice Barak. Saying "what the law is" encompasses an educative function closely tied to the work of developing a constitution. This work is commonly perceived to be within the jurisdiction of the Knesset, the legislative source of basic law in Israel. But the decisions of the Court may influence the substance of the basic laws (e.g., *Neiman*), and the judicial review of administrative acts creates what can with ample justification be described as constitutional guarantees.

In reflecting on the constitutional import of these guarantees it is helpful to consider Ronald Dworkin's comparison of the task of judging in hard cases to the writing of a chain novel. The latter activity involves the creation of a novel *seriatim*, where each novelist in the chain contributes a chapter with the intent of producing a coherent piece of work that could be construed as the achievement of a single author. As in the model of law as integrity, each contributor seeks to make the novel the best it can be by adopting an interpretive stance that places a premium on textual coherence. Whatever creative departures are undertaken by one of the authors must demonstrate continuity with the preceding chapters, as well as "fit" with the concept of the work as a whole. "The distinction between author and interpreter [is] more a matter of different aspects of the same process."[110]

Justice Barak has found this comparison appealing. "The judicial creation

---

[110] Dworkin, *Law's Empire*, p. 229.

is a book written by a number of authors, with each writer contributing one chapter to the joint creation."[111] For him, too, judicial creativity (which he, unlike Dworkin, sees as involving considerable discretion) needs to be constrained by the obligation to preserve the coherence of the legal system as a whole. "Like the writing of a book in serial installments," this creative activity "has no beginning and no end and is all continuity."[112]

The literary analogy serves a role similar to the concept/conception distinction of Dworkin's earlier work.[113] A concept is a specific moral-constitutional principle (e.g., equality)—specific, that is, in the minds of its authors—the application of which may yield different results, or conceptions, depending on the circumstances and context in which it occurs. The conceptions that are derived from concepts represent the particular application of modernized principles. Elsewhere I have criticized Dworkin's use of this distinction because of the way in which it permits the interpreter to inject his or her own moral philosophy into the Constitution while still asserting claims of fidelity to text and original intent.[114] The result is often a transvaluation of the document. Similarly, in the chain novel metaphor, the interpreter may easily define the narrative's plot at such a high level of abstraction that the authors of succeeding chapters are largely unconstrained in their creative efforts to produce the best possible novel.

As we have seen, the Israeli constitution is perhaps unique in the sense that, by design, it is *in fact* evolving chapter by chapter. Under these circumstances it is more reasonable to claim on behalf of Israeli judges, as opposed to their American counterparts, a position of coauthorship of the constitutional text. They are directly engaged in a serial creation. Justice Barak's use of Dworkin's analogy provides a more satisfactory jurisprudential result in Israel than Dworkin himself achieves in the American constitutional setting, where adjudication takes place within a more stable, textually circumscribed legal context. But as we have also seen, there are risks. The Israeli interpreter confronts a narrative with a very complex story line involving intriguing subplots. To develop one subplot at the

[111] Barak, *Judicial Discretion*, p. 164.

[112] Ibid., p. 165.

[113] Specifically in *Taking Rights Seriously* (Cambridge: Harvard University Press, 1977). Justice Barak has used the same distinction in his work. "What we seek is the fundamental perception rather than the individual application—the abstraction, the principle, the policy and purpose. We are interested in the Legislature's *concept* as to the purpose of the Law, and not in its *conception* as to the resolution of the specific dispute before the court." From Justice Barak's opinion in *Of Ha' Emek* v. *Ramat Yishai Local Council*, 40 (1) P.D. 113, 144 (1985).

[114] Gary J. Jacobsohn, "Modern Jurisprudence and the Transvaluation of Liberal Constitutionalism," *Journal of Politics* 47 (1985): 414.

expense of the other may produce a failed novel and may even provoke a hostile reaction from the reading public. As attractive are the opportunities for creative achievement, so too are the possibilities for improvident assertions of power.

CONCLUSION

Recall Justice Hugo Black's advice to Attorney General Haim Cohen: "Make a constitution immediately, and make it so stringent that no Supreme Court can evade it." This recommendation, with its emphasis on the salutory constraints that a written constitution imposes on the judiciary, mirrors the sentiments expressed by the justice in many of his opinions on the Court. In *New York Times Co.* v. *United States* (the Pentagon Papers case), a decision that, like *Schnitzer*, rejected a governmental claim that national security considerations justified a prior restraint on press publication, Black focused much of his opinion on the issue of judicial lawmaking. He dismissed the "contention that the courts should take it upon themselves to 'make' a law abridging freedom of the press in the name of equity, presidential power and national security, even when the representatives of the people in Congress have adhered to the command of the First Amendment and refused to make such a law."[115] He also suggested that the executive branch had ignored the history surrounding the adoption of the Bill of Rights. "The amendments were offered to *curtail* and *restrict* the general powers granted to the Executive, Legislative, and Judicial Branches two years before in the original Constitution. The Bill of Rights changed the original Constitution into a new charter under which no branch of government could abridge the people's freedom of press, speech, religion, and assembly."[116]

If one contrasts the approach taken by Justice Black with that of Justice Barak in *Schnitzer*, the principal difference lies in the American judge's refusal to engage in any balancing of competing interests. Well might he have been concerned with the impact of balancing on the role of judges, as it has been described by Barak. "The 'sovereign prerogative of choice' grows when the judge is required, as a precondition to locating the point of balance, to assign relative weights to the accepted values that are competing for the upper hand."[117] In the Pentagon Papers case, Black observed,

[115] *New York Times Co.* v. *United States*, 403 U.S. 713, 718 (1971).
[116] Ibid., 716.
[117] Barak, *Judicial Discretion*, p. 70.

173

"The word 'security' is a broad, vague generality whose contours should not
be invoked to abrogate the fundamental law embodied in the First Amendment."[118] Whatever balancing needed to be done had been accomplished
by the authors of the First Amendment, who had determined that real
security is not achieved by withholding secrets from the public, and who
had left it for others to apply the guarantee's categorical language in a
straightforward, uncomplicated way. Moreover, this stricture applies to the
rest of the Bill of Rights as well.

> I believe . . . that the Framers themselves did this balancing when they
> wrote the Constitution and the Bill of Rights. They appreciated the risks
> involved and they decided that certain rights should be guaranteed regard-
> less of these risks. Courts have neither the right nor the power to review this
> original decision of the Framers and to attempt to make a different evaluation
> of the importance of the rights granted in the Constitution. Where conflict-
> ing values exist in the field of individual liberties protected by the Constitu-
> tion, that document settles the conflict, and its policy should not be changed
> without constitutional amendments by the people in the manner provided by
> the people.[119]

Black's absolutist interpretation of the First Amendment was never embraced by a majority on the Court (and thus most of his colleagues were
inclined to balance security against a free press), but his textualist approach, while unique in some ways, embodies the inner logic of a formal
written constitution, much as Barak's ad hoc balancing, identified more
with him than any other Israeli justice, epitomizes constitutional interpretation in its absence.

That the two approaches achieve a similar outcome in these two cases is
beside the point. For Justice Black, the Court would be just as much
engaged in inappropriate lawmaking if, in the absence of explicit constitutional language, it extended the domain of individual rights, as it would be
here, if it had in the face of such language contracted the domain. In
comparative terms, the significance of the Black-Barak contrast has to do
with what it suggests about the degree of interpretive freedom available to,
and appropriate for, judges deciding constitutional cases. To be sure, Israeli
judges have often displayed Black-like judicial proclivities, and even more
American judges have projected a jurisprudential profile matching that of
Barak. Thus, it could be argued that Black's textualism may even fall out-

---

[118] *New York Times Co.*, 403 U.S. at 719.
[119] Black, "The Bill of Rights," p. 879.

side the judicial mainstream in the United States, since most judges have found the language of the Constitution to be more opaque, or at least less specific, than Black's literalist theory would have it. But it does not follow from this that his fundamental insight, that a written document containing a specific enumeration of rights must be seen as constraining judges as much as any other political actors, is wrong. Indeed, constitutional theorists like Dworkin, who find fault with the "narrow interpretivism" of Black, implicitly accept his claim about the obligations of textual fidelity, even while proposing an alternative understanding of the text.

But if Dworkin and Black can so easily be made to fall under the same jurisprudential rubric, is there much point in distinguishing the Israeli and American models, particularly if an Israeli judge like Barak is, in all but one important respect, Dworkinian in constitutional approach? The one important respect—Barak's much more categorical acceptance of judicial discretion—is, however, critical. "Judicial discretion is the power and the authority to choose and to create."[120] Highlighted here are the potential jurisprudential stakes involved in committing to constitutional language the particular limits that are to be imposed on political power. This point emerges also from an interview with Justice Cohn, who pointed out, in the course of expressing some reservations about the desirability of adopting a bill of rights, that "today all laws must be interpreted in the light of the Declaration of Independence, but with a constitution that ends, and all laws must then be interpreted according to the clauses of the constitution."[121] (Thus, many years after his conversation with Justice Black, Justice Cohn was still resisting the American jurist's advice.)

Of course one could challenge the assumption that with the adoption of an American-style constitution, the interpretive significance of the Declaration would disappear. But to do so one should try to account for the fact that in the United States this is precisely what has happened; one rarely encounters any references to it in constitutional opinions.[122] Justice Barak's frequent application of the Israeli Declaration in cases like *Schnitzer* and *Neiman* is not paralleled by similar usage of the American Declaration in analogous cases like *New York Times Co.* v. *United States* and *Powell* v.

---

[120] Barak, *Judicial Discretion*, p. 91.

[121] Interview with the author, December 11, 1988.

[122] Lincoln's understanding of the connection between the two documents is, as far as the current constitutional orthodoxy is concerned, admired at best at a very considerable distance. Perhaps the most explicit renunciation of the constitutional significance of the Declaration may be found in John Hart Ely's account, where the document is seen purely as a brief for independence. *Democracy and Distrust*, p. 49.

McCormack. This is not simply a reflection of the difference between statutory construction and constitutional interpretation, for one would have to look long and hard before finding any American case where statutory meaning was established through the interpretive prism of the Declaration. Justice Black was surely correct in his Pentagon Papers opinion; "the Bill of Rights changed the original Constitution into a new charter," one of the jurisprudential consequences of which was to sever specific constitutional rights from their philosophical underpinnings. If and when in Israel "all laws [are] interpreted according to the clauses of the constitution," the role of the Court will change, both in limiting and expanding its potential for influence in the broader society.

Doctrinal Diversions: Speech, Democracy, and the American Way

> The principle of freedom of expression is closely bound
> up with the democratic process.
> —*Justice Shimon Agranat*

The Rabbi and the Survivor's Son

United States District Court, 1978: "We live in a society that is very conscious of racial and religious differences, in which open discussion of important public issues will often require reference to racial and religious groups, often in terms which members of those groups, and others, would consider insulting and degrading." And later: "The [Supreme] Court has made it clear that speech may not be punished merely because it offends."[1]

Israeli Supreme Court, 1986: "A near certainty that the feelings of a religious or ethnic minority be really and harshly hurt, by publication of a deviant speech, is enough to justify limiting that speech. Therefore . . . it would be justified to prevent a demonstration of Petitioners, if it intends to pass through Arab populated areas, and a near certainty of a real injury exists because of the racist content of Petitioners' message."[2]

The petitioners in these two cases were doubly victorious: they won in court and they attracted great amounts of valuable publicity to their respective causes. On the face of it, no two causes—Nazism and Jewish ultranationalism—could be more different. Nevertheless the principals in these legal episodes are perhaps fated to share a specific role, at least in jurisprudential circles. They both traded in the rhetoric and tactics of hate, and as a result posed a common challenge to their respective political systems: how far must a constitutional order go in tolerating expressive activities that have as their principal purpose the vilification of particular groups in the society? In Israel and in the United States, these activities

---

[1] *Collin v. Smith*, 447 F. Supp. 676, 691, 697 (1978).

[2] *Kahane v. Broadcasting Authority*, 41 (3) P.D. 255, 295–96 (1986).

have been instrumental in the development of political and constitutional approaches to the question of free speech.

Any comprehensive assessment of the American contribution to Israeli free speech law would have to include the fact that Rabbi Meir Kahane emigrated to Israel from the United States. As a founder and leader of the Jewish Defense League, Kahane was well known upon his arrival in Israel in 1971, and he quickly established himself as a thorn in the side of the Israeli political establishment. He attracted a small but devoted following that eventually grew to sufficient numbers that he was able in 1984 to gain election to the Knesset.[3] The principal features of his program called for the denial of civil rights for Israeli Arabs, their transfer from Israeli territory, and the total separation of Jews and non-Jews (including imprisonment for sexual relations). Accompanying this agenda was a distinctive pattern of behavior entailing provocative acts directed at Arabs, including abusive speech, hostile demonstrations, and support for terrorism. Predictably, Kahane frequently was the subject of legal controversy, including his appeal of a ruling by the Israel Broadcasting Association to ban him from the airwaves, the case from which the second of the above quotes is taken.

Kahane's election to the Knesset frightened many Israelis, who found it increasingly difficult to dismiss him and his movement as simply an annoying irrelevancy. Frank Collin, on the other hand, the American Nazi whose plan to lead a small band of followers through the streets of Skokie, Illinois, captured the attention of the nation, was more pathetic than frightening. This twisted soul, it turns out, is the son of a Jewish survivor of the Holocaust, whose pursuit of the National Socialist dream is doubtless best understood by applying the tools of psychopathology. But the marginality of his personal and political status was more than compensated for by the centrality of the constitutional issues he raised after the Village of Skokie, a community that was home to a large population of death camp survivors, refused to issue him a permit to march. Indeed, as one of the many commentators on the case has observed, "Skokie boiled down to a debate over fundamental or first principles of liberal, constitutional democracy."[4] And testifying to the difficulty of the issues involved, it is a debate that, in much

[3] Kahane's party list, "Kach," was able to secure one seat in the 1984 election, held by Kahane himself. A number of estimates indicate that had Kach not been banned (as a result of legislation passed subsequently) from the 1988 election, it would very likely have secured as many as three or four seats.

[4] Donald Alexander Downs, *Nazis in Skokie: Freedom, Community, and the First Amendment* (Notre Dame: University of Notre Dame Press, 1985), p. 119.

the same way as the controversy over Kahane in Israel, has divided the normally united civil liberties community.[5]

The issues raised by the Kahanes and Collins of the world—people for whom expressive behavior often functions as an assault weapon—speak directly to the conceptual differences that distinguish the pluralistic legal-political environments of Israel and the United States. This is illustrated by the opening excerpts of this chapter. Judge Decker, the author of the federal district court's Skokie opinion, acknowledged the heterogeneous character of American society and, following Supreme Court precedent, concluded in effect that this very heterogeneity precludes punishment of speech that may be offensive to particular groups. To protect discussion of public issues it is necessary to tolerate insulting and degrading speech, for such speech is the inevitable by-product of public discourse in a diverse and open society. The decision is designed to safeguard the interests of both individuals (Collin and his followers) and the society as a whole, the latter being the beneficiary of an unrestricted, uninhibited discussion of matters affecting the public interest. Groups, however, are not recognized as having a corporate interest that commands judicial or constitutional consideration.

Justice Barak's opinion in the Broadcasting Association case also acknowledged social heterogeneity, but it appeared to draw a different entailment from this reality. The sensitivities of minority groups are a factor to consider in any final assessment of the free speech interests involved in a given case. In this particular case, such sensitivities were not implicated, but in Justice Barak's hypothetical of a Kahane-led demonstration through Arab-populated areas, the Court, he suggested, would be justified in limiting speech if there was a near certainty that the racist content of the speech might cause real injury. The acknowledgment of group diversity is accompanied by a respect for the communal integrity of minorities, to the extent that it could call for the trumping of the individual's right of free expression.

While it would be tempting to infer from this initial comparison a fundamental divergence in the basic orientations of the two courts on questions of free speech, it would also be misleading. Justice Barak's dictum is never elaborated on, certainly not in the detailed and deliberate manner in which

---

[5] The situations are not entirely analogous. The defense of the Nazis by the American Civil Liberties Union precipitated numerous resignations, as well as a significant withdrawal of financial support. On the matter of Kahane, the Association for Civil Rights in Israel (a much smaller organization) was divided over what position to take, but its division was confined to internal debate.

179

other justifications for limiting speech are discussed elsewhere in his lengthy opinion. Indeed, his opinion is in most particulars consonant with the jurisprudential and philosophical premises of the prevailing American First Amendment approach. This is not surprising; perhaps in no other area of constitutional law have doctrinal developments in the United States had more influence in Israel than with regard to matters of speech and expression.[6] This does not mean that there has been a systematic appropriation of American First Amendment jurisprudence by Israeli judges. Moreover, differences that have emerged are not only a reflection of the absence of an Israeli First Amendment; they have also to do with the contrasting sociopolitical and ideological environments within which the two Supreme Courts adjudicate. But the allure of the American approach has been very important, so much so that it has, for better or worse, made it difficult to discern a distinctively Israeli approach, one that is as much a reflection of the pluralist elements of the larger system of which it is a part as the American orientation is of *its* pluralist world.

If one turns, for example, to the proposed test advanced by Justice Barak for resolving his hypothetical—a "near certainty of a real injury"—it may sound vaguely familiar to American ears. Actually it is a modification of the American "clear and present danger" test, a sort of compromise between the "imminence" requirement of that test and the "probability" requirement of one of its main competitors.[7] What is not familiar is its application to "the feelings of a religious or ethnic minority." In the context of a demonstration, questions of imminence, near certainty, or probability have in the United States been associated with specific acts of violence and civic unrest. The violation of the sensitivities of particular groups has not, in this constitutional context, been held to constitute criminally liable injurious behavior, in part because it would require judicial scrutiny of the "racist content" of expression. On the other hand, when the Court has had to concern itself with offensive content—in the area of obscenity—it has not searched for a specific speech-injury connection; that is, it has typically proceeded without recourse to proximity tests. The "patently offensive"

---

[6] See, for example, David Kretzmer, "The Influence of First Amendment Jurisprudence on Decision-making in Israel," unpublished paper. Kretzmer points out that "reference to American authorities [by Israeli judges] both on the demands of free speech theory and its boundaries has become almost standard practice." (p. 19).

[7] Justice Brandeis, in his dissent in *Whitney v. California*, 274 U.S. 357 (1927), first elaborated on the "imminence" requirement; and the so-called "clear and probable danger" test was initially introduced to the Supreme Court by Chief Justice Vinson, writing for a plurality in *Dennis v. United States*, 341 U.S. 494 (1951).

nature of the expression *itself*, its lack of "redeeming social value" as measured against community standards, is sufficient to criminalize it. Were the
American Court to equate racist expression with pornographic expression,
in the sense of being offensive and socially worthless, it follows that, as with
obscenity, the subsequent judicial examination would be confined to an
independent or self-contained evaluation of the particular substantive
merits of the questionable expression.

Pursuing the analogy further, if, as the more libertarian view would have
it, the only valid governmental concern in connection with obscenity is
whether it causes sexual violence, then the Court, consistent with precedent, would be inclined to broaden the inquiry by focusing on the specific
nexus between speech and violence. Justice Barak's reliance on a proximity
test in the circumstances of a targeted racist demonstration therefore raises
the following question: What is the nature of the "real injury" that may
justify a ban on the demonstration? Is it the hurt feelings of an offended
minority, or is it rather the breach of peace that would almost certainly
accompany these hurt feelings? The choice of a "near certainty" test suggests the latter, but Justice Barak's language strongly indicates that racist
speech may "be punished because it offends." Then why not, it may be
asked, follow through fully on this clear difference with the American
approach by proposing a more content-oriented test?[8] Could it be that the
fundamental premises underlying the American reluctance to examine
content remain appealing to Justice Barak in spite of the fact that Israeli law
clearly differs from American law in its recognition that groups require
protection against hateful speech?[9] If so, then doctrinal transplantation
may be seen as a judicial strategy designed to reconcile and accommodate
the indigenous positive law with the philosophical premises underlying the
reigning constitutional interpretation of another system.

---

[8] Let me not be misunderstood here. I do not mean to say that judges should be oblivious
to context when questions of this sort arise. David Kretzmer, for one, is correct in distinguishing between offensive demonstrations held in general areas and others held in specific locales
(e.g., Nazis in Skokie). David Kretzmer, "Demonstrations and the Law," *Israel Law Review* 19
(1984): 106. The argument is that in these latter instances it is *the expression itself* that must be
the basis for determining its legality or illegality. Another factor to consider in this connection
is that when reviewing the offensiveness of racist expression in the context of the feelings of a
community, the most important injury may be long term, taking some time to manifest itself,
and thus rendering problematic an official's dependence on a "near certainty" standard.

[9] Here are two questions worth reflecting on: "What could be more natural for a state that
arose from the ashes of a racist holocaust than to declare incitement to racism a criminal
offense?" Editorial, *Jerusalem Post*, February 2, 1986. "What could be more natural for a state
that continues to confront the legacy of racist slavery than to declare incitement to racism a

This chapter, then, is concerned with the intersection of constitutional doctrine and political culture, and with the transplantation to the Israeli system of a doctrinal model with roots in the soil of contemporary American liberal constitutionalism. The argument will not be that, to the extent this transplantation is occurring in the area of free expression, the effort is necessarily misguided or ill advised. One could, for example, begin with the simple proposition that the political culture (in this instance referring to our two pluralist models) is sufficiently supple to accommodate a range of constitutional possibilities, and that the direction that may initially possess the greatest "fit" with the broader sociopolitical context may not be the best way to go. Thus, the fact that the American approach is reflective of deeper currents in American society does not by itself discredit the criticism that is often directed at that approach. Indeed, it might be helpful to the critics to be able to cite a coherent, cogently argued formulation of the preferred alternative that has been developed elsewhere. As has been wisely pointed out, "Comparative law does not provide blueprints or solutions. But awareness of foreign experiences does lead to the kind of self-understanding that constitutes a necessary first step on the way toward working out our own approaches to our own problems."[10] One logical place for critics to go for a critique of the prevailing constitutional orthodoxy in the United States is Israel, where an understanding of the political culture might suggest a congenial jurisprudential environment for nurturing this alternative. But as we shall see, the very example of the American model has to some extent impeded the flowering of such an alternative.

LESSONS FROM THE FIRST AMENDMENT

The "Consensus on Untouchable Content"

In her comparative study of the law respecting abortion and divorce, Mary Ann Glendon convincingly demonstrates that "the United States . . . often

---

criminal offense?" The first state has in fact criminalized incitement to racism, whereas the second state has not; but it is more than the knowledge of this particular fact that likely would lead most people to accept the rhetorical form of the first query and challenge it in the second. Nor is it necessarily a comparative assessment of the evils of slavery and the Holocaust that would adequately account for the differential response. It is, rather, that in the case of the second state what has come to be viewed as "natural," insofar as the law is concerned, is the toleration of hateful speech even when it is directed at those most closely associated with a shameful past.

[10] Mary Ann Glendon, *Abortion and Divorce in Western Law* (Cambridge: Harvard University Press, 1987), p. 142.

occupies an extreme end of the spectrum when cross-national comparisons are made on specific issues."[11] She finds the radically individualist American approach to these questions to be expressive of the deepest ideological and cultural commitments of the society, just as she finds European alternatives similarly revealing. Appealing to Tocqueville, she is not surprised that in "a country where liberty has been severed from other republican virtues,"[12] the emphasis in law and policy should be so decidedly upon satisfying the expectation of personal autonomy.

Glendon's work has implications for the issue of free speech. Here too the United States must be placed on the extreme end of the spectrum when cross-national comparisons are made. For example, most Western European countries have laws against incitement to racial hatred; but the American antipathy to this sort of a prohibition is so strong that at international conventions on racial discrimination, the United States highlights its extreme position by refusing to accept any interpretation that would require it to ban racist speech in contravention of the First Amendment.[13] Such refusals suggest a further analogy to Glendon's discussion of the abortion issue, which is that on both questions the debate is often structured by an insistence that compromise is impossible. Thus, one of Frank Collin's ACLU lawyers argued that "the First Amendment to the United States Constitution *is* democracy."[14] In effect he was saying that unless *his* reading of the First Amendment is adopted, we will not have democracy.

In what sense is there compromise, however, if the abortion restrictions imposed in most Western European jurisdictions, like the prohibitions against racist speech permitted in these same places, do very little (as in fact is the case) to deter either abortions or racist speech? With regard to abortion, Glendon reasons that the law may have important symbolic and pedagogic value apart from any specific impact it might have on the practice of abortion. "[A] legal norm, even though it seems ineffective, can help to create a climate of opinion which impedes more extensive violations of the norm."[15] The law, according to this view, communicates the seriousness of

[11] Ibid., p. 2.

[12] Ibid., p. 119.

[13] This is pointed out by Lee C. Bollinger, who cites American participation at the Convention on the Elimination of All Forms of Racial Discrimination for illustrative purposes. Article 4 of the Convention contains extensive prohibitions against racist speech activities, a fact that has impelled a number of commentators to recommend against ratification of the agreement. Lee C. Bollinger, *The Tolerant Society: Freedom of Speech and Extremist Speech in America* (New York: Oxford University Press, 1986), p. 253.

[14] David Hamlin, *The Nazi/Skokie Conflict: A Civil Liberties Battle* (Boston: Beacon Press, 1980), p. 175.

[15] Glendon, *Abortion and Divorce in Western Law*, p. 60.

abortion as a moral issue. With regard to racist speech, it signals that there are certain matters about which a democratic community cannot afford to remain neutral. In so doing, it embodies critical definitional dimensions of a democratic ethos. In the end it makes more sense to say that democracy *is* the First Amendment, that our interpretation of the constitutional guarantee expresses the way in which we understand the polity in which we live.

But there is, according to respected scholarly opinion, a "lack of consensus in our society concerning the basic purposes and values underlying the First Amendment."[16] How then can one speak of a prevailing view, much less one that embodies an important political teaching? The *Skokie* outcome, for example, embodies a lesson on democracy, but in what sense can it be said to reflect any sort of orthodoxy within judicial and scholarly circles? With the flow of books and articles on First Amendment theory having reached torrential proportions, it is, after all, safe to assume that these writings do not simply provide us with a continuous reaffirmation of the same set of orthodox principles.

Justice Brandeis's famous concurrence in *Whitney* v. *California* is a good place to begin in order to understand this question. It is among the most oft-quoted opinions on the subject of free expression; not surprisingly, both Judge Decker and Justice Barak included extended excerpts in their decisions:

> Those who won our independence believed that the final end of the State was to make men free to develop their faculties; and that in its government the deliberative forces should prevail over the arbitrary. They valued liberty both as an end and as a means. They believed liberty to be the secret of happiness and courage to be the secret of liberty. They believed that freedom to think as you will and to speak as you think are means indispensable to the discovery and spread of political truth; that without free speech and assembly discussion would be futile; that with them, discussion affords ordinarily adequate protection against the dissemination of noxious doctrine; that the greatest menace to freedom is an inert people; that public discussion is a political duty; and that this should be a fundamental principle of the American government.[17]

One can readily understand why this statement is so frequently cited, for apart from its great eloquence, it includes a concise statement of the princi-

---

[16] Franklyn S. Haiman, *Speech and Law in a Free Society* (Chicago: University of Chicago Press, 1981), p. 185.

[17] *Whitney*, 274 U.S. at 375.

pal justifications for free speech. Indeed, the lack of consensus in contemporary American free speech theory has mainly to do with disagreement over the relative importance to be assigned to the various rationales cited by Brandeis. But rarely are the traditional justificatory arguments seen as mutually exclusive. Instead, one commentator will emphasize the intrinsic value of speech; another will conceptualize it more instrumentally, often in relation to the pursuit of truth. One will stress self-fulfillment; another self-government. It seems almost obligatory that, whatever one's own particular preference, a serious consideration of the issue must begin with an assessment of the strengths and weaknesses of the three standard defenses of free speech.

To discover a dominant teaching requires going beyond this initial level of disagreement over justification. For each of the standard defenses it is possible to reach different conclusions about the extent to which speech should remain unrestricted. Someone who values free speech because it is a basic human right may believe either that self-fulfillment is an inherently subjective concept requiring complete autonomy in how one chooses to express oneself through speech, or that limits to speech may legitimately be imposed at the point where speech is no longer *free*, that is, expressive of our specifically *human* nature. Likewise, the argument for free speech that rests on its contribution to the pursuit of truth may lead one to the "marketplace of ideas," where regulation may be justified only to ensure a more diverse hearing; or to official policies that pursue truth by encouraging what is good and discouraging what is bad. And finally, the claim that self-government implies free speech may suggest a system of absolute protection for speech (at a minimum, certainly, of the kind that may be deemed "political"), or selective protection, depending on whether the speech has the potential to undermine the regime's commitment to self-government.

The common fault line in all three of these sets of possibilities centers on the question of *content*; more specifically, whether it is proper for government to take the substance of what someone says into account when deciding the limits of free speech. Thus, whatever one's view on the relative importance of the three justifications, there is a strong likelihood that, on the critical issue of content-neutrality, a consistent pattern of response will be forthcoming, meaning that someone who believes such neutrality is vital to one justification will also see it as vital to the others. As the following comments by leading free speech theorists suggest, the prevailing wisdom is to be found on the side of content-neutrality. Archibald Cox: "The first amendment gives speech and related forms of expression virtually absolute protection against restriction based upon the dangerous character of the words."[18] Laurence H. Tribe: "If the constitutional guarantee is not to be trivialized, it must mean that government cannot justify restrictions on free expression by reference to the adverse consequences of allowing certain ideas or information to enter the realm of discussion and awareness."[19] Thomas I. Emerson: "To say that [any speech is] of 'slight social value as a step to truth' is to inject the Court into value judgments concerned with the content of expression, a role foreclosed to it by the basic theory of the First Amendment."[20] Harry Kalven, Jr.: "The point [about the First Amendment is] that the state is not to umpire the truth or falsity of doctrine; it is to remain neutral."[21] Kenneth L. Karst: " 'Equality of status in the field of ideas' is not merely a first amendment value; it is the heart of the first amendment."[22] Frederick Schauer: "The decision not to allow free speech protection to turn on the point of view adopted by the speaker goes to the epistemological and political cores of free speech theory."[23]

Brandeis's opinion is basically consistent with these statements. As the coauthor of a classic article on privacy that extols the virtues of being let alone, his libertarian views on expression do not come as a surprise.[24] At least one key sentence in his opinion, however, lends itself to an interpretation that suggests what the view on the other side of the fault line looks like, a view that has become increasingly hard to find, both from a scholarly and a judicial vantage point: "Those who won our independence believed that the final end of the State was to make men free to develop their faculties; and that in its government *the deliberative forces should prevail over the arbitrary*" (emphasis added). Today it is difficult to imagine this to mean something other than that any interference by public authority in the expressive choices of individuals is arbitrary and hence incompatible with the design of the framers of the Constitution. But within the natural rights context of the framers, the triumph of deliberative forces over arbitrary ones meant that liberty, rightly understood in contradistinction to license,

[18] Cox, *Freedom of Expression*, p. 48.

[19] Tribe, *American Constitutional Law*, p. 581.

[20] Thomas I. Emerson, *The System of Freedom of Expression* (New York: Vintage Books, 1970), p. 326.

[21] Harry Kalven, Jr., *A Worthy Tradition: Freedom of Speech in America* (New York: Harper & Row, 1988), p. 10.

[22] Kenneth L. Karst, "Equality as a Central Principle in the First Amendment," *University of Chicago Law Review* 43 (1975): 43.

[23] Frederick Schauer, "Categories and the First Amendment: A Play in Three Acts," *Vanderbilt Law Review* 34 (1981): 284.

[24] S. Warren and L. Brandeis, "The Right to Privacy," *Harvard Law Review* 4 (1890).

was predicated on the rule of reason over the passions. As Rogers M. Smith has pointed out, "When early liberals described the state as a human creation aimed at furthering men's own ends . . . they were not justifying it as a means of enabling each man to pursue whatever he wished, or even as a means for each to do so consistently with the like rights of others. The liberal state was instead justified as a means of enabling each to freely pursue activities in accord with reason."[25] Smith carefully distinguishes the liberalism of the founding period from the quite different notion of autonomy prevailing today, while indicating that from the very beginning it was difficult sustaining the natural rights view against the fairly relentless onslaught of competing currents of thought.[26]

It is wrong, then, to say of the decision to keep the Nazis from marching that "what Skokie wanted most to do was the one thing which two hundred years of American political tradition and law flatly forbid— . . . to censor an idea based on the content of that idea."[27] A more accurate conclusion is that the various Supreme Court cases cited in the decision to support a position of viewpoint neutrality are in fundamental harmony with the broad thrust of philosophic movement in twentieth-century American intellectual opinion. Judge Decker, for example, quoted from the Court's opinion in *Gertz* v. *Welch*: "Under the First Amendment there is no such thing as a false idea."[28] He expressed some misgivings about this particular formulation, but he affirmed its basic message when he quoted the Supreme Court's view in *Police Department of Chicago* v. *Mosley*: "Above all else . . . the government has no power to restrict expression because of its message, its ideas, its subject matter, or its content."[29] And he relied heavily on *Cohen*

[25] Rogers M. Smith, "The Constitution and Autonomy," *Texas Law Review* 60 (1982): 179. See also Murray Dry, "Free Speech and Modern Republican Government," *Constitutional Commentary* 6 (1989). Dry uses Locke and Spinoza to argue against the libertarian thrust of contemporary free speech doctrine.

[26] "The turn from liberty to autonomy reflects a shift from higher law views that justified the liberal state as the means of achieving a specific substantive goal, securing natural rights, to more relativistic stances that defend the state because it allows for the pursuit of self-chosen ends, now held to be the only ends that are legitimate." Smith, "The Constitution and Autonomy," p. 177. The most decisive assault on the older view was delivered by the pragmatists and their intellectual colleagues in sociological jurisprudence. I have described these developments at length in *Pragmatism, Statesmanship, and the Supreme Court* (Ithaca: Cornell University Press, 1977). Smith's work suggests a need to make an important qualification of Glendon's conclusion that personal autonomy is fundamental to American philosophical commitments. One clause should do it—*as these commitments have evolved.*

[27] Hamlin, *The Nazi/Skokie Conflict*, p. 58.

[28] *Gertz* v. *Welch*, 418 U.S. 323, 339 (1974).

[29] *Police Department of Chicago* v. *Mosley*, 408 U.S. 92, 95 (1972).

187

v. *California*, which is well known for its assertion that "it is . . . often true that one man's vulgarity is another's lyric."[30]

When one adds to this the further commonly held presumption (as reflected in Brandeis's opinion) that the official indifference to viewpoint has a special importance when applied to political speech, the connection to the older liberalism of the framers becomes even more tenuous.[31] That is because, as Walter Berns has argued, the founders established the United States upon a clear political creed, declaring certain propositions to be self-evident, that is, true.[32] This led them to distinguish between political and religious speech, providing greater latitude for intervention in the first kind, for in the case of religion, the regime's neutrality was an essential cornerstone of the entire constitutional edifice they had created.[33] Politics, in this view, was different in the decisive sense that all ideas were not equal. To argue, as Harry Kalven, Jr., has, that the religion clauses of the First Amendment should serve as a model for interpreting the speech and press clauses[34] may or may not be good advice, but its conformity to the thinking of the framers is highly questionable. Perhaps more consistent with these early liberal (but now illiberal) views is Lincoln's position that the political truth concerning the equality of all men meant that all ideas were not equal, which in turn meant that the Constitution did not necessarily afford them equal protection.[35]

---

[30] *Cohen* v. *California*, 403 U.S. 15, 25 (1971).

[31] Obviously I cannot agree with this observation of Kent Greenawalt. "Although the perceived justifications for free speech were not articulated in a systematic way, an assessment based on writings that were then highly respected suggests that the Framers' reasons for valuing speech were connected to those which dominate modern adjudication." Kent Greenawalt, *Speech, Crime, and the Uses of Language* (New York: Oxford University Press, 1989), p. 175.

[32] Walter Berns, *The First Amendment and the Future of American Democracy* (New York: Basic Books, 1976), p. 82. More typical of modern commentators is Thomas I. Emerson, who contends that the Declaration of Independence supports content-neutrality. See Emerson, *The System of Freedom of Expression*, p. 7.

[33] Berns, *The First Amendment*, p. 146.

[34] Kalven, *A Worthy Tradition*, p. 10. Kalven was intent on establishing the presence of a "consensus on untouchable content" in regard to First Amendment interpretation. He rightly observed, in connection to religious controversies, that "*In America there is no heresy, no blasphemy*" (p. 7). But he made a questionable move in extending this to the political sphere.

[35] I have considered Lincoln's "liberal intolerance" elsewhere. See Jacobsohn, *The Supreme Court and the Decline of Constitutional Aspiration*, pp. 106–7. It is also worth noting here that the Court has defended its neutrality position on the content of speech by linking the equal protection clause of the Fourteenth Amendment to the free speech guarantee of the First Amendment. See *Police Department of Chicago*, 408 U.S. 92. Kenneth L. Karst has

The Supreme Court has not ruled that all *speech* is equal. Certain categories of speech are of such "low value" that they either fall outside of the protective ambit of the First Amendment (obscenity, for example) or are entitled to only a limited degree of protection (as in the case of certain types of commercial speech). However, within the area of protected speech, there is a presumption that all ideas are equal, a corollary of the core requirement that "government may not aim at the communicative impact of expressive conduct."[36] As one of the leading academic exponents of the doctrine of content-neutrality has noted, "Outside the realm of low-value speech, the Court has invalidated almost every content-based restriction that it has considered in the past thirty years."[37] Obviously this two-track approach entails inquiry into the content of speech, but only to ascertain that the subject matter of the contested speech places it in one category or another. This means, for example, that if you are an adherent of the "marketplace of ideas" rationale for free speech, you may proceed uncompromisingly in the knowledge that the restrictions imposed on speech do not improperly remove ideas from the competitive arena.[38] As the Court said in the landmark case of *Chaplinsky* v. *New Hampshire*, "Such utterances [referring to obscenity, profanity, libel, and 'fighting' words] are no essential part of any exposition of ideas, and are of such slight social value as a step to truth that any benefit that may be derived from them is clearly outweighed by the social interest in order and morality."[39]

The doctrinal path to these categorical distinctions is not always clear. Either it leads to the application of what amounts to a legal fiction—that

---

argued, "Just as the prohibition of government-imposed discrimination on the basis of race is central to equal protection analysis, protection against governmental discrimination on the basis of speech content is central among first amendment values." Karst, "Equality as a Central Principle in the First Amendment," p. 35. Thus, as far as the First Amendment is concerned, the who and the *what* of civic identity are equally irrelevant.

[36] Tribe, *American Constitutional Law*, p. 672.

[37] Geoffrey R. Stone, "Content-Neutral Restrictions," *University of Chicago Law Review* 54 (1987): 48. Stone's other articles on the subject are "Restrictions of Speech Because of Its Content: The Peculiar Case of Subject-Matter Restrictions," *University of Chicago Law Review* 46 (1978); and "Content Regulation and the First Amendment," *William and Mary Law Review* 25 (1983).

[38] This understanding does not find acceptance by some of the critics of the two-level approach. For example, Kenneth L. Karst contends that "the two-level theory rejects the principle of equality in the marketplace of ideas." Karst, "Equality as a Central Principle in the First Amendment," p. 31. See also Martin H. Redish, "The Content Distinction in First Amendment Analysis," *Stanford Law Review* 34 (1981).

[39] *Chaplinsky* v. *New Hampshire*, 315 U.S. 568, 571 (1942).

judicial inquiry is not concerned with ideas—or it accepts, following *Chaplinsky*, that the ideas in some speech are not *essential* to the good of society. This latter interpretation seems to invite, or at least make possible, the addition to the original list of other types of speech, a prospect that explains why, among other reasons, *Chaplinsky* is not held in high regard today by many commentators. In both cases, however, the immunity of speech that has any *political* content is preserved; in the first instance because political speech communicates ideas, and in the second because, *as* political speech, it is presumed to be essential to the conduct of the public's business. In *Skokie*, the village rested its case on the claim that the Nazi propagation of racial hatred was unprotected speech (despite the unfortunate fact that the community's ordinances employed *context*-based exceptions to the First Amendment). This did not impress the Court, which observed that the "determination of whether speech is valueless and therefore unprotected inevitably involves to some extent an inquiry into its content, and this raises the possibility that the speech will be suppressed in part because of the offensiveness of the ideas it conveys."[40] It adopted the Supreme Court's narrow interpretation of *Chaplinsky*, emphasizing that "care must be taken to insure that what is restricted is insulting and offensive *language* not the communication of offensive ideas."[41]

Once the presumption was made that the Nazis were communicating ideas, and especially ideas that had political content, their free speech rights under the modern interpretive dispensation were basically unassailable. "It seems unlikely," wrote the philosopher T. M. Scanlon, Jr., "that expression so deeply offensive to bystanders would be deemed to be protected by freedom of expression if it did not have a political character."[42] The way to challenge the court's ruling was not to depict the ugly quality of Nazi political ideas, but to deny that they were political. Thus a fairly typical critical reaction concedes that "if the Nazi march is political . . . it cannot be prohibited under the First Amendment."[43] But if it is seen as an "instigation to violence," then it falls "outside the protection of the First Amendment."[44] Both sides, in other words, accept the same rules of the game regarding political speech, and thereby implicitly acknowledge an

[40] *Collin*, 447 F. Supp. at 689.

[41] Ibid., 690.

[42] T. M. Scanlon, Jr., "Freedom of Expression and Categories of Expression," *University of Pittsburgh Law Review* 40 (1979): 538.

[43] Irving Louis Horowitz and Victoria Curtis Bramson, "Skokie: The ACLU and the Endurance of Democratic Theory," *Law and Contemporary Problems* 43 (1979): 336.

[44] Ibid.

important consensus of understanding.[45] What generally separates expansive and restrictive interpretations of the First Amendment is how broadly to define what is political, rather than whether or not the position of political speech is sacrosanct.[46]

The viewpoint-neutrality approach, and its special place in connection with political speech, is the free speech doctrine of the "procedural republic." In the American context, the work of someone like John Hart Ely suggests the message of the current constitutional orthodoxy. Ely is widely known for his process-oriented constitutional jurisprudence, an approach that views the democratic commitment of our political system as irreconcilable with a judicial role that includes enforcement of specific substantive values. "The original Constitution's . . . strategy . . . can be loosely styled a strategy of pluralism."[47] From this pluralism Ely deduces the following lesson: "If the First Amendment is even to begin to serve its central func-

[45] Not many other interpretations would unite Robert H. Bork and many of his harshest libertarian critics. Bork writes, without claiming as he usually does that original intent is clear on the issue, that "constitutional protection should be accorded only to speech that is explicitly political." Robert H. Bork, "Neutral Principles and Some First Amendment Problems," *Indiana Law Journal* 47 (1971): 20. The agreement of course is not that protection should be limited to explicitly political speech, but that political speech is the First Amendment's principal concern. Bork goes on to say, "There is no basis for judicial intervention to protect any other form of expression, be it scientific, literary or that variety of expression we call obscene or pornographic" (p. 20). This is where he parts company with almost everyone who has written on the subject. The viewpoint-neutrality principle that Bork would attach to explicitly political speech is extended by most contemporary commentators to other forms of expression, and often for reasons—for the sake of self-fulfillment, for example—that Bork considers illegitimate.

[46] Obscenity is likely to produce the greatest disagreement. Michael J. Perry, for example, argues that "certainly there is no denying that obscene pornography constitutes a political-moral vision." Michael J. Perry, "Freedom of Expression: An Essay on Theory and Doctrine," *Northwestern University Law Review* 78 (1984): 1182. Many others view pornography as unprotected speech precisely because it is physiologically, rather than rationally, oriented. In this regard, Cass R. Sunstein makes an interesting observation about the feminist antipornography argument: "In one respect . . . the feminist case for regulation of pornography might seem, quite paradoxically, to weaken the argument for regulation. The feminist argument is that pornography represents an ideology, one that has important consequences for social attitudes. Speech that amounts to an ideology, one might argue, cannot be considered low-value, for such speech lies at the heart of politics. If pornography indeed does amount to an ideology of male supremacy, it might be thought to be entitled to the highest form of constitutional protection." Cass R. Sunstein, "Pornography and the First Amendment," *Duke Law Journal* 1986 (1986): 607.

[47] John Hart Ely, *Democracy and Distrust: A Theory of Judicial Review* (Cambridge: Harvard University Press, 1982), p. 80.

tion of assuring an open political dialogue and process, we must seek to minimize assessment of the dangerousness of the various messages people want to communicate."[48] Ely's general thesis has been widely acclaimed, but it has also been the object of extensive and heated attack, particularly from those critical of the separation of process and substance. But his pluralist constitutional framework can easily accommodate a more substance-oriented approach, as the free speech deduction illustrates. Thus, someone believing that the central function of the First Amendment is to assure each person's self-fulfillment, or that free speech is an intrinsic good, would likely, in today's intellectual climate, reach precisely the same conclusion as Ely concerning the role of government in assessing the content of speech. To achieve the substantive goal of autonomy requires the affirmation of process.

The district court's opinion in *Collin* v. *Smith* exemplifies this pluralist vision. Judge Decker conceived of the polity in purely procedural terms, having no authority to assess the substantive merits of speech, even when this speech is employed for the purpose of vilifying a specific community. "Defendants have no power to prevent plaintiffs from stating their political philosophy, including their opinions of black and Jewish people, however noxious and reprehensible that philosophy may be."[49] As Donald A. Downs has correctly noted, "In essence, survivors asked the courts to heed the claims of substantive justice in the case rather than limiting their legal considerations to the issue of procedural justice, or equal protection in the public forum. Yet the courts abided by the requirements of the content neutrality rule, which prohibited a consideration of substantive justice."[50] What is at issue here is a profound commitment to a particular conception of a liberal polity, one that holds that a free society may not endorse an official or public orthodoxy. The community may not exercise its authority to establish the illegitimacy of certain ideas. "If there is any fixed star in our constitutional constellation, it is that no official, high or petty, can prescribe

[48] Ibid., p. 112.

[49] *Collin*, 447 F. Supp. at 686.

[50] Downs, *Nazis in Skokie*, p. 5. For a critique of Downs's argument, see Edward L. Rubin, "Nazis, Skokie, and the First Amendment as Virtue," *California Law Review* 74 (1986). Rubin's main contention is that content-neutrality is a reflection of the "quasi-absolute" right of free speech, and that therefore upholding the Nazis' right to march is not "procedural" at all. Elsewhere Downs has wisely pointed out that "the liberal tradition is not encapsulated by the brand of individualism that underlies modern First Amendment law." Donald A. Downs, "Beyond Modernist Liberalism: Toward a Reconstruction of Free Speech Doctrine," in *Judging the Constitution: Critical Essays on Judicial Lawmaking*, ed. Michael W. McCann and Gerald L. Houseman (Glenview, Ill.: Scott, Foresman & Co., 1989), pp. 317–18.

what shall be orthodox in politics, nationalism, religion, or other matters of opinion."[51]

Pluralism and the Sensibilities of Others

If there were a civil liberties Hall of Fame, Justice Jackson's eloquent statement, like Justice Brandeis's, would surely be a treasured exhibit. Whether the justice himself would gain admittance is not as clear, since his opinions did not always sit well with the organized civil liberties community.[52] For example, in *Kunz* v. *New York*, involving the fulminations of an anti-Semitic speaker, Jackson wrote, "To blanket hateful and hate-stirring attacks on races and faiths under the protections for free speech may be a noble innovation. On the other hand, it may be a quixotic tilt at windmills which belittles great principles of liberty. Only time will tell. But I incline to the latter view."[53] When juxtaposed with his earlier opinion in *Barnette*, Jackson's observation raises the interesting question of whether a high official, such as a Supreme Court justice, may declare as a matter of political orthodoxy the illegitimacy of hateful speech.

To proscribe is also to prescribe; the fact, in other words, that *Kunz*, unlike *Barnette*, did not involve governmental action in *support* of a particular orthodoxy is irrelevant to the critical issue of whether the polity should serve as a neutral forum for the expression of all points of view. In *Barnette*, Justice Jackson affirmed "the right to differ as to things that touch the heart

[51] Justice Jackson in *West Virginia* v. *Barnette*, 319 U.S. 624, 642 (1943). Of course the statement has a built-in contradiction in the sense that its very declaration is an attempt to establish an official orthodoxy, namely that no orthodoxies are to be permitted under the Constitution, that content-neutrality is our political truth. This might be considered in connection with what we have seen in Chapter 2, that the acquisition of American citizenship is predicated on acceptance of the principles of the Constitution.

[52] For an analysis of Justice Jackson's First Amendment views, see Walter F. Murphy, "Mr. Justice Jackson, Free Speech, and the Judicial Function," *Vanderbilt Law Review* 12 (1959). Murphy portrays an enigmatic Jackson, pointing out, "There is no doubt that Jackson's ideas about free speech . . . cannot be fitted into the common classifications of libertarian or anti-libertarian" (p. 1019). See also C. Herman Pritchett, *Civil Liberties and the Vinson Court* (Chicago: University of Chicago Press, 1954): "The unpredictability of Jackson's performance leads one to question whether he has developed any systematic theories about civil liberties or the judicial function" (pp. 228–29). Another interesting perspective on Jackson's free speech views may be found in Murray Dry, "Flag Burning and the Constitution," *Supreme Court Review 1990* (Chicago: University of Chicago Press, 1991), pp. 100–102.

[53] *Kunz* v. *New York*, 340 U.S. 290, 295 (1951). It may very well be that Jackson's recent experience as chief U.S. prosecutor at Nuremberg made him more sensitive to the sort of speech involved in this case.

of the existing order."[54] In *Kunz*, he implied that the heart of the existing order consisted of great principles of liberty, principles that should not be distorted by incorporating within them the toleration of hateful verbal attacks on races and faiths, or, in Harry Kalven, Jr.'s phrase, "ideological fighting words."[55] The first opinion seems very much in the spirit of the modern constitutional right to personal autonomy; the second seems to be informed by the older equation of liberty with reasoned order.

The distinction has particular relevance to the sort of group-targeted expression implicated in the *Skokie* affair. The rejection of the community's claim by the court has been both celebrated and denounced as a triumph of individualism over communitarianism. On one level, certainly, this reading is correct; Collin's individual right was upheld against the community's defensive actions. But viewed from another level, this interpretation obscures the sense in which the individualist strain ingrained in the rational liberty of the Declaration of Independence may also be used to dispute Collin's free speech argument. In this older conception, the claims of the individual and the community are not inherently competitive or conflictual; indeed, they can be mutually supportive. Thus, the aspect of group vilification that renders it most offensive is not so much its failure to respect the integrity of the group as its denigration of those attributes of the human personality that are common to all people and not just specific groups.[56] From this perspective, group libel laws and antihate legislation aim to uphold the fundamental liberty rights of individuals. The fact that today these laws are often associated with the communitarian agenda of a republican revival in American political and jurisprudential thought, rather than with traditional liberal concerns, is witness to the ascendance of autonomy to a special position in constitutional law and theory.

---

[54] *West Virginia v. Barnette*, 319 U.S. at 642.

[55] Kalven, *A Worthy Tradition*, p. 81.

[56] See Mark S. Campisano, "Group Vilification Reconsidered," *Yale Law Journal* 89 (1979). The author disputes the common view that group libel is speech protected by the First Amendment, arguing that laws against it do "not violate, but . . . rather fulfill, the ideal of deliberative self-government that underlies the First Amendment" (p. 332). The author, however, does not base the argument on the content of any ideas implicit in group vilification; indeed, such speech "trades not in ideas but in pernicious and undeliberated passions" (p. 322). There is a further sense in which communal and individual rights may be viewed as mutually supportive rather than in conflict. "When we think about speech we imagine not only individual speakers . . . but also a community of shared understanding, sustained communication, collective representations, and collective self-expression and self-understanding. Thus, communality is a necessary dimension of the speech value." Ronald Garet, "Communality and Existence: The Rights of Groups," *Southern California Law Review* 56 (1983): 1023.

But the communitarian approach, to the extent that its primary focus is on the group rather than the individual, will have a difficult time competing on the playing field of American pluralism. Our constitutional law, as we have seen, simply does not acknowledge that groups possess rights. In their critique of the *Skokie* decision, Horowitz and Bramson advance the concept of "community privacy" as an urgent matter for constitutional consideration.[57] Privacy, they claim, is not a purely individualist phenomenon. Maybe so, but the thrust of modern legal opinion is in the opposite direction, equating privacy with individual autonomy, which means, as far as the First Amendment is concerned, that it is the speaker's "privacy right" that commands judicial protection. For example, David A. J. Richards, a libertarian constitutional theorist who espouses a contractarian model of the polity, bases his objection to group libel laws on the premise that these actions represent an attack on the "central ideas of the political and moral legitimacy of the state and community."[58] These ideas are identified with individual conscience and autonomy, which are rendered vulnerable by group libel laws because such laws require the state to make evaluative judgments regarding the merits of communicative content.[59] While the same objection might be raised against individual libel actions, Richards distinguishes it from the unconstitutional variety by contending, as others have, that the former do not "express general conscientious views of speakers and audiences."[60]

The court in *Collin* v. *Smith* reached essentially the same conclusion. In the process it presented dictum to the effect that the controversial 1952 Supreme Court decision in *Beauharnais* v. *Illinois*, upholding a group libel statute, is, in light of subsequent decisions, no longer good law.[61] One of its reasons for viewing the case as "obsolete by modern standards" is that group defamation touches on questions that are the subject of legitimate

[57] Horowitz and Bramson, "Skokie," p. 338.

[58] David A. J. Richards, *Toleration and the Constitution* (New York: Oxford University Press, 1986), pp. 191–92.

[59] Ibid., p. 191.

[60] Ibid. For a criticism of the distinction, see Hadley Arkes, "Civility and the Restriction of Speech: Rediscovering the Defamation of Groups," *Supreme Court Review 1974* (Chicago: University of Chicago Press, 1975), p. 296.

[61] The Court appealed, in this regard, to the widely held belief among First Amendment scholars. In his last work, Harry Kalven, Jr., wrote, "Although the Court has never again been confronted with the group defamation question, the continued vitality of *Beauharnais* is highly questionable." Kalven, *A Worthy Tradition*, p. 117. For a minority view, see Kenneth Lasson, "Racial Defamation as Free Speech: Abusing the First Amendment," *Columbia Human Rights Law Review* 17 (1985).

public debate. "It is obvious," said one commentator after the 1952 ruling, "that group libel is one means—albeit it an unethical one—of conducting the public discussion necessary to the democratic process; consequently . . . the First Amendment should apply, since it was especially designed to protect discussion of public issues."[62] This is a view that one repeatedly encounters in the First Amendment literature.[63] It is so popular because it implicates all three of the standard justifications for free speech and fits comfortably within the modern individualist ethos of content-neutrality. On the other hand the republican or communitarian challenge to this dominant interpretation raises the specter of viewpoint censorship. "[Republicans] stress the close identity of the person with the group. So to attack a group . . . is no mere abstraction for them, nor is group libel an outmoded idea. We *are* our families and groups, say Republicans; they form us in our youth and membership in them defines us after we mature."[64]

The difference between this republican account and the early individualist view is that the latter imagines the individual apart from the group and finds in the vilification of the group a denigration of the individual members of the group as equal constituents of the social order. Both are ultimately concerned with personal dignity, but they approach the problem from different angles. In the end, there is more that unites than divides them, a fact often obscured by the efforts of the republican revivalists to locate their position within a tradition distinct from the early Federalists. Thus the moderate republican argument, as opposed to a more radical version in

[62] Loren Beth, "Group Libel and Free Speech," *University of Minnesota Law Review* 39 (1955): 172.

[63] See, for example, Carl Cohen, "The Case Against Group Libel," *Nation*, June 24, 1978; Emerson, *The System of Freedom of Expression*, p. 397; D.F.B. Tucker, *Law, Liberalism, and Free Speech* (Totowa, N.J.: Rowman & Allanheld, 1985), p. 140; and Haiman, *Speech and Law in a Free Society*, p. 96.

[64] John Arthur, *The Unfinished Constitution: Philosophy and Constitutional Practice* (Belmont, Calif.: Wadsworth Publishing Co., 1989), p. 91. This is consistent with Justice Frankfurter's opinion in *Beauharnais*: "It is not within our competence to confirm or deny claims of social scientists as to the dependence of the individual on the position of his racial or religious group in the community. It would, however, be arrant dogmatism . . . for us to deny that the Illinois legislature may warrantably believe that a man's job and his educational opportunities and the dignity accorded to him may depend as much on the reputation of the racial and religious group to which he willy-nilly belongs, as on his own merits." *Beauharnais* v. *Illinois*, 343 U.S. 250, 263 (1952). If *Beauharnais* is to be revived, the chances are that it will occur in the context of the feminist critique of pornography. With a change of pronouns, Justice Frankfurter's observation is very much in line with this critique. On the relationship between group libel and pornography, see William Brigman, "Pornography as Group Libel: The Indianapolis Sex Discrimination Ordinance," *Indiana Law Review* 18 (1985).

which the community's interests are distinct from the individual's, is reconcilable with an individualism that is itself distinguishable from the radically individualist focus on autonomy. With respect to the issue of antihate legislation (which may or may not take the form of a group libel law), they both require judicial attention to the substance of speech, even where the threat of immediate social disorder is not implicated.

This is because, as Harry Kalven, Jr. once noted, "Group libels would be exactly as odious, antisocial, and dangerous even though there were never to be a breach of peace."[65] "Unlike other troublesome speech, it does not advocate or incite, its words are not 'triggers of action.' Its evils are slower, and corrosive."[66] It is, then, significant that, according to Judge Decker, "The [Supreme] Court views speech which defames racial and religious groups merely as a special category of language likely to cause breaches of the peace."[67] Again, mainstream academic opinion is in agreement; Kent Greenawalt, for example, writes that "if racial or religious epithets are to be proscribed it must be primarily because they amount to fighting words or because they do some other immediate harm."[68] This is consistent with the general trend in the judicial treatment of offensive speech, which has been to focus almost exclusively on behavioral considerations—acts as opposed to feelings.[69] The upshot is that, for all practical purposes, group-targeted defamation is immune from liability in the United States. This explains why in Great Britain legislation concerned with racial vilification is now framed in terms of "offensiveness" and not breach of the peace. Section 6 of the British Race Relations Act of 1965 specifically removed the requirement for a probable breach of the peace that had been central to the Public Order Act of 1936.[70] It is a provision very similar to the one struck down by the district court in *Collin* v. *Smith*.

Embedded in the prevailing American approach to group defamatory speech is a specific teaching on pluralist democracy that conceives of the

---

[65] Kalven, *The Negro and the First Amendment*, p. 44.

[66] Ibid., p. 13.

[67] *Collin*, 447 F. Supp. at 697.

[68] Greenawalt, *Speech, Crime, and the Uses of Language*, p. 284.

[69] See Mark C. Rutzick, "Offensive Language and the Evolution of First Amendment Protection," *Harvard Civil Rights–Civil Liberties Law Review* 9 (1974). Rutzick argues that the prevention of physical violence is a valid and fundamental interest of a free society, but that the interest in "sensibilities," because it cannot be given "an objective fixed meaning," represents a potential threat to such a society (p. 7).

[70] See the discussion in Eric Barendt, *Freedom of Speech* (Oxford: Oxford University Press, 1987), pp. 162–64. French and German law are even less tied to the breach-of-the-peace model.

public domain as a mirror to society, reflecting with minimal distortion all of its jagged edges, abrasive surfaces, and jarring discontinuities. Flattering images and ugly images present themselves with equal clarity; nothing is to be done to enhance the appearance of one at the expense of the other. Were it permitted, for example, to adjust the contours of the mirror (amusement park–style) in order to eliminate the most offensive reflections, we would confront a basic challenge to the foundational premises of a viable pluralist democracy. "In a polyglot society we cannot—repeat, cannot—threaten to punish angry speech about groups, even when allegedly defamatory, and expect to keep democracy healthy."[71]

In response to this it might be said that racial defamation has nothing to do with democracy. It is one thing to value verbal free-for-all in the public arena, quite another to tolerate verbal or expressive assault. The latter is a form of intimidation that, like other forms of intimidation, is calculated to achieve silence, which is not a result ordinarily associated with democracy. For this reason it has been called "subversive speech," subversive, that is, of the older pluralism of the framers.[72] They had been concerned, as Madison put it, with those passions and interests that "divided mankind into parties, inflamed them with mutual animosity, and rendered them much more disposed to vex and oppress each other than to co-operate for their common good."[73] Speech intended to intimidate, frighten, and wound is a destructive force undermining the Madisonian aspiration of an open polity dedicated to the pursuit of the common good. The framers feared the natural tendency of groups to pursue their particular ends without their members acknowledging the common humanity of others whose associations were different. Where the public forum is distinguished by incivility and distrust, where the fundamental integrity of fellow citizens is questioned on the basis of ascriptive group affiliation, the political process is corrupted in a way that diminishes its ability to mediate conflict and advance the public good.

Civility is a value that has on occasion been recognized by the Supreme

[71] Cohen, "The Case Against Group Libel," p. 758.

[72] Lasson, "Racial Defamation as Free Speech," p. 23. On intimidation, see Justice Powell's dissent in *Rosenfeld* v. *New Jersey*, 408 U.S. 901 (1972): "The shock and sense of affront, and sometimes the injury to mind and spirit, can be as great from words as from some physical attacks" (909). Silence as a goal of verbal intimidation is particularly worth considering in the academic environment, where it is often said that the university's tradition of free and open inquiry precludes any restriction on communication. Indeed, the strongest argument *for* restriction of racist speech on campus is that it may *advance* the cause of intellectual inquiry.

[73] Lodge, *The Federalist #10*, p. 54.

Court. In a 1972 opinion, Justice Powell wrote, "The preservation of the right to free and robust speech is accorded high priority in our society and under the Constitution. Yet, there are other significant values. One of the hallmarks of a civilized society is the level and quality of discourse. We have witnessed in recent years a disquieting deterioration in standards of taste and civility in speech."[74] That this observation appears in a dissenting opinion is altogether fitting, because civility has not been a virtue especially valued in contemporary First Amendment jurisprudence. One year earlier, Justice Harlan, by all accounts one of the most civil justices ever to have sat on the Court, struck what several commentators claim was a devastating blow to civility as an interest commanding significant constitutional consideration.[75] His majority opinion in *Cohen* v. *California* has become critically important in the evolution of free speech doctrine, and its libertarian message is an eloquent embodiment of the suppositions of contemporary American pluralism.

Cohen had expressed himself in vivid fashion by attaching the memorable sentiment "Fuck the Draft" to the back of his jacket. Justice Harlan found that the First Amendment protected communication serving an emotive function as well as speech that was cognitive in content. It was not to be regretted, he maintained, that on occasion the air may seem "filled with verbal cacophony."[76] Indeed, this was a sign of strength; offensive speech may reflect a healthy political vitality. While in this case profanity was centrally involved, the issue of civility should not be made to hinge on the use of profane speech, for if it does, a serious matter may easily be trivialized by its reduction to a concern over whether the sensibilities of the majority happen to be bruised by a particular use of language. A deference to the majority in matters of this kind itself can become evidence for the claim of insensitivity to minorities, as was illustrated in a subsequent case, when Justice Brennan found regulatory action against profanity to be "another of the dominant culture's inevitable efforts to force those groups who do not share its mores to conform to its way of thinking, acting, and speaking."[77] When civility is allowed to become a synonym for politeness or comfortableness, its significance to a theory of democratic pluralism may very well go unappreciated. As Montesquieu explained, "Civility is . . . of

[74] *Rosenfeld* v. *New Jersey*, 408 U.S. at 909.

[75] See, for example, Arkes, "Civility and the Restriction of Speech," p. 315; Downs, *Nazis in Skokie*, p. 11; and Robert C. Post, "The Social Foundations of Defamation Law: Reputation and the Constitution," *California Law Review* 74 (1986): 734.

[76] *Cohen*, 403 U.S. at 24.

[77] *FCC* v. *Pacifica Foundation*, 438 U.S. 726, 777 (1978).

more value than politeness. Politeness flatters the vices of others, and civility prevents ours from being brought to light. It is a barrier which men have placed within themselves to prevent the corruption of each other."[78]

Montesquieu's reflections on civility were made in reference to China, where legislators once provided rules of civility in order to have people "filled with a veneration for one another, that each should be every moment sensible of his dependence on society, and of the obligations he owed to his fellow-citizens."[79] While the rulers of China had options available to them that should be forbidden in a liberal democracy, their ostensible goal is one that, with modification, has relevance to the modern democratic predicament. If we substitute respect for veneration, and sensitivity for obligation, then civility emerges as a goal both appropriate and desirable for a liberal pluralist polity. But in a polity where pluralism and autonomy have evolved in tandem, it is not a legitimate predicate for restricting speech. In this setting, "One must begin with the premise that government may not justify the suppression of speech because its content or mode of expression is offensive to some members of the audience."[80]

Robert C. Post has argued that the "the constitutional 'premise of individual dignity' upon which *Cohen* is grounded is . . . a form of individual 'autonomy.' "[81] He distinguishes this understanding of dignity from that which underlies defamation law, where dignity "derive[s] from membership in an orderly and cohesive community defined by the reciprocal observance of rules of civility."[82] Justice Harlan's opinion made clear that the official enforcement of civility rules was incompatible with the freedom of

[78] Montesquieu, *The Spirit of the Laws*, p. 301.

[79] Ibid., p. 300.

[80] Tribe, *American Constitutional Law*, p. 619.

[81] Post, "The Social Foundations of Defamation Law," p. 734. Justice Harlan had said, citing *Whitney*, "The constitutional right of free expression is powerful medicine in a society as diverse and populous as ours. It is designed and intended to remove governmental restraints from the arena of public discussion, putting the decision as to what views shall be voiced largely into the hands of each of us, in the hope that use of such freedom will ultimately produce a more capable citizenry and more perfect polity and in the belief that no other approach would comport with the premise of individual dignity upon which our political system rests." *Cohen*, 403 U.S. at 24. See also Robert C. Post, "The Constitutional Concept of Public Discourse: Outrageous Opinion, Democratic Deliberation, and *Hustler Magazine* v. *Falwell*," *Harvard Law Review* 103 (1989–90). Here Post argues that the ideal of rational deliberation is ultimately dependent on the continuing viability of community norms.

[82] Post, "The Social Foundations of Defamation Law," p. 734. "For the Supreme Court explicitly to incorporate into its constitutional analysis the principles underlying the concept of reputation as dignity . . . would require it to embrace values that directly fly in the face of the essential premise of constitutional autonomy" (p. 737).

individual choice mandated by the First Amendment. "The ability of government, consonant with the Constitution, to shut off discourse solely to protect others from hearing it is . . . dependent upon a showing that substantial privacy interests are being invaded in an essentially intolerable manner."[83] A substantial public interest—for example, civility—would not, presumably, justify shutting it off. The pluralist theory emerging from his constitutional interpretation is one that sees in the rich diversity of the society the possibility for the multiple expression of personal identities, and expects that any curtailment will be consistent with that end. It is irrelevant whether such expression manifests the absence of any regard for the sensibilities of others. Of course in *Cohen* the *others* had no referent more specific than the society at large. On the other hand, in *Skokie*, which relied heavily on the authority of *Cohen*, it was precisely toward the violation of the sensibilities of a specific group of others that the expression of individual opinion was directed.

Post has elsewhere presented a communitarian approach to group defamation. He labels it "pluralist," but it is not the pluralism of constitutional autonomy. How far it is from prevailing doctrinal orthodoxy is suggested by his use of blasphemy to illustrate its legal implications. To be sure, it is not the common law definition of blasphemy, designed to protect the hegemonic position of Christianity, that is his model; rather, it is the reformulated version articulated by Lord Scarman in an important 1979 British case. In that case, Lord Scarman conceived of blasphemy as an attack on the integrity of *any* religious group. He considered it vital "in an increasingly plural society" for the law to enforce respect for the "religious beliefs, feelings, and practices of all."[84] For Lord Scarman, the purpose of blasphemy law was "to protect religious feelings from outrage and insult."[85] Post contrasts this perspective with that of the Supreme Court in the famous case of *Cantwell* v. *Connecticut*, in which the fact of a diverse society led the Court "in exactly the opposite direction, toward the constitutional requirement that the law tolerate 'exaggeration,' 'vilification,'

---

[83] *Cohen*, 403 U.S. at 21.

[84] Robert C. Post, "Cultural Heterogeneity and Law: Pornography, Blasphemy, and the First Amendment," *California Law Review* 76 (1988): 313. Compare to Israel's Penal Law, section 173, making the publication of matter that would grossly hurt the religious feelings and beliefs of others a misdemeanor. The prohibition extends to the pronouncement of such statements verbally in public or within the hearing range of an individual whose religious feelings would be grossly hurt.

[85] Ibid., p. 311.

and even 'excesses and abuses.' "[86] He portrays *Cantwell* as paradigmatic of individualist law, which is premised on the autonomous choices of individuals. This is one way of putting it; another is to understand the work of the Court as a reflection of contemporary pluralist premises. Again, Ely's work is representative. Where Lord Scarman's pluralism leads him to want to protect religious feelings from outrage and insult, Ely's pluralism says, "Allowing people to assault our eardrums with outrageous and overdrawn denunciations of institutions we treasure will inconvenience, annoy, and infuriate us on occasion, even set us to wondering about the stability of our society: that's exactly what such messages are meant to do, and exactly the price we shouldn't think twice about paying."[87]

Would it make any difference if, instead of institutions like the Selective Service, it was a racial or religious group that was the object of outrageous denunciation? Almost assuredly not, for in both cases the social interest in "robust and uninhibited" debate would be compromised, and so would the right of the individual to select whatever message he or she chose to communicate. The fact that social groups have feelings and bureaucracies (presumably) do not should have no effect on the constitutional equation. The parallel to the placement of emotive speech under the protective umbrella of the First Amendment is the constitutional irrelevance of the nonviolent emotional reaction that might be evoked in a specific audience. Just as it is important that we experience the emotive dimension of speech, which, according to *Cohen*, "may often be the more important element of the overall message sought to be communicated,"[88] it is also vital that we not be deprived of the entire range of emotions that may be stimulated by speech. That within this range is included the wrenching psychological trauma that may surface upon exposure to vivid reminders of a nightmarish past is, as Ely says, part of the price we must be willing to pay for democracy.

Blasphemy refashioned in communitarian guise is no more likely to be incorporated within the doctrinal contours of contemporary First Amendment jurisprudence than is its older incarnation. According to the prevailing view, whatever the loss in civility resulting from abusive and offensive group-targeted speech is more than made up for in the security gained against governmental intrusion into the lives of individuals based on the content of their expressive choices. In rejecting the suggestion that pluralism requires a "rhetorical nonaggression pact," Michael Walzer has argued

[86] Ibid., p. 319.
[87] Ely, *Democracy and Distrust*, p. 116.
[88] *Cohen*, 403 U.S. at 26.

that this would lead to "public life on tiptoe," an unacceptable state of affairs for a free society.[89] But he also wonders whether there are no limits on democratic discourse, whether we should not "worry about insult, contempt, vilification—for the sake of some minimal civility."[90] The answer of American constitutional law has for the most part been to worry more about other things. It is an answer that may very well be consistent with what had, at least until recently, been seen as the long-term decline in the significance of race, ethnicity, and religion in American social life, so that the costs alluded to by Walzer could be expected progressively to diminish as the facts producing them faded into the background of the cultural landscape.

But the prevailing jurisprudential view has come under attack in the last few years, much as the resurgence in some sectors of American social life of ethnic, racial, and religious identities has caused even the most confident prognosticators of assimilation to reassess the future course of cultural development. That this attack has not yet extended much beyond the gates of academia is understandable, for it is mainly in the educational arena that the challenge to liberal pluralist assumptions has been vigorously pursued. Many colleges, as part of their commitment to a vibrant multicultural academic environment, have adopted speech codes (of varying degrees of specificity) intended to curb offensive and abusive expression. They have produced some interesting political alignments, generating opposition from libertarian conservatives and First Amendment liberals, and evoking support from liberal and radical defenders of oppressed minorities, as well as cultural conservatives with an interest in promoting a discourse of civility.

As far as First Amendment jurisprudence is concerned, the debate might usefully be placed within the context of our earlier discussion of pluralist alternatives.[91] Recall, for example, Iris Young's notion of "differential citizenship," which she advances in opposition to orthodox constitutionalism's blindness to group-based perspectives, and what she sees as its failure to acknowledge the irreducible differences in the life experiences of

---

[89] Michael Walzer, "The Sins of Salman," *New Republic*, April 10, 1989, p. 14.

[90] Ibid.

[91] For example, in justifying its speech code, the Massachusetts regents concluded that "there must be a unity and cohesion in the diversity which we seek to achieve, thereby creating an atmosphere of pluralism." This prompted a critic of such codes to observe that "this 'pluralism' is not to be confused with the version endorsed by the First Amendment." Chester E. Finn, Jr., "The Campus: 'An Island of Repression in a Sea of Freedom,'" *Commentary*, September 1989, p. 17.

diverse groups. Then consider that the law review article that has become the centerpiece of debate on the subject of hate speech is premised on the telling of "the victim's story."[92] Beginning with the testimonies of particular victims of hate speech, and connecting these experiences with the broader experience of subordination in the United States, Mari J. Matsuda proposes a rethinking of liberal views on freedom of expression that will, if embraced, lead to a greater willingness to prohibit hate speech. Doctrinal reconstruction in this area of the law is an important part of the development of an "outsider's jurisprudence," which rejects, as do Young and other feminist legal theorists, the "false universalism" of liberal constitutionalism. What is necessary is a "highly contextualized analysis," one that "recognizes that the experience of racism, of persecution for membership in a group, makes the group's consciousness the victim's consciousness, all of which is relevant in assessing the harm of racist speech."[93]

But how relevant is it likely to be in the courts? A student leader at Stanford University told a reporter, "What we are proposing is not completely in line with the First Amendment, but I'm not sure it should be. We . . . are trying to set a standard different from what society at large is trying to accomplish."[94] The student's assessment of constitutional requirements has already been judicially confirmed, even if the accompanying normative gloss has not. The University of Michigan's policy on discriminatory harassment of students was invalidated by a federal district court on First Amendment grounds. To be sure, the university's policy was an easy target because its regulations were unusually vague and overbroad. So while the question of how a more narrowly focused policy might fare in the courts is still arguable, the court's opinion, which scrupulously follows Supreme Court precedents, suggests just how powerful is the constitutional orthodoxy against which the alternative pluralist voices in the academy are arrayed.[95] "What the university could not do . . . was establish an anti-

---

[92] Mari J. Matsuda, "Public Response to Racist Speech: Considering the Victim's Story," *Michigan Law Review* 87 (1989). See also Charles R. Lawrence III, "If He Hollers Let Him Go: Regulating Racist Speech on Campus," *Duke Law Journal* 1990 (1990). "We see a different world than that which is seen by Americans who do not share [our] historical experience. We often hear racist speech when our white neighbors are not aware of its presence" (p. 435).

[93] Matsuda, "Public Response to Racist Speech," p. 2373.

[94] Finn, "The Campus," p. 17.

[95] In an unusual addendum to the district court's opinion, *Doe* v. *University of Michigan*, 721 F. Supp. 869 (E.D. Mich. 1989), Judge Cohn mentioned Matsuda's paper, indicating that for some inexplicable reason the court had not been aware of its existence until after its opinion had been docketed. He then enigmatically suggested that an earlier awareness would have "sharpened the Court's view of the issues" (869).

discrimination policy which had the effect of prohibiting certain speech because it disagreed with ideas or messages sought to be conveyed."[96] The opinion went on to quote with favor from another university report that concluded that "freedom of expression is a paramount value, more important than civility or rationality."[97] In the face of such sentiments it is difficult to imagine the advocates of hate speech criminalization finding a welcome reception in the courts for their alternative doctrinal recommendations. The pluralist assumptions of modern liberal constitutionalism are not so easily dislodged. As the appeal on behalf of a teenager charged with violating a local ordinance prohibiting hateful displays asserts, "Displays of racial, ethnic, religious or gender intolerance reflect varied political viewpoints within our pluralistic society and are not susceptible to constitutionally valid restrictions."[98] The question, as we now turn to Israel, is how well the teaching of American First Amendment jurisprudence fits the circumstances of an alternative pluralist environment.

FREE SPEECH AND THE "VISION AND CREED OF THE PEOPLE"

The U.S. Supreme Court did not speak directly to the meaning of the First Amendment's free speech clause until 1919, or 127 years after the adoption of the Bill of Rights. Free speech issues, some of considerable importance, had arisen in the interim, but none of them led to a ruling by the Supreme Court. This history contrasts sharply with that of Israel, where the Supreme Court decided its first free speech case only five years after independence. In fact it was a landmark case, arguably the most important decision ever handed down by that Court. Indeed, it stimulates one to wonder whether a decision of similar significance would have resulted had the American Court ruled at a comparable time in its history on the constitutionality of the Sedition Act of 1798.[99] Would the Court have used the

[96] Ibid., 863. This conclusion was based on the content-neutrality principle of earlier cases. Among others cited were *Texas* v. *Johnson*, *Chicago Police Department* v. *Mosley*, *Cohen* v. *California*, *West Virginia State Board of Education* v. *Barnette*, and *Hustler Magazine* v. *Falwell*.

[97] Ibid., 868.

[98] *New York Times*, June 11, 1991. The appeal is from a case, *R.A.V.* v. *St. Paul*, which, as of this writing, has just been accepted for review by the Supreme Court. It has already received a great deal of attention; for example, in its lead editorial *The New Republic* (July 8, 1991) advocated its resolution along the lines of the *Skokie* case.

[99] This speculation leads to an obviously affirmative answer if we imagine the Court invalidating the Sedition Act, thus having it establish judicial review while it was also enlightening

opportunity to break with the English doctrine of seditious libel, thus affirming what many have later claimed was the intent of the framers to adopt a more libertarian position on free speech? Or would they have been, at this formative period, reluctant to depart from the familiar Blackstonian view that freedom of speech consists entirely in the freedom from prior restraints?

Whatever the result of such speculations, the fact remains that the Court began to address questions relating to the content of free speech protection only after the judiciary's role in American politics had crystallized. The one speculative response to the question of what might have been the result of an early intervention by the Court into the domain of free speech that seems virtually sure is that the decision would have become enmeshed in the web of uncertainties surrounding the Constitution's federal structure of power. In other words, the Court would have had to contend not only with the vexing matter of the relationship of American law to English common law, but also with the even more basic question of just what type of regime it was adjudicating for.

These large issues were precisely the ones facing the Israeli Court in the formative years of the state. [100] Both courts confronted a postindependence constitutional order that had not as yet received the defining imprint of the broader political culture. But there are important differences in the relevant American and Israeli histories, not the least of which was the absence in Israel of a written constitution. Also important in distinguishing them, especially in relation to free speech, was the *presence* in Israel of a viable and attractive alternative model, one that had emerged from some thirty years of judicial and scholarly development in the United States. Nothing analogous to this presented itself to the fledgling U.S. Supreme Court as a possible inducement for it to forge new legal paths. So if it had addressed the First Amendment issue, the Court would not have had the benefit of an alternative doctrinal history to draw on in guiding its own evolving interpretations.

---

us on the meaning of the First Amendment. However, unlike *Marbury* v. *Madison*, which we probably would not remember had the Court upheld Section 13 of the Judiciary Act of 1789, a decision to uphold the Sedition Act might still have provided us with a memorable moment in constitutional history.

[100] One could argue that the passage of forty years has done little to clarify the regime question, that the tensions embodied in the Declaration of Independence remain as intractable as ever. But then the forty years after the U.S. Constitution went into effect only brought the nation that much closer to civil war. In the face of the failure to resolve the profound issues dividing the country, it would have been difficult for the American Court to have resolved the free speech questions that had been spawned by the slavery issue.

But as beneficial as this judicial option may appear, one should still consider what Justice Agranat referred to in his *"Kol Ha'am"* opinion as the "well-known axiom that the law of a people must be studied in the light of its national way of life."[101] One way to view the long judicial delay in addressing the question of free speech in the United States is that it afforded the Supreme Court the opportunity to develop its doctrinal approaches in light of the accumulated wisdom of a mature political system. Absent the emulative lure of successfully functioning constitutional solutions in faraway lands, the Court's interpretive stance toward speech could be said to represent a genuinely indigenous achievement expressive of the unique features of the American political culture. The remainder of this chapter will focus on the much more eclectically oriented Israeli Court, with a view toward assessing the limitations and possibilities of constitutional transplantation.

Taking Liberties with License

"The very polarization between 'liberty' and 'license' implies authoritarianism."[102] This according to Pnina Lahav, author of a detailed and thoughtful analysis of American influence on Israeli free speech jurisprudence. Her observation appears in the context of an evaluation of Justice Shimon Agranat's *"Kol Ha'am"* opinion, in which she argues that the justice's artful transplantation of American free speech doctrine to the Israeli legal scene effectively renounced the licentiousness doctrine, the position that some speech by its very nature is illegitimate. Regrettably, from her point of view, this negation failed to take hold, leading to a somewhat erratic pattern of decisions, reflective of the fact that "the core postulates of *"Kol-Ha'am"* have not yet [as of 1981] been internalized in Israel's jurisprudence."[103]

One explanation for this failure is that Justice Agranat never explicitly rejected the licentiousness doctrine. Indeed at one point he wrote, "The right to freedom of expression does not mean that a person is entitled to proclaim, by word of mouth or in writing, in the ears and eyes of others, whatever he feels like saying. There is a difference between freedom and license."[104] According to Lahav, this apparent acceptance of the liberty-license distinction was only a tactical maneuver by Agranat, who was concerned that his constitutional innovations not be viewed as parasitic on foreign sources. Thus the legitimacy of the Court depended in no small

---

[101] *"Kol Ha'am"* Co. Ltd. v. *Minister of Interior*, 7 P.D. 871, 884 (1953).

[102] Pnina Lahav, "American Influence on Israel's Jurisprudence of Free Speech," *Hastings Constitutional Law Quarterly* 9 (1981): p. 63.

[103] Ibid., p. 65.

[104] *"Kol Ha'am,"* at 878.

measure on its ability to convey a sense that it was *interpreting* the law as a national creation, not *making* it on the basis of nonindigenous—particularly American—precedents. "In a judicial system heavily influenced by legal formalism, this would have been a charge of some significance. Hence the licentiousness doctrine was 'discovered' in Israeli law, and Israeli precedents and statutes were invoked. This respectable, seemingly conservative attire was needed in order to perform the task which lay ahead."[105]

What was this task? In doctrinal terms, it was the transplantation of the "clear and probable danger" test, the doctrine against prior restraint, and the doctrine against seditious libel. In jurisprudential terms, it was the importation of "interest balancing," and more generally, the "Grand Style" of American sociological jurisprudence.[106] But most important, it was the achievement of a goal inspired by Justice Agranat's "sense of mission—to build a solid body of case law suitable for making the dream of a free democratic Jewish homeland come true."[107] By focusing on this most fundamental of objectives, Lahav is understandably persuaded that the underlying assumptions of "*Kol Ha'am*" imply a repudiation of the licentiousness doctrine; after all, it is a doctrine that denotes authoritarianism, which of course is a contradiction of the democratic message of the Court's decision. If there is a principled connection between the liberty-license distinction and political authoritarianism, then there is sound logic in Lahav's argument. "The principle of free expression," wrote Agranat, "is closely bound up with the democratic process."[108] How then could such a principle tolerate a constitutional doctrine under which certain speech is by its very nature illegitimate?

[105] Lahav, "American Influence on Israel's Jurisprudence of Free Speech," p. 44. There was also a more pressing reason for proceeding cautiously. The case involved a decision by the government to suspend publication of two communist newspapers that, in the opinion of the minister of interior, were publishing articles that endangered the public peace. The government justified its action by appealing to a section of a 1933 statute that gave the minister of interior the authority to suspend publication "if any matter appearing in a newspaper is, in the opinion of the [minister of interior] likely to endanger the public peace." Based on its interpretation of the word *likely*, the Court overturned the order, thus placing itself in direct conflict with the government. So for political as well as jurisprudential reasons, the Court had good reason to be careful in how it chose to deliver its ruling.

[106] The term is borrowed from Karl Llewellyn and contrasted with the "Formal Style." Unlike the latter, the Grand Style approach relies on both legal and nonlegal sources in the adjudication of cases.

[107] Lahav, "American Influence on Israel's Jurisprudence of Free Speech," p. 35. Lahav points out that this sense of mission was shared by the other members of the Court.

[108] "*Kol Ha'am*," 7 P.D. at 876.

The question should be considered in the light of our discussion of American free speech jurisprudence. Lahav correctly observes that "the notion that speech which is intuitively perceived to be 'bad' may be legitimately suppressed" was undermined by American twentieth-century free speech law.[109] Of that achievement it may also be said that it was closely bound to a vision of the democratic process. But as we have seen, it is a particular vision of the democratic process, one refracted through the prism of modern pluralist individualism. While it is this pluralism that is typically identified with the democratic vision, it is not a necessary or inevitable identification, as the examples of the early liberal and the communal republican understandings were meant to suggest. This is pertinent to Lahav's remark that "the distinction between liberty and license rests on the distinction between acceptable and unacceptable community standards."[110] In light of the equation between the licentiousness doctrine and authoritarianism, this means that a further equation, between democracy and enforceable community standards, is logically implausible. Thus, Lahav's interpretation of Justice Agranat's free speech position comes down to this: his transplantation of American constitutional doctrine, broadly conceived, involves the embrace of a particular democratic vision that is, in a vital respect, antithetical to the precepts of communal pluralism and rational liberalism.

The principal constitutional innovation in Justice Agranat's opinion is his use of the Israeli Declaration of Independence. That document provided him with the necessary principles—or at least offered important support—for resolving the free speech issue democratically. Prior judicial decisions, as we have seen, had dismissed its legal significance, but for Agranat the Declaration assumed a salient role in constitutional decision making, one that has become increasingly instrumental in the Supreme Court's protection of individual rights. The specific occasion for his appeal to the Declaration was the Court's rejection of the "bad tendency" approach to limiting speech, an approach that Agranat found suitable only to "an autocratic or totalitarian regime."

The system of laws under which the political institutions in Israel have been established is indeed a state founded on democracy. Moreover, the matters set forth in the Declaration of Independence, especially as regards the basing of the State "on the foundations of freedom" and the securing of freedom of conscience, mean that Israel is a freedom-loving State. . . . [I]nsofar as it

109 Lahav, "American Influence on Israel's Jurisprudence of Free Speech," p. 56.
110 Ibid., p. 63.

"expresses the vision of the people and its faith," we are bound to pay attention to the matters set forth in it when we come to interpret and give meaning to the laws of the State.[111]

The passage then goes on to resolve the case's key statutory question—what is meant by "likely to endanger the public peace"—by discarding the "bad tendency" test and replacing it with the more libertarian "probability" test. According to Lahav, the latter is distinguishable from the licentiousness doctrine because it breaks "from the notion of 'acceptable speech' and focus[es] on *concrete* harms to society."[112] It may not be as dramatic a break as is involved in the older, more familiar "clear and present danger" test; nevertheless it is a decisive democratic step toward eliminating governmental suppression of speech on the basis of the offensiveness of what is said.

Justice Agranat, however, was notably vague in his discussion of the democratic "vision of the people." A "freedom-loving State" is not a distinctive description of any particular conception of democracy. This vagueness calls for caution in assenting to Lahav's contention that the various post–"*Kol Ha'am*" opinions, in which the licentiousness doctrine was applied in their authors' belief that they were being faithful to the "*Kol Ha'am*" legacy, were actually violating the spirit of the Agranat opinion and the transplanted American doctrines that were at its core.[113] In one such opinion Justice Landau wrote, "There is a consensus that one purpose of the theatre is to criticize negative social phenomena, and satire is a known means to do so. But under Israeli law even a playwright is not absolved of the duty not to hurt the feelings of others. This duty stems directly from the reciprocal obligation of tolerance among free citizens of different creeds, without which a pluralist democratic society like ours cannot survive. So important is this obligation, that even the basic principle of free expression must be withdrawn."[114] Landau was one of the judges who had joined in Agranat's

---

[111] "*Kol Ha'am*," at 884.

[112] Lahav, "American Influence on Israel's Jurisprudence of Free Speech," p. 64. One should note here that at the time the U.S. Supreme Court was developing and refining the doctrines that were the object of Justice Agranat's transplantation, *Chaplinsky* v. *New Hampshire* was good law. In other words, there was at the time no problem in recognizing speech as unacceptable absent a demonstration of its probable connection to a concrete societal harm.

[113] Ibid., p. 64. Among those who, according to Lahav, at one time or another failed to internalize Justice Agranat's "*Kol Ha'am*" theories was Agranat himself (p. 67).

[114] Ibid., p. 67. The quotation is from Justice Landau's opinion in *Keynan* v. *Cinematic Review Board*, 26 (2) P.D. 811, 814 (1972).

opinion. Presumably, therefore, his views on censorship were written in the belief that they were consistent with the Declaration of Independence. But that would be the case only if the "vision and faith of the people" embraced a conception of pluralist democracy in which the interest in communal integrity was of such importance that it might justify governmental suppression of speech. Landau, for example, might have distinguished between speech that allegedly threatens state security (as in "*Kol Ha'am*") and speech that is blatantly offensive to a particular religion or creed by requiring a demonstration of probable danger in the first instance but not in the second, where the licentiousness of the speech is *per se* sufficient to restrict it. A distinction of this kind may be vulnerable to criticism, but unless one insists on a model of pluralism that emphasizes individual autonomy, it should not be attacked for being either incoherent or undemocratic. Lahav's operational definition of democracy is clearly of this latter sort, and she may very well be correct in associating it with Agranat (although the evidence here is inconclusive); but for someone like Landau, whose conception of pluralist democracy is more group oriented, the explicit adoption of the liberty-license distinction in "*Kol Ha'am*" may be viewed as having a principled justification rather than simply a clever tactical one.[115]

This emerges more clearly in another landmark free speech case, *Electric Company* v. *Ha'aretz*, decided by the Israeli Supreme Court in 1978. At issue was a libel suit instituted by the director general of the government-controlled Electric Company against an important and influential daily newspaper. The Court addressed the matter in two stages. In its initial ruling in 1974 (*Ha'aretz I*),[116] a three-judge panel decided by a two-to-one majority in favor of the newspaper; a further hearing in 1978 (*Ha'aretz II*)[117] led to a four-to-one reversal and reinstatement of the original libel verdict. According to Lahav, Justice Landau's majority opinion in the reconsideration restored the "spirit of licentiousness" to a predominant position in Israeli law.[118] This restoration followed directly from his refusal to partake in the transplantation of American free speech doctrine, espe-

---

[115] One of the areas cited by Justice Agranat in his formal acceptance of the licentiousness doctrine was "the prevention of outrage to religious feelings." Applying the Landau conception of pluralist democracy, it is very easy to see why the Criminal Code Ordinance that addressed this issue is reconcilable in principle with the Declaration of Independence.

[116] 31 (2) P.D. 281 (1974).

[117] 32 (3) P.D. 337 (1978).

[118] Lahav, "American Influence on Israel's Jurisprudence of Free Speech," p. 76. That spirit, she argues, had been revived in Justice Miriam Ben-Porath's dissent in *Ha'aretz I*.

cially the determination that free expression enjoys a preferred position in a constitutional democracy.[119] In this case it meant that a person's right to reputation was entitled to the same consideration as another's right to speech.

A concern for personal reputation, particularly of public officials, that is so deeply ingrained in legal doctrine that it may override the public interest in free speech is presumptively suspect in an American constitutional context. "Thinking of the reputation of public figures as a public good, in need of protection, seems to run head on into another requirement of a free society—that we scrutinize the actions of our public servants and hold them accountable."[120] The clear preference of American law, therefore, has been to construe reputation as a private affair, as an individual asset that does not directly implicate the public good.[121] To think otherwise is to invite the criticism that one is insufficiently attentive to the requirements of a democratic polity; or in the case of Justice Landau, that one is an advocate of an "elitist model [of democracy that] places a high value on governmental stability and authority and admits little faith in the ability of the ordinary citizen to contribute actively to political decisionmaking."[122] From this perspective, the failure to transplant American law implies a rejection of the classical democratic vision to which that jurisprudence is historically connected.

If Justice Landau harbored elitist sentiments, it is not so obvious that ruling in favor of the established institutional press would have revealed more egalitarian republican sympathies. Robert Bellah has argued that "the *reputation* of public officials and public figures is an important matter

[119] In his majority opinion in *Ha'aretz I*, Justice Shamgar relied heavily on American sources, particularly *New York Times* v. *Sullivan*. Although in sympathy with his position, Lahav faults Shamgar for his judicial craftsmanship in transplanting American doctrine. While he was substantively following in the path of Justice Agranat, his transplantation was not nearly as sophisticated as his predecessor's. One of the reasons this is disturbing to Lahav is that it provided an easy target for Justice Landau in *Ha'aretz II*.

[120] Robert N. Bellah, "The Meaning of Reputation in American Society," *California Law Review* 74 (1986): 745.

[121] One of the first to appreciate this was David Reisman, who pointed out in 1942 that "the American attitude towards reputation is unique." David Reisman, "Democracy and Defamation: Control of Group Libel," *Columbia Law Review* 42 (1942): 730. While the United States may no longer be unique in this regard, its individualist orientation in regard to the question of defamation still stands out in any comparative legal context. Reisman's observations are, if anything, more accurate as applied to the post–*New York Times* v. *Sullivan* legal state of affairs: "Our law of defamation, such as it is, is conceived of only as a protection against individual injury, as the law of assault and battery is a protection for individual life and limb" (p. 730).

[122] Lahav, "American Influence on Israel's Jurisprudence of Free Speech," p. 106.

in a democratic republic and . . . of late the relation between the public figure, reputation, and the media is far from what it ought to be."[123] A deference to authority is not the only reason for protecting the reputations of public officials; once it is recognized that effective execution of the *public trust* is connected to the high esteem in which officials are held, the interest in protecting reputation takes on a more republican cast. And if the concern for reputation is more broadly connected to the "reciprocal obligation of tolerance" that sustains a "pluralistic democratic society," then resistance to embracing American doctrines that seem hostile (or at least indifferent) to this interest may be as much (or more) an indication of a communally oriented pluralistic commitment than it is of authoritarian proclivities. Let us, then, look more closely at Landau's opinion.

From a doctrinal perspective the opinion is notable chiefly for its determination to elevate the right to reputation out of its subordinate position vis-à-vis the right of free expression. The lesser status of the right to one's good name had been affirmed in *Ha'aretz I* by Justice Shamgar in an opinion that drew heavily on the landmark American decision *New York Times v. Sullivan.* Justice Landau sought to replace a "vertical grading of a superior right against an ordinary right [with] a horizontal approach to equally important rights, without preference of one right, as defined in a statute, over another right."[124] He therefore cautioned against being "taken in by the American decision in *New York Times*,"[125] an admonition that Lahav interprets as integral to his "offensive on American law," but which Landau views as simply "a refusal to follow blindly whatever the U.S. Supreme Court decides."[126]

This same refusal obviously applies to those courts that *are* obliged to follow the Supreme Court, namely the lower courts in the American judicial system. In particular, Justice Landau pointedly referred to the *Skokie* case as an example of an American decision that should not become a model for Israeli jurisprudence. The decision of the American courts to prohibit a ban on a Nazi march through a predominantly Jewish suburb was made, he

[123] Bellah, "The Meaning of Reputation in American Society," p. 748. For Justice Landau, too, individual reputation is inseparable from consideration of the social good. He recommends the work of the New Zealander Zelman Cowen, who has written that there is no necessary conflict between "an individual and a public or social interest; both are social interests and the interest in individual reputation is an interest in the reputation of every man." Zelman Cowen, *Individual Liberty and the Law* (Dobbs Ferry, N.Y.: Oceana Publications, 1977), p. 26.

[124] *Ha'aretz II*, 32 (3) P.D. at 343. Translation by Pnina Lahav.

[125] Ibid., 344.

[126] Personal correspondence with the author, September 28, 1989.

said, "because the Justices saw themselves bound by the First Amendment. We should better reflect on the phenomenon."[127] Lahav correctly finds in this disagreement with the *Skokie* outcome a distancing from the orthodox American political justification for free speech, but then curiously she accuses him of "evad[ing] the theory behind the principle of free expression in democratic society."[128] She wonders, "What in the context of *Skokie* so disturbed Justice Landau?"[129] After failing to discover a satisfactory response to her question, she concludes, "It seems clear that the confusion in his opinion arises from the tremendous aversion to Nazism, an aversion so powerful in Jewish existence as to generate an impulsive repulsion of anything tolerant of it."[130]

Lahav's effort to explain Justice Landau's treatment of *Skokie* as the product of an obsession with Nazism earns initial plausibility in the fact that the case is introduced at an odd moment in the opinion. It appears in the context of a discussion of the Nazis' successful campaign "to destroy the Weimar regime [with the aid of] unrestrained defamation of the elite."[131] After quoting David Reisman to the effect that German libel law was an important factor in the Nazi rise to power, the justice expressed the "fear that history will repeat itself."[132] However strained this reference might seem in connection with allegations about a relatively obscure public official's improper purchase of a luxury car, it is at least linked to the earlier example by the offense of seditious libel. But the *Skokie* affair had nothing to do with seditious libel; it involved group defamation, verbal assault on a targeted (and psychologically vulnerable) community. If the ultimate purpose of Landau's defense of reputation was, as Lahav suggests, to underline the critical importance of governmental stability and authority, then why confuse the issue with a reference to an example of defamation occurring within the private arena?

The answer may very well be related to the principle of free expression in democratic society, but not perhaps the one that follows from the constitutional premises of contemporary liberalism. Respect for duly constituted authority is a consideration surely present in Justice Landau's opinion; it is a concern, however, that should be viewed in the context of a general family of concerns related to the survival of "a pluralist democracy like ours." Here the protection of individual reputation—one's good name—is linked to the

---

[127] *Ha'aretz II*, 32 (3) P.D. at 347.
[128] Lahav, "American Influence on Israel's Jurisprudence of Free Speech," p. 105.
[129] Ibid.
[130] Ibid.
[131] *Ha'aretz II*, 32 (3) P.D. at 346–47.
[132] Ibid., 347.

defense of groups against libelous and defamatory expression by an interest in supporting civility as an important attribute of democratic pluralism.[133] It is worth recalling Post's observations regarding the communitarian basis of defamation law, in particular the derivation of human dignity from membership in a community characterized by reciprocal observance of rules of civility. In contrast, the concept of autonomy, which has been vital to the development of American free speech jurisprudence, "assumes that the significant aspects of individual identity are those that are authentically self-created, even if what is created contradicts community values."[134] Post points out that the *New York Times* case was a clear-cut example of defamation law being used "solely to enforce civility rules and to punish deviants."[135] While this example should perhaps instruct us about some of the dangers inherent in the communitarian argument, it also suggests the possibility that Landau's criticism of *New York Times* v. *Sullivan* involved concerns extending well beyond an elitist deference to public authority.

What in the context of *Skokie* so disturbed Justice Landau? Painful memories, to be sure, but also, it would appear, a constitutional solution that failed to accommodate the interest in freedom of expression to the political realities of Israeli democracy. His admonition in *Keynan* v. *Cinematic Review Board* that the survival of pluralistic democracy in Israel depended on reciprocal tolerance among citizens of different creeds—which in this case justified censorship—indicates that the discussion of *Skokie* is consistent with a coherent political vision as well as a visceral reaction to the Holocaust. It suggests, too, that the insertion of the discussion in the context of seditious libel may not be as farfetched as upon first glance it appeared, that an unwarranted attack on a *government* official may poison the atmosphere of democratic discourse in ways not dissimilar to the public display of intolerance directed at racial, ethnic, or religious groups. *New York Times* v. *Sullivan* stood for "the principle that debate on public issues should be uninhibited, robust, and wide open," a fact noted by Judge Decker in striking down the Skokie ordinance punishing language that

---

[133] Reputational considerations are at the heart of Charles R. Lawrence III's efforts to persuade us that *Brown* v. *Board of Education* is in one sense a free speech case. Beginning with pluralist assumptions that are closer to Justice Landau's than to prevailing American constitutional assumptions, he observes, "*Brown* is a case about group defamation. The message of segregation was stigmatizing to black children. To be labelled unfit to attend school with white children injured the reputation of black children, thereby foreclosing employment opportunities and the right to be regarded as respected members of the body politic." Lawrence, "If He Hollers Let Him Go," p. 463.

[134] Post. "The Social Foundations of Defamation Law," p. 735.

[135] Ibid., p. 737.

intentionally incites hatred.[136] But without inhibitions, what are the prospects for reciprocal tolerance? The common thread in Justice Landau's juxtaposition is this: to the extent that the good name of the public official and the good name of the group are both potential victims of a lack of restraint, pluralist democracy in Israel suffers. Enforcing the distinction between liberty and license in a democratic political context thus presumes that support for healthy inhibitions is not, in the end, incompatible with robust and wide-open debate.

Democracy and Toleration

In his opinion in the case arising from Rabbi Kahane's dispute with the Broadcasting Authority, Justice Barak asserted that "democracy is based on tolerance." He went on to point out that "in a pluralistic society like ours, tolerance is the force that unites us, and enables us to live together."[137] Without pausing to focus on the special qualities of this pluralism, Barak insisted on a societal obligation of tolerance for the expression of nasty and derogatory views directed at specified groups.

But as we have seen, alternative pluralisms may suggest alternative perspectives on toleration. A few blocks from where Justice Barak works is the Old City of Jerusalem, where, in Amos Elon's account, "the crowds mingle on terms of reciprocal antipathy. Few other people, save perhaps the Irish, live so intimately together, yet each with his distant, mutually antagonistic past."[138] This depiction of historically rooted "reciprocal antipathy" could easily lead one to conclude that "to live together" in such an environment requires an intolerance of expression that evinces contempt for the principle of toleration. Or put differently, the pluralist reality is such that it may make sense to affirm the greater importance of tolerance of group differences to tolerance of expression that, by virtue of its group vilifying character, blatantly subverts a viable democratic community. The recent controversy in Israel over the film *The Last Temptation of Christ* highlights the dilemma.

The controversy was generated by the decision of the Censorship Board to ban the film. To many people that decision seemed bizarre—after all, countries with Christian majorities had permitted the film to be shown,

---

[136] *Collin*, 447 F. Supp. at 692.

[137] *Kahane*, 41 (3) P.D. at 277.

[138] Amos Elon, *Jerusalem: City of Mirrors* (New York: Little, Brown, 1989), p. 177. See also Michael Romann and Alex Weingrod, *Living Together Separately: Arabs and Jews in Contemporary Jerusalem* (Princeton: Princeton University Press, 1991).

albeit in the face of considerable protest. In an interview the chairman of the board, Yehoshua Justman, defended the decision in terms of the uniqueness of the Israeli social and historical predicament. Israel, and in particular Jerusalem, he maintained, holds a special significance for Christians as well as for Jews.[139] It was therefore especially important, so went the argument, that public authority be cognizant of the sensibilities of the various communities for whom the place meant so much. He also argued that the unique historical suffering of the Jewish people should make them acutely sensitive to material that (in the view of the board) deeply offends the core beliefs of a religious minority. He acknowledged that in the United States these arguments would carry much less weight, but that in Israel a credible claim can be made for the state providing guarantees that the public space exhibit respect for each of the varying cultures that constitute the overall society. Therefore, from this perspective pluralism justifies censorship, whereas in the United States it suggests just the opposite.[140]

To this claim, and perhaps implicit within it, is a further consideration that extends from the Declaration's affirmation of the Jewishness of the state of Israel. Ruth Wedgwood has argued that the formal identification of the state with a particular ethnoreligious group means that the distinction between state action and private action, a distinction central to liberal constitutionalist thought, is much less clear than in the United States, where official neutrality among groups prevails. She argues that the tolera-

[139] At least one Christian spokesman supports Justman on this point. Bishop Timothy of the Greek Orthodox patriarchate wrote, "This is the cradle of Christianity. They should not show, in this holy place, a film which insults the followers of Jesus." *Jerusalem Post*, June 24, 1989.

[140] The findings of a major comparative study of political tolerance in the United States, Israel, and New Zealand are instructive in this regard. The authors conclude that the United States is characterized by "pluralistic intolerance," a relatively benign phenomenon in which an intolerant majority is "held in check by its own lack of agreement about the targets of its intolerance." John L. Sullivan, Michal Shamir, Patrick Welsh, and Nigel S. Roberts, *Political Tolerance in Context: Support for Unpopular Minorities in Israel, New Zealand, and the United States* (Boulder, Colo.: Westview, 1985), p. 111. On the other hand, Israel reflects a pattern of "focused intolerance," most of which is directed toward its Arab minority, and most of which is attributable to a high degree of objective and subjective threat. (p. 142). There is, as it were, a self-corrective Madisonian dynamic at work in the American context, in which the very diffuseness of target groups mitigates the destructive effects of intolerance. This suggests that public officials can without too much risk to the public welfare adhere to a policy of tolerating intolerance. The First Amendment of course both facilitates and legitimates this policy. But in Israel, where an official commitment to cultural autonomy must contend with a basic hostility to a substantial minority (of a kind that, in addition, may not always pose a clear and present danger), the case for such a policy of benign neglect may not appear so obvious.

tion by public authority of hostile private actions directed against Israeli Arabs comes very close to being governmental action.[141] Applying this reasoning, which is consistent with our depiction of the specific character of Israeli pluralism, to the controversy over *The Last Temptation of Christ*, the failure of the government to regulate a film that is offensive to the Christian minority will then (rightly or wrongly) be taken by that group as a tacit acceptance of its message on the part of the favored ethnic majority. The failure to act in these circumstances in effect amounts to state action. Thus the Jewish identity of the state imposes special obligations on the Censorship Board when the sensibilities of a non-Jewish group have been violated by offensive expression. Or to be more precise (since it cannot be reasonably contended that any or all expression that offends a minority group should necessarily be proscribed), a presumption of illegality attaches to this sort of communication.

But these claims did not impress the Supreme Court, which could see no logic in the fact that a film that had been screened widely in Christian countries had been banned in Israel because it was deemed offensive to Christian sensibilities. It overturned the board's ruling on the ground that there was no evidence of a "near certainty" of a serious impairment of the public order.[142] Indeed, the very fact of its distribution in Christian countries indicated that the "near certainty" standard had not been met. This is not to say, according to the Court, that the board acted improperly in seeking to protect religious sensibilities; the section of the Penal Law that made it a crime to offend religious feelings could not be ignored. But the various opinions of the justices agreed that a restriction on free speech was

[141] Ruth Wedgwood, "Freedom of Expression and Racial Speech," *Tel Aviv University Studies in Law* 8 (1988): 336. Mari J. Matsuda has also argued that the failure of the government to prosecute racist speech is tantamount to its support of such speech, that its passivity amounts to state action. "State silence . . . is public action where the strength of the new racist groups derives from their offering legitimation and justification for otherwise socially unacceptable emotions of hate, fear, and aggression." Matsuda, "Public Response to Racist Speech," p. 2378. But Matsuda's argument is significantly less powerful than Wedgwood's, because in the American legal environment that she is addressing, the state is not officially identified with any particular group. To be sure, her case is stronger in the case of blacks than it is for the other "outsiders" she wishes to protect, but even in this instance of a group that was once a legally mandated outsider, the claim that the state today sanctions through its silence the vitriol that bigots hurl at it is difficult to sustain. For a rejoinder to the state action argument that embodies the traditional American civil libertarian position, see Nadine Strossen, "Regulating Racist Speech on Campus: A Modest Proposal?" *Duke Law Journal* 1990 (1990): 544–47.

[142] *Universal City Studios v. Censorship Board*, 43 (2) P.D. 22 (1989).

such a serious matter that it could not proceed absent clear evidence of likely damage to a legitimate countervailing public interest.

This decision was followed in a matter of weeks by a further constriction of the powers of the Censorship Board. The Knesset eliminated (for a two-year trial period that is likely to remain permanent) the board's authority to censor plays, a move that is perhaps best understood as a concession to the legal realities created by Supreme Court decisions in support of freedom of expression.[143] In the leading case, Justice Barak gave voice to the increasingly familiar (in Israel) libertarian jurisprudential (if not popular) view of the relationship between toleration and democracy: "We live in a democratic state, and the searing of the heart lies at the very core of democracy. The force of democracy lies not in acknowledging my right to hear what pleases my ear. It recognizes the right of the other to utter words that hurt my ears and cause pain in my heart. 'Freedom of speech,' said Justice Holmes, 'is toleration of what we hate.'"[144]

But how applicable is Holmes's view in the Israeli context? Under the mandate of the First Amendment it may very well be that, like it or not, one must tolerate what one hates even if it hurts one's ears and causes pain in one's heart. Certainly, as we have seen, that is consistent with the dominant legal and scholarly interpretation of the Amendment, even if it has been critically questioned by some dissenting voices in the scholarly community. In Israel, however, it is illegal to cause outrage to religious feelings. Public order is defined much more broadly than in the United States, where it is largely synonymous with public peace. The Censorship Board, as the Court has repeatedly acknowledged, possesses the legal authority to protect group sensibilities. The Court may differ with the board's application of the law to a specific set of facts (as in its ruling on *The Last Temptation of Christ*), but that does not obviate the fact that Israeli law, in its criminalization of various types of offensive speech, resists a Holmesian toleration of what we hate, at least to the extent that what we hate is speech involving

---

[143] The principal decision here is not the *Last Temptation of Christ* case (which in time may lead to a similar result as far as films are concerned), but the 1986 case *Laor v. Film and Play Supervisory Board*, 41 (1) P.D. 421 (1986). That decision, which overturned the board's banning of the controversial play *Ephraim Returns to the Army*, convinced many in the legal and artistic communities that theater censorship had become a practical impossibility. In this they were following the lead of the justices themselves. Justice Netanyahu said of the principal opinion by Justice Barak that it "raises the question whether there is any point any more for the existence of censorship on plays, and perhaps the legislature should consider this" (444). And more critically, Justice Maltz thought it best to abolish censorship entirely, since "the rigid tests [of the Court] render the entire business of censoring plays (and films) a farce" (445).

[144] *Laor*, 41 (1) P.D. at 441.

the deliberate infliction of pain on members of religious (or racial) groups. If, in other words, the searing of the heart lies at the core of democracy, then there is reason to believe that Israeli democracy remains an unfulfilled aspiration.

The makers of the film may have offended some Christian sensibilities, but it surely was not their intention to do so. Meir Kahane, on the other hand, rarely missed the opportunity to sear the heart with speech whose content was suffused with bigotry and hatred. The Broadcasting Authority had ample reason to believe that given the opportunity to disseminate his views through the airwaves, Kahane would engage in illegal speech. Moreover, their awareness that incitement to racism is a crime punishable by five years imprisonment understandably contributed to their concern that, should Kahane be prosecuted for what was said in one of their broadcasts, they too would be susceptible to criminal liability. Where the Broadcasting Authority erred, however, was in its blanket exclusion of Kahane (not including news coverage of his activities), so that even in the unlikely event that he might be interested in airing a perfectly legitimate message, he would not be permitted to have that opportunity. All three judges agreed that this exceeded the BA's authority, but as an editorial in an Israeli newspaper put it, the Court left "the central issue unresolved: is enunciation of racist doctrine itself sufficient ground for denial of access to the state media, or must it pass a pragmatic test of its likely baneful impact in every instance before it is so declared."[145]

On this critical matter there was division on the Court, although the decision was handed down according to the opinion of Justice Barak, who maintained that the Broadcasting Authority could not impose a policy of excluding the broadcast of racist views and sentiments on the basis of content alone. His position was criticized by Justice Gabriel Bach, usually a jurisprudential ally, who was perplexed by his colleague's "near certainty" test for racist speech: "Can racist incitement somehow *not injure* the feelings of the public, or at least that part of the public, it is levelled at? And that not just with '*near certainty*,' which would be enough to ban it, but with *absolute certainty*? Therefore, it seems to me that including publication of racist incitement in the list of topics protected by the principle of freedom of expression is unjustified and artificial."[146] In short, according to Bach, the type of racist speech that Kahane was known for should be categorized as unprotected speech.

[145] *Jerusalem Post*, July 30, 1987.
[146] *Kahane*, 41 (3) P.D. at 312.

As in many contemporary Israeli free speech cases, the First Amendment drew attention from the justices. Not surprisingly, its appeal varied in proportion to the extent to which content-neutrality was seen to fit the doctrinal needs of the Israeli legal system. Under prevailing American doctrine the racist content of someone's speech does not render it unprotected, no matter the degree of its capacity to offend and violate the sensibilities of a targeted community. Justice Barak cited eighteen American cases (and fourteen scholarly works), some of which provoked Justice Bach to say that "one should not apply these decisions to the case at bar, which deals with the right of public authorities to prevent broadcasts of specific programs banned by an explicit law."[147] Embedded in a disagreement over the appropriate limits of democratic tolerance was a debate over the limits of constitutional transplantation.

The statutory authority of the Broadcasting Authority stems from the BA Act of 1965. Among the stated roles of the BA is that of furthering "the aims of public education as described in the Public Education Act, 1953." According to this latter act, these aims include grounding education in "a desire for a society based on liberty, equality, tolerance, mutual aid and love of neighbors."[148] However, another section of the BA Act adds that "the Authority will ensure that the broadcasts will properly reflect the various views and opinions prevailing in the public and broadcast trustworthy information." Justice Barak indicated the interpretive difficulty posed by these two sections: "Does good citizenship [the fostering of which is assigned to the BA] require reflecting every opinion, including an opinion that spreads hatred between people and races? The aims of the Public Education Act also creates an ambiguity. What is the 'liberty' youths should be educated on? Does it not include freedom of speech, including Petitioners' freedom of speech? Does 'equality' not mean broadcasting all views and opinions? Should a society based on tolerance not be tolerant of views that foster intolerance?"[149] He then correctly observed that to discover a consistent purpose in these two sections requires an inquiry into the basic principles of the legal system. That will illuminate the question of whether the mandate of the Broadcasting Authority requires it to reflect the opinions of even those who express an ugly hatred of their neighbors.

As was suggested by Justice Agranat in "*Kol Ha'am*," such an inquiry must begin with the premise that Israel is a democratic state. The appropri-

[147] Ibid., 316.
[148] Ibid., 265.
[149] Ibid., 266.

ate limits on speech and tolerance should then reflect democratic requirements. But what is democracy? The many references to American sources
in Justice Barak's opinion make it clear that his operational definition is
fundamentally consonant with the prevailing model of American constitutional theory. [150] Thus, liberty and equality are to be framed by the constitutional requirement of neutrality; in the words of Justice Marshall (in a case
cited by Barak), "There is an 'equality of status in the field of ideas,' and
government must afford all points of view an equal opportunity to be
heard." [151] Which also means, as far as the First Amendment is concerned,
"that government has no power to restrict expression because of its message, its ideas, its subject matter, or its content." [152]

There is no question that the application of this principle would lead to
the following law being declared unconstitutional: "(a) Whoever publishes
anything, intending to incite to racism, shall serve five years in prison. (b)
For the purposes of this section, it does not matter if the publication led to
racism or not or whether it was true or not." [153] The law clearly places public
authority in a position where it cannot help but restrict expression on the
basis of content. It blatantly challenges the doctrine of viewpoint-
neutrality. It is, however, good law in Israel, where, as Justice Barak perhaps grudgingly acknowledged, "No constitutional provision determining the permissible limits on freedom of speech has yet been enacted.
Therefore, every law limiting freedom of speech is constitutionally
valid." [154] While some may see it violating the spirit of Israeli democracy—
particularly because the prohibition does not specify a need to demonstrate
a near certainty of a real danger to the public order—the law is as valid, in a
legal sense, as any other law that might be thought of as embodying the
essence of that spirit.

Justice Barak's opinion does not attack this law—at least not openly. He

---

[150] American sources of course are not the only ones cited by Justice Barak. Israeli precedents also figure prominently in the opinion. However, it is worth noting that Justice Shamgar
is the Israeli justice who is quoted most frequently and at greatest length; and it is Shamgar
who, with Barak, is known for his heavy reliance on American sources in matters of civil
liberties. At one point, for example, his views are presented as similar to the familiar observation of Justice Jackson that "freedom to differ is not limited to things that do not matter much.
That would be a mere shadow of freedom. The test of its substance is the right to differ as to
things that touch the heart of the existing order." *Kahane*, 41 (3) P.D. at 279.

[151] *Police Department of Chicago*, 408 U.S. at 96.

[152] Ibid., 95.

[153] Section 144(B) of the Penal Act of Israel.

[154] *Kahane*, 41 (3) P.D. at 283.

rests his argument that the BA cannot, in effect, hide behind it to prevent Kahane's broadcasts on the ground that this constitutes an improper exercise of prior restraint. "The centrality of freedom of speech means that only a near certainty of a real danger to the public peace, justifies limiting freedom of speech prospectively."[155] But there is something circular about this argument. If the ambiguity about the BA's right under its grant from the Knesset to ban certain views from the airwaves is to be resolved through inquiry into the principles of the polity, then it is certainly pertinent to ask whether another statute passed by the Knesset—in this case a criminal one—that attaches liability to the propagation of views purely on the basis of their content does not, in the first instance, shed light on the intent of the legislature, and in the second, suggest something important about the principles of the polity. The exercise of prior restraint on the basis of content alone contradicts the centrality of freedom of speech only because, in Barak's view, democracy requires neutrality with respect to the substance of ideas. Obviously the Knesset did not share this view, a fact that in itself is not dispositive of the issue of principle, but one that certainly entitles the alternative legislative view to a serious hearing.[156]

This is not to say that Justice Barak gives inadequate consideration to the arguments for limiting freedom of speech. The "near certainty" test emerges from an elaborate balancing process involving the weighing of the interests in freedom of speech (the traditional three arguments) against the interests (falling under the rubric of public order) that may recommend its restriction. "The balancing formula, by which limits are set on freedom of speech, depends on the essence of the competing values."[157] Here Barak is careful to point out that "the task of balancing belongs first and foremost to the legislature."[158] In other words, the *degree* to which freedom of speech is to be protected is primarily a matter for the Knesset to determine. But as far as the *scope* of freedom of speech is concerned—that is, its coverage or, as Barak puts it, the "internal essence" of the principle—the legislative view appears to get short shrift. The Court determines, on the basis of its insights into democratic theory, that "deviant speech, namely speech that

---

[155] Ibid., 299. This would be the case even if what threatened the public peace was not a crime. On the other hand, in the absence of a near certainty, prior restraint is unjustifiable even if the criminal prohibition applies to the speech.

[156] This difference is another example of the potentially creative tension between the judicial and legislative branches that was discussed in Chapter 5.

[157] Ibid., 285.

[158] Ibid., 284.

annoys and hurts, spreads hatred and anger, based on racial and national/ethnic origin—is included within freedom of speech."[159] As we have seen, however, this assertion as to the scope of the principle does not describe the statutory situation, where laws pertaining to the permissible limits of speech clearly exclude deviant speech—in this instance speech with a racist content—from the scope of the free speech principle.

This distinction between scope and degree goes directly to the question of constitutional transplantation. American courts have not as yet followed the lead of Matsuda and others and produced a test for judicial application in cases of religiously or racially injurious speech that fails to endanger the public peace. A "near certainty" that a group of people will have their feelings seriously violated by someone's hate-filled speech will not support governmental suppression of such speech. It will in Israel, at least in theory, because preventing a violation of this kind is thought to be a sufficiently weighty interest that it should be a part of any equation for ascertaining the degree of free speech protection. Thus the particular circumstances of Israeli sociopolitical life dictate the elements of the appropriate constitutional equation. As Justice Barak advises, "We should learn from the experience of others, but our approach to freedom of speech we should have on our own experience, our political strength, moral health, and national culture."[160] This admonition, he would probably say, applies with equal force to the scope of freedom of speech; yet the evidence suggests that here the American experience has become more than just a source for study, but a model for emulation.

[159] Ibid., 285.

[160] Ibid., 282. Justice Barak is fond of quoting Justice Sussman's observation in *Shalit* that law is "a creature in its environment." Ibid., 266. That environment includes accepted principles reflecting the social consciousness of the Israeli people. In this regard, notice should be taken of the Canadian example, where promoting hatred against an identifiable group is a violation of the Canadian Criminal Code. It has been pointed out that the American melting pot approach to cultural diversity has been rejected in Canada in favor of a mosaic approach. Thus Canada's charter of Rights and Freedoms differs from the American Bill of Rights in explicitly pursuing a multicultural pluralist vision. Section 27 calls for interpretation of the Charter in a manner consistent with Canadian multiculturalism, thus legitimating criminalization of hate speech as, in effect, an extension of Canadian pluralism. See the colloquium remarks of Kathleen Mahoney in "Language as Violence v. Freedom of Expression: Canadian and American Perspectives on Group Defamation," *Buffalo Law Review* 37 (1988–89): 347. To which it may be said that however deeply rooted is the diversity of the Canadian multicultural experience, it pales in comparison with the entrenched tribal-like antagonisms of Israel; hence, the logic behind the Canadian approach applies with even greater force to the Israeli legal experience.

CONCLUSION

The Israeli legal scholar David Kretzmer points out that "the frequent citation of [American] sources in a constitutional system which is ostensibly so different from the American system is hardly insignificant."[161] Its significance is not that one can predict how the Israeli Supreme Court will resolve a given free speech issue on the basis of knowing how the U.S. Supreme Court has decided cases involving a comparable question. The fact that the Court in Israel does not sit *en banc* means that the deference accorded American judgments can vary tremendously on the basis of which judges happen to be hearing a particular case. And even among those judges, such as Barak and Shamgar, who are well known for their admiration of American civil liberties jurisprudence, an appreciation of the indigenous features of the Israeli legal system prevents any reflexive incorporation of American doctrinal innovations.

The significance of the frequent references to American sources is that they have contributed to the failure of the Israeli Supreme Court to develop a free speech jurisprudence that reflects the character of the larger pluralist democracy of which it is a part. This failure is not to be regretted (that is, it is not really a *failure*) if the prospect of having a less than satisfactory fit between doctrine and political culture is viewed as desirable in contemporary Israel. As we saw in the previous chapter, the practice of judicial activism in Israel involves a self-consciously pedagogical commitment premised on the felt need to instill habits of Western democratic participation in a body politic that on the whole is inexperienced in the ways of democracy. The American model can thus serve to facilitate the realization of these democratic aspirations.

But Western notions of democratic participation are not defined, or certainly limited, by the American example. On the issue of racist speech, for example, the United States stands virtually alone in the latitudinous extent to which it protects those engaged in such expression. In constitutional terms, its current emphasis on viewpoint-neutrality and the autonomy of the speaker contrasts sharply with other Western democracies where the right to give offense is afforded decidedly less legal protection, and where a more sympathetic official solicitude for the virtue of civility

---

[161] Kretzmer, "The Influence of First Amendment Jurisprudence on Judicial Decision-making in Israel," p. 21. For Kretzmer its significance is that it has been important in placing Israeli judicial decision making somewhere between the American and English models.

exists. For instance, Donald Kommers writes of the former Federal Republic of Germany, "As seen through the eyes of the Federal Constitutional Court, the political system is composed not of autonomous voters but of active and informed citizens involved in public affairs, striving for the creation of a socially cohesive and politically integrated 'free democratic basic order.' "[162] The German Criminal Code punishes speech that reviles religions or advocates racial hatred and genocide. Kommers points out that these laws incorporate the communitarian ethic that inheres in the concept of the "moral order" within the meaning of the Basic Law (i.e., the Constitution).[163] The jurisprudence of free speech reflects the German historical experience; that which may appear illiberal to some is, in German constitutional terms, the altogether appropriate defense by a democratic polity of the political principles to which it is committed.

The fact that regimes we recognize as democratic are not confined to one response on the issue of freedom of speech is not always apparent from reading Israeli opinions. A valid restriction on speech—for example, in the case of a near certainty that racist speech will result in real injury—tends to be explained as a prudential limitation on the necessarily relative principle of freedom of speech. "The accepted view in Israel as well as in other democracies is that freedom of speech is not absolute. It is a relative freedom."[164] But if the free speech principle were defined so as to incorporate limits on certain kinds of speech within its meaning (i.e., the distinction between speech and the freedom of speech), then there would be less grounds for asserting the inherently relativistic character of the principle. If the Israeli Court, for example, were to follow the example of democratic polities in which the scope of the principle did not extend as far as covering speech with racially or ethnically defamatory content, then a restriction on some of the expressive activities of a Rabbi Kahane would be seen not as a limitation on the free speech principle but as an affirmation of its core meaning.

In this context the example of the earlier liberal tradition has suggestive possibilities for Israeli free speech jurisprudence. The communally ori-

---

[162] Donald P. Kommers, "The Jurisprudence of Free Speech in the United States and the Federal Republic of Germany," *Southern California Law Review* 53 (1980): 678. Kommers finds that "the pluralism [envisioned by the U.S. Supreme Court to be] less integral than that envisioned [by the German court]." As a result, "In the American view [as contrasted with the German], the community has no valid claim upon the individual person, particularly in the domain of mind and morals" (694).

[163] Ibid., p. 685.

[164] *Kahane*, 41 (3) P.D. at 283.

ented nature of Israeli pluralism makes it a polity well constituted for sustaining a rational liberal (or as we have explained, moderate republican) approach to freedom of speech. Unlike the United States, where individual autonomy now occupies an elevated constitutional position reflective of long-term trends in the society that are likely to prevail over recent separatist challenges, limited communal autonomy is still a vital Israeli sociopolitical phenomenon.[165] Thus, the claims of the individual and the community do not present themselves in inherently conflictual terms; for example, the defense of the group against outrageous verbal assault can readily be assimilated into an argument for individual liberty rightly understood. And as a result, the achievement of civility can become a central goal of free speech jurisprudence rather than a casualty of a radically individualist doctrinal constitutional solution.

[165] As one surveys the current multicultural challenge to traditional liberal pluralism, a challenge basically emanating from the political Left, one cannot help but note that this coincides with the ascendance in the United States of the political Right, and especially its firm control over the federal judiciary. It is in the light of these developments that J. M. Balkin's observation that " 'pluralism' and 'free speech' are being slowly co-opted by the right today" is particularly useful in projecting the continuing hegemony of the orthodox First Amendment position. J. M. Balkin, "Some Realism about Pluralism: Legal Realist Approaches to the First Amendment," *Duke Law Journal* 1990 (1990): 393.

CHAPTER SEVEN

Conclusion

> Solon being asked if the laws he had given to the
> Athenians were the best, he replied, "I have given
> them the best they were able to bear."
> —*Montesquieu*

SOLON'S RESPONSE was echoed in Publius's summary appraisal of what the
Constitution's framers had wrought: "I am persuaded that it is the best
which our political situation, habits, and opinions will admit."[1] The Constitution, in other words, would have been better if the circumstances
surrounding its creation had been more propitious, but then again it would
have been worse if these conditions had not been as favorable as they were.
In this simple statement is the answer to the question raised in the opening
paragraph of Publius's first essay: whether constitutions might follow from
"reflection and choice" as well as from "accident and force." The teaching of
The Federalist would seem to be that people can choose a constitution that
reflects their reasoned judgment as long as they are prepared to accept the
inevitable limits and accommodations that chance imposes. Or in a more
contemporary vocabulary, political culture (i.e., situation, habit, and opinion) is a significant factor in determining the extent to which constitutional
choices will be implemented.

The defense of the Constitution did not require that all allegations regarding the document's shortcomings be denied; in the disarming refrain of
the political realist, Publius indicated that "I never expect to see a perfect
work from imperfect men."[2] It is not only imperfection in the circumstances attendant to constitution making, but also imperfection in those
doing the constitution-making, that accounts for the distance between the
best constitution and the best attainable constitution. In addition, this
emphasis on human deficiencies highlights the essence of modern constitu-

---

[1] Lodge, *The Federalist* #85, p. 547.

[2] Ibid., p. 548. Apparently, however, some men are capable of transcending their own
imperfection to at least appreciate how far their efforts fall short of the absolute best constitution. We may not wish to push the logic of this point too far, since if all were perfect there
would be no need for a written constitution.

tionalist theory, that the common interest requires that all power be limited by the rule of law. The American solution has arguably been the most successful response to the problem that constitutionalism seeks to address; hence it is not surprising that for many it has become a model for what the constitutional polity should look like. The irony here is that the founders of this model themselves recognized the compromised status of their creation, appreciating that local conditions necessitated departures from *their* understanding of what the best entails. Their own experience reveals the fallacy of assuming *a* constitutional path, or that any particular feature of their solution—for example, federalism, judicial review, a bill of rights— must be a component of what should be prescribed for a genuinely constitutional regime.

To a great extent this awareness of the range of possibilities for constitutional governance was rooted in a political understanding informed by a careful comparative study of other regimes. "Nations," Seymour Martin Lipset has said, "can be understood only in comparative perspective."[3] As the frequent references in *The Federalist* to the experience of other nations, past and present, suggest, the *making* of a nation can also benefit from the perspective provided by a knowledge of alternative political arrangements. Indeed, in the American case, an understanding of the nation as a commitment to fulfill certain ideas and principles structured the choices that the founders made regarding institutions and practices that had been tried elsewhere. Publius makes clear that in considering constitutional possibilities, these framers' decisions about whether it was wise to borrow from foreign sources did not depend on an assessment of how well this or that worked in its native environment, but rather on an analysis of how well it was likely to serve the ends or vision incorporated in the collective self-understanding of the newly emerging American polity. They understood that constitutionalism entails a commitment to limited government (although where the limits are set may vary from regime to regime); beyond this basic requirement, however, the constitutional configuration it might assume in any particular place should be compatible with the spirit of a given people.[4]

[3] Seymour Martin Lipset, *Continental Divide: The Values and Institutions of the United States and Canada* (New York: Routledge, 1990), p. xiii. For an elaboration of Lipset's views on the centrality of comparative analysis for an understanding of national character and political culture, see his *Consensus and Conflict: Essays in Political Sociology* (New Brunswick, N.J.: Transaction Books, 1985).

[4] Vernon Bogdanor has put it well: "[A] constitution . . . to survive must remain congruent with the broad way of life of a community, a way of life whose meaning . . . is to be found as

To a great extent this is what the debate in Israel over the desirability of adopting a formal written constitution that includes a bill of rights, judicial review, and electoral reform is all about. On one side are those whose passionate advocacy of a new constitution leads them to express their impatience with what they see as the constraining logic of political culture. Accordingly, Baruch Susser, one of the consultants for the widely discussed and circulated draft constitution for Israel, contends, "Arguments from political culture are so often, in the end, sophisticated forms of a mystical fatalism. . . . One cannot fight ghosts. The more political culture becomes vaporized into generalities, the more academics and others can simply say, well, there really is nothing to be done."[5] The basic premise of his argument is that constitutions "need to set the standard rather than merely [express] the prevailing one."[6] His ire is directed at those whose opposition to constitutional change is not based for the most part on legal objections, but rather political ones, for example, that the weakness of the democratic consensus in Israel would not be able to support fundamental reform in the direction of Western constitutionalist norms. Moreover, he is not flailing at imagined foes, since critiques of the reform position do indeed frequently begin with political culture. Whether it is the attribution of antidemocratic Middle Eastern sensibilities to the Israeli body politic or the emphasis on a Jewish tradition that is depicted as inconsistent with the premises of liberal constitutionalism, some significant feature of the political culture is often found to stand in the path of adopting a revised constitutional arrangement.[7]

much in pre-constitutional norms as in the document itself." Vernon Bogdanor, "Introduction," in his *Constitutions in Democratic Polities*, p. 10.

[5] Baruch Susser, "A Proposed Constitution for Israel," in Elazar, *Constitutionalism*, p. 181. Doing nothing is precisely what is to be avoided. "Above all, for those moved by a sense of urgency (and we were certainly moved by such a sense), the idea of attacking this amorphous thing called political culture meant dooming the entire project to failure. Institutional change appeared the fastest and most effective route to cultural transformation" (p. 182).

[6] Ibid.

[7] As of this writing, the proposed bill of rights (or Basic Law on Human Rights) is stuck in a committee of the Knesset. This is less the result of a successful campaign of political culture arguments than it is a reflection of the electoral system, namely the disproportionate influence wielded by the small religious parties which are capable of bringing down the government in power. It was the Likud's own justice minister, Dan Meridor, who in May 1989 presented a bill of rights to the cabinet for its adoption. Initially it received government support, but ultimately mounting pressures forced Meridor to table his bill. Amnon Rubinstein of the Shinui-Center Movement then submitted an identical bill, which passed its first reading with substantial support from both major parties. However, in December 1989 the Likud withdrew its

The choice is not between a rejection of political culture or a slavish adherence to whatever constitutional implications may seem to extend from it. Montesquieu observed of the laws that they "should have relation to the degree of liberty which the constitution will bear; to the religion of the inhabitants, to their inclinations, riches, numbers, commerce, manners, and customs."[8] Much later on he wrote, "It is the business of the legislature to follow the spirit of the nation, when it is not contrary to the principles of government; for we do nothing so well as when we act with freedom, and follow the bent of our natural genius."[9] These sentiments can be usefully applied to an understanding of constitutionalism that speaks directly to our comparison of the Israeli and American systems. They might be reformulated in the following way. The raison d'etre of constitutional government is the preservation of liberty; whatever other goals it may have, a regime that identifies itself as constitutional, but fails to pursue this goal, is simply not what it purports to be.[10] If, therefore, the pursuit of liberty (the minimum condition of which is protection against arbitrary rule) should be inconsistent with the spirit of the nation, and if deference to the latter prevents the realization of the former, then the obligations of constitutionalism require some departure from the path of national spiritual fulfillment. But every effort should be made to integrate the pursuit of liberty with a polity's particular cultural and historical commitments; in other words, a basic congruence between the demands of political culture and constitutionalism ought to be established. Where the political culture itself strongly incorporates the core principle of constitutionalism, as it does in the United States, the task will of course be simpler. Where, as in Israel, the principle is more weakly incorporated within a political culture that also includes other prominent commitments with which it may be in tension, the effort will pose more of a challenge. The choice, then, is not

---

support for the bill, leaving the legislation in limbo in the Constitution, Law and Justice Committee.

[8] Montesquieu, *The Spirit of the Laws*, vol. 1, p. 6.

[9] Ibid., p. 294.

[10] Gordon J. Schochet has noted the declining significance of the term *constitutionalism*," relating this development to its use in connection with regimes that are autocratic. "There is little point in discussing constitutionalism as a significant and distinct political concept; its apparent universality has rendered it vacuous." Gordon J. Schochet, "Introduction," in *Constitutionalism—Nomos XX*, ed. J. Roland Pennock and John W. Chapman (New York: New York University Press, 1979), p. 5. Students of constitutionalism should not succumb to this trend; rather, they must insist on criteria that make it very clear when the term is being abused.

between "reflection" and "accident," but between the reconciliation of principle and circumstance versus the abandonment of one for the other.

CONSTITUTIONALISMS

According to one of the leading contemporary practitioners of constitution making, "American constitutionalism is America's most important export."[11] While no doubt reassuring to Americans who worry that they are best known abroad for Coca-Cola and McDonald's, it may be less comforting to those abroad who fear the penetration of their societies by an alien cultural tradition. In his study of the Indian Constitution, Granville Austin points out that "the most frequently expressed fear, and the most easily understandable, was that the largely foreign origin of the Constitution would make it unworkable in India."[12] The fear was certainly grounded in reality, since the Indian Constitution was pointedly modeled after other systems, with the American example exerting the strongest influence. "The pervasive influence of United States legal ideals began with the very process of the formulation of the Indian Constitution."[13] Moreover, as Andzrej Rapaczynski notes, "It is one of a few cases of a massive borrowing by a country with a vastly different tradition that has had lasting effects on the legal and political culture of the borrowing country, yet took place without American control or pressure."[14]

Nevertheless, commentators on the Indian constitutional experience have not found the concerns about foreign origins to have been justified by subsequent history. Austin, for example, finds that "while most of the Constitution is plainly non-Indian . . . this is different from being un-Indian, or being inconsistent with Indian ways of thought and action."[15] Soli J. Sorabjee quotes from an Indian Supreme Court opinion to the effect

---

[11] Albert Blaustein, "Contemporary Trends in Constitution-Writing," in Elazar, *Constitutionalism*, p. 171.

[12] Granville Austin, *The Indian Constitution: Cornerstone of a Nation* (Oxford: Oxford University Press, 1966), p. 325.

[13] Soli J. Sorabjee, "Equality in the United States and India," in Henkin and Rosenthal, *Constitutionalism and Rights*, p. 96. See also, in the same volume, Andrzej Rapaczynski, "Bibliographical Essay: The Influence of U.S. Constitutionalism Abroad." Rapaczynski describes the influence of American constitutionalism on India, particularly with respect to fundamental rights and judicial review, as "massive and the borrowings direct" (p. 449).

[14] Ibid., p. 447.

[15] Austin, *The Indian Constitution*, p. 326.

that the judicial process of applying American principles of constitutional equality "would not [entail] incorporating principles foreign to [their] Constitution."[16] While others are not as sanguine in their assessments of the Indian constitutional condition—Harvey Wheeler, for example, calls it "a doubtful member of the family [of constitutional regimes]"[17]—the general thought seems to be that the Indians have managed the process of constitutional transplantation well, demonstrating that critical differences in sociopolitical background do not necessarily preclude deriving satisfactory results from the importation of principles and practices from one constitutional milieu to another.

The Indian case has suggestive implications for the Israeli—American comparison, not the least of which is the potential it reveals for parallel constitutional development in very different political cultures.[18] The transferability of constitutional concepts and practices across national boundaries is not as limited as a narrow focus on political culture might lead one to expect. The wisdom of transplantation is another matter, for the fact that something can survive does not mean that it ought to. This was not lost on the makers of the Indian Constitution. The visit of Haim Cohn to the U.S. Supreme Court has its analogue in late 1947 in a similar trip by the Indian constitutional adviser B. N. Rau. Rau met with Justices Vinson, Hughes, Frankfurter, Burton, Murphy, and Judge Learned Hand; and much like Cohn, Rau had the experience of being persuaded by Frankfurter (not that Cohn needed much persuasion) to avoid specific features of the American model—in the Indian case, of not following the conception of due process prevalent in the United States. The advice was heeded, highlighting the pattern of selective borrowing from American precedent in accordance with the perceived needs of the Indian polity. Similarly, in Australia, which has been among the most open of the English-speaking Commonwealth nations to American constitutional influence, there is no bill of rights, a reflection of the fact that American individual rights jurisprudence has not (unlike in some other areas like federalism) penetrated very deeply into Australian constitutional development. That a bill of rights could be

[16] Sorabjee, "Equality in the United States and India," p. 102.

[17] Harvey Wheeler, "Constitutionalism," in *Handbook of Political Science*, ed. Fred I. Greenstein and Nelson W. Polsby (Reading, Mass.: Addison-Wesley, 1975), p. 2. Wheeler then goes on to suggest that Israel is a similar case in this respect.

[18] Harvey Wheeler has suggested that Americans "assume that constitutionalism is the exclusive property of the Anglo-American nations." Ibid. While India's experiment in constitutional government is hardly an unmitigated success, it surely causes one to question the validity of this assumption.

adopted in Australia (or Great Britain for that matter) is not in doubt; whether it should be cannot so confidently be affirmed.[19]

There is also nothing inevitable or necessary about the Israeli failure to adopt an entrenched bill of rights, although, as we have seen, when one looks closely the reasons for it are not obscure. Why a polity such as India, which at first glance possesses at least as many ethnic, tribal, and religious problems as Israel, should so quickly move in the direction of an American model of rights enforcement may seem odd in light of our discussion of alternative pluralisms. It is, however, worth noting that the Indian Constituent Assembly was able with very little difficulty to draft a constitution with a bill of rights because, as Granville Austin points out, its "members disagreed hardly at all about the ends they sought and only slightly about the means for achieving them."[20] Whatever the explanation for this achievement—Austin, for example, says that "the roots of accommodation rest in the soil of Indian thought"[21]—it was evidently not replicated at the Israeli Constituent Assembly, where disagreement about ends and means figured prominently in the postponement of formal constitution making. In this Assembly the conflicting visions embodied in the Declaration of Independence impeded the process of creating a written constitution. The individualist tradition of liberal constitutionalism, with its cardinal prescription of generality as the signature attribute of law, collided with, or at least posed a serious challenge to, the communitarian rationale for the state, with its recognition of the privileged status of one particular group, and its commitment to the semiautonomous condition of all major groups. To be sure, the Indian Constitution, much like the recently enacted Canadian Charter of Rights and Freedoms, makes provision for group rights, and thus diverges in a notable way from the American preference for avoiding any official cognizance of diversity. Nevertheless, the thrust of both documents is libertarian; as Lipset remarks about the Canadian adoption of a bill of rights, it was "perhaps the most important step that Canada has taken to Americanize itself."[22]

---

[19] Ronald Dworkin has recently written of the need for Great Britain to adopt a bill of rights. He argues that in a "culture of liberty" there must be certain freedoms "exempt from the ordinary process of balancing and regulation." Ronald Dworkin, *A Bill of Rights for Britain* (London: Chatto & Windus, 1990), p. 10. Maybe so, but this in itself does not indicate the advisability of moving to a bill of rights.

[20] Austin, *The Indian Constitution*, p. xiii. Significantly, too, as Sori J. Sorabjee notes, "The framers of India's Constitution were quite clear that there should be no place for state religion, nor for official patronage of any particular religion." Sorabjee, "Equality in the United States and India," p. 106.

[21] Austin, *The Indian Constitution*, p. 320.

[22] Lipset, *Continental Divide*, p. 225.

In Israel, much of the legal community has long lamented the absence of a bill of rights. Among them is Itzhak Zamir, the former Israeli attorney general and noted civil libertarian, who has referred to such an enumeration as "the very heart of constitutionalism worth its name."[23] Taken literally, this means that Israel cannot be considered a constitutional regime. It is a judgment that parallels views expressed on the other side of the Atlantic; for example, Richard B. Morris, in his examination of the influence of the American Revolution abroad, writes of the failure of Israel to adopt "a formal written constitution along the American model," and contends that "the religious issue, along with the tense military situation, have conspired to postpone for Israel her day of constitutionalism."[24] For Zamir, as for many Israelis, the time for following the American model is long overdue.[25] This does not mean that the specific content of the Bill of Rights must be duplicated in Israel, only that there be some constitutional entrenchment of rights that can be judicially enforced against those who act in the name of the state. For example, the much-discussed Tel Aviv draft constitution goes beyond the American example in making provision for workers' rights, subsistence rights, and rights to education and medical treatment. But the notion that the structure of constitutionalism has a specific formulaic content is of dubious value. There is no litmus test for constitutionalism; for example, the presence of a bill of rights can be, and often is, a misleading indicator of constitutional freedom. That there are regimes where the provision of guarantees in a bill of rights in fact guarantees very little may be taken to mean one of two things: either a necessary condition of constitutionalism has been achieved while sufficient conditions remain to be fulfilled; or the presence or absence of such a document is not essential to a determination of whether constitutionalist claims are legitimate. The latter

[23] Itzhak Zamir, "Two Contrasting Constitutional Experiences," in Elazar, *Constitutionalism*, p. xix. Zamir's views reflect his own experience in the public arena. In an interview with the author, he emphasized that, apart from its role in the judicial enforcement of rights, a bill of rights "would be a great tool of the attorney general in enforcing the rule of law against the government." Interview, Jerusalem, November 30, 1988. Zamir had been replaced as attorney general after he insisted on prosecuting the General Security Service officials suspected of participating in the bus incident in which two captured terrorists were killed.

[24] Richard B. Morris, *The Emerging Nations and the American Revolution* (New York: Harper & Row, 1970), p. 198.

[25] Zamir, "Two Contrasting Constitutional Experiences," p. xiii. In this introductory essay, Zamir uses the occasion of the fortieth anniversary of the state of Israel and the bicentennial of the U.S. Constitution as an opportunity to call on Israelis to follow the American example by completing the work of constitution making with the adoption of a bill of rights. An interesting omission is any acknowledgment of the fact that the bicentennial celebration was honoring a document that, using the year 1787 as the benchmark, did not include a bill of rights.

view seems particularly appropriate in the case of a regime such as Israel, where a commitment to liberal democratic principles is to be reconciled with the establishment of the state as a homeland for a particular people. Very few Israeli Jews would countenance the abandonment of this latter goal as an essential foundational block of any constitutional solution. Even the proposed draft constitution establishes as its first "basic tenet" that "the State of Israel is the state of the Jewish people, founded on this people's eternal right to sovereign existence in Eretz Israel."[26] Not surprisingly, this critical assertion of identity and purpose is not included in the draft's bill of rights. With the exception of one provision that provides that the guarantee of equality shall not be construed as contradicting the Law of Return, the section on human rights does not advert to the particularistic commitments of the polity. Included are familiar guarantees such as that "every person has the right to freedom of expression."[27] It is only much later, under the section on political parties, that the right to found a party that subscribes to "the negation of the existence of the State of Israel as the state of the Jewish people" is denied.[28] So it turns out that in effect everyone does not have the right to freedom of expression (even as to content), but one has to wait until getting well past the bill of rights to make this discovery.

This provision incorporates the language of the amended Basic Law on the Knesset discussed in Chapter 5 and reflects the incongruity in the Israeli polity between nationality and citizenship. The inherent logic of a bill of rights incorporates a rejection of this incongruity. Indeed its ultimate purpose is not only to transcend nationality (understood in ethnoreligious terms), but also to push beyond citizenship itself toward recognition of the sanctity of universal rights. In its pure form a bill of rights, following the American model that has inspired many of the principal human rights treaties in international law, should not even take cognizance of the noncitizen status of individuals.[29] It has been said that "liberal politics is constitutionalism."[30] If Giovanni Sartori is correct in this contention, then the constitutional enumeration of rights is a perfectly natural, if not inevitable, extension of the philosophical premises on which such a politics rests.

[26] A Constitution for the State of Israel (Chairperson, Uriel Reichman), p. 1.

[27] Ibid., sec. 24(b), p. 8.

[28] Ibid., sec. 190 (b)(1), p. 45. This section also outlaws parties that negate the democratic character of the state and that incite to racism.

[29] For a discussion of this point, see Guy S. Goodwin-Gill, "The Status and Rights of Nonnationals," in Henkin and Rosenthal, Constitutionalism and Rights.

[30] Giovanni Sartori, The Theory of Democracy Revisited (Chatham, N.J.: Chatham House, 1987), p. 309.

These premises, however, make it difficult to accommodate political experiments that do not flow from the same set of universalistic principles.[31] An inversion of Sartori's point—"constitutionalism is liberal politics"—would require substantial qualification to fit the description of those regimes, like Israel, that incorporate a mix of universal and particularistic principles. Here the *absence* of a bill of rights, while also not inevitable (or perhaps even desirable), should not be taken to signify the absence of constitutionalism. Provided that there are reasonably effective judicial and other protections for individual rights, it should rather indicate the awkwardness of coming to terms in a coherent constitutional way with political aspirations that are in some considerable tension. Constitutionalism is definitely not *illiberal* politics, but its conceptualization should not be confined only to polities that embody an unambiguous, robust commitment to the ends of liberal democracy.

It is of course reasonable to ask "whether a constitutional arrangement can exist where it is impossible to have one people."[32] One can construe the United States as the prototypical constitutional regime because its conception of nationhood is based on certain political ideas and principles whose affirmation (in most cases tacit) establishes a common relationship of all citizens to the central political authority. Shared membership in the political community constitutes the only membership that carries with it any formal recognition. Imagining for a moment the enactment of even the most secular and minimalist interpretation of the Israeli Law of Return into American law will illustrate what is at stake. Suppose a law were to grant automatic citizenship to all Protestants immigrating to the United States. They, unlike all others who would have to comply with the extended pro-

---

[31] Here I agree with Robert A. Goldwin's observations: "In the philosophies of modern democratic liberalism going back to the teachings of John Locke . . . , there is a determined effort to universalize the principles of government, by emphasizing the principles of human nature that are common to all and that transcend particular nations or groups or nationalities." He goes on: "Nothing in John Locke helps us to think about [the problem of powerful particularities] or to know what to do when faced by it." Robert A. Goldwin, comments from Goldwin, Kaufman, and Schambra, *Forging Unity Out of Diversity*, pp. 429–30.

[32] Comments of William T. Coleman, in Goldwin and Kaufman, *Constitution Makers on Constitution Making*, p. 456. In particular, "In the Israel—Palestine situation, can one think of a constitutional arrangement that would recognize and take into account the basic differences there" (p. 456)?. It is not clear from Coleman's remarks if he is addressing the question of the occupied territories or of Israel proper, although his general concern about constitutionalism in countries without *a* people suggests the latter. This is also suggested by a distinction he makes between a country like Yugoslavia and those in the Middle East, where, he maintains, the problems of difference are more intractable.

cedures required of all immigrants under prevailing legislation, could become Americans simply because of who they were. Among the effects of such a law would undoubtedly be a transformation in the way religious groups in the society viewed themselves in relationship to one another and to the government. Grave constitutional concerns would surely be raised; ultimately the identification of one people in this manner for special benefit and consideration would evoke doubts as to the viability of constitutionalism in America. These doubts would not flow simply from a focus on the law itself, but would be generated by placing the law in the broader context of American political aspirations and historical development. It would then be seen as a violation of traditional principles of liberal governance, a particularly grievous violation precisely because it offended historic notions of American nationhood. It would be offensive to abstract precepts of political justice as well as to the spirit of the nation.

The Israeli Law of Return is both the constitutional legacy of a tragic past and a concession to the intractability of communal difference, what William T. Coleman means when he speaks of the impossibility of having one people. Establishing the state as the state of the Jewish people is understandably offensive to many in Israel who are not Jews, but unlike the analogous American hypothetical, the argument that supports it bears the legitimating claim of history. Bernard Lewis has said that there are different ways to make a constitution; writing one is the most obvious way, but you can also grow one. " 'Growing' a constitution . . . is building on the basis of the historical experience of a nation or of a society."[33] Not all such constitutions are legitimate by the standards of constitutionalism that emerge from the philosophic tradition of political liberalism; on the other hand, some *are* legitimate even though by an ahistorical application of criteria from this tradition they would not be so considered. Constitutionalism rightly understood has room for contrasting constitutionalisms.

BORROWINGS

There is one apparent exception in the U.S. Constitution to the presumption of modern constitutionalist theory that the exercise of all power will be constrained by law. Article II, section 2, states that the president "shall have Power to grant Reprieves and Pardons for offenses against the United States, except in cases of impeachment." The unique character of this

[33] Comments of Bernard Lewis in ibid., p. 175.

delegation was made clear by a decision of the Supreme Court: "To the executive alone is entrusted the power, and it is entrusted without limit."[34] For many Americans the extraordinary nature of this executive prerogative was revealed in President Ford's pardon of his predecessor for offenses that Richard Nixon committed or *may* have committed during his tenure in office. That a pardon could occur before President Nixon had been convicted of anything was in accord with the intentions of the framers of the Constitution, who in their consideration of the pardon power specifically chose not to include the words "after conviction" subsequent to the words "reprieves and pardons."[35]

The framers were familiar with abuses associated with the pardoning power; they had, after all, rebelled against a monarchy that had, through its royal governors, left them with bitter memories of this kingly prerogative. They were also familiar, through their acquaintance with Montesquieu and Blackstone, with the serious theoretical objections to the existence of executive pardons in a republican regime. Crimes perpetrated in a monarchy were a direct offense against the king, but in a popular government it was the people who were the victims of criminal acts. Why then provide the executive with the authority to frustrate the will of the people, as expressed both in legislatively derived criminal penalties and in convictions handed down by popular juries? And more to the point of our immediate concern, why adopt a practice for a new Constitution that embraced a set of conceptual suppositions more consonant with the theory of governance associated with the old rejected order?

To the first question, an opinion of Justice Holmes accurately reflects what appears to have been the dominant view at the Constitutional Convention. "A pardon in our days is not a private act of grace from an individual happening to possess power. It is a part of the Constitutional scheme. When granted it is the determination of the ultimate authority that the public welfare will be better served by inflicting less than what the judgment fixed."[36] To the second question, James Iredell's reply to the objec-

---

[34] *United States v. Klein*, 80 U.S. 128, 147 (1871).

[35] Luther Martin had moved to insert these words, but he withdrew his motion after being persuaded by James Wilson that a "pardon before conviction might be necessary, in order to obtain the testimony of accomplices." Quoted in William F. Duker, "The President's Power to Pardon: A Constitutional History," *William and Mary Law Review* 18 (1977): 501.

[36] *Biddle v. Perovich*, 274 U.S. 480, 486 (1927). This public welfare interpretation was meant to correct Chief Justice Marshall's early account of the pardon power as "an act of grace." According to Marshall, "It is the private, though official act of the executive magistrate, delivered to the individual for whose benefit it is intended." *United States v. Wilson*, 32 U.S.

tions of George Mason suggests the circumstances under which it is appropriate to borrow from the practice of a discredited monarchy. "[It is a wise aim], in forming a general government for America, to combine the acknowledged advantages of the British constitution with proper republican checks to guard as much as possible against abuses."[37] Thus in Great Britain the king may not be impeached, whereas in the United States the president not only can be, he may not be pardoned if so convicted. Or to rephrase and elaborate upon Iredell's point: in the case of two significantly different polities, constitutional transplantation is both justified and desirable when that which is adopted by one from the other will serve the interests of the new constitutional venture and not undermine its essential character.

The appropriateness of using the British experience with pardons as a model for American constitutional practice has long been the basis of intense debate on the Supreme Court. In an 1856 case, *Ex parte Wells*, involving the pardon of a capital offender under the condition that he accept a sentence of life imprisonment, Justice Wayne's majority opinion upholding President Fillmore's pardon argued for following the prevailing British understanding: "At [the time of the adoption of the Constitution] both Englishmen and Americans attached the same meaning to the word pardon. At the convention which framed the Constitution, no effort was made to define or change its meaning, although it was limited in cases of impeachment."[38] Wayne also quoted from Chief Justice Marshall's opinion in *United States* v. *Wilson*: "As the power has been exercised from time immemorial by the executive of that nation whose language is our language, and to whose judicial institutions ours bears a close resemblance, we adopt their principles respecting the operations and effect of a pardon, and look into their books for the rules prescribing the manner in which it is to be used by the person who would avail himself of it."[39]

Justice McLean's dissenting opinion saw the issue differently: "The executive office in England and that of this country is so widely different, that doubts may be entertained whether it would be safe for a republican chief

---

(7 Pet.) 150, 160–61 (1833). Alexander Hamilton's explanation in *The Federalist* would tend to support the public welfare view: "The principal argument for reposing the power of pardoning . . . to the Chief Magistrate is this: in seasons of insurrection or rebellion, there are often critical moments, when a well-timed offer of pardon to the insurgents or rebels may restore the tranquility of the commonwealth." Lodge, *The Federalist* #74, p. 465.

[37] Quoted in Duker, "The President's Power to Pardon," p. 502. In addition, for historical examination of the pardoning power, see G. Sidney Buchanan, "The Nature of a Pardon Under the United States Constitution, *Ohio State Law Journal* 39 (1978); and Kathleen Dean Moore, *Pardons: Justice, Mercy, and the Public Interest* (New York: Oxford University Press, 1989).

[38] *Ex parte Wells*, 18 How. 307, 311 (1856).

[39] Ibid., 311.

magistrate, who is the creature of the laws, to be influenced by the exercise of any leading power of the British sovereign. . . . A safer rule of construction will be found in the nature and principles of our own government."[40] And if Wayne could appeal to Marshall, McLean could cite Joseph Story, who had written, "The whole structure of our government is so entirely different, and the elements of which it is composed are so dissimilar from that of England, that no argument can be drawn from the practice of the latter, to assist us in a just arrangement of the executive authority."[41] It was an argument later echoed in the dissenting opinion of Justice Thurgood Marshall, who contended in the important 1974 case *Schick* v. *Reed* that "the historical status of the pardon power in England [does not] supply any relevance here."[42] For Marshall, "The primary resource for analyzing the scope of Article II is our own republican system of government."[43] In contrast, Chief Justice Burger's majority opinion urged adherence to the British model and, like Wayne, quoted John Marshall to that effect.

But the two views in this debate, represented by Marshall, Wayne, and Burger on one side, and Story, McLean, and Thurgood Marshall on the other, are similarly problematic. Both seem to miss the point of Iredell's remark, that determining the wisdom of constitutional borrowing from a historically linked but politically disparate regime should not be premised on a simple recitation of similarities and differences. Rather, the proposed object of transplantation should be evaluated in terms of its functional prospects within the political and philosophical context of the constitutional setting for which it is being considered. Chief Justice Marshall mischaracterized the pardoning power in the U.S. Constitution as a private act of grace because his analysis was too narrowly focused on the operation of the power in England. But those who rejected the broad executive power were similarly inattentive to the alternative rationale offered by the framers, one intended, in part, to republicanize the pardoning power. Edward S. Corwin points out that "whereas Blackstone was thinking of pardon as an instrument only of clemency, and so more or less opposed to the law, the Framers regarded it as also an instrument of law enforcement."[44] In other words, for them it was proper to borrow from the existing array of royal prerogatives, but only with the clear understanding that the exercise of any such prerogative should serve, or at least not be in con-

---

[40] Ibid., 318.

[41] Ibid., 321.

[42] *Schick* v. *Reed*, 419 U.S. 256, 276 (1974).

[43] Ibid., 276.

[44] Edward S. Corwin, *The President: Office and Powers* (New York: New York University Press, 1964), p. 159.

tradiction to, republican ends. This ultimately is the significance of the pardon's inapplicability to impeachment.

And now back to Israel, where a similar judicial debate over the pardoning power has been conducted. The occasion was the granting of a pardon by the state president to the head of the General Security Service and three members of that service in connection with the so-called bus no. 300 incident, which was referred to in Chapter 5. What made this pardon so controversial was that it was issued prior to any trial or conviction. The president claimed in his public statement explaining the reasons for his decision that the public interest (the war against terrorism) required that the General Security Service be spared the damage that would follow from any further investigation into the incident. He therefore acted pursuant to the language of section 11(b) of the Basic Law: The President of the State, which reads: "The President of the State shall have power to pardon offenders and to lighten penalties by the reduction or commutation thereof."

The case pitted against each other two justices, Barak and Shamgar, who are often judicial allies, particularly in matters relating to individual rights. Here they differed on several important questions, including the relevance to Israel of the American and British experience with the pardoning power. Shamgar's majority opinion, upholding the president's action, drew inspiration from precedents in the United States and Great Britain affirming the legitimacy of preconviction pardons. In response to the charge that this power was inconsistent with the rule of law, he wrote, "It should be remembered that we are dealing here with legally valid constitutional arrangements of the kind found today in countries of recognized democratic character, and to say that the existence of an effective rule of law is negated by reason of a pardoning power of full scope, where it exists, is an extreme proposition lacking any real foundation."[45] Shamgar's readers were not

---

[45] *Barzilai*, 40 (3) P.D. at 563. Shamgar traced his reliance on American and British experience to an earlier pardon case, *Attorney-General* v. *Matana*, where the majority, in an opinion by Justice Agranat, contended that the presidential pardoning power was shaped according to the Anglo-American model (although it should be noted that today the power of the British monarch does not extend to pardon before conviction). Already in that decision, however, the alternative view was presented, as Justice Landau's dissenting opinion maintained: "I doubt whether . . . we should follow the precedents of the United States in interpreting the Constitution of that country. And particularly in regard to the powers of the President of the State and the President of the United States there exists in my view a fundamental difference between the constitutional characters of these institutions here and in the United States which excludes any possibility of drawing comparisons between the two." *Attorney-General* v. *Matana*, 16 (1) P.D. 430, at 461 (1960). Justice Barak's opinion in *Barzilai* makes a similar argument; however, Landau, as compared to Barak, has been much more insistent on applying its logic to the sphere of individual liberties as well.

being misled about the legality of the broad pardoning power in certain other democratic countries, although they would not have known from his trivialization of the opposing position that serious judicial voices have not only found a *real* foundation for their objections, but in their minds a very strong one. For example, not noted in his appeal to foreign sources are the concerns once raised by American critics of the pardoning power (and revived with the Nixon pardon), that following the British approach meant compromising that which people most admire about the United States, its commitment to the rule of law. Shamgar's approving citation of Chief Justice Burger's opinion in *Schick* v. *Reed* is an example of borrowing from foreign sources that are themselves based on foreign sources—doubtless a not uncommon occurrence, but one that calls for skepticism in evaluating the lessons to be learned from the precedent directly cited. In the instance of the pardon, a controversial assimilation of one country's tradition to another (e.g., John Marshall's assertion about the close resemblance of American and British judicial institutions) then serves to legitimate the embrace of an "Anglo-American model" by a third country, although by the time this occurs, distinctions between Anglos and Americans in terms of their salient regime differences have long since disappeared.[46]

Not surprisingly, Justice Barak felt more comfortable with Justice Marshall's opinion in *Schick*, which he cited to support his strongly held views about the interpretive significance of foreign sources: "The pardoning power forms part of the fabric of our democratic life"; thus, "we can gain but limited interpretive guidance from the situation in other countries."[47] He was particularly taken by Marshall's notion that a nation's own republican system of government should be the "the primary resource" for analyzing the scope of the pardoning power.[48] However, in his eagerness to establish the distinctiveness of the Israeli republican experience, he like Shamgar merged the American and British practices, so that we find him quoting from Justice Wayne's opinion (but not Justice McLean's) in *Ex parte Wells*, to the effect that the shared tradition of the two societies had led the

---

[46] For two critiques of the approach of the *Barzilai* majority that touch on the use of foreign precedents, see Paul F. Occhiogrosso, "The Shin Beth Affair: National Security versus the Rule of Law in the State of Israel," *Loyola of Los Angeles International and Comparative Law Journal* 11 (1989); and Mordechai Kremnitzer, "The General Security Service Pardon: A Test for the High Court of Justice," *Tel Aviv University Studies in Law* 8 (1988). Kremnitzer, for example, says that "not every scheme that bears a label of British or American manufacture is necessarily consistent, on account of its origin, with the rule of law" (p. 172).

[47] *Barzilai*, 40 (3) P.D. at 595–96 . Barak was particularly taken by Marshall's notion that "the primary resource for analyzing the scope [of the pardoning power] is our own republican system of government."

[48] Ibid., 595.

constitution makers in the United States consciously to emulate the old country. But finally for Barak, the telling consideration in avoiding the Anglo-American model is that in Israel the president is not the chief executive charged with the enforcement of the law, but rather he is the occupant of a largely symbolic office that places him above the political battleground where responsibility for executing the law lies. Furthermore, the president is not a constitutional part of the administration of criminal justice; as a result his intervention prior to conviction is an improper invasion and interruption of the rightful authority of other constitutional actors.

The strength of Justice Barak's opinion lies in his effort to relate the purpose of the pardon to the distribution of constitutional power within the structure of government. His approach was patterned after Justice Holmes, whose emphasis on structure and context had led him to revise Chief Justice Marshall's justification of the executive use of the pardon. "The presidential power of pardon must be seen as a component in the complex of governmental powers comprising the 'constitutional scheme.' "[49] However, Barak's acceptance of the public welfare rationale leaves uncertain why the constitutional scheme is not better served if a nonpartisan figure like the state president acts in pursuit of the public welfare, as opposed to a political figure like the president of the United States, who could more reasonably be suspected of seeking to advance his own partisan interests behind the rhetoric of the common interest.[50] Would Israeli democracy be better off if it had been the prime minister who had brought the criminal investigation of the General Security Service to a premature ending through his exercise of the pardoning power? Maybe so, if the health of democracy was largely a function of formal compliance with strict separation of powers guidelines. But in fact Barak's problem with this pardon extended much more deeply into the substance of the rule of law. As he wrote in his concluding words, "The rule of law is negated where there is discrimination between equals."[51] Thus where grave offenses have been alleged against members of the executive branch, the rule of law requires that the investigation and prosecution of these offenses be fully pursued.

[49] Ibid.

[50] At one point in his opinion Justice Barak devalued the worth of constitutional transplantation in this instance by suggesting that the power to pardon in England and the United States "is based on an approach that differs entirely from our own." Ibid., 600. But this is not convincing. At least in the American and Israeli cases, while the structural context differs markedly, the common approach to exercising the power to pardon involves, rightly or wrongly, pursuing the public welfare as defined by the pardoning official.

[51] Ibid., 622.

This is a sensible and admirable position to take, and its eloquent artic-ulation in Justice Barak's opinion is consistent with the pedagogical role of adjudication that we discussed in Chapter 5. The basic position is not, in Justice Marshall's words, that a premature pardon is offensive to "our own republican system of government," but that it contravenes the principles of republican government, pure and simple. In this respect the debate as conducted here over the American and British experience is essentially tangential. Justice Shamgar evidently believed that citing the Anglo-American practice would enhance the persuasive power of his opinion, and thus Barak was forced to respond to his argument. This he effectively did by distinguishing between the structural characteristics of the Israeli and for-eign systems. But since his real objection to the pardon before conviction was the threat it posed to the principles of constitutional government (rather than to the particular structure of *this* constitutional government), what he may inadvertently have demonstrated is that this sort of executive prerogative is even more difficult to reconcile with the less conflicted (than Israel's) constitutional principles underlying the American polity. This also means that Shamgar's argument would have been stronger (in theory if not effect) had he emphasized the *differences* between the two regimes rather than their similarities; that is to say, if in the United States constitutionalist principles can be compromised to the extent of permitting public welfare claims to legitimate a preconviction pardon, then surely in Israel, where the urgency of the security interest is so explicitly bound up in the constitu-tional premises of the regime, the power to pardon must be construed in a manner sufficiently expansive to uphold the actions of the state president.

In the end *Barzilai*, like the American pardon cases, reinforces the insight of the Indian constitutional scholar P. K. Tripathi, who wrote that "foreign precedents, which even at their best are possessed of persuasive value only, seem sometimes to become such flexible and absolutely dispen-sable tools in the hands of judges as to be mere ornaments to embellish a previously and independently reached conclusion rather than guides to lead and direct a court to it."[52] This is not to diminish the potential value of such borrowings; persuasion, after all, is essential to democratic politics. It is also essential, as we have seen, to the educational enterprise of constitu-tional adjudication. As we have also seen in the examples of Justice Barak and others, Israeli judges have drawn liberally and productively from for-eign, especially American, sources as a basis for instructing their fellow

[52] Pradyumna K. Tripathi, "Foreign Precedents and Constitutional Law," *Columbia Law Review* 57 (1957): 328.

citizens in the ways of constitutionalism. Thus Barak, for example, even as he disputed the relevance of American constitutional policy on pardons, paid homage to the inspirational value of American understandings of individual rights. "We . . . can learn from the American recognition of the fundamental human rights, since both our countries have democratic regimes committed to the rule of law and the separation of powers."[53] What *we* have learned is that the differences in democratic regimes should also be acknowledged as part of the processes of constitution making and interpretation. These differences, standing alone, do not establish the wisdom of any specific appeal for inspirational guidance, but they do provide a necessary context within which the adaptive processes of transplantation can most fruitfully occur.

The fragment from Lincoln's writings that was quoted at the outset of this book, and from which its title is taken, remains something of a mystery. There is, according to the editor of Lincoln's writings, some reason to think that it was written in the months immediately prior to the First Inaugural Address, and that it may have been a part of the preparation for that speech. What *is* known is that no speech employing its language has been located. Thus, its meaning will likely never possess the clarity that is typically present in Lincoln's completed works.

For example, the opening lines of the fragment read, "All this is not the result of accident. It has a philosophical cause. Without the *Constitution* and the *Union*, we could not have attained the result; but even these, are not the primary cause of our great prosperity. There is something back of these, entwining itself more closely about the human heart. That something, is the principle of 'Liberty to all'—the principle that clears the *path* for all—gives *hope* to all—and, by consequence, *enterprize*, and *industry* to all."[54] Presumably "this" in the first sentence refers to "our great prosperity," but in the end we are left to wonder about the precise content of a prosperity that maintains its hold on the imagination of one who is about to lead his nation into a bloody and protracted struggle for survival. Is it a prosperity that is the common property of all, or only of those who accept it, or who are its most obvious beneficiaries? If standing behind this pros-

---

[53] *Barzilai*, 40 (3) P.D. at 600. It is worth contrasting this perspective with that of P. K. Tripathi, who in his 1957 study of the use of foreign precedents in several countries, wrote, "We . . . see that despite all divergences of tradition, form of government, and text, the American principles relating to the law of freedom of speech could be imported by the courts in Israel." Tripathi, "Foreign Precedents and Constitutional Law," p. 347.

[54] Basler, *Collected Works*, vol. 4, pp. 168–69.

perity is the rationally derived principle of "liberty for all," then how potent a "philosophical cause" could it have been that was unable to persuade the slaveholder who denied it, or to unburden the slave for whom it had so little effect? Lincoln's depreciation of "accident" as an explanation for American well-being is in the tradition of Publius's account of the founders' basic commitment to "reflection and choice" in their establishment of constitutional government. They had made it in juxtaposition with "accident and force," but as the tragic history over which Lincoln was to preside reveals, their commitment was only partially realized. Force was to prove necessary to secure the fruits of reason and reflection.

Despite the enormous price, few today would deny that it was worth paying. The principle of liberty in the Declaration of Independence—the "apple of gold"—had, as Lincoln suggested, "clear[ed] the *path* for all," which meant that a philosophical commitment that emerged out of the dominant political culture would ultimately prevail over a resistant counterculture. Without the eventual incorporation of the latter into the former, "our great prosperity," which is really an aspirational commitment to national self-realization, would have been squandered. It is the Constitution that serves as the instrument of this self-realization, which is to say, the achievement of nationhood; and it is that document, interpreted in the spirit of the principles that gave it life, that still provides "*hope* to all." As the "picture of silver" created to preserve a precious fruit, the Constitution is both the product of its political culture and the necessary instrument of its perpetuation.

To speak of "our great prosperity" in Israel would also mean, for most Israelis, taking pride in the commitment to realizing democratic aspirations. But no comprehensive assessment of prosperity in Israel could fail to highlight its most distinctive achievement, the building of a state for the Jewish people. Lincoln's assertion that behind the great prosperity is something "entwining itself more closely about the human heart" has universal resonance, but in Israel a particular content that, in comparison with the United States, bears a weaker imprint of philosophical principle and a more pronounced sense of primordial connectedness. There is a tension between the two, nothing like (except perhaps in their most extreme versions) the contradiction between liberal constitutionalist ideals and the practice of slavery. One need not, therefore, triumph over the other; rather, they appear destined for a long, if not always harmonious, coexistence. The process of constitutional evolution will reflect this tension, the inner dynamic of philosophical principle constantly straining against, but not always in opposition to, the various drives that fuel the engine of communal identity. How an Israeli constitution enters into the securing of this "great prosperity" is, as we have seen, much less clear than it is in Lincoln's reflections on American constitutionalism. A number of possible outcomes are possible, all involving the relative muting of one of the two principal strands in the Israeli political culture. Of at least one thing, however, we may be reasonably sure: whatever finally emerges from the fires of constitutional struggle will justify someone in saying, "All this is not the result of accident."

Afterword

No DOUBT the reader has noticed that there is no mention in this book of the Israeli and American elections of 1992. That, alas, is a function of the publication timetable, an annoying reality that all authors writing about changing situations must confront. As of September 1992, knowing the results of the Israeli election, readers should simply register the fact that with the victory of the Labor Party under the leadership of Yitzak Rabin, the political climate for significant constitutional reform in Israel is as propitious as it has ever been.

Such reform might very well include the adoption of an entrenched bill of rights. Already, in advance of the election, moves in that direction had occurred. In March 1992, the Knesset passed two new Basic Laws, the first providing for Freedom of Occupation, and the second concerning Human Dignity and Freedom. Only the first is entrenched, which means that it cannot be amended without an absolute majority of the Knesset.

Interestingly, these developments have been described as "a constitutional revolution" that provides Israel with "legal norms of preferred constitutional status—much like the situation in the United States, Canada, and many other countries" (*Jerusalem Post*, International Edition, June 6, 1992). The characterization comes from Justice Barak, whose enthusiasm for the enactments is understandable in light of our earlier discussion of his constitutional views. But it is difficult to see wherein the revolutionary significance of these laws lie, unless the Supreme Court follows Justice Barak's lead by following an activist judicial agenda under the legitimating authority of the new legislation. Aside from being unentrenched, the Human Dignity and Freedom statute explicitly provides that nothing in it will affect existing legislation, and it includes important qualifications, such as the possibility of its infringement "by a statute that befits the values of the State of Israel," and when there exists a state of emergency as proclaimed "under section 9 of the Law and Administration Ordinance" of 1948. Justice Barak says of the laws that "They bind the Knesset itself." Perhaps in a moral or political sense this is true, but nothing could be clearer than that the most far reaching of the two Basic laws does not constitutionally bind the Knesset. It is, then, quite different from an amendment to the United States Constutition.

As for the United States, the reader should take note of one significant recent development. The hate speech litigation referred to in Chapter Six has been decided by the Supreme Court in a unanimous judgment striking down St. Paul, Minnesota's Bias-Motivated Crime Ordinance (*R.A.V.* v. *City of St. Paul, Minnesota*). The Court, however, split 5–4 on its reasoning, with the majority opinion by the Court's most conservative member, Justice Scalia, outlining a maximalist position on the scope of the presumption against content discrimination. The outcome is further evidence for the strength of the pluralist assumptions of modern liberal constitutionalism.

Appendix

THE PROCLAMATION OF THE STATE OF ISRAEL

The Land of Israel was the birthplace of the Jewish people. Here their spiritual, religious and national identity was formed. Here they achieved independence and created a culture of national and universal significance. Here they wrote and gave the Bible to the world.

Exiled from Palestine, the Jewish people remained faithful to it in all the countries of their dispersion, never ceasing to pray and hope for their return and the restoration of their national freedom.

Impelled by this historic association, Jews strove throughout the centuries to go back to the land of their fathers and regain their Statehood. In recent decades they returned in their masses. They reclaimed the wilderness, revived their language, built cities and villages, and established a vigorous and ever-growing community, with its own economic and cultural life. They sought peace yet were prepared to defend themselves. They brought the blessings of progress to all inhabitants of the country.

In the year 1897 the First Zionist Congress, inspired by Theodore Herzl's vision of the Jewish State, proclaimed the right of the Jewish people to national revival in their own country.

This right was acknowledged by the Balfour Declaration of November 2, 1917, and reaffirmed by the Mandate of the League of Nations, which gave explicit international recognition to the historic connection of the Jewish people with Palestine and their right to reconstitute their national home.

The Nazi holocaust, which engulfed millions of Jews in Europe, proved anew the urgency of the reestablishment of the Jewish State, which would solve the problem of Jewish homelessness by opening the gates to all Jews and lifting the Jewish people to equality in the family of nations.

The survivors of the European catastrophe, as well as Jews from other lands, proclaiming their right to a life of dignity, freedom and labor, and undeterred by hazards, hardships and obstacles, have tried unceasingly to enter Palestine.

In the Second World War the Jewish people in Palestine made a full contribution in the struggle of the freedom-loving nations against the Nazi evil. The sacrifices of their soldiers and the efforts of their workers gained them title to rank with the peoples who founded the United Nations.

251

On November 29, 1947, the General Assembly of the United Nations adopted a resolution for the establishment of an independent Jewish State in Palestine, and called upon inhabitants of the country to take such steps as may be necessary on their part to put the plan into effect.

This recognition by the United Nations of the right of the Jewish people to establish their independent state may not be revoked. It is, moreover, the self-evident right of the Jewish people to be a nation, like all other nations, in its own sovereign state.

Accordingly, we, the members of the National Council, representing the Jewish people in Palestine and the Zionist movement of the world, met together in solemn assembly today, the day of the termination of the British Mandate for Palestine, and by virtue of the natural and historic right of the Jewish people and of the resolution of the General Assembly of the United Nations, hereby proclaim the establishment of the Jewish State in Palestine, to be called Israel.

We hereby declare that as from the termination of the Mandate at midnight, this night of the fourteenth of May, 1948, and until the setting up of the duly elected bodies of the State in accordance with a Constitution, to be drawn up by a Constituent Assembly not later than the first day of October 1948, the present National Council shall act as the Provisional State Council, and its executive organ, the National Administration, shall constitute the Provisional Government of the State of Israel.

The State of Israel will be open to the immigration of Jews from all countries of their dispersion, will promote the development of the country for the benefit of all its inhabitants; will be based on the precepts of liberty, justice and peace taught by the Hebrew prophets; will uphold the full social and political equality of all its citizens, without distinction of race, creed or sex; will guarantee full freedom of conscience, worship, education and culture; will safeguard the sanctity and inviolability of the shrines and Holy Places of all religions; and will dedicate itself to the principles of the Charter of the United Nations.

The State of Israel will be ready to cooperate with the organs and representatives of the United Nations in the implementation of the Resolution of the Assembly of November 29, 1947, and will take steps to bring about the Economic Union over the whole of Palestine.

We appeal to the United Nations to assist the Jewish people in the building of its State and to admit Israel into the family of nations.

In the midst of wanton aggression, we yet call upon the Arab inhabitants of the State of Israel to return to the ways of peace and play their part in the development of the State, with full and equal citizenship and the representation in all its bodies and institutions, provisional or permanent.

We offer peace and amity to all the neighboring states and their peoples, and invite them to cooperate with the independent Jewish nation for the common good of all. The State of Israel is ready to contribute its full share to the peaceful progress and development of the Middle East.

Our call goes out to the Jewish people all over the world to rally to our side in the task of immigration and development and to stand by us in the great struggle for fulfillment of the dream of generations—the redemption of Israel.

With trust in the Rock of Israel, we set our hand to this Declaration, at this Session of the Provisional State Council, in the city of Tel Aviv, on this Sabbath eve, the fifth of Iyar, 5708, the fourteenth day of May, 1948.

Bibliography

BOOKS

Abramov, S. Zalmon. *Perpetual Dilemma: Jewish Religion In the Jewish State*. Rutherford, N.J.: Fairleigh Dickinson University Press, 1976.

Agresto, John. *The Supreme Court and Constitutional Democracy*. Ithaca: Cornell University Press, 1984.

Akzin, Benjamin. *State and Nation*. London: Hutchinson University Library, 1964.

Arian, Asher. *Politics in Israel: The Second Generation*. Chatham, N.J.: Chatham House Publishers, 1985.

Arkes, Hadley. *Beyond the Constitution*. Princeton: Princeton University Press, 1990.

Arthur, John. *The Unfinished Constitution: Philosophy and Constitutional Practice*. Belmont, Calif.: Wadsworth Publishing Co., 1989.

Austin, Granville. *The Indian Constitution: Cornerstone of a Nation*. Oxford: Oxford University Press, 1966.

Avineri, Shlomo. *The Making of Modern Zionism: The Intellectual Origins of the Jewish State*. New York: Basic Books, 1981.

Banting, Keith G., and Richard Simeon, eds. *Redesigning the State: The Politics of Constitutional Change*. Toronto: University of Toronto Press, 1985.

Barak, Aharon. *Judicial Discretion*. New Haven: Yale University Press, 1989.

Barber, Sotirios A. *On What the Constitution Means*. Baltimore: Johns Hopkins University Press, 1984.

Barendt, Eric. *Freedom of Speech*. Oxford: Oxford University Press, 1987.

Basler, Roy, ed. *The Collected Works of Abraham Lincoln*. New Brunswick, N.J.: Rutgers University Press, 1953.

Beeman, Richard, Stephen Botein, and Edward C. Carter II, eds. *Beyond Confederation: Origins of the Constitution and American National Identity*. Chapel Hill: University of North Carolina Press, 1987.

Bellah, Robert N., Richard Madsen, William M. Sullivan, Ann Swidler, and Steven M. Tipton. *Habits of the Heart: Individualism and Commitment in American Life*. New York: Harper & Row, 1985.

Ben-Gurion, David. *Rebirth and Destiny of Israel*. New York: Philosophical Library, 1954.

Bercovitch, Sacvan. *The American Jeremiad*. Madison: University of Wisconsin Press, 1979.

Berns, Walter. *The First Amendment and the Future of American Democracy*. New York: Basic Books, 1976.

————. *Taking the Constitution Seriously*. New York: Simon & Schuster, 1987.

255

Bickel, Alexander M. *The Least Dangerous Branch: The Supreme Court at the Bar of Politics*. Indianapolis: Bobbs-Merrill Co., 1962.

———. *The Morality of Consent*. New Haven: Yale University Press, 1975.

Black, Jr., Charles L. *The People and the Court: Judicial Review in a Democracy*. Englewood Cliffs, N.J.: Prentice-Hall, 1960.

Bogdanor, Vernon, ed. *Constitutions in Democratic Politics*. Aldershot, Eng.: Gower Publishing Co., 1988.

Bollinger, Lee C. *The Tolerant Society: Freedom of Speech and Extremist Speech in America*. New York: Oxford University Press, 1986.

Boorstin, Daniel J. *The Genius of American Politics*. Chicago: University of Chicago Press, 1953.

Braude, Benjamin, and Bernard Lewis, eds. *Christians and Jews in the Ottoman Empire: The Functioning of a Plural Society*. 2 vols. New York: Holmes & Meier, 1982.

Bryner, Gary C., and Noel B. Reynolds, eds. *Constitutionalism and Rights*. Provo, Utah: Brigham Young University Press, 1987.

Calhoun, John C. *A Disquisition on Government*. Indianapolis: Bobbs-Merrill Co., 1953.

Calvert, Robert E., ed. *"The Constitution of the People": Reflections on Citizens and Civil Society*. Lawrence: University of Kansas Press, 1991.

Clinton, Robert Lowry. *Marbury v. Madison and Judicial Review*. Lawrence: University of Kansas Press, 1989.

Cohen, Erik, Moshe Lissak, and Uri Almagor. *Comparative Social Dynamics*. Boulder, Colo.: Westview Press, 1985.

Cohen, Steven M. *Ties and Tensions: An Update—the 1989 Survey of American Jewish Attitudes toward Israel and Israelis*. New York: American Jewish Committee, 1989.

Corwin, Edward S. *The President: Office and Powers*. New York: New York University Press, 1964.

Cowen, Zelman. *Individual Liberty and the Law*. Dobbs Ferry, N.Y.: Oceana Publications, 1977.

Cox, Archibald. *Freedom of Expression*. Cambridge: Harvard University Press, 1981.

Dainow, Joseph, ed. *The Role of Judicial Decisions and Doctrine in Civil and Mixed Jurisdictions*. Baton Rouge: Louisiana State University Press, 1974.

Dawidowicz, Lucy. *The Jewish Presence: Essays on Identity and History*. New York: Harcourt Brace Jovanovich, 1978.

Deloria, Jr., Vine. *Behind the Trail of Broken Treaties: An Indian Declaration of Independence*. Austin: University of Texas Press, 1985.

Deloria, Jr., Vine, and Clifford M. Lytle. *American Indians, American Justice*. Austin: University of Texas Press, 1983.

Devine, Donald J. *The Political Culture of the United States: The Influence of Member Values on Regime Maintenance*. Boston: Little, Brown, 1972.

Dicey, A. V. *Introduction to the Law of the Constitution.* London: St. Martin's Press, 1961.

Downs, Donald Alexander. *Nazis in Skokie: Freedom, Community, and the First Amendment.* Notre Dame: University of Notre Dame Press, 1985.

Dworkin, Ronald. *A Bill of Rights for Britain.* London: Chatto & Windus, 1990.

———. *Law's Empire.* Cambridge: Harvard University Press, 1986.

———. *Taking Rights Seriously.* Cambridge: Harvard University Press, 1971.

Elazar, Daniel J., ed. *The Constitution of the State of Israel.* Jerusalem: Jerusalem Center for Public Affairs, 1986.

———. *Constitutionalism: The Israeli and American Experiences.* Lanham, Md.: University Press of America, 1990.

———. *Israel: Building a New Society.* Bloomington: Indiana University Press, 1986.

Elon, Amos. *Jerusalem: City of Mirrors.* New York: Little, Brown, 1989.

Elon, Menachem, ed. *The Principles of Jewish Law.* Jerusalem: Keter Publishing House, 1974.

Ely, John Hart. *Democracy and Distrust: A Theory of Judicial Review.* Cambridge: Harvard University Press, 1982.

Emerson, Thomas I. *The System of Freedom of Expression.* New York: Vintage Books, 1970.

Esman, Milton J., and Itamar Rabinovich, eds. *Ethnicity, Pluralism, and the State in the Middle East.* Ithaca: Cornell University Press, 1988.

Fisher, Louis. *American Constitutional Law.* New York: McGraw-Hill Publishing Co., 1990.

Fishman, Hertzel. *American Protestantism and a Jewish State.* Detroit: Wayne State University Press, 1973.

Ford, Paul L., ed. *The Works of Thomas Jefferson.* New York: Putnam's, 1905.

Friedrich, Carl J. *The Impact of American Constitutionalism Abroad.* Boston: Boston University Press, 1967.

Funston, Richard. *A Vital National Seminar: The Supreme Court in American Political Life.* Palo Alto: Mayfield Publishing Co., 1978.

Geertz, Clifford, ed. *Old Societies and New States: The Quest for Modernity in Asia and Africa.* London: Free Press, 1963.

Glendon, Mary Ann. *Abortion and Divorce in Western Law.* Cambridge: Harvard University Press, 1987.

Goldwin, Robert A., and Art Kaufman, eds. *How Does the Constitution Protect Religious Freedom?* Washington D.C.: American Enterprise Institute for Public Policy Research, 1987.

Goldwin, Robert A., Art Kaufman, and William A. Schambra, eds. *Forging Unity Out of Diversity: The Approaches of Eight Nations.* Washington, D.C.: American Enterprise Institute of Public Policy Research, 1989.

Gordon, Charles, and Ellen Gittel Gordon. *Immigration and Nationality Law.* New York: Matthew Bender, 1986.

Gotein, E. David, ed. *Selected Judgments of the Supreme Court of Israel, Vol. 1, 1948–1953*. Jerusalem: Ministry of Justice, 1962.

Greenawalt, Kent. *Speech, Crime, and the Uses of Language*. New York: Oxford University Press, 1989.

Greenstein, Fred I., and Nelson W. Polsby, eds. *Handbook of Political Science*. Reading, Mass.: Addison-Wesley, 1975.

Haiman, Franklyn S. *Speech and Law in a Free Society*. Chicago: University of Chicago Press, 1981.

Halpern, Stephen C., and Charles M. Lamb, eds. *Supreme Court Activism and Restraint*. Lexington, Mass.: D. C. Heath & Co. 1982.

Hamlin, David. *The Nazi/Skokie Conflict: A Civil Liberties Battle*. Boston: Beacon Press, 1980.

Hartz, Louis. *The Liberal Tradition in America*. New York: Harcourt, Brace & World, 1955.

Henkin, Louis, and Albert Rosenthal, eds. *Constitutionalism and Rights: The Influence of the United States Constitution Abroad*. New York: Columbia University Press, 1990.

Hertzberg, Arthur, ed. *The Zionist Idea: A Historical Analysis and Reader*. Garden City, N.Y.: Doubleday & Co., 1959.

Hofstadter, Richard. *The Idea of a Party System: The Rise of Legitimate Opposition in the United States, 1780–1840*. Berkeley: University of California Press, 1969.

Horowitz, Dan, and Moshe Lissak. *Trouble in Utopia: The Overburdened Polity of Israel*. Albany: State University of New York Press, 1989.

Horwitz, Robert H., ed. *The Moral Foundations of the American Republic*. Charlottesville: University Press of Virginia, 1977.

Hume, David. "Of National Characters." In *The Philosophical Works*, ed. Thomas Hill Green and Thomas Hodge Grose. Vol. 3. Darmstadt, Ger.: Scientia Verlag Aalen, 1964.

Huntington, Samuel P. *American Politics: The Promise of Disharmony*. Cambridge: Harvard University Press, 1981.

Isaacs, Harold R. *Idols of the Tribe: Group Identity and Political Change*. New York: Harper & Row, 1975.

Jacobsohn, Gary J. *Pragmatism, Statesmanship, and the Supreme Court*. Ithaca: Cornell University Press, 1977.

———. *The Supreme Court and the Decline of Constitutional Aspiration*. Totowa, N.J.: Rowman & Littlefield, 1986.

Kalven, Jr., Harry. *The Negro and the First Amendment*. Chicago: University of Chicago Press, 1965.

———. *A Worthy Tradition: Freedom of Speech in America*. New York: Harper & Row, 1988.

Karst, Kenneth. *Belonging to America: Equal Citizenship and the Constitution*. New Haven: Yale University Press, 1989.

Kelly, Alfred H., Winfred A. Harbison, and Herman Belz. *The American Constitution: Its Origins and Development*. New York: W. W. Norton & Co., 1983.

Kettner, James H. *The Development of American Citizenship, 1608–1870.* Chapel Hill: University of North Carolina Press, 1978.

Kimmerling, Baruch, ed. *The Israeli State and Society: Boundaries and Frontiers.* Albany: State University Press of New York, 1989.

Konvitz, Milton R. *Judaism and the American Idea.* Ithaca: Cornell University Press, 1978.

Konvitz, Milton, ed. *Judaism and Human Rights.* New York: W. W. Norton & Co., 1972.

Kraines, Oscar. *The Impossible Dilemma: Who Is a Jew in the State of Israel?* New York: Bloch Publishing Co., 1976.

Kretzmer, David. *The Legal Status of the Arabs in Israel.* Boulder, Colo.: Westview Press, 1990.

Kurland, Philip B., ed. *Of Law and Life and Other Things That Matter: Papers and Addresses of Felix Frankfurter, 1956–1963.* New York: Atheneum, 1969.

Kurland, Philip B., and Ralph Lerner, eds. *The Founders' Constitution.* Vol. 1. Chicago: University of Chicago Press, 1987.

Levinson, Sanford. *Constitutional Faith.* Princeton: Princeton University Press, 1988.

Levy, Leonard W. *Original Intent and the Framers' Constitution.* New York: Macmillan Publishing Co., 1988.

Levy, Leonard W., Kenneth L. Karst, and Dennis J. Mahoney, eds. *Encyclopedia of the American Constitution.* Vol. 3. New York: Macmillan, 1986.

Liebman, Charles S. *The Ambivalent American Jew: Politics, Religion, and Family in American Jewish Life.* Philadelphia: Jewish Publication Society of America, 1973.

Liebman, Charles S., and Stephen M. Cohen. *Two Worlds of Judaism: The Israeli and American Experiences.* New Haven: Yale University Press, 1989.

Lijphart, Arend. *Democracy in Plural Societies: A Comparative Exploration.* New Haven: Yale University Press, 1977.

Lipset, Seymour Martin. *Consensus and Conflict: Essays in Political Sociology.* New Brunswick, N.J.: Transaction Books, 1985.

———. *Continental Divide: The Values and Institutions of the United States and Canada.* New York: Routledge, 1990.

———. *The First New Nation: The United States in Historical and Comparative Perspective.* New York: Basic Books, 1963.

Locke, John. *A Letter concerning Toleration.* Edited by Mario Montouri. The Hague: Martinus Nijhoff, 1963.

Lodge, Henry Cabot, ed. *The Federalist.* New York: Knickerbocker Press, 1888.

Lowi, Theodore J. *The End of Liberalism: Ideology, Policy, and the Crisis of Public Authority.* New York: W. W. Norton & Co., 1969.

Lustick, Ian. *Arabs in the Jewish State: Israel's Control of a National Minority.* Austin: University of Texas Press, 1980.

Lutz, Donald S. *The Origins of American Constitutionalism.* Baton Rouge: Louisiana State University Press, 1988.

259

McCann, Michael W., and Gerald L. Houseman, eds. *Judging the Constitution: Critical Essays on Judicial Lawmaking.* Glenview, Ill.: Scott, Foresman & Co., 1989.

McKitrick, Eric L., ed. *Slavery Defended: The Views of the Old South.* Englewood Cliffs, N.J.: Prentice-Hall, 1963.

McWilliams, Wilson Carey. *The Idea of Fraternity in America.* Berkeley: University of California Press, 1973.

Mann, Arthur. *The One and the Many: Reflections on the American Identity.* Chicago: University of Chicago Press, 1979.

Mar'i, Sami Khalid. *Arab Education in Israel.* Syracuse: Syracuse University Press, 1978.

Migdal, Joel S. *Strong Societies and Weak States: State-Society Relations and State Capabilities in the Third World.* Princeton: Princeton University Press, 1988.

Miller, Charles A. *The Supreme Court and the Uses of History.* New York: Simon & Schuster, 1969.

Minow, Martha. *Making All the Difference: Inclusion, Exclusion, and American Law.* Ithaca: Cornell University Press, 1990.

Montesquieu. *The Spirit of the Laws.* New York: Hafner Publishing Co., 1966.

Moore, Kathleen Dean. *Pardons: Justice, Mercy, and the Public Interest.* New York: Oxford University Press, 1989.

Morris, Richard B. *The Emerging Nations and the American Revolution.* New York: Harper & Row, 1970.

Myrdal, Gunnar. *An American Dilemma.* New York: Harper & Row, 1962.

Pangle, Thomas L. *The Spirit of Modern Republicanism: The Moral Vision of the American Founders and the Philosophy of Locke.* Chicago: University of Chicago Press, 1988.

Paterson, William, Michael Novak, and Philip Gleason. *Concepts of Ethnicity.* Cambridge: Harvard University Press, 1982.

Pennock, J. Roland, and John W. Chapman, eds. *Constitutionalism—Nomos XX.* New York: New York University Press, 1979.

Perry, Michael J. *Morality, Politics, and Law: A Bicentennial Essay.* Oxford: Oxford University Press, 1988.

Price, Monroe E. *Law and the American Indian: Readings, Notes and Cases.* Indianapolis: Bobbs-Merrill Co., 1973.

Pritchett, C. Herman. *Civil Liberties and the Vinson Court.* Chicago: University of Chicago Press, 1954.

Prucha, Francis Paul. *The Great White Father: The United States Government and the American Indians. Vol. 2.* Lincoln: University of Nebraska Press, 1984.

Rabinovich, Itamar, and Jehuda Reinharz, eds. *Israel in the Middle East: Documents and Readings on Society, Politics and Foreign Relations, 1948–Present.* New York: Oxford University Press, 1984.

Rackman, Emanuel. *Israel's Emerging Constitution, 1948–1951.* New York: Columbia University Press, 1955.

Richards, David A. J. *Toleration and the Constitution*. New York: Oxford University Press, 1986.

Romann, Michael, and Alex Weingrod. *Living Together Separately: Arabs and Jews in Contemporary Jerusalem*. Princeton: Princeton University Press, 1991.

Rostow, Eugene V. *The Sovereign Prerogative: The Supreme Court and the Quest for Law*. New Haven: Yale University Press, 1962.

Roth, Sol. *Halakhah and Politics: The Jewish Idea of the State*. New York: Yeshiva University Press, 1989.

Rubinstein, Amnon. *The Zionist Dream Revisited*. New York: Schocken Books, 1984.

Sabine, George H. *A History of Political Theory*. 3rd ed. New York: Holt, Rinehart & Winston, 1961.

Sartori, Giovanni. *The Theory of Democracy Revisited*. Chatham, N.J.: Chatham House, 1987.

Schaar, John H. *Loyalty in America*. Berkeley: University of California Press, 1957.

Schlesinger, Jr., Arthur M. *The Disuniting of America: Reflections on a Multicultural Society*. Knoxville: Whittle Direct Books, 1991.

Schuck, Peter H., and Rogers M. Smith. *Citizenship without Consent: Illegal Aliens in the American Polity*. New Haven: Yale University Press, 1985.

Shipler, David K. *Arab and Jew: Wounded Spirits in a Promised Land*. New York: Penguin Books, 1986.

Shklar, Judith N. *American Citizenship: The Quest for Inclusion*. Cambridge: Harvard University Press, 1990.

Smooha, Sammy. *Israel: Pluralism and Conflict*. Berkeley: University of California Press, 1978.

Snowiss, Sylvia. *Judicial Review and the Law of the Constitution*. New Haven: Yale University Press, 1990.

Snyder, Louis L. *Varieties of Nationalism*. New York: Holt, Rinehart, & Winston, 1976.

Sollors, Werner. *Beyond Ethnicity: Consent and Descent in American Culture*. Oxford: Oxford University Press, 1986.

Storing, Herbert. *What the Anti-Federalists Were For*. Chicago: University of Chicago Press, 1981.

Sullivan, John L., Michal Shamir, Patrick Welsh, and Nigel S. Roberts. *Political Tolerance in Context: Support for Unpopular Minorities in Israel, New Zealand, and the United States*. Boulder, Colo.: Westview, 1985.

Syrett, Harold C., ed. *The Papers of Alexander Hamilton*. Vol. 3. New York: Columbia University Press, 1961.

Tec, Nechama. *In the Lion's Den: The Life of Oswald Rufeisen*. New York: Oxford University Press, 1990.

Tocqueville, Alexis de. *Democracy in America*. Edited by Phillips Bradley. New York: Vintage, 1945.

Tribe, Laurence H. *American Constitutional Law*. Mineola: Foundation Press, 1978.

261

Tucker, D.F.B. *Law, Liberalism, and Free Speech.* Totowa, N.J.: Rowman & Allanheld, 1985.

Vital, David. *Zionism: The Crucial Phase.* Oxford: Oxford University Press, 1987.

Walzer, Michael, Edward T. Kantowicz, John Higham, and Mona Harrington. *The Politics of Ethnicity.* Cambridge: Harvard University Press, 1982.

———. *Spheres of Justice.* New York: Basic Books, 1983.

Washburn, Wilcomb E. *Red Man's Land/White Man's Law.* New York: Charles Scribner's Sons, 1971.

Watson, Alan. *Legal Transplants.* Edinburgh: Scottish Academic Press, 1974.

Wiecek, William. *Liberty Under Law: The Supreme Court in American Life.* Baltimore: Johns Hopkins University Press, 1988.

Wilkinson, Charles F. *American Indians, Time, and the Law: Native Societies in a Modern Constitutional Democracy.* New Haven: Yale University Press, 1987.

Wood, Gordon S. *The Creation of the American Republic, 1776–1787.* Chapel Hill: University of North Carolina Press, 1969.

Zelinsky, Wilbur. *Nation into State: The Shifting Symbolic Foundations of American Nationalism.* Chapel Hill: University of North Carolina Press, 1988.

Zucker, Norman. *The Coming Crisis in Israel: Private Faith and Public Policy.* Cambridge: MIT Press, 1973.

ARTICLES

Abram, Morris B. "Why U.S. Jews Care about 'Who's a Jew.'" *Jerusalem Post,* December 2, 1988.

Aleinikoff, T. Alexander. "Citizenship, Aliens, Membership and the Constitution." *Constitutional Commentary* 7 (1990): 9–34.

———. "Theories of Loss of Citizenship." *Michigan Law Review* 84 (1986): 1471–1503.

Amar, Akhil Reed. "The Bill of Rights as a Constitution." *Yale Law Journal* 100 (1991): 1131–1210.

Apelbom, A. M. "Common Law à l'Americaine." *Israel Law Review* 1 (1966): 562–79.

Arkes, Hadley. "Civility and the Restriction of Speech: Rediscovering the Defamation of Groups." In *Supreme Court Review 1974,* 281–335. Chicago: University of Chicago Press, 1975.

Balkin, J. M. "Some Realism about Pluralism: Legal Realist Approaches to the First Amendment" *Duke Law Journal* 1990 (1990): 375–430.

Barak, Aharon. "Freedom of Speech in Israel: The Impact of the American Constitution." *Tel Aviv University Studies in Law* 8 (1988): 241–48.

Baron, Salo W. "Who Is a Jew?: Some Historical Reflections." *Midstream* 6 (Spring 1960): 5–16.

Bellah, Robert N. "The Meaning of Reputation in American Society." *California Law Review* 74 (1986): 743–51.

Berns, Walter. "The Constitution and the Migration of Slaves." *Yale Law Journal* 78 (1968): 198–228.

Berry, Christopher J. "Nations and Norms." *Review of Politics* 43 (1981): 75–87.

Beth, Loren. "Group Libel and Free Speech." *University of Minnesota Law Review* 39 (1955): 167–84.

Black, Hugo L. "The Bill of Rights." *New York University Law Review* 35 (1960): 865–81.

Bork, Robert H. "Neutral Principles and Some First Amendment Problems." *Indiana Law Journal* 47 (1971): 1–35.

Brest, Paul. "The Fundamental Rights Controversy: The Essential Contradictions of Normative Constitutional Scholarship." *Yale Law Journal* 90 (1981): 1063–1109.

Brigman, William. "Pornography as Group Libel: The Indianapolis Sex Discrimination Ordinance." *Indiana Law Review* 18 (1985): 479–505.

Buchanan, G. Sidney. "The Nature of a Pardon Under the United States Constitution." *Ohio State Law Journal* 39 (1978): 36–65.

Burnett, Jr., Donald L. "An Historical Analysis of the 1968 'Indian Civil Rights' Act." *Harvard Journal on Legislation* 9 (1972): 557–626.

Burt, Robert A. "The Constitution of the Family." *Supreme Court Review 1979*, 329–95. Chicago: The University of Chicago Press, 1980.

———. "Inventing Judicial Review: Israel and America." *Cardozo Law Review* 10 (1989): 2013–97.

Campisano, Mark S. "Group Vilification Reconsidered." *Yale Law Journal* 89 (1979): 308–32.

Cherrick, Jordan B. " 'Constitutional' Adjudication in Israel? The High Court Speaks Out for Prisoner' Rights." *International and Comparative Law Quarterly* 30 (1981): 835–61.

Clinton, Robert N. "Isolated in Their Own Country: A Defense of Federal Protection of Indian Autonomy and Self-Government." *Stanford Law Review* 33 (1981): 979–1068.

Cohen, Carl. "The Case Against Group Libel." *Nation*, June 24, 1978: 757–61.

Cohn, Haim H. "The Spirit of Israel Law." *Israel Law Review* 9 (1974): 456–62.

Corwin, Edward S. "*Marbury* v. *Madison* and the Doctrine of Judicial Review." *Michigan Law Review* 12 (1914): 538–72.

Dayan, Yael. "Agenda We Share with U.S. Jewry." *Jerusalem Post*, November 24, 1988.

Dry, Murray. "Flag Burning and the Constitution." *Supreme Court Review 1990*, 69–103. Chicago: University of Chicago Press, 1991.

———. "Free Speech and Modern Republican Government." *Constitutional Commentary* 6 (1989): 351–66.

Duker, William F. "The President's Power to Pardon: A Constitutional History." *William and Mary Law Review* 18 (1977): 475–538.

Elman, Peter. "Comment." *Israel Law Review* 4 (1969): 565–69.

Epstein, Richard A. "Modern Republicanism—or the Flight from Substance." *Yale Law Journal* 97 (1988): 1633–50.

Finn, Jr., Chester E. "The Campus: An Island of Repression in a Sea of Freedom,' " *Commentary* (September 1989): 17–23.

Fiss, Owen M. "Groups and the Equal Protection Clause." *Philosophy and Public Affairs* 5 (1975): 107–77.

Frantz, Laurent B. "The First Amendment in the Balance." *Yale Law Journal* 71 (1962): 1424–50.

Friedman, Daniel. "Independent Development of Israel Law." *Israel Law Review* 10 (1975): 515–68.

Galanter, Marc. "A Dissent on Brother Daniel." *Commentary* 36 (1963): 10–17.

Garet, Ronald. "Communality and Existence: The Rights of Groups." *Southern California Law Review* 56 (1983): 1001–75.

Gavison, Ruth. "The Controversy Over Israel's Bill of Rights." *Israel Yearbook on Human Rights* 15 (1985): 113–54.

Gordon, Milton M. "Models of Pluralism: The New American Dilemma." *Annals of the American Academy of Political and Social Sciences* 454 (1981): 178–88.

Greenfield, Meg. "The Fellowship of Patriotism." *Newsweek* (July 8, 1991): 68.

Grey, Thomas C. "Origins of the Unwritten Constitution: Fundamental Law in American Revolutionary Thought." *Stanford Law Review* 30 (1978): 843–93.

Hart, Herbert L. A. "Between Citizen and State." *Israeli Democracy*, Winter 1987: 27–29.

Hartog, Hendrik. "The Constitution of Aspiration and 'The Rights That Belong to Us All.' " *Journal of American History* 74 (1987): 1013–34.

Heimowitz, David. "Can Israel be a Real Democracy?" *Jerusalem Post*, March 16, 1991.

Henkin, Louis. "Infallibility Under Law: Constitutional Balancing." *Columbia Law Review* 78 (1978): 1022–49.

Hirsch, H. N. "The Threnody of Liberalism: Constitutional Liberty and the Renewal of Community. *Political Theory* 14 (1986): 423–49.

Horowitz, Dan. "Dual Authority Politics." *Comparative Politics* 14 (1982): 329–49.

Horowitz, Irving Louis, and Victoria Curtis Bramson. "Skokie, the ACLU and the Endurance of Democratic Theory." *Law and Contemporary Problems* 43 (1979): 328–49.

Horwitz, Morton J. "Republicanism and Liberalism in American Constitutional Thought." *William and Mary Law Review* 29 (1987): 57–74.

Isaacs, Harold R. "The New Pluralists." *Commentary* (March 1972): 75–78.

Jacobsohn, Gary J. "Abraham Lincoln 'On This Question of Judicial Authority': The Theory of Constitutional Aspiration." *Western Political Quarterly* 36 (1983): 52–70.

———. "Modern Jurisprudence and the Transvaluation of Liberal Constitutionalism." *Journal of Politics* 47 (1985): 405–26.

264

Karp, Judith. "Finding an Equilibrium." *Israeli Democracy*, Fall 1990: 29–31.

Karst, Kenneth L. "Equality as a Central Principle in the First Amendment." *University of Chicago Law Review* 43 (1975): 20–68.

———. "Paths to Belonging: The Constitution and Cultural Identity." *North Carolina Law Review* 64 (1986): 303–77.

Kay, Richard S. "The Illegality of the American Constitution." *Constitutional Commentary* 4 (1987): 57–80.

Kommers, Donald P. "The Jurisprudence of Free Speech in the United States and the Federal Republic of Germany." *Southern California Law Review* 53 (1980): 657–95.

———. "Liberty and Community in American Constitutional Law: Continuing Tensions." Indiana University Bicentennial of the U.S. Constitution Lecture Series, 1986: 3–16.

Kremnitzer, Mordechai. "The General Security Service Pardon: A Test for the High Court of Justice." *Tel Aviv University Studies in Law* 8 (1988): 157–84.

Kretzmer, David. "Demonstrations and the Law." *Israel Law Review* 19 (1984): 47–153.

———. "Forty Years of Public Law." *Israel Law Review* 24 (1990): 341–55.

———. "The Influence of First Amendment Jurisprudence on Decision-making in Israel." Unpublished paper.

———. "Judicial Review of Knesset Decisions." *Tel Aviv University Studies in Law* 8 (1988): 95–156.

Lahav, Pnina. "American Influence on Israel's Jurisprudence of Free Speech." *Hastings Constitutional Law Quarterly* 9 (1981): 21–108.

———. "Foundations of Rights Jurisprudence in Israel: Chief Justice Agranat's Legacy." *Israel Law Review* 24 (1990): 211–269.

———. "The Press and National Security." *Israeli Democracy*, Winter 1989: 28–32.

———. "The Supreme Court of Israel: Formative Years, 1948–1955." *Studies in Zionism* 11 (1990): 45–66.

Lasson, Kenneth. "Racial Defamation as Free Speech: Abusing the First Amendment." *Columbia Human Rights Law Review* 17 (1985): 11–55.

Lawrence III, Charles R. "If He Hollers Let Him Go: Regulating Racist Speech on Campus." *Duke Law Journal* 1990 (1990): 431–83.

Lerner, Ralph. "The Supreme Court as Republican Schoolmaster." *Supreme Court Review 1967*, 127–80. Chicago: University of Chicago Press, 1968.

Levinson, Sanford. " 'Veneration' and Constitutional Change: James Madison Confronts the Possibility of Constitutional Amendment." *Texas Tech Law Review* 21 (1990): 2443–60.

Liebman, Charles S. "Conceptions of 'State of Israel' in Israeli Society." *Jerusalem Quarterly* 47 (1988): 95–107.

Likhovski, Eliahu. "The Courts and the Legislative Supremacy of the Knesset." *Israel Law Review* 3 (1968): 345–67.

Lynch, Judy D. "Indian Sovereignty and Judicial Interpretations of the Indian Civil Rights Act." *Washington University Law Quarterly* 1979 (1979): 897–918.

McFadden, Patrick M. "The Balancing Test." *Boston College Law Review* 29 (1988): 585–656.

Mahoney, Kathleen. Colloquium remarks, "Language as Violence v. Freedom of Expression: Canadian and American Perspectives on Group Defamation." *Buffalo Law Review* 37 (1988–89): 337–73.

Matsuda, Mari J. "Public Response to Racist Speech: Considering the Victim's Story." *Michigan Law Review* 87 (1989): 2320–81.

Michelman, Frank. "Law's Republic." *Yale Law Journal* 97 (1988): 1493–1537.

Murphy, Walter F. "Mr. Justice Jackson, Free Speech, and the Judicial Function." *Vanderbilt Law Review* 12 (1959): 1019–46.

———. "Who Shall Interpret? The Quest for the Ultimate Constitutional Interpreter." *Review of Politics* 48 (1986): 401–23.

Nimmer, Melville B. "The Uses of Judicial Review in Israel's Quest for a Constitution." *Columbia Law Review* 70 (1970): 1217–60.

Note. "The Indian Bill of Rights and the Constitutional Status of Tribal Governments." *Harvard Law Review* 82 (1969): 1343–73.

Note. "Membership Has Its Privileges and Immunities: Congressional Power to Define and Enforce the Rights of National Citizenship." *Harvard Law Review* 102 (1989): 1925–47.

Occhiogrosso, Paul F. "The Shin Beth Affair: National Security versus the Rule of Law in the State of Israel." *Loyola of Los Angeles International and Comparative Law Journal* 11 (1989): 67–116.

Peretz, Martin. "Comfort of Strangers." *New Republic* (June 24, 1991): 43.

Perry, Michael J. "Freedom of Expression: An Essay on Theory and Doctrine." *Northwestern University Law Review* 78 (1983): 1137–1211.

Post, Robert C. "The Constitutional Concept of Public Discourse: Outrageous Opinion, Democratic Deliberation, and *Hustler Magazine* v. *Falwell*." *Harvard Law Review* 103 (1990): 601–86.

———. "Cultural Heterogeneity and Law: Pornography, Blasphemy, and the First Amendment." *California Law Review* 76 (1988): 297–335.

———. "The Social Foundations of Defamation Law: Reputation and the Constitution." *California Law Review* 74 (1986): 691–742.

Powell, H. Jefferson. "Reviving Republicanism." *Yale Law Journal* 97 (1988): 1703–11.

Redish, Martin H. "The Content Distinction in First Amendment Analysis." *Stanford Law Review* 34 (1981): 113–51.

Riesman, David. "Democracy and Defamation: Control of Group Libel." *Columbia Law Review* 42 (1942): 727–80.

Rubin, Edward L. "Nazis, Skokie, and the First Amendment as Virtue." *California Law Review* 74 (1986): 233–60.

Rubinstein, Amnon. "Israel Nationality." *Tel Aviv University Studies in Law* 2 (1976): 159–89.

———. "Who's a Jew, and Other Woes." *Encounter*, March 1971: 84–93.

Rutzick, Mark C. "Offensive Language and the Evolution of First Amendment Protection." *Harvard Civil Rights–Civil Liberties Law Review* 9 (1974): 1–28.

Sarid, Yossi. "Only Yourselves to Blame." *Jerusalem Post*, December 1, 1988.

Scanlon, Jr., T. M. "Freedom of Expression and Categories of Expression." *University of Pittsburgh Law Review* 40 (1979): 519–50.

Schauer, Frederick. "Categories and the First Amendment: A Play in Three Acts." *Vanderbilt Law Review* 34 (1981): 265–307.

———. "Community, Citizenship, and the Search for National Identity." *Michigan Law Review* 84 (1986): 1504–17.

Schwartz, David S. "The Amorality of Consent." *California Law Review* 74 (1986): 2143–71.

Shamgar, Meir. "On the Written Constitution." *Israel Law Review* 9 (1974): 467–76.

———. "The Supreme Court of Israel: Present Trends and Concepts." *Israel Law Review* 20 (1985).

Shamir, Michal, and John L. Sullivan. "The Political Context of Tolerance: The United States and Israel." *American Political Science Review* 77 (1983): 911–28.

Shammas, Anton. "A Stone's Throw." *New York Review of Books*, March 31, 1988: 9–10.

Shapira, Amos. "Judicial Review without a Constitution: The Israeli Paradox." *Temple Law Quarterly* 56 (1983): 405–62.

Shapiro, Allan E. "Changing Times and the High Court." *Jerusalem Post*, January 11, 1992.

———. "Power to the Court Over the Knesset?" *Jerusalem Post*, February 22, 1992.

Sherry, Suzanna. "The Founders' 'Unwritten Constitution.' " *University of Chicago Law Review* 54 (1987): 1127–77.

Shetreet, Shimon. "Developments in Constitutional Law: Selected Topics." *Israel Law Review* 24 (1990): 368–430.

———. "Reflections on the Protection of the Rights of the Individual." *Israel Law Review* 12 (1977): 32–65.

Smith, Rogers M. "The 'American Creed' and American Identity: The Limits of Liberal Citizenship in the United States." *Western Political Quarterly* 41 (1988): 225–51.

———. "The Constitution and Autonomy." *Texas Law Review* 60 (1982): 175–205.

Sokoloff, Yitzhak. "A Jewish Timebomb." *Jerusalem Post*, November 28, 1988.

Soper, Philip. "Dworkin's Domain." *Harvard Law Review* 100 (1987): 1166–86.

Stone, Geoffrey R. "Content-Neutral Restrictions." *University of Chicago Law Review* 54 (1987): 46–118.

———. "Content Regulation and the First Amendment." *William and Mary Law Review* 25 (1983): 189–252.

———. "Restrictions of Speech Because of Its Content: The Peculiar Case of Subject-Matter Restrictions." *University of Chicago Law Review* 46 (1978): 81–115.

Strossen, Nadine. "Regulating Racist Speech on Campus: A Modest Proposal?" *Duke Law Journal* 1990 (1990): 484–573.

Sunstein, Cass R. "Beyond the Republican Revival." *Yale Law Journal* 97 (1988): 1539–90.

———. "Pornography and the First Amendment." *Duke Law Journal* 1986 (1986): 589–627.

Tripathi, Pradyumna K. "Foreign Precedents and Constitutional Law." *Columbia Law Review* 57 (1957): 319–57.

Walzer, Michael. "The Sins of Salman." *New Republic*, April 10, 1989: 13–15.

Warren, S., and L. Brandeis. "The Right to Privacy." *Harvard Law Review* 4 (1890): 193–220.

Wedgwood, Ruth. "Freedom of Expression and Racial Speech." *Tel Aviv University Studies in Law* 8 (1988): 325–38.

"Whose America?" *Time* (July 8, 1991): 12–27.

Young, Iris Marion. "Polity and Group Difference: A Critique of the Ideal of Universal Citizenship." *Ethics* 99 (1989): 250–74.

Cases

Israeli Cases

Attorney-General v. *Matana*, 16 (1) P.D. 430 (1960).

Avshalom Ben Shlomo v. *Minister of Interior*, 43 (3) P.D. 353 (1989).

Barzilai v. *Government of Israel*, 40 (3) P.D. 505 (1986).

Ben Shalom v. *Central Committee for the Elections of the Twelfth Knesset*, 43 (4) P.D. 221 (1988).

Beresford v. *Ministry of Interior*, 23 (4) 793 (1989).

Bergman v. *Minister of Finance*, 23 (1) P.D. 693 (1969).

Cohavi v. *Beker*, 11 P.D. 225 (1959).

Cohen v. *Minister of Labor and Welfare*, 41 (2) P.D. 540 (1987).

Committee for the Protection of the Expropriated Nazareth Lands v. *Minister of Finance* 9 P.D. 1261 (1955)

Dalal Rassi v. *Attorney-General* 7 P.D. 790 (1953).

Dweikat v. *Government of Israel*, 34 (1) P.D. 1 (1979).

Electric Company v. *Ha'aretz* (I), 31 (2) P.D. 281 (1974).

Electric Company v. *Ha'aretz* (II), 32 (3) P.D. 337 (1978).

Flatto-Sharon v. *Knesset Speaker*, 35 (4) P.D. 118 (1981).

Hadashot, Inc. v. *Minister of Defense*, 38 (2) P.D. 477 (1984).

Jabotinsky v. *Weizmann*, 5 P.D. 801 (1951).

"*Kach Party Faction*" v. *Hillel*, 39 (3) P.D. 141 (1985).

Kahane v. *Broadcasting Authority*, 41 (3) P.D. 255 (1986).

Keynan v. *Cinematic Review Board*, 26 (2) P.D. 811 (1972).

"*Kol Ha'am*" *Co. Ltd.* v. *Minister of Interior*, 7 P.D. 871 (1953).

Laor v. *Film and Play Supervisory Board*, 41 (1) P.D. 421 (1986).

Leon v. *Gubernik*, 1 P.D. 58 (1948).

Miari v. *Knesset Speaker*, 41 (4) P.D. 169 (1985).

Mitrani v. *Minister of Transportation*, 37 P.D. (3) 337 (1983).

Muhammad Sa'id Burkaan v. *Minister of Finance*, 32 (2) P.D. 800 (1978).

Neiman and Avneri v. *Chairman of the Central Elections Committee for the Eleventh Knesset*, 39 (2) P.D. 225 (1984).

Of Ha' Emek v. *Ramat Yishai Local Council*, 40 (1) P.D. 113 (1985).

Poraz v. *Mayor of Tel Aviv—Yafo*, 42 (2) P.D. 309 (1988).

Ressler v. *Minister of Defense*, 42 (2) P.D. 441 (1988).

Rufeisen v. *Minister of Interior*, 16 P.D. 2428 (1962).

Sa'ar v. *Minister of Interior*, 34 (2) P.D. 169 (1979).

Schnitzer v. *Chief Military Censor*, 42 (4) P.D. 617 (1989).

Shalit v. *Minister of Interior*, 23 (2) P.D. 477 (1970).

Stern v. *Shamir*, 12 P.D. 421 (1958).

Tamarin v. *State of Israel*, 26 (1) P.D. 197 (1972).

Universal City Studios v. *Censorship Board*, 43 (2) P.D. 22 (1989).

Vogel v. *Broadcasting Authority*, 31 (3) P.D. 657 (1976).

Yardor v. *Chairman of the Central Elections Committee for the Sixth Knesset*, 19 P.D. 365 (1965).

Yosifof v. *Attorney—General*, 5 P.D. 481 (1951).

Zeev v. *Gubernik*, 1 P.D. 85 (1948).

American Cases

Adamson v. *California*, 332 U.S. 46 (1947).

Afroyim v. *Rusk*, 387 U.S. 253 (1967).

American Party of Texas v. *White*, 415 U.S. 767 (1974).

Beauharnais v. *Illinois*, 343 U.S. 250 (1952).

Biddle v. *Perovich*, 274 U.S. 480 (1927).

Chaplinsky v. *New Hampshire*, 315 U.S. 568 (1942).

Cherokee Nation v. *Georgia*, 30 U.S. (5 Pet.) 1 (1831).

Cohen v. *California*, 403 U.S. 15 (1971).

Collin v. *Smith*, 447 F. Supp. 676 (1978).

Cooper v. *Aaron*, 358 U.S. 1 (1958).

Davis v. *Beason*, 133 U.S. 333 (1889).

Dennis v. *United States*, 341 U.S. 494 (1951).

Doe v. *University of Michigan*, 721 F. Supp. 869 (E.D. Mich. 1989).

Dred Scott v. *Sandford*, 60 U.S. (19 How.) 393 (1857).

Ex parte Wells, 18 How. 307 (1856).

FCC v. *Pacifica Foundation*, 438 U.S. 726 (1978).

Gertz v. *Welch*, 418 U.S. 323 (1974).

Goldman v. *Weinberger*, 475 U.S. 503 (1986).

Graham v. *Richardson*, 403 U.S. 365 (1971).

Graves v. *O'Keefe*, 306 U.S. 466 (1938).

INS v. *Chadha*, 462 U.S. 919 (1983).

Katzenbach v. *Morgan*, 384 U.S. 641 (1966).

Kunz v. *New York*, 340 U.S. 290 (1951).

McLean v. *Arkansas*, 529 F. Supp. 1255 (1982).

Marbury v. *Madison* 5 U.S. (1 Cranch) 137 (1803).

Miller v. *California*, 413 U.S. 15 (1973).

Minor v. *Happersett*, 88 U.S. 162 (1874).

New York Times Co. v. *United States*, 403 U.S. 713 (1971).

Plyler v. *Doe*, 457 U.S. 202 (1982).

Police Department of Chicago v. *Mosley*, 408 U.S. 92 (1972).

Powell v. *McCormack*, 395 U.S. 486 (1969).

Reynolds v. *United States*, 98 U.S. 146 (1879).

Rochin v. *California*, 342 U.S. 165 (1952).

Rosenfeld v. *New Jersey*, 408 U.S. 901 (1972).

San Antonio Independent School District v. *Rodriguez*, 411 U.S. 1 (1973).

Santa Clara Pueblo v. *Martinez*, 436 U.S. 49 (1978).

Schick v. *Reed*, 419 U.S. 256 (1974).

Schneiderman v. *United States*, 320 U.S. 118 (1943).

Shapiro v. *Thompson*, 394 U.S. 618 (1969).

The Slaughter-House Cases, 83 U.S. (16 Wall) 36 (1873).

Talton v. *Mayes*, 163 U.S. 376 (1896).

Trop v. *Dulles*, 356 U.S. 86 (1958).

United States v. *Fisher*, 6 U.S. (2 Cranch) 358 (1805).

United States v. *Klein*, 80 U.S. 128 (1871).

United States v. *Nixon*, 418 U.S. 683 (1974).

United States v. *Seeger*, 380 U.S. 163 (1965).

United States v. *Thind*, 261 U.S. 204 (1923).

United States v. *Wilson*, 32 U.S. (7 Pet.) 150 (1833).

United States v. *Wong Kim Ark*, 169 U.S. 649 (1898).

Welsh v. *United States*, 398 U.S. 333 (1970).

West Virginia v. *Barnette*, 319 U.S. 624 (1943).

Whitney v. *California*, 274 U.S. 357 (1927).

Williams v. *Rhodes*, 393 U.S. 23 (1968).

Wisconsin v. *Yoder*, 406 U.S. 205 (1971).

Worcester v. *Georgia*, 31 U.S. (6 Pet.) 515 (1832).

Index